MAKING MUSIC FOR MODERN

SOURCE READINGS COMPILED

AND EDITED BY

KATHERINE TECK

MAKING MUSIC FOR MODERN DANCE

Collaboration in the Formative Years of a New American Art

OXFORD
UNIVERSITY PRESS

OXFORD
UNIVERSITY PRESS

Oxford University Press, Inc., publishes works that further
Oxford University's objective of excellence
in research, scholarship, and education.

Oxford   New York
Auckland   Cape Town   Dar es Salaam   Hong Kong   Karachi
Kuala Lumpur   Madrid   Melbourne   Mexico City   Nairobi
New Delhi   Shanghai   Taipei   Toronto

With offices in
Argentina   Austria   Brazil   Chile   Czech Republic   France   Greece
Guatemala   Hungary   Italy   Japan   Poland   Portugal   Singapore
South Korea   Switzerland   Thailand   Turkey   Ukraine   Vietnam

Published by Oxford University Press, Inc.
198 Madison Avenue, New York, New York 10016

www.oup.com

Oxford is a registered trademark of Oxford University Press.

Library of Congress Cataloging-in-Publication Data
Making music for modern dance: collaboration in the formative years of a new
American art / source readings compiled and edited by Katherine Teck.
p. cm.
Includes bibliographical references and index.
ISBN 978-0-19-974321-6; 978-0-19-974320-9 (pbk.)
1. Modern dance music—United States—20th century—History and criticism.
2. Modern dance—United States—History—20th century.   I. Teck, Katherine.
ML3411.5.M35 2011
781.5'560973—dc22   2010042145

9 8 7 6 5 4 3 2 1
Printed in the United States of America
on acid-free paper

FOR WILLIAM MOULTON

Preface

The era when modern dance came into being was a time of exciting creative ferment, and collaboration with living composers was an important ingredient in the development of new concert dance styles in America during the earlier decades of the twentieth century. Choreographers wanted to distance themselves from both ballet and popular entertainment genres, while collaborating composers searched for ways to make music suitable for dancers' individualistic styles. Both musicians and dance artists experimented with expressivity and techniques in ways that began to differentiate their works from earlier European models and offer a stronger "American" flavor. Yet dancers beginning with Isadora Duncan also expanded their options by drawing from existing concert music of Europe's past, as well as from folk and classical traditions developed in other parts of the world.

During this period, there were few journalists who specialized in dance as a theatrical genre, and reviews of concert dance programs were often written by music or drama critics who lacked familiarity with dance movement as an art.[1] Partly as a consequence of this, there came to be unusually fiery discussions among creative artists—as well as carefully written published consideration of such topics as: how could dance movement and music relate to each other; what working procedures were most practical; and how could theatrical dance works best express then-contemporary feelings and concerns.

Today's dancers, musicians, students, and audience members have much to gain by learning about those nurturing times and challenging creative concerns. Unfortunately, arts enthusiasts have been hampered in such explorations because some old periodicals are on crumbling paper in a few university libraries, or because various comments on collaboration may be scattered within sections of books that have another focus.

This volume of edited articles brings together a representative sampling of some vibrant firsthand accounts. Drawn mostly from periodicals and books of the times, these on-the-scene observations allow readers of today to share the deeply emotional questioning, the careful consideration of technical crafting, and the dreams of possibilities that those artists were mulling over as they sought to merge their innovative styles of dance and music. This collection also includes several excerpts in which writers offer retrospective observations (such as those of choreographers Agnes de Mille, Erick Hawkins, and Alvin Ailey, as well as composers Virgil Thomson and Vivian Fine). Additionally, choreographer Paul Taylor and composer Leonard Bernstein delve into fundamental questions pertaining to the very spark of creativity, and pioneer choreographer Doris Humphrey provides her personal introduction to basic relationships of music and dance.

The fifty-two readings (though written in various years) focus on the creative work in dance and music spanning roughly 1910 to the early 1960s. Some essays are quoted briefly; some have been edited lightly or abridged somewhat to maintain a focus; and others are presented in their entirety. Some spellings have been changed to maintain consistency, but a few idiosyncrasies of capitalization and punctuation have been left alone because they seem to impart a certain flavor from earlier times. A few chapter titles were changed to delineate their focus better. For source details, see notes and permissions.

The selections provide an arc of experience, beginning with the statements of Émile Jaques-Dalcroze, Isadora Duncan, and Ted Shawn all yearning for greater masterpieces and new relationships between music and dance—and drawing toward a close with dancer-choreographer José Limón's 1967 convocation address to students at the Juilliard School, in which he reviews what *had* been accomplished, and what changes *had* taken place during the preceding half century in regard to using music for theatrical dance.

Among the distinctive and important voices heard in this collection is that of Louis Horst, composer-accompanist for Martha Graham and many other early modern dancers. Through his music-making, mentoring, and writing, he came to be considered a pivotal figure in the development of modern dance itself. It was he who conceived and edited *Dance Observer*, an influential periodical published from 1934 to 1964, from which a number of articles in this book are drawn.

The early 1960s seemed a good cutoff point in regard to the artistic activities that are the focus of articles in this collection. In the view of some chroniclers, the end of an era was marked by the death of Horst himself in 1964, which also spelled the end to publication of *Dance Observer*.

Moreover, throughout the 1960s, uptown and downtown in New York City and elsewhere, new generations of choreographers and dancers began another cycle of questioning, radical experimentation, and invention, veering far away from mainstream traditions of staged modern dance. Subsequently dance historians started using the label "postmodern" to demarcate the changing attitudes, techniques, and styles that were related in many ways to trends in other performing and visual arts, as well as to the general turmoil during the years of the Vietnam War. These are all beyond the scope of this book but are touched upon briefly in the afterword.

Another demarcation that had to be made regards geographic focus. There is much that could be explored about musical aspects of dance activity outside of New York and the West Coast, particularly in regard to the work of college teachers who participated in summer festivals at the Bennington School of the Dance and then went on to establish academic dance departments plus regional performance groups around the country. But because a great deal of professional modern dance emanated from the two coasts, it seems reasonable to focus attention initially upon articles that reflect activities of the artists who came to work there. Moreover, then (as now), New York City was considered the mecca of dance, and one reason groups from around the world have always wanted to perform in New York is precisely because of the published reviews they could garner from major arts critics. Consequently, a number of the following articles reflect the New York scene and are drawn from sources published there.

In this collection, here from among the finest collaborative composers of those times is Norman Lloyd telling about his work with pioneer choreographers Doris Humphrey and José Limón. Here also are Wallingford Riegger, collaborator for Hanya Holm; Vivian Fine, composer for Doris Humphrey and Charles Weidman; Lehman Engel, eager composer for Martha Graham; and Lucia Dlugoszewski, long-time composer-musician for Erick Hawkins, musing on the wide range of options open to collaborators by midcentury.

As a witness to the somber social context in which some artistic efforts were taking place, here is folksinger Woody Guthrie (who married Marjorie Mazia, one of Martha Graham's dancers) underscoring

his intensive dedication to the World War II effort, while also report-
ing his struggles to perform a ballad and guitar piece the same way
twice in a row for dancers' rehearsals. Attention is also drawn to another
wartime collaboration, *Appalachian Spring*, with a score by Aaron
Copland for Martha Graham.

Focusing on the legacy of West Coast choreographer-teacher Lester
Horton are recollections of those who worked with him, with spotlights on dance artists Carmen de Lavallade and Alvin Ailey, and on
the composer Kenneth Klauss.

Here also are comments on the debates about the appropriateness
of using religious music by the Baroque composer Johann Sebastian
Bach for Doris Humphrey's choreography, plus innovative practical
hints from composer Henry Cowell, explaining his concept of "elastic
form" (in effect, music that could be stretched as needed to fit dancers'
choreographic needs). And in response to the dancers' desires for new
sound qualities, here are Franziska Boas (daughter of the noted
anthropologist Franz Boas) suggesting how to use percussion instruments from around the world; West Coast composers John Cage and
Lou Harrison questioning basic ways of organizing musical compositions; Otto Luening and Alwin Nikolais sharing their early explorations into electronic soundscores; and Merce Cunningham's solo
dancer Carolyn Brown candidly remembering what it was like to perform in tandem with sounds such as those of a chair being scraped
across the floor.

Throughout this period, collaboration with dancers was regarded
as important to the composers' careers, and in exchange for the experience and performance opportunities, they often accepted low fees or
contributed their efforts. (Some more atypical business arrangements
are chronicled in Aaron Copland's letters included here, about his
commission for a ballet for Martha Graham.) Most compelling, however, is the sense that composers entered into their dance collaborations with gusto and minds open to experimental procedures.

This collection of articles is not meant to be comprehensive but
rather to provide a representative sense and flavor of collaborative
efforts during the earlier years of modern dance in America. For those
who want to delve more deeply into the subject, the notes provide
further information, documentation, and recommended resources.

Additionally, brief part introductions are provided to help readers
put the selected articles into broader perspective. Typically, books on
the history of dance do not devote much space to musical aspects, while
histories of music usually concentrate on vocal and symphonic concert

forms and may mention dance only in passing. Therefore, the introductory remarks are intended to provide historical context and to focus attention on threads of styles and practices that helped shape the artistic scene inherited by these collaborating artists.

A sense of the challenges faced by the collaborators for early modern dance can be gathered from the editorial of the very first 1934 issue of *Dance Observer*, which explained the reason for the publication:

> *The Dance Observer* is established to fill a need as yet unfilled by any other publication in the United States. A definite injury is being done to the dance in America by both the dearth of unprejudiced critical writing and the publication of much that is pernicious. The most offensive are the reviews of dance recitals that appear in the daily press, too often written by a third string music critic with all the qualifications of a sports writer. As a result of this and other factors, the public is led to believe in many fanciful contentions and false propositions: that the dance by its very nature is merely a decorative divertissement; that the modern dance because it strives to be an expressive art defies the principles of decoration and is therefore bad; that the only good modern dancers are Europeans, and that even these Europeans, because they are modern, are bad; that the highest decorative dance form is the ballet; that there should be an American ballet; that there will be an American ballet and that this American ballet will rightly be patterned after and directed by Europeans.
>
> But we will assail the claim of foreign superiority *per se*; not only by presenting the single instance of Isadora Duncan but by pressing discussion and criticism into every phase and style of the dance. We affirm that America has and will produce great dancers; that these dancers will be the product of modes and styles conditioned by current life, not the techniques related to a distant past.
>
> We hope that our efforts will serve to secure those young and experimental dancers a proper recognition of their importance. And we hope, finally, to make the dance audience more fully aware of the contributions now being made by our contemporary American dancers in the belief that this encouragement and understanding may lead to greater achievement.

It would seem that this belief was well-placed. In any case, artists of today continue to be influenced by pathbreakers of the previous century. For audience members and students as well: this is a story of cultural history in which we are an ongoing part.

Acknowledgments

This volume has reached publication only because of the assistance of many people, and I am grateful for their help.

Foremost in my appreciation are the editors and staff at Oxford University Press, especially Norman Hirschy, who provided exceptional guidance in the shaping of this collection. Heartfelt thanks to Janet Soares, Greg Presley, and the peer scholars for Oxford University Press, for reading early versions of the manuscript and making suggestions.

Special thanks go to George Boziwick, head of the Music Division, and the professional staffs of both the Music Division and the Jerome Robbins Dance Division at the New York Public Library for the Performing Arts, for their knowledgeable assistance and for all they do to make these unusual collections available to the public.

Extra thanks to Charles Humphrey Woodford, who published my previous book *Ear Training for the Body* and gave permission to use writings of his mother, Doris Humphrey, for this one.

For the inclusion of the delightful caricatures by Aline Fruhauf, I am particularly grateful to the artist's daughter, Deborah Vollmer. The drawings all first appeared in various issues of *Dance Observer.*

My colleagues in the International Guild of Musicians for Dance have offered a forum for the sharing of information and artistry for more than two decades, and all of us are indebted to the organization's founding president, William Moulton, to whom this book is dedicated.

In trying to locate heirs and representatives of literary estates, I am grateful to many people for their generous help, as well as to members of publishing staffs and not-for-profit organizations who paid attention to many details that helped to make this collection possible.

Ongoing appreciation is extended to those identified below who granted permission to reprint these articles and excerpts. All abridgments and editing of materials were made with the knowledge and approval of those granting permission to reprint.

Permissions

Copyright renewed 1953 by the author. Excerpts abridged and reprinted courtesy of the Jacob's Pillow Dance Festival Archives.

8. Louis Horst, "Music and Dance," appeared in *Dance Observer*, May 1935.

9. "Louis Horst," interview by Henry Gilfond, from *Dance Observer*, February 1936. Reprinted with the assistance of the author's daughter, Pamela Gilfond.

10. Gertrude Lippincott, article originally titled "A Quiet Genius Himself: Louis Horst, the Permanent Patron of Modern Dance," from the 1969 issue of *Focus on Dance* published by the American Alliance for Health, Physical Education, Recreation and Dance (AAHPERD). Adapted with permission from the National Dance Association, an affiliate of AAHPERD.

11. Wallingford Riegger, "Synthesizing Music and the Dance," from *Dance Observer*, December 1934. Reprinted with abridgment by permission of the estate of Wallingford Riegger.

12. Ernestine Stodelle, "Sensing the Dancer's Impulse," from *Art Times*, November 1993. Abridged and reprinted by permission of *Art Times*, a literary journal and resource for the fine and performing arts in print and online at www.arttimesjournal.com.

13. Vivian Fine, originally untitled essay on her scores for modern dance, in *Composer/Choreographer, Dance Perspectives*, 16 (1963). Reprinted by permission of Dance Perspectives Foundation and the composer's daughter, Peggy Karp.

14. Doris Humphrey, article originally titled "Music for an American Dance," from *American Composers Alliance Bulletin*, Vol. 8, No. 1, 1958. Reprinted with permission from American Composers Alliance, sole publishers, and from Charles Humphrey Woodford.

     Doris Humphrey, "The Relationship of Music and Dance," originally a speech given to dance students at The Juilliard School of Music on November 7, 1956. First published in Doris Humphrey, *New Dance: Writings on Modern Dance*, selected and edited by Charles Humphrey Woodford, Princeton Book Company, Publishers © 2008. Reprinted by permission of the publisher.

15. Lehman Engel, "Under Way," from *This Bright Day: An Autobiography*, published by Macmillan Publishing Company, 1974. Excerpt abridged and reprinted by permission of Russell & Volkening as agents for the author. Copyright © 1974 by Lehman Engel, renewed in 2002 by the Estate of Lehman Engel.

26. Aaron Copland, letters to Harold Spivacke concerning *Appalachian Spring*, reproduced by permission of The Aaron Copland Fund for Music, Inc., copyright owner.

27. Gail Levin, excerpts from *Aaron Copland's America*, by Gail Levin and Judith Tick, copyright 2000 by Gail Levin and Judith Tick. Used by permission of Watson-Guptill Publications, a division of Random House, Inc., and with the assistance of Gail Levin.

28. Richard Philp, editorial concerning a revival of *Appalachian Spring*, from *Dance Magazine*, August 1998. Reprinted by permission of *Dance Magazine*.

29. "Lester Horton: Of Money, Music and Motivation" is drawn partially from an untitled section of *The Dance Theater of Lester Horton*, *Dance Perspectives* 31 (1967). These excerpts are reprinted with permission of Dance Perspectives Foundation, Inc. and with permission of Anne Warren. The letter from Lou Harrison is reprinted with permission from the Lou Harrison Archive, the University of California at Santa Cruz. Three additional very brief quotations are drawn from Larry Warren, *Lester Horton: Modern Dance Pioneer*, originally published by Marcel Dekker in 1977, and are reprinted here by permission of Anne Warren.

30. Katherine Teck, "Kenneth Klauss: Musician for California Dancers," is a new article written in 2009 especially for this book and is included here with the approval of Kenneth Klauss.

31. Katherine Teck, "Carmen de Lavallade: Dancing to Many Musical Styles," is a new article written in 2009 especially for this book and is included here with the approval of Carmen de Lavallade.

32. Alvin Ailey's poem "Instructions: How to Play the Drums" is reprinted courtesy of the Alvin Ailey Dance Foundation, Inc.

33. Jennifer Dunning, "Alvin Ailey's *Revelations*," from *Alvin Ailey: A Life in Dance*, copyright 1996 by Jennifer Dunning. Abridged excerpts reprinted with permission from Perseus Books Group.

34. Alvin Ailey with A. Peter Bailey, "*Revelations*," from *Revelations: The Autobiography of Alvin Ailey*, 1995. Abridged excerpt reprinted with permission from A. Peter Bailey.

35. Franziska Boas, article originally titled "Percussion Music and Its Relation to the Modern Dance: Fundamental Concepts," from *Dance Observer*, January 1940. Abridged and reprinted with permission from the author's daughter, Gertrud M. Michelson.

36. Henry Cowell, "East Indian Tala Music," from *Dance Observer*, December 1939. Reprinted by permission of The David & Sylvia Teitelbaum Fund, Inc.

37. Lehman Engel, "Choric Sound for the Dance," from *Dance Observer*, April 1934. Copyright © 1934 by Lehman Engel. Reprinted by permission of Russell & Volkening as agents for the author.

38. John Cage, "Goal: New Music, New Dance," from *Dance Observer*, December 1939. © John Cage Trust. Reprinted with permission from the John Cage Trust.

39. Otto Luening, description of his electronic music for Doris Humphrey's *Theatre Piece No. 2*, from the composer's book *The Odyssey of an American Composer: The Autobiography of Otto Luening* © 1980 Otto Luening and published by Charles Scribner's Sons. Abridged excerpt reprinted with permission from Catherine Luening, the Otto Luening Trust.

40. Alwin Nikolais, "My Total Theater Concept," originally an untitled section from *Nik: A Documentary*, ed. Marcia B. Siegel, *Dance Perspectives*, 48 (Winter 1971). Reprinted with permission from the Nikolais-Louis Foundation and from Dance Perspectives Foundation, Inc.

41. John Cage, "Experimental Music," excerpt from speech given in 1957, © John Cage Trust and reprinted with permission from the John Cage Trust.

42. John Cage, "Communication," excerpt abridged from a lecture first given in 1958, © John Cage Trust and reprinted with permission from the John Cage Trust.

43. Carolyn Brown, excerpts from *Chance and Circumstance: Twenty Years with Cage and Cunningham*, copyright 2007 by Carolyn Brown. Used by permission of Alfred A. Knopf, a division of Random House, Inc., and with the approval of the author.

44. Leonard Bernstein, article originally "Music and the Dance," from *Dance Magazine*, June 1946. © Amberson Holdings LLC. Used by permission of The Leonard Bernstein Office, Inc.

45. Paul Taylor, "Why I Make Dances," appeared in the *Wall Street Journal*, February 23, 2008, and is reprinted with permission from both the author and the Dow Jones Company, Inc.

46. Carlos Surinach, essay originally untitled, in *Composer/Choreographer*, *Dance Perspectives*, 16 (1963). Reprinted with permission from Dance Perspectives Foundation.

47. Lou Harrison, essay originally titled "Music for the Modern Dance," from *American Composers Alliance Bulletin*, October 1952. Retitled and reprinted with permission from both the American Composers Alliance and the Lou Harrison Archive at the University of California at Santa Cruz.

Contents

Introduction

Threads of America's Heritage in Music and Dance

I wanted, in all my arrogance, to do something in dance uniquely American.

—Martha Graham

I F UNTIL THE twentieth century America lacked the kinds of schools, companies, theaters, and funding that supported artistic dance at the sometimes lavish levels found in Europe, the country *could* claim a diverse heritage rich in both music and dance styles. Modern concert dance did not spring up in isolation, nor did the musical styles from which choreographers drew, and from which they also departed.

In the United States, the threads of heritage include folk songs and fiddle tunes; church hymn singing and spirituals; work songs; children's play chants; classical European chamber and symphonic music; operas and operettas; instrumental ensemble music for European court and peasant dances; solos for keyboards, including harpsichords, pianos, and organs; marching and concert bands; community choral groups; American Indian traditional chanting, drumming, and flute playing; military fifes and drums; guitars of Mexico; the pounding sticks and pocket violins of professional dance masters and their accompanists; West African singing and playing of percussion as well as stringed instruments; academic training from European conservatories of music; melodies from French ballet schools; minstrelsy; popular theatrical musicals; lush scores from Russian story ballets; the sounds of clog dancing; piano and band arrangements for Latin American social dance; instruments from around the world—and a spirit of invention.[1]

Enter the Modern Dance Pioneers

Nobody can know exactly what the music of the ancients sounded like to accompany all those intriguing dancing figures seen on Greek vases in museums. But inspired by them, Isadora Duncan (1877–1927) led the way in departing from nineteenth-century traditions of theatrical dance. She was the first to draw upon purely instrumental concert music and spurned the dramatic interest of nineteenth-century European story-ballets in favor of dancing that emphasized gesture, form, and emotional nuance. At one point she did arrange with the American composer Ethelbert Nevin (1862–1901) to allow her to dance to several of his short pieces.[2] But mostly she used older classic works by European composers: Chopin, Brahms, Schubert, Tchaikovsky, and Gluck.

Establishment Tastes and New Challenges

Aside from Ethelbert Nevin, why had American concert art composers contemporary to Isadora Duncan failed to capture interest of this vibrant dancer who was attracting audiences on both sides of the Atlantic?

Summing up a prevalent long-term cultural milieu in America, Henry and Sidney Cowell made this general observation: "Because music teaching in this country was suffering under a rigid, second-hand German academicism, the average American's experience of art music during most of the nineteenth century was so overwhelmingly dull, stiff, and meaningless, that only 'popular' music—stage, dance, and folk music—had any vitality."[3]

And as pointed out by music historian Michael Broyles, before the Civil War, few Americans aspired to be composers at all. Indicating some of the challenges, he observed:

> American composers had three agendas or challenges in the second half of the nineteenth century. The first was acceptance. Throughout

the nineteenth century the American public continued to assume that if a composer was American, he was inferior. A European education solved this issue in the short term. Beyond intrinsic benefits to a composer, European study provided a stamp of approval to a public very unsure about the art. It legitimized American musicians. The second challenge facing the composer was opportunity. Americans could learn their craft in Europe, they could be sanctioned by names such as Liszt, Berlioz, or Chopin, but that did little good if their compositions could not be heard.

The third challenge was identity. Only after American composers had gained the requisite craft, had secured a pedigree, and found at least a potential audience, was the call for a uniquely American musical art heeded seriously.[4]

Regarding the second challenge, that of finding audiences to listen, it can now be reported that in the early decades of the twentieth century, a number of classically trained American composers were to find an outlet for their talents precisely in their collaborations with the choreographers of new styles that came to be called simply "modern dance."

Before such collaborations, however, earlier modern dance works tended to have an "interpretive" relationship to the preexisting music selected and to emphasize expressive emotional nuances. In contrast, as the decades went along, dance artists focused on structural form and then went on to explore, in tandem with their composer colleagues, many other ways of relating musical sound and dance movement. By the latter part of the century, the avant-garde composer John Cage and the choreographer Merce Cunningham agreed that, fundamentally, their only common denominator would be clocked time.

For the most part, the early modern dancers collaborated with classically trained musicians. However, from the 1920s on, some symphonists also drew from popular styles of jazz, for instance, the composer William Grant Still with his orchestrally scored ballets. By midcentury, West Coast choreographer Lester Horton used music by jazz musician Duke Ellington (his *Liberian Suite*), and in 1955 choreographer Anna Sokolow premiered her *Rooms*, with bassist Charles Mingus among the instrumentalists performing the jazz of Kenyon Hopkins. Increasingly as the century progressed, choreographers and their collaborating musicians felt that it was appropriate, as urged especially by the composer Henry Cowell, to draw from the whole world of music.

The making of a new sound-art for the new dance included not only the reappraisal of basic ingredients of musical styles and structure but also a tremendous expansion in the use of instruments, notably percussion. And with the advent of electronic technologies, composers increasingly employed whatever means were at hand to enhance the scores for theatrical dance.

From the beginning, questions abounded. As the composer Henry Cowell observed in 1934:

> Arguments occupying half the night and getting nowhere, fights lasting half the rehearsal time and still getting nowhere, comments from all sides in the dance press: these frequent happenings are but symptoms of the puzzling problems presented today in the relation of music to the dance. Each dance leader will have some sort of solution to offer.[5]

The articles in this collection offer a sampling of some of the "solutions" suggested by choreographers and composers as they forged their new collaborative art.

PART ONE

MUSICAL COLLABORATION FOR A NEW ERA IN DANCE

The composer who would write music for the modern dance starts literally from scratch. In the annals of music there is nothing to parallel the procedure, nothing to help him in the technique involved in the new creative process of the modern dance as developed here in America.

—Wallingford Riegger

Overview

The Question of Using Old Music for New Dance

I N THE FORMATIVE years of modern dance, a notable departure from past theatrical practice was the use of classical concert music as an aural backdrop for "interpretive" dance movement. With her first appearances in London in 1900, Isadora Duncan was seen as the originator of this heretofore unthought-of combination. For some audience members, the mix was unacceptable, as they felt that instrumental masterworks were complete in themselves and should not be used for dance purposes. But dancing to masterworks was precisely what Isadora Duncan did. Those who could put aside scruples of "pure" music adored her, and she achieved fame on both sides of the Atlantic. Similarly, the Japanese dance artist Michio Ito used mostly European classical music for his performances in both Europe and America, though he did have some new scores written especially for him.

It was left to the Denishawn company of Ruth St. Denis and Ted Shawn to forge ahead in eliciting new music from their contemporary composers. They continued Duncan's example of an expressive "interpretive" relationship to the music, but in Denishawn productions there were also important aspects of narration and of projecting characters. Often the music borrowed suggestive elements from traditions beyond the European mold to help evoke exotic settings.

Because of Ted Shawn's interest in American Indian dance, he sometimes wanted scores for Denishawn that could suggest a native aura.

Indeed, early in the century, there were a number of composers whom music historians subsequently labelled "Indianists" because of their efforts to incorporate or imitate sounds of indigenous North American music.[1] Among these composers was Charles Wakefield Cadman, mentioned in this part's article by Shawn. Yet most Indianist music sounded quite European and reflected the then-current sensibility that European traditions of the previous 200 years were the "norm" to emulate. Well into the twentieth century, American concert composers pursued study in Europe, for the stamp of approval it gave as well as for the knowledge of craft. Their artistic focus was on symphonies, chamber music, and vocal works, including opera.

Operas usually included scenes where ballet would be introduced for local color. Late nineteenth-century ballet music in operas, however, was something that twentieth-century American choreographers tended to deplore as trivial. After the great ballet scores by Delibes and Tchaikovsky, there did not seem anything of equal quality—until impresario Sergei Diaghilev's ballet dancers burst onto the Paris scene in 1909, followed in 1911 by the formation of his ongoing troupe, the Ballets Russes. If anyone needed a role model of fresh collaboration for theatrical dance, this was it. Employing the talents of Europe's top dance artists, visual artists, and symphonic composers, the Ballets Russes included in its repertoire music by Igor Stravinsky, Maurice Ravel, Sergei Prokofiev, Claude Debussy, Nicolai Rimsky-Korsakov, Erik Satie, Manuel de Falla, Darius Milhaud, and other leading composers of the time. Especially after the first American tour by the Ballets Russes in 1916, dance artists in the United States also began to search for composers with whom they might create fresh and exciting theatrical works, but with an American spirit.

Simultaneously, some choreographers began to look at music from the past in a new way, focusing on its architectural aspects. Within the Denishawn company, there were experiments with "music visualization," in which the formal structure of the music would be mirrored by the dance patterns. After she left Denishawn, Doris Humphrey continued such experiments, choreographing dances to music by J. S. Bach (1685–1750) and, in so doing, stirring controversy.

Part of the controversy involved politics and world events. From the late nineteenth century there had been a tremendous influx of German musicians into America, and they enriched the nation's symphonies, choirs, conservatories, and concert halls with their considerable talents as both performers and teachers. Yet because of twentieth-century wars, the anti-Germanic view took such a hold, that no German opera was allowed to be discussed in New York City public schools during World War I, and as new war clouds formed in the 1930s, even performance of music by Bach was not immune to censure. Hence the particular emphasis in this part's article by Norman Cazden.

But along with such seriousness, there were also dances with a lighter touch, drawing on existing works of American composers such as Louis Moreau Gottschalk (1829–69) and Nathaniel Dett (1882–1943), as well as on fiddle tunes from rural mountain areas. It will be seen that even in the early days of modern dance, there existed what today might be termed "crossovers" between more popular folk styles and art styles.

The search for skilled collaborative composers can also be seen as part of the efforts by American choreographers to have their new styles of concert dance be considered on a par with other expressive arts. There was a yearning for greatness (as expressed quite clearly by Ted Shawn) and a recognition that music was an important ingredient—but one that often set unnecessary limitations upon the dance, mainly because the form of most concert music involved exact repetitions, which were not necessarily supportive of the more "unfolding" nature of dance.

Another need felt early in the century (as indicated in the article by Émile Jaques-Dalcroze), was for systematic dance training in physical technique and for ways to nurture a deeper awareness of both expressive qualities and structure in music.

Concurrently, in the United States there was a sense that musicians did not understand very much about how concert dances were made or about how music might contribute to this multifaceted theatrical art. Consequently, as composers were engaged more and more to work with choreographers, there was experimentation with various collaborative procedures, as well as with the basic ingredients of movement and sound. Some results of such experimentation are discussed in Part Two, but many basic questions and observations set forth by articles in this first part become themes that reoccur throughout this collection.

ONE

How to Revive Dancing; Music and the Dancer

Émile Jaques-Dalcroze

DESPITE THE STATED *desire of some choreographers to evolve a truly "American" expression in their work, there was always some transatlantic artistic exchange and fertilization. From the time of her London recitals in 1900, the American dancer Isadora Duncan affected the aesthetic views of Europeans. In a reverse flow, one strong influence upon early American modern dance was the study of eurhythmics developed by Viennese-born educator Émile Jaques-Dalcroze (1865–1950), who taught in Hellerau (a quarter within Dresden) until the outbreak of war in 1914, when he moved to Geneva to found his own institute.[1] His method was not intended as dance training but rather as a way of using natural movements of the body to experience musical ingredients and relationships. The ultimate goals were kinesthetic awareness and theoretical understanding rather than polished dance performance. His teaching had international influence, which continues today with Dalcroze organizations, training, and events in many locations.*

It seems that Americans and Europeans alike had complaints about the general quality of both music used for theatrical dance and the training of dancers early in the twentieth century. As the author observed, the time was ripe for something different, and many aspiring dancers came to him for training. Among them was the Japanese dancer Michio Ito, who studied with this master in Hellerau, soon taking his knowledge and awareness to New York and later to California. Hanya Holm (who had first trained with the German modern dancer Mary Wigman) earned a degree from Dalcroze and also brought that background to her dance and teaching in New York.[2]

And so, though it may seem surprising to begin a collection of readings about American modern dance by presenting a view from a European musician, nevertheless, here is Émile Jaques-Dalcroze, writing as observer, practitioner, and visionary. The questions he raises in these essays were continued as dialogues and explorations by dance artists and musicians across the ocean in America. He concludes with some questions that were especially widely debated: whether dance could do everything in silence; whether it had to "submit" to various elements of its accompanying music; or whether, by moving in varying contrasts to music, the dance could become more strongly expressive.

***

HOW TO REVIVE DANCING (1912)

There exist, and there will always exist, exceptional beings who, naturally gifted in music and moving plastic, imbued with the joy of living, and permeated with the profound impression of beauty derived from human emotions, contrive to render sound rhythms visible, and to re-create music plastically, without any special training, guided solely by their intuition, and by the unconscious subordination of their physical faculties to their imaginative and emotional capacities.[3]

Numerous normal individuals are attracted to the art of choreography by a natural taste for plastic expression—frequently for mere bodily movement—and devote themselves to dancing, without acquiring the numerous faculties necessary for the practice of this independent and profoundly human art. For these, the training in vogue among dancers is hopelessly inadequate. The possibility of raising the standard of this training is my present concern; only by the raising of this standard, and, in consequence, this mentality of dancers, can the dance be restored to its ancient glories.

The notable efforts of Isadora Duncan to revive Greek dancing seems to some audiences all that is required to reform the art of ballet; they do not notice that these dances are quite uninfluenced by music, and could dispense with music altogether!

The music of movement, like the music of sound, aims at expressing the common emotions of humanity. The music that is within us, and which is composed of our natural rhythms, and of the emotions that determine the sensations peculiar to our temperament, may assume different forms, according to the capacities of individuals. In dancing, it must transpose itself at once into sound and movement.

In the modern ballet, music and dancing are separated owing to the isolation of musical and choreographic training. This has been the case for so long that there exists very little ballet music suitable for dancing, and very few bodily rhythms involved in dancing that can inspire composers with original musical ideas. There is no common ground between dancers and composers for the ballet, nor any *rapport* between rhythms in time and those in space.

Both dancer and public should be trained in feeling for bodily forms; the courageous and noble efforts of Isadora Duncan and her disciples to restore plastic purity, by the idealization of the quasi-nudity of the human body, must not be allowed to succumb to the clamor of protests from hypocritical or ignorant Philistines. Bodies trained in the refined realization of rhythmic sensations must learn to assimilate thought and absorb music.

Doubtless it will be possible one day, when music has become ingrained in the body and is at one with it, when the human organism is impregnated with the many rhythms of the emotions of the soul, and only requires to react naturally to express them plastically by a process of transposition, in which only appearances are changed—doubtless it will be possible at that stage to dance without the accompaniment of sound. The body will suffice to express the joys and sorrows of men, and will not require the cooperation of instruments to dictate their rhythms—itself comprising all rhythms and expressing them naturally in movements and attitudes.

Meanwhile, the body must submit to the intimate collaboration of music, or rather, be willing to yield, without restriction, to the discipline of sounds in all their metrical and pathetic accentuations, adapting their rhythms to its own, or, better still, contriving to oppose plastic to sound rhythms in a rich counterpoint never before undertaken, and which must definitely establish the unity of gesture and symphony. And thus the dance of tomorrow will become a medium of expression and poesy, a manifestation of art, emotion, and truth.

MUSIC AND THE DANCER (1918)

There is an intimate connection between sound and gesture, and the dance that is based on music should draw its inspiration at least as much, and even more, from its subjective emotions as from its external rhythmic forms.

Music is the basis of the most conventional dance, and we have a right to demand from dancers that elements of musical phrasing, shading, time, and dynamics should be observed by them as scrupulously as practicable. To dance in time is not everything. The essential is to penetrate the musical thought to its depths, while following the melodic lines and the rhythmic pattern, not necessarily "to the letter"—which would be pedantic—but in such a way that the visual sensations of the spectator may not be out of harmony with those of his auditive apparatus. Music should be to dancers not a mere invitation to the play of corporal movements, but a constant and profuse source of thought and inspiration. Music should reveal to the dancer inner and higher forces that any intellectual analysis or pursuit of the picturesque can only weaken. It will serve his purpose only so long as he does not exploit it in the interests of an exclusively ratiocinative [exactly reasoned] expression.

Any direct revelation of inner feeling by means of moving plastic can only assist the sound expression, where it is a spontaneous emanation, and manifests itself in a naturally emotive, eloquent, and distinct form. In so doing it qualifies as music itself, since the art of music is only, in R. Pasmanik's definition, the "revelation of the quintessence of the universe."

But just as music may be allied to the word in the form of music drama or ballad, so it may be combined with plastic to express elementary emotion in a mixed language. In the one case as in the other, music must be kept within bounds, and obliged to diminish its expressive power to enable the element with which it is associated to assert itself, not with redundancy but in collaboration.

There remains for us to indicate under what conditions there might be created—as a contrast to absolute music—a special music adapted to gesture, and which, while distinct from the music of pantomime, would, like it, be deprived of all technical development, constructed on simple and regular lines, and would leave—at considerable sacrifice—a large scope for the collaboration of human movements. Its function would consist in inspiring and animating the body—the source of its own inspiration and animation—in acting both as its master and its servant, identifying itself with it, while preserving its own individuality.

A difficult and complex task, no doubt, but one that will certainly be accomplished, once the dancer has become a musician and can persuade the composer to spare him the effects of merely decorative music, and to devote his gifts along the lines of a more human and vital art. A new style will have to be created, product of the collaboration of two equally expressive arts, with the potential participation of a whole public trained to cooperate with the artist, and to assume a responsible part in his performances. The time is ripe.

TWO

Dancing to Beethoven's Seventh Symphony

Isadora Duncan

*A*S ÉMILE JAQUES-DALCROZE *observed, the time indeed was ripe for change. The artist generally credited with ushering in the modern era of concert dance was Isadora Duncan (born in San Francisco 1877, died in France, 1927). Inspired by images of the ancient Greeks, she in turn inspired the next generation of barefoot modern concert dancers. In her autobiography, she recalled her mother playing piano music of Chopin and other European composers. For her emotionally charged interpretive dancing, Duncan was a pathbreaker in using European concert repertoire of the past, and (as chronicled in this excerpt) she at times enjoyed the highest quality of live musical accompaniment.*

Among the highlights of her career were performances in 1908 and 1911 with the New York Symphony conducted by Walter Damrosch. This orchestra had been founded in 1878 by Damrosch's father, and in 1928 it merged with the New York Philharmonic, which continues into the present. Walter Damrosch not only followed in his father's path as assistant conductor at the Metropolitan Opera; he also did much to transform the musical life of New York and to encourage new music. It was he who persuaded Andrew Carnegie to build the world-famous Carnegie Hall, and as chronicled in the dancer's account, it was also Damrosch who had the vision to approach Duncan and offer her the opportunity to perform with his orchestra, onstage at the Metropolitan Opera House and Carnegie Hall in New York City, and on tour elsewhere.

——— FIRST APPEARANCE OF THE SEASON ———

CARNEGIE HALL

WEDNESDAY AFTERNOON, FEBRUARY 15th

AT THREE O'CLOCK

Reserved Seats $2.00 to 75c.   Boxes at $15.00 and $18.00

On Sale at Carnegie Hall Box Office, the New York Symphony Society Office, Number
One West 34th Street, and at the Office of the Management.

Duncan-Damrosch Tour

SYMPHONIC MUSIC

AND THE DANCE ═══

Miss Isadora Duncan

WITH THE

New York Symphony Orchestra

Mr. Walter Damrosch

CONDUCTOR

During her present American Tour Miss Duncan will dance and interpret
in pantomime an entirely new and remarkable series of programs which she
has been developing for the past three years

Management, HAENSEL & JONES

ONE EAST FORTY-SECOND STREET   -   -   NEW YORK

FIGURE 2.1 Carnegie Hall program of February 15, 1911, showing Isadora Duncan and conductor Walter Damrosch. From the collection of the Jerome Robbins Dance Division, The New York Public Library for the Performing Arts, Astor, Lenox and Tilden Foundations.

In the following excerpt from her memoirs, Isadora Duncan conveys the ecstatic emotions she experienced while performing to music of Wagner and Gluck, and to Beethoven's Seventh Symphony, which had been called "the apotheosis of the dance" by the composer Richard Wagner (1813–83). The opening press review is included here exactly as Duncan cited it. For some interesting contrasting reviews of Duncan's performances, see the notes for this chapter in the back of the book.

***

The Editor of an Art Magazine (Mary Fanton Roberts) speaks ecstatically what Miss Duncan admits has been the most pleasing summing up of her work that she has read:

> It is far back, deep down the centuries, that one's spirit passes when Isadora Duncan dances; back to the very morning of the world, when the greatness of the soul found free expression in the beauty of the body, when rhythm of motion corresponded with rhythm of sound, when the movements of the human body were one with the wind and the sea, when the gesture of a woman's arm was as the unfolding of a rose petal, the pressure of her foot upon the sod as the drifting of a leaf to earth. When all the fervour of religion, of love, of patriotism, sacrifice or passion expressed itself to the measure of the cythara, the harp or the timbrel, when men and women danced before their hearthstones and their gods in religious ecstasy, or out in the forests and by the sea because of the joy of life that was in them, it had to be that every strong, great or good impulse of the human soul poured from the spirit to the body in perfect accord with the rhythm of the Universe.

One day there arrived in the studio a man who was to be instrumental in gaining for me the enthusiasm of the American public. This was Walter Damrosch. He had seen me dancing an interpretation of the Seventh Symphony of Beethoven at the Criterion Theatre, with a small, bad orchestra, and he had the understanding to realize what would be the effect of this dancing when inspired by his own fine orchestra and glorious conducting.[1]

My studies of the piano and of the theory of orchestral composition as a child must have remained in my subconsciousness. Whenever I lie quiet and shut my eyes, I can hear the whole orchestra as plainly as if they were playing before me, and for each instrument I see a god-like figure in movement of fullest expression. This orchestra of shadows danced always in my inner vision.

Damrosch proposed to me a series of representations at the Metropolitan Opera House and on tour for a month, to which I joyfully assented.

I was very proud to travel with an orchestra of eighty men, conducted by the great Walter Damrosch. This tour was particularly successful, as there reigned throughout the orchestra such a feeling of goodwill towards the chief and towards myself. Indeed, I felt such sympathy with Walter Damrosch that it seemed to me when I stood in the centre of the stage to dance, I was connected by every nerve in my body with the orchestra and with the great conductor.

How can I describe the joy of dancing with this orchestra? It is there before me—Walter Damrosch raises his baton—I watch it, and, at the first stroke there surges within me the combined symphonic chord of all the instruments in one. The mighty reverberation rushes over me and I become the Medium to condense in unified expression the joy of Brunhilde awakened by Siegfried, or the soul of Isolde seeking in Death her realization.[2] Voluminous, vast, swelling like sails in the wind, the movements of my dance carry me onward—onward and upward, and I feel the presence of a mighty power within me which listens to the music and then reaches out through all my body, trying to find an outlet for this listening. Sometimes this power grew furious, sometimes it raged and shook me until my heart nearly burst from its passion, and I thought my last moments on earth had surely arrived. At other times it brooded heavily, and I would suddenly feel such anguish that, through my arms stretched to the Heavens, I implored help from where no help came. Often I thought to myself, what a mistake to call me a dancer—I am the magnetic centre to convey the emotional expression of the Orchestra. From my soul sprang fiery rays to connect me with my trembling, vibrating Orchestra.

There was a flutist who played so divinely the solo of the Happy Spirits in *Orpheus* that I often found myself immobile on the stage with the tears flowing from my eyes, just from the ecstasy of listening to him, and the singing of the violins and the whole orchestra soaring upwards, inspired by the wonderful conductor.[3]

Louis of Bavaria used to sit alone listening to the orchestra at Bayreuth, but if he had danced to this orchestra, he would have known an even greater delight.

There was a marvelous sympathy between Damrosch and me, and to catch one of his gestures I instantly felt the answering vibration. As he augmented the crescendo in volume, so the life in me mounted and overflowed in gesture—for each musical phrase translated into a musical movement, and my whole being vibrated in harmony with his.

Sometimes when I looked down from the stage and saw the great brow of Damrosch bent over the score, I felt that my dance really resembled the birth of Athena, springing full-armed from the head of Zeus.

In Washington I was met by a perfect storm. Some of the Ministers had protested against my dance in violent terms.

And then, suddenly, to the astonishment of everyone, who should appear in the stage box on the afternoon of a matinee but President [Theodore] Roosevelt himself. He seemed to enjoy the performance and led the applause. He afterwards wrote to a friend:

> What harm can these Ministers find in Isadora's dances? She seems to me as innocent as a child dancing through the garden in the morning sunshine and picking the beautiful flowers of her fantasy.

THREE

Music for Isadora Duncan's Dance

Baird Hastings

*A*S ACKNOWLEDGED BY *Isadora Duncan herself, critics were sometimes extremely harsh about her use of older concert music, suggesting that she detracted from the aural completeness of the classics. In this article (written in connection with a museum exhibit devoted to photographs of Duncan's dancing), Baird Hastings offers a resounding rebuttal to such criticism, plus an admiring tribute to the dancer's instincts in performing to Beethoven's Seventh Symphony and other orchestral masterworks.*

Baird Hastings (1919–2007) was just out of Harvard when he wrote this article. He went on to serve in the military and to study at both the Paris Conservatory and the Salzburg Mozarteum. Subsequently he became a noted conductor especially of Mozart's works. In addition to being founding editor of Dance Index, *Hastings also authored 400 articles plus ten books on music, including one on collaboration for choreography. Later on he taught at the Juilliard School and administered the orchestral library there. The following article (written long after Duncan's death in 1927) certainly indicates what was to become a lifelong passion for Hastings, namely, the relation of music to dance movement.*

***

If Isadora's dance was unique, her choice of music and subject was even more amazing. She was the first soloist to dance to great music.

Isadora was soundly rated by music critics for dancing to music which they did not consider dance music, just as she was admired by artists, writers, composers for giving visual expression to their art. Specifically critics objected to her not employing Greek music when her dance was inspired by Greek vases in the Louvre. Duncan realized the justification of this criticism, but she felt that the original music could not add to her derivative dance. She felt it would be more appropriate to commission new scores or dance to existing music which would complement her dance with an aural quality which the audience could understand. She found what was ideal music for many of her ideas in Gluck's operas *Orfeo ed Euridice* and *Iphigenia in Aulis*.

The classical period of her career came to an end with her first journey to Germany. In her Paris days an impresario had offered her 1000 marks a night to dance with a symphony orchestra billed as the World's First Barefoot Dancer. She had refused and said that one day she would dance for the countrymen of Goethe for more than that. She was right. In 1904 she danced the Bacchanal in Wagner's *Tannhauser* at Bayreuth. This was the beginning of her dancing to the music of Wagner. *Liebestod* [from Wagner's opera *Tristan und Isolde*] was on her final program in 1927 along with music by Liszt, Chopin, and Schubert.

Over 30 years before Massine choreographed Beethoven's Seventh Symphony, Duncan danced the second, third, and fourth movements— with the first played by the orchestra alone. She undoubtedly became interested in this work because of Liszt's and Wagner's analysis of it as the Apotheosis of the Dance on account of its compelling rhythms. Isadora herself declared that dancing this symphony under the baton of Walter Damrosch was one of her most thrilling moments, and there is ample testimony that the large audiences who came to the special concerts of the New York Symphony were profoundly moved. On other programs with Damrosch she danced to the music of Gluck, Chopin, and Wagner. In this period of her life she greatly enlarged her repertoire to include works by Berlioz, Bach, Grieg, Brahms, Mozart, Monteverdi, Schumann, Scriabin, Lanner, Johann Strauss, Franck, and Rachmaninoff.

After 1920 she again ventured into the realm of symphonic repertoire for her music, dancing Schubert's *Unfinished Symphony* and Tchaikovsky's *Pathétique*. For these large symphonic works she used a group of girl dancers.

Those interested in Duncan's movements alone will point out that she danced to poetry, trash, gypsy music, great music, and to no music at all, and conclude that music was of no importance to Isadora; but they would be wrong. She demonstrated that dancing to great music was an inspiration.

FOUR

The Dance Poems of Michio Ito

The White Peacock, to Music by Griffes

by Helen Caldwell

*J*APANESE-BORN MICHIO ITO (1892–1961) *excelled in a dance career on three continents. After studying piano as well as classical Japanese dance from childhood, he went to Paris in 1911 to study singing. However, upon witnessing performances by both Vaslav Nijinsky (with Diaghilev's Ballets Russes) and Isadora Duncan, he changed his life's focus and enrolled as a student in the Jaques-Dalcroze school for eurhythmics in Germany. Fleeing to London before World War I, he subsequently pursued a brilliant career for a dozen years in New York City, encompassing not only dance performance but also scenic design, choreography, and either directing or taking part in diverse theatrical productions including opera.[1] He developed a very fluid style of movement and presented his solo works as "dance poems"*

Ito danced to music drawn mostly from European classical repertoire, but he also used contemporary scores such as The White Peacock *by Charles Tomlinson Griffes (1884–1920), an American considered one of the great impressionist composers of his time.[2] Griffes died young from influenza, but luckily he was able first to both compose for Ito and perform with him. The* White Peacock *was a piano piece originally, from* The Roman Sketches. *The composer made an orchestral arrangement in 1919.*

Helen Caldwell (1904–87) made her career as professor of classics at the University of California at Los Angeles. However, earlier in life she had studied and performed with Michio Ito for a number of years and developed a deep understanding of his artistry, as witnessed by the following evocative

FIGURE 4.1 Michio Ito, ca. 1916. Photograph by Alvin Langdon Coburn. Courtesy of George Eastman House, International Museum of Photography and Film.

description. Summing up the aesthetics of Ito's style, Caldwell observed: "His dances strike responsive chords in almost all spectators through a use of universal symbolism expressed by strong, unusual gestures in a symmetry of continuous movement that is at one with the music."

***

In Ito's dance poems (that is what he called them), music regulates and controls the movement. As Dalcroze stated, gesture in itself is nothing. Its whole value depends on the emotion, the idea, that inspires it. A dance then, in Ito's definition, is the music's idea rendered visible; and this visible form is the "poem," is the idea; and it is movement. Ito's dance poems are continuous movement, gesture moving inevitably into gesture, and a briefly held gesture within a dance serving only to punctuate the movement's meaning.

Nor does the movement, that is, the dance, end with the final gesture or pose at its conclusion. Ito's final gesture is never final; it merely enters the spectator's mind, where it beckons the imagination into the future.

FIGURE 4.2 Charles Tomlinson
Griffes, composer. Photographer,
Albert Meyer. From the
collection of the Music Division,
The New York Public Library
for the Performing Arts, Astor,
Lenox and Tilden Foundations.

Ito and Charles Griffes, the composer of *The White Peacock*, were friends. During the last three years of Griffes's life they were associated in theatrical ventures in which Griffes performed his own compositions, so that Ito must have heard him play the piano version of *The White Peacock* a good many times. But the idea for the dance as we know it seems to have come to him later. He awoke early one morning, he said, and, in that state where sleep and dream are not yet quite gone, saw "whiteness" to the remembered sound of Griffes's music. Just so, the dance conjures up an infinite whiteness which our thought—our emotion at least—inhabits without effort, for it is an infinity within our own psyche. William Butler Yeats wrote of Ito: "He was able, as he rose from the floor where he had been sitting cross-legged, or as he threw out an arm, to recede from us into some more powerful life...he receded but to inhabit as it were the deeps of the mind."

By the same path, this dance finds its way unerringly into our inmost thought. Although sharp step, feathery hands, and sweeping wing bear traces of the bird's characteristic movement, rhythmic restraint renders these gestures formal and of a godlike dignity and grandeur, so as to suggest such flight as no peacock ever knew. The beautiful birdlike creature is a manifestation of the eternal in all creatures: pure beauty, pure love, pure life caught in a momentary vision of delicately flashing white. Yet throughout the dance there is a pervasive tenderness and a sense of brotherhood in all life, reminding us that we too have a part in nature's scheme.

Nature in its manifold aspects, the universe as a whole, is present in Ito's dance poems. Against the backdrop of nature, and merging with it, moves some human concept in visible shape. It is often individual man himself, curious, eager, frightened in the presence of Nature, defying her, compromising with her, loving her, adoring her, surrendering self to his adoration, but never going down to abject defeat before her. As Ito remarked, "Art gives a spiritual interpretation to the visible, and material signification to the invisible; the artist *must* make these two relations manifest."

White Peacock is somewhat different in nature, or at least in degree, from the other dances. It is highly abstract; line and movement absorb, almost obliterate, symbolic gesture. As within the other dances, there are splendid shifts of emotion; but there is not the same orderly progression of emotion or idea. Rather, before our eyes, but almost without our being aware of it, the idea unfolds in its entirety. The dance is a kind of epiphany, a radiance that vanishes from our sight as imperceptibly as it appeared; but it vanishes into us, where it continues to glow and vibrate before our inner eye.

In April 1918 Ito gave three recitals as part of which he interpreted Griffes's *White Peacock*, with Charles Griffes at the piano. Griffes had been trying for two years to obtain a favorable hearing and a critical review of this beautiful piece. As with *Sho-Jo*, it is apparent, Ito's dance created an audience for the music. It was now on its way not only to critical acclaim but also to popularity.

Ito's dances at this time betray the influence that Noh exerted on his art. In August 1917 he had described his way of composing dances. It was his desire, he said, to bring together East and West in a style of his own. Like a sculptor he worked over every gesture until it meant what he would have it mean.

Reflecting on the impact of Michio Ito's resulting performances, Ted Shawn commented: "Ito, a Japanese, was truly one of the American modern dance pioneers."

FIVE

The Denishawn Aesthetic

America and the Dance; Music Visualization

Unattributed

*W*HILE MICHIO ITO *brought his Pacific culture and European training to bear upon his poetic dance creations in America, the dancers in the American touring troupe of Denishawn conjured up theatrical evocations of exotic foreign places, with lavish costumes and settings designed to please the large vaudeville audiences for their popular productions. The company was the joint venture of Ruth St. Denis (1879–1968) and Ted Shawn (1891–1972), and its repertoire reflected the interest of St. Denis in sacred rituals of the East, as well as Shawn's explorations of American Indian culture and his desire to bring skilled composers into the creation of new dances.*

Few films of the early dances by Ted Shawn and Ruth St. Denis exist, and one must do a bit of searching to hear some of the music they used.[1] Yet we can gain a sense of their style from other materials, such as the 1924–25 program book for Denishawn performances. This included the following commentaries touching upon aesthetic values and use of music for the dances.

At that point, Louis Horst (a musician who was to become important in the nurturing of modern dance as an art form) had been with Denishawn since 1916. He functioned as both accompanist and conductor, and additionally arranged scores for such dances as Ishtar of the Seven Gates, *a spectacular success with music drawn from the works of Charles Tomlinson Griffes. Many other musical choices are noteworthy in view of the intent expressed in the program notes, to develop a repertoire created by American artists*

FIGURE 5.1 Ruth St. Denis and Ted Shawn, from the 1924 souvenir program booklet of Denishawn. From the collection of the Jerome Robbins Dance Division, The New York Public Library for the Performing Arts, Astor, Lenox and Tilden Foundations.

(though composers' stylistic inspiration might be drawn from traditions of Europe or the Orient).

The second program excerpt explains briefly the procedure of music visualization, in which movement would parallel specifically musical structure in an abstract way. This was a departure from theatrical dances based on expressivity or narrative stories. Remarks in the excerpts indicate that the Denishawn dancers and musicians were quite aware that they were forging a new approach and a new artistic era in the use of music for their dances.

***

AMERICA AND THE DANCE

The fact that we are actually in a period which in relation to the whole history of the Art of the Dance is analogous to the Renaissance in poetry, painting and sculpture which took place some few centuries ago in Europe is generally accepted. The art of the Dance, after a long and terrible period of being the Cinderella among the arts, is now being recognized as one of the great arts, if not the greatest.

A large share of credit is due American dancers for helping to bring this about. Among the several pioneers who broke away from the outworn traditions of the classic ballet and revitalized this dance, is Ruth St. Denis. Believing that the Dance was the finest medium of religious expression, and that the whole body was truly "The Temple of the Living God," she dared to appear in bare feet, uncorsetted, and clad only in a costume of jewels, at a time when this was considered shocking. The position which she occupies in the world of art today is the most convincing testimony of the sincerity of her purpose, and the quality of her gift of beauty to the world.

Some few years later she was joined by Ted Shawn, himself the first American man dancer to win serious recognition as an artist. A year after this artistic wedding, they jointly founded Denishawn and their own school of the dance. Prior to this, America had no school of the dance not headed by foreign teachers or whose system and technique was not borrowed from or founded upon the technique of foreign schools. The intention of Denishawn is to use the techniques of all known styles and systems of dance, but merely as a compost out of which America's own message in the art of the dance may grow.

The attention of Miss St. Denis and Mr. Shawn is being given to those fields of inspiration which are indigenous to this continent. The Indian races furnish the theme for three ballets. *The Huskin' Bee*, an idealization of American country dances, is also to be offered to the public next season, as well as a symphonic dance poem inspired by the "Leaves of Grass" of our great Walt Whitman.

Furthering the American idea, this season Miss St. Denis and Mr. Shawn are offering one complete production with music entirely by American composers. Starting with our American classic, Edward MacDowell, the dancers visualize the "Sonata Tragica" and the "Polonaise." R. S. Stoughton, who wrote the score for Miss St. Denis's "Spirit of the Sea," is best known as a composer for the organ and has won for himself an enviable reputation through his compositions of Oriental inspiration. Charles Wakefield Cadman is well known as the greatest authority on American Indian music. His opera "Shanewis" was produced by the Metropolitan Opera Company, and his songs are beloved everywhere. The music of the "Cuadro Flamenco" is arranged from native manuscripts (brought by Mr. Shawn from Spain) by Louis Horst, who has for eight years been the Musical Director of the Denishawn School, and Conductor of Orchestra for Ruth St. Denis and Ted Shawn. In the section "American Sketches" three American composers are represented—Dent Mowrey ("Danse Americaine"), Nathaniel Dett ("Juba Dance") and Louis Gottschalk ("Pasquinade"). The music of "Ishtar of the Seven Gates" has been arranged by Mr. Horst entirely out of the compositions of Charles Tomlinson Griffes.

With this organization of dancers, American born and American trained, accompanied by music composed by American musicians, and with a repertoire of ballets the costumes and scenery for which have been designed by American artists, Miss St. Denis and Mr. Shawn expect in a few more years to tour the world, offering to the world America's contribution to the dance—not for comparison, or in the spirit of competition, but merely claiming a place in the sun.

MUSIC VISUALIZATION

The symphony being the highest of music forms, Ruth St. Denis turned her attention some years ago to its more adequate translation into visible dance form. It seemed obvious at the start that one dancer could no more visualize a symphony than one violin could play it. And so she created her "Synchoric Orchestra," an organization of dancers—one for each instrument in a symphony orchestra—and first visualized the two movements of Schubert's "Unfinished" symphony—a pioneering effort at a real orchestration of movement.

Following this first great experiment—using smaller numbers, she visualized Beethoven's "Sonata Pathetique"; compositions of Brahms, music by other early classic composers, and a wide variety of the best in music down to our moderns.

Following very closely to the actual architectural construction of the music, she made a closer relation between the written page of the music and its dance rendition than heretofore the habit of the "interpretive" and classic dancers, while also giving dramatic expression to the emotional content of the composition.

Following in her footsteps, Mr. Shawn visualized many of the Bach Inventions and Fugues, using one group of dancers for each part or voice—and brought out in visible grouping the contrapuntal phrases of Scarlatti's "Pastorale and Capriccio." His "Revolutionary Etude" [of Chopin] so dramatically gripping, holds very closely to the music visualization principle. This season he has visualized the MacDowell "Polonaise" for himself and four Denishawn boys.

Doris Humphrey, who has worked with Miss St. Denis for many years in this music visualization phase of the dance, because of her own creative ability, her intellect and great talent as a dancer, has been enabled to do a magnificent piece of dance writing in the "Sonata Tragica" of MacDowell. Thus a new school of choreography has been established by Ruth St. Denis in which many dance composers may create beautiful and vital works.

SIX

On Dancing to Bach

Humphrey-Weidman Programs

Norman Cazden

*A*S A MEMBER *of Denishawn, Doris Humphrey (1895–1958) had choreographed a few music visualizations. After she teamed with another Denishawn dancer, Charles Weidman (1901–75) to form a new company in 1928, she continued exploring possible structural relationships between music of the past and new dance. Some of her works set to the music of J. S. Bach continue to be performed and are considered masterpieces. But after some initial performances, the influential New York critic John Martin was rather harsh.*

When he wrote this rebuttal, Norman Cazden (1914–80) was music director for the Humphrey-Weidman Company.[1] Cazden himself went on to compose for both dance and purely musical concert performances; to teach at the university level; and to collect folk music of the Catskill region. Another of his particular scholarly interests was the study of consonance and dissonance. But here are his fervent convictions about the use of Bach's masterworks for theatrical dance. Along the way he offers observations on the stylized instrumental dance suites of Baroque times plus traditions of dance in organized religion—and distances the spirit of Bach from the increasing horrors of Nazi Germany, while confirming Bach's music as part of a universal heritage.

In regard to the production concerns mentioned, readers might keep in mind that in those days there was no amplification to allow musicians to stay behind the scenes. And finally, the mention of Ralph Kirkpatrick (1911–84) is noteworthy: he became one of the outstanding harpsichordists of his day.

***

In John Martin's "minority report" on the current all-Bach programs being presented by the Humphrey-Weidman Company, he raises several issues of importance in the understanding of modern dance, and particularly of the role of music in the dance.[2] On cursory view he appears to claim that it is simply not possible to dance to Bach; upon which one may immediately reply that it may be impossible, but it is being done. Artists are stopped neither by the impossible nor the incredible.

It is not within the writer's province to discuss the success of the choreography in the Bach program, nor the effectiveness of its rendition. But he does feel some clarification is needed on the problem of the music itself, its choreographic potentialities, and its special meaning for the modern dance.[3] His viewpoint is that of a student of music and a lover of Bach; also, he is in some measure responsible for the current program, as it was planned by Miss Humphrey in consultation with him and with Mr. Ralph Kirkpatrick.[4]

In the first place, most of the numbers—the Passacaglia, the Chaconne and the Partita—are actually dance forms; at least, such is their origin. Now, none of them were used as dances in Bach's time, nor were they intended to be so used. Rather, they are essentially musical compositions with a high degree of artistic elaboration, which use the movement and structure of the dance as a foundation.

Modern choreography, however, is similarly far removed from the village square, the court function and the ballroom in which the Allemandes and Gigues were danced. The modern dance is a stage presentation, in which physical movement in rhythm has been abstracted and heightened and stylized into an art form. Its use of the equally idealized forms such as those found in Bach's Suites is not an attempt to imitate the older social dances. The dances and the music of the all-Bach program are thus based respectively on primary dance patterns and dance music; they are parallel outgrowths reflecting the healthy potency of elementary folk forms for complex artistic superstructures. True, the superstructures do not in every case develop in the same general direction for dance and music; thus, not all of Bach is equally danceable. It is Miss Humphrey's opinion that the music chosen from the inexhaustible material of Bach was distinctly suitable for her purposes.

Another question Mr. Martin raises is the supposed lack of free movement in the rigid architectural form of Bach's music, a fault which if present would certainly react strongly against the natural tendencies of the dance. But here he seems to be adopting a very limited interpretation of Bach's music. It is precisely because of its remarkable structure, its inexorable logic and self-consistency, its tremendous rhythmic unity on the large scale combined with the utmost precision and clarity of proportion in detail, that Bach's music is the pinnacle of musical freedom—yes, and not only musical. The fugue, for instance, is the most exactly regulated and prescribed of musical forms, and is at the same time the form that allows the greatest sweep of free movement and imagination. Freedom in art forms does not mean anarchy; it means limitation, selection, rigorous elimination of the irrelevant, and concentrated organization of its intrinsic material.

It is noteworthy that the emphasis on structural unity, on "classic" proportion found in Bach is precisely the outstanding quality of important tendencies in modern dance, and of modern music as well. That the ideals of modern art are closer to those of the eighteenth century than of the nineteenth, and especially to those of Bach, is as evident in the strivings toward architectural clarity in modern dance. It is a many-sided urge toward communal unity, elevated to artistic formalization and integrated harmony and proportion, that mirrors the vital current meaning of Bach's music.

When Bach wrote seemingly stylized elaborations of the chorales "From the Deepest Need I Cry to Thee" and "In Thee Is Joy," or when he intoned "Why do ye tremble, why do ye hesitate," it was in no conventionally religious turn of phrase, as the depth of passion makes clear; it was a practical manifesto. It is in terms of this meaning of Bach for the human drama of his day that our present attraction to his music finds expression. It is this heritage which in Germany itself is being destroyed by the Nazis.[5] The new barbarians aim to eradicate the hopes of the German people of Bach's time from the memory of those living; they seek to burn out from history the advance of communal faith of which the Chorales were the foremost expression. For us, on the other hand, the Chorales become a part of our cultural heritage, a heritage which it is our prerogative as artists of a free people to affirm, and on which it is natural for us to build. The extension and fruition of those dreams becomes the goal of our highest art.

The presentation of an all-Bach program in modern dance is not only highly justifiable, but also a powerful contribution to the significant art of our time. From the start the writer has anticipated the enthusiastic response which Miss Humphrey's presentation received. Part of this may be due to the attraction of the music itself, and so much the better. The independent power of the music is not necessarily a distraction emphasizing the separateness rather than the unity of the sister media. Bach's music is broad enough in human feeling to encompass the dance, and the modern dance is strong enough to absorb the music. Only in the Chaconne was the presence of Mr. Totenberg on the stage a noticeable over-balance of the music, and that was dictated by a technical problem—the solo violin would not be effectively heard from the wings.

Some musicians, as well as dancers, are skeptical of the justice of dancing to Bach. Possibly they fear the evils of the romantic "interpretive" dance that has ruined several symphonies for them. Possibly they find it difficult to tear themselves away from the tradition, almost as old as Christian ceremonial, that affirmation of faith through the dance is somehow unholy. Not all lovers of music can immediately grasp the fact that the beauty and human passion of Bach's music is truly moving in a more literal sense than they have hitherto assumed. The writer, for one, is gratified to find Miss Humphrey's ambitious program shaking loose such preconceptions.

SEVEN

American Music and Composers

What Dancers Need

Ted Shawn

*A*S INDICATED IN *his writing, Ted Shawn (1891–1972) had a deeply held desire to create a concert dance form that would truly reflect American roots, and he felt that an important ingredient was masterful music that in turn was rooted in the forms of new dance. Shawn did much to make such a theatrical art develop: first as cofounder and choreographer of the Denishawn Company (1914–31 with Ruth St. Denis), and subsequently (1933–40) with his company of Ted Shawn and His Men Dancers, based at Jacob's Pillow in Massachusetts.[1]*

In these passages from his book, Shawn imagines the beginnings of music for dance at the dawn of human time and emphasizes the completeness of silent movement. He offers some perspective on the state of music for theatrical dance in his own time, as well as in Europe during the late nineteenth century, and then touches upon specific works that he commissioned for the Denishawn company, with particular attention to composers who could evoke an aura of American Indian life and spirituality.

The reading concludes with advice for would-be collaborators. Drawing attention to the use of repeated sections in many purely musical works, Shawn suggests that music with other kinds of structure might better serve the needs of dance, which usually has a more continuous unfolding in form. Finally, he

FIGURE 7.1 Ted Shawn in *Hopi Indian Eagle Dance*. Reproduced by permission of Jacob's Pillow Dance Festival Archives from Ted Shawn's book *American Ballet* (1926), © renewed.

envisions a flowering of musical composition that would truly complement the new art of modern dance and more fully express America's soul.

***

Fundamentally, the dance is an independent art, complete in itself, and needs no musical accompaniment. This principle Miss St. Denis believed nearly fifteen years ago, but only three or four years ago did she put it into practical expression in the form of the silent dance on the Denishawn programs. The dance is a complete, synthetic art which embraces in itself all the other arts. The dance makes music. The dance is sculpture and painting. The dance is poetry before it is spoken. The dance is the parent of drama. In the progress of the art of the dance from its first complete condition, the dancer moved rhythmically without the accompaniment of music of any kind, before there was music.[2] The first thing that he naturally and automatically did was to sing with his dancing. Eventually other people watching him found themselves pounding on hollow logs with sticks, and then the drum was invented. Later he learned to make sounds by blowing into hollow reeds, and still later, stringed instruments were made of gut stretched over a hollow bowl, and a bow was drawn over the stretched string to produce a musical tone. But all of these came about as accompaniments for the dance and were offshoots of the dance. All of the possibilities of music lay within the dance at its beginning, and through a great many years the music was subordinate to the dance and used only as accompaniment. Music as a separate art developed much later and achieved its first forms and its most interesting forms out of dance rhythms.

As we come down into modern European music, music which is written down in the acknowledged style of writing today, we find that many compositions are based upon the dance. Composers like Bach, Mozart, and Haydn wrote their best compositions as gavottes, pavanes and minuets, all of which were dance forms and dance rhythms originally developed purely as accompaniment to actual dancing.

Then through studying these rhythms and steps, they wrote music in a more finished art form, and as the growth of the art of music continued, we found the tables being turned—the interest of the world lessening toward the dance and increasing toward music—and now we have in our concert field thousands of pianists, violinists, and singers, but comparatively few dancers and only one or two ballet companies.

During that century which saw the beginning of modern music, the ballet was the center of public interest. The stars of the ballet were the great stars of the theater and idols of the public, and the singers were rather subordinate. It was only after the ballet began to degenerate into a fixed and unprogressive system of dancing that the singers had any chance at all.

In Europe within the last twenty-five years we have seen that the foremost composers found the renaissance of the dance so interesting that they began to compose for the dance. For about a hundred years previously when a composer wrote an opera and for theatrical reasons introduced a ballet into the opera, he felt that he had to write down to the ballet. The ballet had grown so doggerel that when he thought of the ballet, he thought of mechanical repetitions of steps, and so for the ballet he wrote music which was on a lower order than the music of the opera.

About twenty years ago, composers began to evince interest in the dance again as they saw new forms beginning to appear in the dance world. Stravinsky has written his best things for the dance, and among the other Russians were Rimsky-Korsakov, Scriabin and Tchaikovsky, who in many cases have produced almost their finest compositions from the inspiration of the ballet. And so the Romantic Revolution which took flower and produced the Ballets Russes under the leadership of Diaghilev was accomplished because of the collaboration of great composers of the day. The Diaghilev ballet would have been considerably reduced in interest if the music had been of a low order. A great many people found quite as much interest in Stravinsky's scores as they did in the way those scores were interpreted by the dancers.

In America we probably suffer from the lack of music more than any other one thing—I mean in relation to the dance. We have a great many composers, but we have not yet produced a man who has been accepted by the world at large as a really colossal composer; we have not produced a man who is equal to Stravinsky or Debussy. If the dance in America is going to reach the heights that it should, we must as a nation produce composers to keep pace with what we are doing in the world of dance. There are big ideas for productions which will remain unborn until original compositions are written for them. And some of them will never be born because we do not know the composer who can or will touch the themes.

In a resumé of American composers, one of the first names to come to my mind is that of Edward MacDowell, who, of all Americans, came the nearest to true greatness.[3] His published works which survive provide some fine things that can be visualized by dancers. Another really great composer, an American, also deceased, is Charles T. Griffes, who I understand among musicians ranks almost highest of any American composer. Miss St. Denis's ballet *Ishtar*, the legend of the Babylonian Aphrodite, was accompanied by an arrangement of the works of Griffes. He composed in the so-called modern manner, with those harmonies and rhythms which are still slightly strange to our ears.

Of the living composers one of the first ones to consider is Charles Wakefield Cadman, a composer of American Indian themes. He has given a great deal of study to the subject and really knows his field. He has harmonized and developed the Indian themes according to our classic standard of what constitutes music. A great many other composers of Indian subjects and themes criticize Cadman for this very thing. They say that he has left the actual Indian themes and made his compositions too sophisticated and complicated and too musical. Be that as it may, he has written some very interesting music. It was my privilege to have Cadman write a ballet to my order. I provided him with the details of my

Hopi Indian dance drama, and he created the score, which was musically very well received by critics throughout the country.

Among composers of Indian themes, Homer Grunn stands in my mind quite on a par with Cadman. He composed the music for my ballet *Xochitl*, and it has certain qualities of vitality and strength and more original Indian feeling than even Cadman's music has. As I said before, there are many composers who are interested in American Indian themes, but none of them have so far produced work which has had great national recognition.

Leaving the American Indian theme and getting into the purely abstract forms of music composition, one of the foremost men of the day is Henry Hadley. Selections from his ballet *Cleopatra* are beautiful in the accepted European manner. He has not, as yet, branched into any creative or progressive field of music, but has been content to follow the established forms. The same is true of a great many other American composers. They are concerned in writing grand opera, concertos, sonatas and etudes—all of the accepted, standardized forms of musical composition—and that type of musician very rarely responds to the dance as a field of composition, because he has that old European attitude of the dance that in writing for the ballet he must write for mechanical steps, four to the right and four to the left.

Eastwood Lane is one composer who has broken away from European forms and is composing music that is purely American because its inspirational idea is American, with its form following none previously established. In the spring and summer, Mr. Lane spends three or four months in the Adirondacks, fishing, so his music gets inspiration and color from this region and its human types. He has written a suite called *Adirondack Sketches*, and I have been using some of the music of his *Five American Sketches*. His *Boston Fancy* was written especially for me; I brought back the pattern and rhythm and some of the simple dance themes that were played by country fiddlers, showed him the dances, and he created music which adapted itself to the model. We are working together on a big ballet, which deals with the legend of Paul Bunyan. Mr. Lane's point of view is absolutely American—he will go a long way in the field of American composers.

Another American composer from whom we may expect bigger things is Deems Taylor. He has written considerable music for various New York productions—the ballet music for *Casanova*, incidental music such as *The Thieves' Song* in *Liliom*, a ballet pantomime in *Beggar on Horseback*—and he has done things that are fresh and novel in their handling and point of view. He is not the homey type of American that Mr. Lane is; his things are more abstract but no less American.

Another composer who has done some very interesting work is John Alden Carpenter, who has written some ballets for Adolph Bolm, one of which is *Krazy Kat*, based on the comic strip. Mr. Carpenter's music has not a great deal of appeal for me personally, but I like the way he works. I like the freshness and novelty of his ideas and the fact of his daring to take a theme from a comic strip and make it into a serious work of art. The word "serious" does not necessarily mean lugubrious and dull—it may be great art even though it is funny.

Among other composers who have done some interesting things is Dent Mowrey, who wrote the music for *Danse Americaine*, which I created for Charles Weidman.

Victor Herbert, in addition to his light opera genius, composed many piano pieces which it would be well for us to revive and use as material for music visualization. In the *Red Man* from the suite *Dwellers in the Western World*, I have found an Indian composition which for popular appeal based on real intrinsic merit is without equal.

Nathaniel Dett, a negro composer, is another real factor among American composers. I used his *Juba Dance* on tour four seasons ago. Mr. Dett has the deepest feeling for the dance, and in his *Enchantment Suite* has shown rich imagination, romance, color, mystery and primitive passion.

R. S. Stoughton achieved his first reputation as a composer for the organ. It was one number from his *East Indian Suite* which Miss St. Denis chose for her *Dance of the Black and Gold Sari*, and later Stoughton wrote especially for her the score for *The Spirit of the Sea* and for our Algerian ballet *The Vision of the Aissoua*. His feeling for Oriental rhythms and strange harmonies is unequalled by any modern composer, and his exquisite and poignant melodies linger in one's memory for years.[4]

I believe if a composer really composes for the dance, he should study with dancers, live and work with them, and learn the principles of the dance from the ground up. He should learn the human body and the possibilities that are within the body and then forget the limitations of the established forms of music writing. All of the technique and all of the knowledge that they may have learned in their periods of study and periods of apprenticeship, and even in their best compositions, should be put to the service of tonalizing forms which the dancer creates unimpeded by music. If we could take a group of dancers and create what we call a silent dance where the rhythms are the rhythms of their own bodies, there would be a continuous unfolding of new forms.

And here is where the dance, left to itself, diverges from classic music forms. The sonata has an opening theme, then a second theme, next a development of the themes, then a return to the original themes. The dance, which is another name for life, does not go back and repeat. In life we do not live our childhood, then our adolescence, and then go back to repeat our childhood, nor in the dance should we—for it is continuously unfolding and the new music must adapt itself to this instructive pattern of great dancing. An American composer, himself sensitive, sympathetic and of big caliber, working thus from the fundamental of the dance, can produce new music forms as epoch-making as those of Beethoven.

At the time of the first pioneering of Isadora Duncan and Ruth St. Denis, the ballet was still pirouetting to the doggerel rhythms of the opera ballet music and dance compositions on that level. These Americans claimed that the bigness of their concept of the dance demanded as accompaniment the most profound music of which the greatest composers were capable. When Miss Duncan danced to the *Andante* of Beethoven's Fifth Symphony, the musicians cried "Sacrilege," but she was right. For the dancing of the truly great dancers there is no music that is not inadequate tonalization of the divine movement of the human body.

There is an infinite complexity of rhythms in the human body. So the composer should study the body to become aware of the music which really emanates from the symphony of its many harmoniously adjusted parts.

I believe that in creating a really great American ballet, we will have to have the most sensitive and thorough cooperation of the greatest composers that we are capable of producing, in spirit as well as in technique, and in actual application.

I have this theme of a great ballet to be based upon the *Leaves of Grass* of Walt Whitman, and as I think of this poem and work on it, ponder, meditate, read and re-read its colossal lines, I realize the ballet must be one of two things. It must be a silent dance, or there must appear a Titan in the American music world to handle adequately the vastness of the Walt Whitman concept. I believe that the America which has produced a Walt Whitman can and will produce the composer who will put into tonal form the same cosmic consciousness that Whitman put into poetry, and it is my constant and sincere prayer that my own consciousness be expanded to the point that I may be a Whitman of the dance.[5]

PART TWO

CREATIVE PROCEDURES AND INGREDIENTS

It is too easy for the dancer and the composer to ruin each other's work in their collaboration because of insufficient understanding of the fusion of their two arts in the dance.

—Lehman Engel

Overview

Some Challenges of Collaboration, and Composers Debate about What Works

C HANGE CAME TO music for modern dance not with fanfares or the sudden burst of a gigantic genius onto the scene (as Ted Shawn and perhaps others may have wished for). Instead, discoveries and change came gradually, through a great deal of experimentation and effort on the part of dedicated composers who often collaborated with dancers for little monetary reward. However, among their discoveries was the fact that frequently audiences for modern dance seemed more welcoming of new sounds than were audiences in the nation's concert halls that featured symphonic and chamber music. Consequently, there were nonmonetary rewards for collaborating composers, in the form of performances and publicity that helped to build their overall careers.[1]

Spearheading much of the investigation and encouraging the participation of his musical contemporaries was a musician little known in the concert music world. Louis Horst is a name still not familiar to many musicians of today. But in the world of concert dance, he is widely considered one of the artists most influential in shaping modern dance styles themselves and in training generations of choreographers, as well as in raising the standards of musical collaboration generally.

Coming out of Denishawn after ten years of touring as accompanist, conductor, and arranger, Horst worked tirelessly for Martha Graham as mentor, composer, and accompanist. Indeed, modern dance historians often point to the date of Graham's first solo dance concert with Horst as the true beginning of the modern dance era. That would be 1926, the same year that Ted Shawn's book was published, with its stated yearning for better American music for dance.

As the years went on, Louis Horst accompanied other leading dancers, as well as helping to train many dance students and—with his longtime friend Ralph Taylor—founding the monthly publication *Dance Observer* in 1934.[2] The pages of this unique magazine featured thoughtful, informed reviews of dance concerts plus profiles of dancers and choreographers. Collaborating composers also reported on their challenges and successes and shared their questioning of basic procedures and aesthetics, as well as their observations on concert dance activities of the time.

In addition to Horst, some composers who were writing new music for the new dance included Wallingford Riegger and Vivian Fine (especially noted for their work with Doris Humphrey); Lehman Engel (in his scores for Martha Graham); Norman Lloyd (especially in his scores for José Limón); and two talents originally from the West Coast: Henry Cowell and Lou Harrison. Other artists became involved too, particularly after the Bennington School of the Dance in the mid-1930s encouraged the study of collaboration as a process and involved both professional and student composers.

The writings of the composers included here offer a representative cross section of the kinds of questions and approaches to collaboration being considered in the formative years of modern dance. Among the topics that these artists mulled over both in private and in print was the question of which should come first: music or movement? Wallingford Riegger pondered this question after his surprise upon entering a dance studio only to find that the movement had already been completely set. In his article here, he proposes the concept of "synthesis" as an approach that could help to bring about satisfying results.

Styles were crucial to dancers. Especially if one were departing from the smooth transitions of traditional ballet and investigating movements that in contrast were sharp, angular, and strong, then the pungent dissonances and jagged rhythms of music by modern composers such as Wallingford Riegger seemed to merge in spirit with the dance. In addition, new scores often served to express the fast urban tempo of the times. But how to merge the two arts in the specifics of both exactly clocked and relative artistic timing: that was an ongoing consideration.

Structure became the focus of much questioning. It may come as a surprise for readers to learn that Louis Horst had his dance students study the forms of pre-classic dances from the Renaissance court styles. Yet such exercises seemed to help the emerging artists to think in terms of broader overall construction for their nonnarrative choreography.

When narrative dances were planned (such as Doris Humphrey's work based on James Thurber, discussed in two of the following articles), character and plot had to be considered by the musicians too. Climaxes in the music could detract from the dance if they did not occur in some kind of relation to the choreographic thrust, and the subject of sectional music versus unfolding choreographic forms was highly debated. Additionally, for dances with more abstract themes, choreographers were finding that precomposed music was often unsatisfactory precisely because dancers had to adjust their movement patterns to the phrasing of the music.

The choreographer Doris Humphrey emphasized her view that the demands of making music for dance were different from those of opera, film, or musicals, due to both physical and psychological considerations. She particularly appreciated the kinesthetic and dramatic sense of her collaborating composer Vivian Fine, whose work is described here. Giving her own viewpoint, Fine mentions an increase in freedom for the composer's invention if what the choreographer presents is a plan for dramatic action in a narrative dance. This became the case, for instance, in some of Martha Graham's later works based on Greek tragedies.

To meet the challenge for music that could be adjusted to the needs of a dancer's more abstract choreography, the composer Henry Cowell came up with the idea of "elastic form," which he explains in his article here. His thought was that musical form could be adapted with changes necessary to meet the dancers' creations, and that the performances could also be flexible in regard to instrumentation available at any particular venue. Cowell's use of his own concept, in a long-distance collaboration with Martha Graham, is described by Norman Lloyd, who along with Louis Horst was surprised to see this new kind of score. It took only about an hour for the specific music to be prepared for a dance premiere at Bennington College.

Dancers no longer felt that their art was a "handmaiden" of music. Just the reverse: sometimes their choreography could exist perfectly well in silence with no musical accompaniment at all. Or the music could be viewed as analogous to the frame for a painting: it should enhance the work of art but not detract from it. The composer Lehman Engel went so far as to state that "the dancer should no more have to consider music in the creation of his composition than the playwright need bother about the color or texture of the scenery and other stage props." However, Engel went on to observe that music *could* add to the energy of the dance.

As suggested in Norman Lloyd's overview, one might become aware of a certain metaphysical "space" surrounding the dancers: a space that should not be infringed upon by the music. In line with this, a new sparseness in instrumental textures seemed to lend itself well to some of the pioneer dancers' styles. On that point, Louis Horst observed: "A good score should have the transparency of primitive music so you can look through it and see the dance."[3]

However, there were specific works (such as *Judith*, a score commissioned from William Schuman by the Louisville Orchestra, intended for Martha Graham as soloist) in which a full orchestral sound seemed appropriate for a single dancer.[4]

Although some composers felt strongly that their collaborative music should be able to stand on its own as concert works, for others, the conviction was that appropriate music for dance might not lend itself to an independent existence.

Looking back over the entire era of early modern dance, the composer-educator Norman Lloyd shared insights from his extensive experience with dancers, in this part's concluding article written in 1961. Drawing on examples from European ballet of past centuries, Lloyd provides a broad framework for understanding both the departures that moderns made from traditions and the consolidation of proven methods upon which they drew—including scenarios, rhythmic charts, suggestions of emotional tone, plans for exact meter and phrasing, and other aids to structure and creative communication.

Lloyd brings the reader up to modern times; describes two examples from among his own collaborations; and strongly suggests that music for dance should not be judged in the same way as purely concert pieces, but rather evaluated for its success in contributing to a total theatrical form. The concluding image that he offers as a quintessential example of good collaboration is of Martha Graham's slowly extended arm in *Frontier*, with the music of Louis Horst's milestone score quivering with excitement as an accompaniment to the dancer's evocation of expansive space and a beckoning future.

EIGHT

Music and Dance

The New Generation's Change in Methods

Louis Horst

*L*OUIS HORST (1884–1964) is widely regarded as a unique and influential figure in the evolution of modern dance and its relation to musical styles.[1] A pianist and violinist, he played ragtime in saloons, improvised for silent movies, and freelanced in theater pits. At thirty-one, he became music director of Denishawn for ten years, accompanying at the piano or conducting for the troupe's performances in vaudeville theaters and other venues all across the United States.

Subsequently, between 1926 and 1948, he took on many professional roles for Martha Graham: as composer, pianist, conductor, critic, and mentor. He also accompanied dance concerts and classes of other artists in New York City and elsewhere. Influencing literally thousands of dancers through his scores, performances, teaching, and coaching, Horst was also author of two books (on pre-classic dance and modern art forms), as well as founding editor of the monthly Dance Observer *from 1934 to 1964.*

Here the musician gives us his 1935 view of how music for theatrical art dance had changed since the time of Isadora Duncan, so that instead of a dancer molding choreography to existing, precomposed music, the composer became, in effect, an interpreter of the dance.

***

During the past generation the dancer's method of meeting his music problem has undergone an inevitable development, and now seems to be on the verge (if not already completely realized) of a most satisfactory solution.

Just a few scant years ago, the dancer, at the interpretative stage of development, depended upon music for practically everything—structure, form, rhythmic pulse and mood. Frankly, music was the sole motivating force. We can easily see why this was so. The dance had fallen into a low state; music had risen to heights of romantic grandiloquence, and the early pioneers of the new dance movement wisely realized that to attain an appearance of importance the dance should ally itself with such a significant art as music. At least this seemed the simplest procedure, and although frowned upon by our contemporary dancers, it nevertheless did achieve occasional happy results.

The next step towards freedom was attained when the dancer created her own idea, and perhaps also had some definite plan as to movement, and then set about finding a suitable piece of music. This also did not always work out satisfactorily. The music was either too long, in which case it was mutilated; or if too short, it had to undergo unnecessary repetition or another composition was added often by a different composer. Though obviously not ideal, this method did produce a higher percentage of important dances. Two fine examples are Doris Humphrey's *Circular Descent* and Martha Graham's *Lamentation*.[2]

The next step was of great importance. Instead of collaborating with the printed page, the dancer now attained the place where he could deal directly with the composer. At first this collaboration was truly so, the dance and the music being fashioned at the same time. However, this was not yet complete freedom, and it was but a short, though great step to the goal wherein the dancer began with movement plus idea, and fashioned the entire structure of his composition without the aid of a note of music. The question might arise here, "Why use music at all?" And one might answer, "Why not music?" The most important factor is the creation of the dance from the stuff of dance—movement, built into a clear and rhythmic form. This independence achieved, the music-less dance exists. If the dancer then elects to have a tonal frame written *to* the dance, much as a painter has a frame made for his painting, it in no way compromises the dancer's achieved freedom, and as demand creates supply, our leading American dancers have found our leading American composers not only willing, but desirous of writing musical scores upon the forms supplied by the choreographers. Among these composers we find George Antheil, Wallingford Riegger, Lehman Engel, Henry Cowell, Paul Nordoff, Aaron Copland, Harvey Pollins, Dance Rudhyar, and the writer.

NINE

Louis Horst

Interviewed by Henry Gilfond

A WELL-RESPECTED POET, *playwright, and scholar as well an editor of* Dance Observer, *Henry Gilfond (1907–2002) came to the U.S. in 1917 from England. Active in his many roles on the New York cultural scene, he was further connected to the modern dance world because his wife Edythe was a costume designer for Martha Graham.*

When Gilfond interviewed Louis Horst for the following profile, Dance Observer *sold for a hefty ten cents a copy, and readers got their money's worth in carefully considered articles about various aesthetic aspects of dance. Here, the interviewer elicits Horst's observations about his work with the early generation of pioneer modern dancers and spotlights the kind of on-the-job learning of musicians who worked in the theater.*

***

Louis Horst was born in Kansas City, Missouri, in 1884. In 1893, with his family, he moved to San Francisco and was raised there. He studied both violin and piano privately, and at eighteen he was a professional musician. His father played trumpet with the San Francisco Symphony Orchestra, and it was consequently in a completely professional atmosphere that he developed.

Musicians play in cafes, theatres, and teach their instruments. Louis Horst complied with the tradition, and this was the manner of his work until 1915, when Ruth St. Denis came to San Francisco; the coming of the dancer proved a turning point in his career. Today he labels the

FIGURE 9.1 Louis Horst. Caricature by Aline Fruhauf, originally published in *Dance Observer*, February 1936. Reproduced by permission of Deborah A. Vollmer.

years before 1915 "B.D. (Before Denishawn)" and the years after "A.D. (After Denishawn)," and the school from which Martha Graham, Doris Humphrey and Charles Weidman emerged was for Louis Horst, as well, in the nature of a molding and maturing crucible.

Ruth St. Denis was having difficulties with her musical director when she arrived in Frisco, and Louis Horst, 31 at the time, was asked to step into the created emergency; the emergency, he thought, was to exist no longer than a few months; it lasted ten years. It was not until the Denishawn Company left for its tour of the Orient that it moved without him. That was in 1925. Louis Horst was 41 and was embarking for Vienna to study composition.

He intended to stay two years; at the end of seven months, he was on his way back across the Atlantic, eager to get back to work. He arrived in time to get into the young and "new" dance movement. In April 1926 he played for Martha Graham's first New York concert.

In October of the same year, he played for the first [Helen] Tamiris concert. When Doris Humphrey and Charles Weidman returned from the East the following year to give their first concert, he played for them. Then followed in rapid succession concerts with Agnes de Mille, Hans Wiener, Michio Ito, Edwin Strawbridge, Doris Niles, the first Harald Kreutzberg and Tillie Losch concert in America, the first Kreutzberg and Yvonne Georgi season in America, Ruth Page,

Ryllis Hasoutra, Ronny Johansson, Berta Ochsner, Jean Berlin, and Adolph Bolm. Sometimes there were two concerts to play in one day, and for the two seasons of its existence he was musical director of the Dance Repertory Theatre (1930–31).

These last years, since 1928, he has been teaching composition in dance form, introducing his work, first, at the Neighborhood Playhouse where it still continues under his direction. For six summers, beginning in 1928, he was musical director of the Perry-Mansfield Camp in Steamboat Springs, Colorado. These last two summers, he has taught at Bennington College in Vermont, and is scheduled to be there again this summer. The music for the completely successful dance festival at Bennington last August was under his direction.

In addition, he has taught these last two years at Sarah Lawrence College, and this last semester at Barnard. Incidentally, it was in 1928 that Louis Horst first developed his popular Pre-Classic Dance Forms as a foundation for the study of modern dance composition.

Before Vienna, for the perfectly adequate reason that he felt there was nothing compelling he wanted to say, Louis Horst had never written music specifically for the dance. It was after his return in 1927 he wrote his first music for choreography, *On Listening to a Flute by Moonlight*, which Martha Graham danced for two seasons.

Then followed *Three East-Indian Poems, Fragments (Tragedy and Comedy), Primitive Mysteries, Chorus for Youth, Tragic Patterns, Celebration, American Provincials*, and *Frontier*, all for Martha Graham. In the interim he also wrote *Japanese Actor 17th Century* for Charles Weidman, *Rhythmic Design* for Portia Mansfield, *Two Balinese Rhapsodies* for Ruth Page, *The Son of God Goes Forth to War* for Edwin Strawbridge, and *Pleasures of Counterpoint No. 2* for Doris Humphrey. He also wrote the music for Pierre Fresnay's *Noah*, performed in New York last February.

His writing has not been prolific, but what little he has written has found a ready audience. We have in mind, especially, his articles on the Pre-Classic Forms. He helped found and does active editorial service, as many of you know, with the *Dance Observer*.

Interviewer: As a pianist and composer, you've devoted yourself almost exclusively to the dance. Just how do you relate your work, music, to dance? Or dance to music? There must be some sort of compromise, adjustment, compensation?

Mr. Horst: Not really. I should say broadly that I am a musician who is interested in music in so far as it is related to dance, and not dance in so far as it is related to music. And as a matter of fact, these last five years I have composed nothing but music for the dance. That doesn't mean that I have relegated music to some secondary and less important position in the relationship of arts. Not at all.

Q: Then there is another slant to this composer and dance question. We won't have to ask which comes first and why?

Mr. H: No. The question isn't relevant. What hasn't been considered is that the dance is creating what we might call a composer-accompanist.

Q: Completely dependent upon the dance?

Mr. H.: No, as a part of the dance. Just as there are virtuoso pianists, and pianist accompanists who developed with the concert singer, so with the dance, there will develop the composer-accompanist.

Q: Such as Norman Lloyd, Estelle Parnas, etc.?

Mr. H.: Quite. We might mention others, and we might add as well that composers are now not only willing but generally eager to compose music for dancers and for dances already created.

Q: Would you say dance needed music?

Mr. H: Dance has obtained its liberty as a creative form. It doesn't need music, just as painting doesn't need a frame. A frame, however, serves a painting well, if it isn't badly constructed.

Q: How far would you carry the analogy?

Mr. H.: Music, of course, is a much more vital frame for dance. It serves, or should, not only to limit, to accentuate, to confine, to deepen the dance choreography, but also specifically to discipline the very plastic instrument of the dancer. The body is not the simplest of instruments. Music is only in the manner of speaking a frame for dance; it enters more directly and is much more a part of the composition.

Q: And should music for dance be capable of standing alone of performance without its associated choreography?

Mr. H.: That, I feel, too, is irrelevant, a problem for the composer. The only legitimate question is—is the music good for the dance? Is it suitable to the choreography, etc.? In Germany such compositions go under the general heading of gebrauchsmusik, functional music. In the composing of music for dance, it should be specific music for a specific choreography, to begin and end with it.

Q: And still I can hum you a couple of fragments from your *Celebration*.

Mr. H.:   Which may mean one of a number of things. But, more directly, it's not likely there'll be another choreography for which the music will be more suitable.

Q: About your music, how would you explain your partiality for woodwinds and the absence of strings?

Mr. H.:   The string is a courtly instrument and has nothing to do with us here. However, it's not altogether inconceivable that strings may be or will be used for dance compositions. Woodwinds are primitive instruments, more suitable to the modern dance.

Q: And modern dance is a primitive art?

Mr. H.:   Neo-primitive. Reed instruments augmented by brass and drums are especially suited to a primitive art form; brass gives it a new vitality.

Q: And for this new vitality of which this modern dance is possessed, how would you explain the use of your pre-classic forms in the study of dance composition, and the popularity of them?

Mr. H.:   Modern dance as yet has no literature that is not historical or inspirational. We have histories and polemics and panegyrics and poetry, but no studies in form, composition, etc.

Q: And music?

Mr. H.:   It is very easy for the musician to procure all sorts of theoretical works, but the absence of this same type of material in dance literature has caused me to use music as form examples (parallel examples) by no means for anything but formal compositions. In a sense we are returning music to dance from which it originated. Most music forms originated in dance. The sonata or the symphony evolved from the old dance suite.

Q: What of the direction of music for dance? Do you see any radical change in the offing?

Mr. H.:   I can see where the dance has already influenced the modern composer to be less verbose and, as the dance, direct. The compositions of the modern composers become more concentrated, and again as the dance, simple in linear statements.

Q: You think this, of course, is movement in the correct direction?

Mr. H.: I believe the composers gain a vitality and their compositions, deleted of useless phraseology, a rhythmic strength from association with dance.

Q: That's a rather large debt you're piling on the composer. Which of your compositions do you feel best answers the demands dance makes on music?

Mr. H.: *Primitive Mysteries* and *Frontier.* I like them best both for the music and the choreography. Maybe I like the music especially because I like the dances best. However, the tone and the movement are perhaps of all choreography to my music best welded in *Frontier* and the *Mysteries.*

TEN

A Quiet Genius Himself

A Dance Teacher's Tribute to Louis Horst

Gertrude Lippincott

BORN IN ST. PAUL, *Gertrude Lippincott (1913–96) initially became immersed in the modern dance world through her training at both Bennington College and New York University. She returned to Minnesota, which became her lifetime base for teaching, choreographing, lecturing, and in general spreading the word about modern dance through her enthusiastic writing.[1] Her memoir here gives us a sense of what Louis Horst's teaching was like—as well as of a younger generation's rebelling attitude toward Horst's approach to choreography.*

***

In the late spring of 1963, I drove into Manhattan after attending a dance program in Bronxville presented by one of my former company members. In the car was my friend's assistant, a young woman whose dance credentials were impeccable, her manner very sure, and her scorn of the older dance generation complete. Her barbs that night were directed mainly toward Louis Horst, whom she considered extremely old hat. There was no doubt that she shared the opinions of many of her peers that any dancer or teacher over thirty should be relegated to the artistic ash heap. Having reached the age of thirty many years before, my personal annoyance was considerable. My reaction to her condemnation of one of America's great teachers of choreography was that of anger, sorrow, and frustration.

FIGURE 10.1 Louis Horst. From the collection of Janet Mansfield Soares.

To those of us who grew up in dance in the 1930s, Louis Horst represented the ultimate in professional integrity and fine teaching. He was teacher, guide, coach, banker, artistic adviser, father-confessor, solicitor-general, escort, and the "tail to our kites," as he had been to Ruth St. Denis, Ted Shawn, and Martha Graham.

We have all known a few truly great teachers in our lives—great because they stimulated us to accomplish more than we thought we could. But compared to the gifted lecturers, the brilliant classroom performers I had known, Louis Horst did not cut much of a figure. He was not eloquent in speech; he was low-keyed in class; his personal appearance was anything but glamorous. Except for his magnificent leonine head of silver-white hair, of which he was justly proud, he looked like a German burgher. There was little in his bearing to reveal his great artistic inclinations and achievements.

His classroom procedure was to sit at the piano, a cigarette drooping from the corner of his rather thick, sensual lips, playing whatever music the dancer had chosen. His heavy eyelids were half-closed. He looked utterly bored and often half-asleep. The whole picture was, of course, entirely deceptive. He was sharply alert and would hurl a caustic remark at the unsuspecting dancer at the moment when he or she least expected it. After the study was presented there was a time of silence; then the blow fell. No one was exempt. All felt the lash of his perceptive criticism. All received what Agnes de Mille called "the Horst treatment."

His memory for the slightest detail of movement was amazing. He could tell a student exactly where changes should be made, to the precise measure and beat. On occasion he would demonstrate what he wanted, moving gracefully with rather small movements despite his bulk. Kind he was not, but tough and penetrating. Though his attacks softened somewhat in later years, he still could hit the target incisively at the age of eighty.

FIGURE 10.2 Paul Manship, *Dancer and Gazelles*, 1916. Gift of Mrs. Houghton P. Metcalf. Photograph courtesy of the National Gallery of Art, Washington, D.C.

One of his stinging jibes at me came after I had given my first Earth Primitive Study, a dreadful piece in which I slithered about on the floor dressed in a black, Wigmanesque divided (midriff) leotard encased in a long, slinky crepe skirt. After a moment of vacuum which followed the end of the movement, he announced sarcastically, "Hmmmm, Hiawatha at the well!" He remembered that I had lived in Minnesota. I was humiliated, frightened, and mad, but knowing that Louis did not like weaklings or weeping women, I summoned up enough courage to reply, "It wasn't Hiawatha. It was Minnehaha. Hiawatha was the man. And it wasn't a well. Hiawatha carried Minnehaha over the creek. There is a statue by Paul Manship in Minnehaha Park to prove it." For a moment he was quiet, and then he said, "And who, pray, is Paul Manship?"[2]

There is hardly an American dancer of my generation and later years who did not go through his hands.

The core of Louis' teaching of choreography lay in his insistence that every dance should have a form which was suitable and recognizable. Structure and style were the keystones of his courses. When his students came to the point where they could think choreographically and structurally, they would possess the necessary aesthetic freedom which form gives them. He thought the body could be "a dangerous instrument and needed to be held in check." Motion and emotion react on each other, he said, and both should be controlled.

He used the music and the dances of the preclassic period as a point of departure—a basis on which beginners could develop their own content and psychological states. While learning a number of authentic forms of the preclassic dances, the students gained an insight into formal structure, and from there they could compose their own individual works.

The class in Modern Forms constituted a remarkable method of showing the relationships between all the modern arts while giving the students insights into space, time, and texture, as well as the attitudes, styles, and idioms of the contemporary artistic era.

In the early stark period of modern dance, Louis was a firm champion of the view that dance movement need not have the beautiful line, the unearthly balance, or the sexual titillation of the ballet. Instead, dance movement was seen to have its origin in the natural posture and gesture of the human body. To be effective, it had to regain the vitality and strength it possessed in the time of primitive man. Louis believed that movement based on the principles of natural tension and relaxation could provide flexibility and a wide range of expressiveness when channeled into an aesthetic form. Thus, the expression of the drives and desires of man could be molded into genuine works of art.

In later years when modern dance and ballet began to infiltrate each other's camps, Louis relaxed his opposition to classical ballet. But he felt strongly that they were really two different manifestations of dance and should not merge.

Louis' reactions to new developments in choreography—the *avant-garde*, nondance, and mixed media—were themselves mixed. He looked upon the lack of form he saw about him with more sorrow than anger. Form, he said, was an absolute necessity, but once learned might be departed from.

He responded to the extremes in dance abstraction by saying that the artistic pendulum constantly swings between the classic and the romantic, and that there would be a return to the body as the instrument of human art expression. But he said that we must have patience and wait. We must never lose faith, even during periods of seeming formlessness. The dance will always produce something of beauty and interest. He believed strongly that there should always be an *avant-garde* movement to keep dance from becoming complacent.

In answering a question put to him on the future of dance and its directions, he replied, "When Petipa was called to Russia, when Diaghilev asked Fokine to choreograph for him, did they know where they were going? Did we know in the late twenties when we felt we had to find a new way of expressing ourselves? What difference does it make where the new dancer is going as long as he is on his way?"

ELEVEN

Synthesizing Music and the Dance

Wallingford Riegger

*I*N CONTRAST TO *the interpretive procedures of earlier artists who set their dances to preexisting music, the composer Wallingford Riegger (1885– 1961) was called in to write scores for dances that had already been fully choreographed.*

Riegger was born in Albany, Georgia, to musical parents, moving first to Indianapolis and then, in 1900, to New York City. He pursued cello and composition in the first class of the Institute for Musical Art (which later became the Juilliard School) and in Germany (where he found positions for several years as a symphony orchestra conductor). Returning to New York before World War I, he became immersed in the New York avant-garde circles. His considerable number of dance scores include, for Doris Humphrey: New Dance, With My Red Fires, Theatre Piece; *for Martha Graham:* Chronicle, Bacchanale, Frenetic Rhythms; *for Hanya Holm:* Cry, City Nocturne, Chromatic Eccentricities, Festive Rhythm, Trend; *for Charles Weidman:* Candide; *and for Erick Hawkins:* The Pilgrim's Progress.[1]

In many of his pieces, there is a strong use of dissonance and rugged rhythms—aspects that struck many of the performers and audience members as complementary to the new dance styles. Here, however, Riegger examines the sequence of creative input, possible relationships between smaller rhythmic subdivisions, and longer phrasing in both music and movement. Finally, he stresses his opinion that the composer's job is a pragmatic one: simply to contribute to a well-rounded work of art.

***

FIGURE 11.1 Wallingford Riegger. Caricature by Aline Fruhauf, originally published in *Dance Observer*, October 1935. Reproduced by permission of Deborah A. Vollmer.

The question of the relationship between music and dance has come into the foreground again through a comparatively recent development in the history of dance, namely the procedure of an increasingly large number of dancers who prefer to create the dance first without music, in other words purely in terms of itself, and then call upon the composer to supply appropriate music.[2] The question then arises, is it the function of the dance to interpret the music or of music to accompany the dance?

Fortunately composers have gone about the matter in an entirely empirical manner, without too much reflection and with the idea of achieving the desired result to the maximum satisfaction of both their own taste and that of the dancer. There has been the invariable sequence: the urge to self-expression, the fulfillment of the creative act and then the arrival of sage and philosopher on the scene, to point out the relation of that particular act to other similar acts, to individual and collective welfare, rationalizing upon its artistic validity or meretriciousness.

How fortunate it is, however, that art does not have to wait for critics to agree. No, the creative act is done without reference to anything in the last analysis but the artist's intuition.

It would be natural to suppose in the present situation that the dance, through its priority of creation, would be of primary importance and that the music would serve in the nature of an accompaniment or embellishment. If this were true, however, we should at once have to place this type of dance in a different category from the interpretative dance, in which it could be held with equal logic that the music, being the starting point, is of primary importance and the dance merely built around it. That this distinction is hardly admissible is proven by the effect in actual performance, where the audience, unless informed, is not aware of a difference between the two methods of approach.

Of course we must distinguish between the classic dance and the interpretative dance, between which lies a vast gulf. In the first type, the dance is directed toward pleasing the eye and is apart from any emotional connotation. In the second, the dancer's subjective reaction to music is brought into play, that is, we have a purely individual expression, as no two dancers react in just the same way to a given piece of music. Here the matter of emotional response enters in, which at once endows the dance with a richer content than that of the set forms. The point then is, shall the composer regard the dance which has been conceived without music in the light of a set form, for which he is to create a background or embellishment, or as one of two factors in an integrated whole, which is neither music nor the dance but a third thing?

Personally I should be inclined to the latter view, which would mean that it is up to the composer to conceive music of which the dance, already composed, could be a possible interpretation, to write music that is on an equal footing, creatively speaking, with the dance, in other words, complete in all its elements.

It might be asserted that the dance, by its nature, would be expected to supply the rhythmic element, and the music the melodic, but before accepting such a viewpoint it would be well to define "rhythm," which could have two fairly distinct connotations: small time units, such as half notes, quarters notes, etc., and larger groupings comparable to phrases and more bound up with the concept of form, line or melody.

While it would be conceivable to have dance music with a virtual absence of the smaller time units, relying on the dancer to express this element, yet for any length of time this procedure would be unsatisfactory. In actual practice we find some dance music played by purely percussive instruments, upon which the dancer is free to improvise the larger, almost melodic lines.

The result of following the larger contours can be a feeling of far greater power than if the tempo beats are rigidly adhered to. A supreme example of this method was shown in the choreographic presentation of Varèse's *Intégrales* by Martha Graham. Here the staccato rhythms of the percussion instruments were by no means always portrayed on the stage, but rather the slow moving groups of dancers created lines of larger flowing rhythms—dance melodies—of inexpressible beauty and power.

It would seem then that the rhythmic component must be at least as pronounced in the music as in the dance, even intensified at appropriate moments, with the employment of smaller rhythmic units than the dancer would attempt to express.

The attitude of the composer wishing to write music for a dance already composed should be similar to that of the dancer about to create a dance from music already written. In the latter case the dancer endeavors to evolve a well-rounded work of art, complete in every aspect, even though inspired through another medium. Should not the composer proceed likewise? *opposite of music visualization*

My own experience in this respect has proved illuminating. I have discovered that it is possible to create music conforming to the preconceived dance patterns, and yet, as it seemed to me, complete in itself as music. I admit there was a resistance to be overcome before I could bring myself to writing music to fit into some such design as this: five bars of four-quarter time, two bars of three-quarter time, with the accent on the second beat of the measure, four bars of five-quarter time with a hold over the last note, ten bars of three-quarter time with an accelerando, etc. The problem was intriguing, however, and a challenge to one's inventiveness. The more I became involved in it, the more strongly I was convinced that the correct solution lay in regarding both the music and the dance as being of equal importance, the dance as a vehicle for the interpretation of the music, and at the same time, the music as a tonal portrayal of the rhythms and mood of the dance, both interwoven to form an organic unit which was neither pure choreography nor pure music, nor their sum, but a fusion into something else for which we have no name.

An analogy exists in opera, which is not drama with the accompaniment of music nor music enlivened by action, not music plus drama, but music drama. Perhaps if the word choreography were used to denote dance action apart from music, the word "dance" itself would be adequate. One then could speak of synthesizing music and choreography to form the dance, regardless of which came first in order of creation.

TWELVE

Sensing the Dancer's Impulse

A Dancer Talks about the Art of Composer-Accompanists

Ernestine Stodelle

*T*HE FOLLOWING RETROSPECTIVE *chronicle offers a sense of firsthand witness. Ernestine Stodelle (1913–2008) in her youth danced with Doris Humphrey and José Limón. Showing equal talent for writing about dance as for performing, Stodelle was noted as well for her later reconstructions and preservations of dance works from the early modern repertoires.[1] In the following article she shines the spotlight on accompanist-musicians in their new relationship to dancers and introduces us to the composer Vivian Fine.*

***

During the first third of our century, a new kind of composer came into being at the request of a new species of dancer. In a dramatic reversal of roles, the dance as an American art form considered itself not the "handmaiden" of music, seeking rhythmic identity with a musician's personal choice of timing or with melodies of an emotionally inspiring nature. In contrast, musical accompaniment would have to relate to the dynamic thrust of the choreographer's ideas—ideas that renounced the popular concept of dance as superficial entertainment and sought instead to create a movement vocabulary out of the rougher, more angular textures of modern life.

It was a period of aesthetic ferment throughout the arts. Musicians, too, were seeking new ways of reflecting the times: to introduce dissonance and unpredictable changes of pace and rhythm more in keeping with the jagged tempo of the day; and to investigate sound itself as a separate entity from the classical musical traditions.

It was also a period of economic shock. The depression was of earthquake size, especially in the large cities where dancers and musicians found survival to be a precarious thing. Grants were non-existent. The new pioneers in modern dance—Martha Graham, Doris Humphrey, Charles Weidman, and later, the Wigman-trained Hanya Holm—had to subsidize their own concerts. Even paying $1 to $1.50 an hour for an accompanist was a burden; but the radical new ideas demanded radical approaches in playing for classes: in short, musicians with a gift for improvising fresh themes and fresh rhythms.

Martha Graham had Louis Horst, her musical director and mentor for the first twenty-two years of her independent career; Doris Humphrey and Charles Weidman had Pauline Lawrence, their manager and costume designer whose musicianship was likewise of concert stature. Soon appeared Vivian Fine, a young musician-composer who would first accompany the Humphrey-Weidman concerts, and then create musical scores for all the aforementioned pioneers.

The success of their early collaborations depended on the validity of the choreographic idea, first, as a dramatic, lyrical, or abstract statement, and then as a dance movement capable of evoking sonic imagery of exciting texture in the mind of the composer. The fact that the dance was created first and the musician had to compose according to pre-established counts might have seemed a thankless musical task. But to Vivian Fine, working with Doris Humphrey and Charles Weidman was overwhelmingly gratifying: "I realize now how rich their dances were. They had a remarkable sense of line. They moved so beautifully…with effortless nuance. Everything was infused with a sense of what movement could be."

THIRTEEN

My Scores for Modern Dance

Tragedy and Comedy

Vivian Fine

L IKE A NUMBER *of other composers, Vivian Fine (1913–2000) began her association with the dance world as a piano accompanist, notably for the concerts of Doris Humphrey and Charles Weidman. Her composing collaborations included* The Race of Life *for Humphrey in 1937;* Opus 51 *for Charles Weidman in 1938; and both* Tragic Exodus *and* They Too Are Exiles *in 1939 for Hanya Holm. Then, as Fine turned her attention to more purely musical creation, there was a hiatus as she garnered large-scale performances and awards for her varied concert works and chamber operas. But in 1960 she wrote the score for Martha Graham's* Alcestis, *and in 1965, she collaborated with José Limón for his dance* My Son, My Enemy.[1]

In the following essay, the composer reflects about the kinesthetic impetus that can spark creation for both music and dance, as well as about fundamental ingredients and relationships between the two arts. She explains how her earlier scores were composed after the choreography and offers her views about how music for dance should differ from music intended only for listening. After contrasting the particular demands of comedy and tragedy, Fine relates her collaborative works to what was happening in the "real" world of dire events.

***

Music and dance are two languages with a common source. They come out of the same stuff—the same stuff, as Shakespeare wrote "as dreams

FIGURE 13.1 "Spring Dance" from *The Race of Life* within *The Seal in the Bedroom and Other Predicaments*, by James Thurber. © 1932 by Rosemary A. Thurber. Reprinted by arrangement with Rosemary A. Thurber and The Barbara Hogenson Agency. All rights reserved.

are made of." Before an idea finds its way into form, there is the as yet unlabelled sensation that one recognizes as the modest herald of a new work. Out of this basic sensation of movement the dancer creates choreography; the composer, music.

What is different in composing for dance is that the initial stimulus is not connected with a sonorous image. But in composing music for dance, the musical ideas are stimulated by ideas the *dancer* has conceived. These may be ideas of a dramatic nature or, as in the earlier works I wrote, the completed choreography. In either case, the body sensations that are the response to an idea (though one is hardly aware of them) are similar for dancer and musician.

The underlying sense of movement is the first expression of a feeling we carry with us always, but keep concealed from our awareness: the feeling of the inexorability of the time-flow. The relationship between music and dance might be called a dialogue concerning silence. It is the silence that is the silent motion of the flow of time. We measure the passage of time by the motion of the stars: we see in this sidereal movement a demarcation of the measureless universe, without end in time or space. So, too, do movement and sound evoke the mystery without beginning or end. Within their ordered measures are framed a portion of unending time and space.

Each art tells of this mystery with its own signs. Music speaks through symbols we hear; dance speaks to the eye. So the two sisters—one having no voice—can both speak at once, each telling us of their mysterious mother.

Evoked by imagery outside the contained world of sound the musician inhabits, music for dance has a special character. This can perhaps be described negatively, as music not having the same intensity or articulation required for "absolute" music. Music for dance can "stand alone," but it still relies to some degree on the choreographic and dramatic ideas that inspired it. The composer articulates the dimensions of his sonorous universe through the musical resources at his command. His burden is less when the movements of dance articulate forms in space.

In modern dance it is not the metrical aspects of rhythm that unite dance and music. In the free interweaving of movement and sound there is a link to deeper rhythm. Free of superficial points of rhythmic contact, music and dance create patterns of inter-relatedness that enhance the total work.

Roger Sessions [the composer] has said: "Music is a gesture." In composing for dance, one must have a willingness to absorb from the dancer his basic gesture and to inflect the musical gesture with the imagery of dance and theatre.

The above speculations are strictly after the fact. I have written for dance intuitively, without theorizing. The problems were no different from those of composing any other music—except that the feeling of "rightness" was related to something outside, rather than to the conscience regulating the sonorous world of the composer.

Of the five principal works I have written for dance, two are in a humorous vein: *The Race of Life*, written for Doris Humphrey, and *Opus 51*, for Charles Weidman. The problem was to capture the kind of comedy involved, the particular area of the human dilemma. In addition, *The Race of Life* (based on drawings by James Thurber) had a story and definite characters, while *Opus 51* had neither. In both works I had to discover the serious musical stance from which humor could be achieved.

In comedy one has an especial sense of being both doer and observer. In Thurber's world, marvelously made to live in the theatre by Miss Humphrey, our fears and foibles are plain. We are able to laugh because

Thurber himself is so very human and intelligent. He shows us the war between men and women, their competitiveness and triangular jealousies. The actions of his people are never threatening, nor do they come close to real anger or hate. While we know these jealous quarrels are no laughing matter in real life, for the moment we see them without fear of consequences. Perhaps it is this dual state of being both actor and spectator that gives an air of elegance to good comedy. All good comedians have a certain meticulousness about them.

Opus 51, lacking story or characters, was almost pure comedy, if there is such a thing. In it Weidman achieved a kind of collage. No attempt was made to create situations leading to a comic "point." Instead, we were shown unrelated actions strung together, the ultimate expression of the absurd. Comedy makes the everyday seem absurd by taking it seriously; leading us close to disaster, and then saying: "but it's not real!" Weidman, using illogical sequences of action, succeeded in making us laugh by treating these sequences as seriously as if they were the normal course of events. In this rearrangement of reality, we sensed that that reality was perhaps just another arrangement, and we enjoyed the upsetting of the proper order of things.

The music for both these dances was written after the dance was composed, although not after the entire work was finished. I would write a section as each new part of the dance was completed. In composing for choreography there is the problem of developing a musical structure and continuity. I was able to do this by not composing for individual movements or patterns, but by sensing the impulse that moved the dancer.

The first of my two works for Hanya Holm, *Tragic Exodus*, was a single movement [musical section] about ten minutes in length. *They Too Are Exiles* was longer, in a number of movements. Both dealt with "social" themes, but the strong emotional drive in these works made musical identification comparatively easy. In *Tragic Exodus*, inspired by the plight of the Jews under Hitler, I used a baritone voice employing only vowel sounds. This recalled Hebrew chants, although no authentic material was used. The piano was plucked, adding to the sense of history with sounds reminiscent of the lyre. *They Too Are Exiles* had sections with a strong ethnic flavor, which presented the problem of creating a homogeneous musical fabric. This large work really needed orchestral support, but in 1940 two pianists at one piano were the principal musical resource of dancer and composer.

Alcestis, written for Martha Graham, was composed from a script prepared by the choreographer, in contrast to the previous works which were composed from the dances themselves. Miss Graham's compelling power is as operative in the composer-dancer relationship as it is in the theatre. But in the working relationship she never overwhelms. Rather, she evokes through the magic of her imagery and feeling. She made me feel I was writing not about an ancient myth, but about the living present. Of all the dance works I have written, I feel *Alcestis* comes off best as a musical work. This is due in good part, I believe, to the fact that my only guide-lines were dramatic, allowing more freedom in the development of the musical material.

Archilochos, in a poetic monologue written in the seventh century B.C., urges himself to "understand the rhythm that holds mankind in its bonds." I have tried to indicate that it is within this bonding rhythm that both dancer and musician find their common ground. To make us aware of flow by stopping it is a basic contradiction in the work of the artist who, like Prometheus, is bound. Chained to the rock of his mortality, the artist seeks to create immortal gesture.

FOURTEEN

The Race of Life: My Side of the Story

The Relationship of Music and Dance

Doris Humphrey

*A*FTER MORE THAN *a decade as a leading dancer with Denishawn, Doris Humphrey (1895–1958) went on to forge a career as a choreographer-performer based in New York, forming a company in professional partnership with Charles Weidman in 1928. She was one of the four leading choreographers at the Bennington School of Dance and for a number of years toured North America with the Humphrey-Weidman Company. When she was no longer able to perform, she continued to be a strong presence in the dance world through her mentorship and work as artistic director for both José Limón and the Juilliard Dance Theater, in addition to serving as head of the dance department at the 92nd Street YM-YWHA in New York.[1]*

In the first brief essay, Humphrey recalls her experience of working with composer Vivian Fine on The Race of Life, *a dance that she had choreographed for herself, Charles Weidman, and José Limón, based on a series of cartoons with the same title, by James Thurber. She also comments on the particular role of music in dances that have plots, and about Vivian Fine's keen understanding of bodily rhythms and dramatic timing.*

In the second more expansive essay, Humphrey presents some of her personal reflections about basic aspects of the two arts. Emphasizing the emotional effect that music can add to theatrical choreography, she also considers rhythmic

FIGURE 14.1 Doris Humphrey and her company in *New Dance*.
Photographer unknown. From the collection of Charles H. Woodford.

*movement in the natural world with regard to details of accent and pause,
and to long time frames that can span eons. Going on to pose questions about
our relative sense of speed, she offers an analytical explanation of how she
thinks dancers experience the time frames of tempo and beat and then turns
attention to phrasing in relation to breath. Echoing concerns of other artists in
this collection, the choreographer touches upon the older "handmaiden" concept; observes how the relationship of music and dance had changed; and suggests kinesthetic considerations that are crucial for both musicians and dancers
if the artists are to work together effectively in the theater.*

***

THE RACE OF LIFE: MY SIDE OF THE STORY

Vivian Fine wrote a score for me some twenty years ago. It was quite
a score and quite an experience. She was a true collaborator in a
field, that of composing for dance, which is so different from other

kinds of program music that it calls for unique qualifications. The dance is an art which, though a part of the theater, has its roots in physical and psychological sources which differ from those of the opera, film, or musicals to a marked degree. All these forms, except programmatic concert music, depend on the word for explicit meaning; consequently music does not bear the full burden of the dramatic idea. Not so in dance, where words are rarely used and movements and music carry all the responsibility of communication. This means, among other things, that the theme must be suitable and intelligible in these terms. Not everything can be danced about. So the first task in a collaboration of this sort is the choice of the idea by the choreographer.

My enthusiasm for James Thurber led me to select one of his series of drawings, at the time brand new, concerning the adventures of a middle class family, called *The Race of Life*. Vivian and I both loved Thurber's dry and improbable humor, and the episodes met all the requirements for dance: plenty of action, contrast, independence from words. The scenes were all quite short, six of them, and had subject matter with a challenging range: the Beautiful Stranger, Night Creatures, Indians, and Spring Song, culminating in the achievement of the goal, a mountain top covered with the heart's desire of gold, jewels and money.

Vivian Fine met all these moods with imagination and a full awareness of their Thurberian gaucherie and humor. Even his Beautiful Stranger is no chic adolescent, but plainly bears the germ of the full-grown Thurber female, rather hard, aggressive and blowzy. To catch such a conception in music was a difficult feat. The composer treated the Indians with a very funny version of an authentic pseudo-Indian popular song. Both in the music and the dance our Indians were phony, gaudy cigar-store fixtures. Night Creatures was handled with grotesquerie, but still with a dreamlike delicacy. At this point she added to the all-piano score a flexatone, whose sliding eeriness exactly met the requirements of the weird scene. In its entirety it was a notable score—bright, humorous, expert.

Among many other pieces written for the dance by Vivian Fine, *Opus 51*, composed for Charles Weidman, stands out. But in all her undertakings in the dance field, she has an uncanny sense of what to choose as sound, and that *sine qua non* for dancer composers: a complete understanding of body rhythms and dramatic timing.

THE RELATIONSHIP OF MUSIC AND DANCE

My Point of View

I come to the dance and music, both of which are my dearest loves, from the theater. I have a theatrical point of view about both of them and this is a very special point of view. I admit that it is a biased point of view too, because music and dance have certain special characteristics which they must have in order to fit into the theater. So I like the music that supports the aims of the theater. The theater's aims are, very briefly and very generally, to arouse emotion. We go to the theater, we see the play, we hear the opera, we see the dancing to be aroused, to feel. So as a consequence of this, I am prejudiced in favor of music that arouses emotion. Thus you will be able to put me in my category, whatever you think it ought to be, and judge my preferences for music. I like music that evokes feeling.

The theater arouses, or should arouse and seek to arouse, feeling. And dance shares in this, and the kind of music that is appropriate to the theater has to be this kind of music too. Flaubert put it in these words, very succinctly. He was thinking of audiences, what audiences want in the theater. He says, "Make me laugh, make me cry, amaze me, delight me, exalt me, make me love, make me hate, make me think." And please note that "make me think" is last. This is not the important part of the list. Because an art that only makes one think is doing badly what science can do extremely well. So that I don't agree with someone like Stravinsky, for example, who says, "The tonal masses are to be regarded objectively by the ear." This is not the kind of music that we in the theater can feel is appropriate.

Rhythm

I like music that relates to thinking, feeling and doing of people. I think of this as two kinds: music that is both rhythmic and melodic, or rhythmic and vocal. These seem to be the first two forms of the art expression of people. Even before there were human beings, in the animal world there was dancing and there was singing and there still are. Birds have courting dances, and beating and fluttering of the wings go along with this; and bird song is one of the delights of the natural world. The insect world has group dances, one of which I based a ballet on, *The Life of the Bee*. This has been described by Maeterlinck in his book as being very well organized, highly geometric and with many figures in it, and is a prime example of rhythmic movement in the insect world.

Who hasn't enjoyed the unfolding of a flower in the slow-motion camera, with its accents that are not smooth, which do not flow openly, smoothly, as would seem to the naked eye? The camera reveals that this has a rhythm, that this has accents and pauses. And also, who hasn't been delighted by the symphonic complexity of a summer afternoon out of doors where the trees and the grasses and the clouds and the flowers and the water are all under the command of the wind, almost like a conductor with a baton? The shadings and the timings and the accents are all in different speeds, all in different dynamics and with different time lengths: a fascinating and highly complex organization of rhythm in nature. Indeed, the scientists tell us that inanimate Nature itself is a vast rhythmic structure of vibration from the atom to the galaxy of stars. Some of these vibrations are too long, too extended. We cannot possibly understand the rhythm of the glacier. The time spaces are so extended and so cosmic we cannot possibly grasp it. We can only grasp all of these rhythmic ideas if they are within the span of our own human perceptions.

It seems to me that rhythm and vocal sound are born right in us. They come to us from untold ages past. And I think, also, that they were the very first arts and they were extant long eons before recent inventions like painting and architecture, language and sculpture. Music (the vocal kind especially) and movement have been linked from the very beginning. They were handmaidens; one accompanied the other. The song was the expression of the emotion, perhaps, of the dance; the dance expressed one kind of emotion and music accompanied it. For twenty or thirty thousand years this wedding of the two arts has certainly existed.

But then there was a change. Roughly by the Middle Ages the two arts seemed to be pulling apart, and they have been pulling apart more and more. They are concerned with their own techniques, with their own theory, with their own procedures. They tend, first of all, not only to drift apart, but also to forget their origins, to forget their heritage. The musicians ignore the physical basis of rhythm and dancers are much too insensitive to music. They not only forget their common origins but also their interdependence. Each is concerned with craft, technique, theory. My branch of the art, theater, is not even a good partner to music, nor the music to dance as good a partner as it could be, because of this tendency to divergence, to concentrate on the isolated problems of each art itself.

I'd like to explain what I mean by lost origins. Take rhythm as an example. Rhythm, it seems to me, can be defined as measured energy, grouped into patterns. How do we perceive this measuring and this energy and these patterns? Through the body. All physiologists and psychologists agree that this is so. Rhythmic perception is gained from sensation through the tensions of the muscles and activity of the body and this, by the way, is a special sense of the body. It has been named: it is called *the kinesthetic sense*. It is a sense added to the five with which everybody is familiar and it is the sense which measures energy, which tells you where you are in space, which judges the amounts of tension, of accent, of time-space, of all things which have a bearing on rhythm.

This kind of rhythmic sense does not come from mathematics. The mathematics comes from it. So that rhythm is not $\frac{3}{4}$ time and $\frac{4}{4}$ on paper. That's a code for the eye to remember these rhythmic sensations. Nor does rhythm come from words, such as *accelerando, ritardando, andante, allegro*. These are also code words to remember the rates of energy that the body has already perceived. I believe that out of the rhythmical structure of movement has grown the rhythmical structure of music.

I would like to make two very simple examples of this. Supposing we had been developed not from the monkey family as we were and finally had grown up to stand on two legs and to free the hands for other uses. Suppose we had developed from the fish family. Suppose we were by now super-fish instead of super-monkeys. We would have an entirely different sense of rhythmic structure. The fish has no idea of beat. There is nothing in his physical makeup, in his organization to make him aware of beat. The fish rhythm would be undulating. We would have faster and slower and we would have been aware of time-space, but the accent, the beat idea would have been quite foreign. I don't think a fish, even a super-fish, would ever be aware of or get any feeling of continuity from the tick of a clock. They are not conscious of anything of this sort in beat. The beat comes from the fact that we are bipeds. Men have walked from time immemorial. There was a binary accent of rhythm in $\frac{2}{4}$ and the feeling of the beat I think comes from the walk, the run, marching, dancing on two feet. The sense of beat comes not only from that, but also from the heartbeat and from other stresses and accents which we use to grasp things, to pull, to strike, to make sharp or smooth accented movements, measured in energy.

Now there is one other example. How do you think we have gained our conception of slow and fast? What is slower? Slower than what?

What is fast? Faster than what? We use these terms in all sorts of situations in human activity, of course in music too. It doesn't seem to me that this is from marks on the metronome. It seems to me that this is from the walk. Everybody has a point of reference in the body itself, so that the walk is what we think of as the common denominator when we say faster. We are unconsciously thinking faster than the normal walk or slower than the normal walk. And anything which pushes us beyond that into a faster tempo than the walk or the heartbeat is faster than anything which retards us, which feels slower. Now, let me show you, as an example, without thinking of this in musical terms at all. Just think of this in the sense of reference to a slower or faster beat. This would be one [handclapping]: clap—   clap—   clap—   clap—   clap—clap. This would be a little slow, I think. The beat of the walk is probably about like this, everybody's common denominator of the walk: [handclapping]   clap—clap—clap—clap—clap—clap—clap—clap—. This feels about in the middle of beating tempos. The next is fast, because it is faster than the normal walk: [handclapping] clap-clap-clap-clap-clap-clap-clap-clap-clap-clap-. Now this one: clap—   clap—clap—   clap—   . This gets so slow it isn't a rhythm at all. We begin to lose the continuity between accents, and it begins to be without a beat. There is accent and then a pause. It loses its connection or its grouping with the other beats; so slow, so far away from the normal rhythm of a human being that it doesn't seem to be a rhythm at all.

Now if it is true, and I believe it is, that rhythm is perceived in the body, then dancing is the best training for encouraging and improving this sense of rhythm, because it is the one activity that not only includes the physical but also the mental and the emotional equipment of the human being. There is total physical awareness, but also the mental and the emotional equipment of the human being. There is total physical awareness, but also these added elements that do not occur in the practice of sports or in any other physical activity that I know of. Havelock Ellis, the eminent British philosopher, has said in *Dance of Life*, "If we are indifferent to the art of dancing we have failed to understand, not merely the supreme manifestation of physical life, but also the supreme symbol of spiritual life."

I do not say that a musician would be without rhythm if he did not dance. This is obviously not true, because a great many musicians have a very fine sense of rhythm, both in the best sense and in the overall sense of the flow of rhythmic phrases. I think that this is because there are a great many individuals who have an instinctive remembrance of these origins of rhythmic movement in the body. But I do say that a musician who does not cultivate the body is overlooking the source and the regulator by which rhythm is perceived. In other words, it could be improved; it could be developed where there is none; it could be very much better.

The conductor is the most physical of all musicians. I am always interested in the kind of dance the conductor is going to do on the podium. The moment he gets in front of his orchestra he begins to use body rhythms to make his meaning clear to the orchestra. He moves, he gets up on the half-toe, he sways the body, makes motion—all expressive movement in the body. This is the only person among musicians who is completely free and completely able to use the body. He isn't tied to an instrument.

I think that dancers are very lacking in some aspects of rhythmic and musical training too. They do have rhythm and phrase sense, but they often do not have good enough ears to relate the movement accurately enough to what they hear.

The Phrase

One more part of music I want to speak of which has its origin in the body, and that is the phrase. The phrase is born of what originally was said, or sung, or spoken on a breath. It seems to me that our sense of the phrase (just as our sense of the beat comes from the walk) comes from the long-ago origin when people spontaneously sang or spoke on a breath. We instinctively like this kind of phrase. The phrase that is in a normal breath-length or even slightly elongated, as the singers use it, is satisfying. It is a comfortable phrase. The phrase that is longer than that is apt to make us feel slightly tired. We're trying to catch up; we don't feel we can take a breath, because the performer isn't taking a breath. I think we find this in literature, too. I myself am absolutely exhausted at the end of reading one of Faulkner's page-long sentences.

The too-short phrase also is not satisfying. It doesn't seem to be complete. We're not borne along with it. We have some breath left which hasn't been used, so the very short phrase seems to be too sudden, too accented, too broken off. We could learn very much about the phrase. The dancers could too, especially. I'm making a very radical suggestion now: I think that dancers should be taught to sing, and I don't mean *solfeggio* and I don't mean just the ordinary song. I mean in the sense of using the voice freely and almost improvisationally, the way it was when our primitive ancestors were making the first song. This would give us a whole new sense of phrase. And I think this wouldn't do the musicians any harm, either, not to be merely confined to the conventional song but to learn to flow, to rise in feeling through the voice and to realize the length of the breath. And in this connection I'd like to pose a question: why do you think the conductor in rehearsal sings the phrase to his orchestra? It is because it isn't on the page and also because very often it isn't in the musician either. But he has the feeling; he is the dancer-conductor.

FIFTEEN

Under Way:
Composing for Martha Graham

Details of Contemporary Collaboration

Lehman Engel

*B*ORN IN JACKSON, *Mississippi, Lehman Engel (1910–82) conducted opera in St. Louis before moving to New York, where his career flourished as both composer and conductor for Broadway musicals, TV, and film. His legacy of encouraging younger composers has lived on through his books and the musical theater workshops sponsored by BMI (Broadcast Music, Inc.).*

Early on, Engel was entranced by the process of collaboration for the theater. In the passages from his memoir, he relates a breezy story of how he associated with vaudeville entertainers and came to compose for Radio City Music Hall dancers, contrasted with his reverential account of how he came to collaborate with Martha Graham.[1]

In the second article, the composer generalizes about changes in musical tastes and working procedures in the dance world around him. He then offers opinions on such topics as the varying functions of music for dance, the pitfalls of simultaneously creating music and choreography, and ways that music can add to the energy of the dance.

***

UNDER WAY: COMPOSING FOR MARTHA GRAHAM

John Martin, critic of *The New York Times*, made me acutely aware of the modern American dance movement, and Harry Losee was the first of many dancers I was to know.[2] Harry and his friends seemed to me both fascinating and evil, and I was dazzled by their cheap glamor. They were the embodiment of the storybook New York, but their behavior—far from being harmful—helped me to grow up, to observe, to learn, to reject what was not compatible with me.

Harry, a tall, well-developed man in his mid-thirties, lived in a cheap hotel, a hangout for infrequently employed vaudevillians. He was always surrounded by other dancers, booking agents, hangers-on (but to God alone knows what). Because of prohibition, he himself produced quantities of gin. We stayed up very late every night.

I wrote music for him, which he used in a free recital at Wanamaker Auditorium—his gesture toward "art." He wanted, as many performers want (in an abstract sort of way), to be a "great" artist, but he was unwilling to sacrifice anything from the frippery of his wasteful life for sustained work.

One engagement brought Harry to Radio City Music Hall early in its existence. Harry worked on a dance number for himself, a female partner, and the resident corps de ballet. A day before the opening performance, it was discovered that the music he had worked with (Ravel, I believe) was not available.

Harry called me to the Music Hall at about midnight prior to a scheduled 10:00 a.m. orchestra dress rehearsal, asking me to compose

FIGURE 15.1 Lehman Engel. Caricature by Aline Fruhauf, originally published in *Dance Observer*, December 1935. Reproduced by permission of Deborah A. Vollmer.

new music. Two exhausted dancers lay on the floor of a small office where I worked at a piano. When I would complete a phrase or two, the dancers would come alive, stand up, try out the steps to the music, then lie down again. A music copyist would appear at regular intervals to take a section at a time to an assembly-line of orchestrators and copyists. (This went on all night.) At 11:00 a.m. the orchestra played the music, and the dancers changed none of their choreography. I was paid seventy-five dollars.

If Harry Losee initiated me into the profane order of the dance (and there were many others like him along the way), it was Martha Graham, who, unknowingly, beckoned as a high priestess.

When I first saw Martha Graham dance (about 1930), I had such an overwhelming experience that it became imperative that I compose music for her. Although we had never met, I was a good friend of John Martin's, and I could therefore claim some common tie with her. I sent her a letter requesting an appointment. She did not reply. I telephoned her studio and wrote to her again. After several months of fruitless pursuit, I was at last given an appointment to meet her and her accompanist, Louis Horst, at the latter's apartment. At the designated time, I rang the doorbell, received no reply, waited an hour, then went away. This did not prevent my writing again.

After several more weeks of trying to see her, she made and kept an appointment at Louis Horst's apartment. They listened intently to my music. Both were sympathetic and promised that we would collaborate.

It was in the fall of 1931 that we actually began work. We did many compositions together during the next three years, and they involved me totally. (*Ceremonials*, 1932; *Ekstasis*, 1933; *Transitions* and *Marching Song* and *Imperial Gesture*, all 1935.)

Martha created most of the choreography in advance of my seeing anything. She would perform alone or with the girls in her group to "counts." I would comprehend an overall mood, write down the counts, notating phrases or accents or climaxes or places where we agreed there should be silence. Martha would talk to me, usually in terms of qualities or general essences like "the stillness of sunrise" or "the sound of a forest at night" and I would go away, wrapped in a kind of magical mood of her making. Then I would compose to this framework of mood and counts and return with what I had written. She would listen, comment (usually enthusiastically) about the style and quality, and then dance to it, counting and listening at the same time. Here she felt there were too many notes. (I would thin them out.) Here the music should sustain while she moved, or the music should move rapidly while she sustained. Always there had to be complementary interaction. Much of the most concrete work was done in the final week and even on the day of performance—in an atmosphere of terror.

But the experience of working with Martha Graham was among the sublime moments of my young life.

Martha of course never had any money. She usually paid me an "outright" fifteen dollars for a score (orchestration included).

In one of our long "collaborations," Martha asked if I would object to begin writing the music of a sizable middle section. She explained that in one part she wanted the music to be like wallpaper—real background without melodic contour or rhythmic interest. After watching her rehearse this section to counts a number of times, I agreed to commence with it. She said there were eighty-seven counts of "seven."

A couple of days later I returned to her studio, where she characteristically sat on the floor (her hands covering her eyes) to hear what I had written. She was very well satisfied with the "feeling," and then decided to "try it on." I played and Martha danced. After two bars we were not together. We tried again with identical results. Finally I asked her to dance to counts aloud. What I heard to my horror was "1-2-3-4-5-6-7-pause." Her "sevens" were "eights"!

Martha not only taught me much about dance and music with dance but also exercised on me a profound influence in an incalculable variety of other ways. I was able to employ her ideas of music-movement complementarity when I began writing incidental music for plays. I merely substituted word motion for body motion, the musical principles being nearly identical. I always recalled her saying that a bodily movement *must* be carried through to completion if it is to have any meaning. This was my most valuable single conducting lesson. It taught me the necessity of full, positive, energetic gestures and the sense of strength especially needed in guiding an orchestra through quiet, seemingly relaxed passages. It was from her that I learned that relaxation in a performance can only *seem*, not *be*.

Because Martha was great, my music was serviceable, and because the newspapers had some good words for me, more dancers wanted me to write music for them. Within three or four years I had written for practically all the concert dancers in America. I had become a vogue. (Almost everyone at some time does become a vogue.)

Martha Graham is a great artist and innovator. Her choreography lives on even without her physical presence as a performer.

DETAILS OF CONTEMPORARY COLLABORATION

A close observer of the dance of, let us say, ten years ago who, by some chance might have disappeared in the interim and then returned to the scene at the present time, would not only have noticed a great change within the dance itself, but more especially would he be inclined to remark about the disappearance of Beethoven, Chopin, Tchaikovsky, Schumann, Grieg and Brahms from the programs of contemporary dance performances. If he were a shrewd observer, he would discover that a majority of the music now employed by our leading dancers has been composed especially for the dance, and if he were extraordinarily shrewd, he would find that a larger percentage of contemporary works appears on dance programs than upon purely musical programs.

Despite the fact that we, even at the present time, have witnessed many excellent dance creations which have been superimposed upon already made musical compositions, it becomes increasingly apparent that from the dancer's point of view, this manner of creation is not the ideal one.

In the first place, the length of the music could not possibly coincide with the length of the dance if the dancer develops his theme entirely out of itself. Most art works which occupy time consist of sections (phrases) and build cumulatively to a climax. The exact point at which this usually transpires, how long it is maintained, and how rapidly it falls are conditions dependent on the theme: its length, its rhythmic, harmonic and melodic contours; the composer's style and temperament; and the kind of formal mold which the composer chooses as logically suited to his musical material.

In much music adopted by dancers, if the actual theme can be lightly considered, the phrase and sectional cadences (psychologically related to breathing), and the climax at least will obtrude violently if they are not treated as such. The matter resolves itself into a consideration of freedom and artistic independence, conditions which any creator within the limits of his own art requires. The dancer should no more have to consider music in the creation of his compositions than the playwright need bother about the color or texture of scenery and other stage props.

A leading contemporary German dancer has her permanent musical director create music for her simultaneously with her working-out of the dance. On the surface, this system would appear to be an ideal one, but a closer examination of its dangers and dance limitations, I believe, renders it less desirable. In the first place, simultaneous creation would require immediate externalization of all ideas—a method which is not compatible to every creator. There is a creative danger, for the two-fold progress of dance with music in creation is bound to result in improvisation of both, and improvisation presents problems of danger. For purposes of exercise and practice, it might be used to a distinct advantage, but creatively, it employs the intellect to a lesser degree than the emotion and is apt to lead both composer and dancer far astray. Any success which might come from such a treatment must be the result of the employment of such simple and constant rhythmic patterns that in a sense, it would be impossible to go astray. In the opinion of this writer, the method of simultaneous composition and dance cannot therefore be widely successful.

What then, may be said of the dancer who plans his choreography alone, puts it into rehearsal, and then engages a composer to write music to it? In this way the dancer is able to develop whatever theme he wishes to express without external hindrance. The phrase-placements are his own; the dynamics are his own; cadence, climax, conclusion all occur as a result of the germination of his own idea. Above all, he is rhythmically free. If he is employing a group of dancers, he can consider polyphony of movement which may be sufficiently complex without any other consideration.

Anyone who has observed even the most elemental kind of dancing in its relationship to music must agree that the music imposes a kind of domination. A strong musical accent produces a like effect on the dancing; a sudden musical pause causes a break in the movement; crescendi or diminuendi exact a corresponding change in the dance; the full musical end brings about an instantaneous conclusion in the dancing. We have grown accustomed to these sorts of things for centuries.

All of this is by way of saying that actually or only apparently, the dancer accepts certain aids from the music. Sometimes it is a rest-impulse, sometimes an impulse of motion. At other times, the music becomes background and background alone, and sometimes it serves as decoration.

Now it is therefore not only possible for the composer who creates *after* the dance to make backgrounds and decorations for the dance through "counterpointing" it, but it is his duty as well to make musical impulses of dance-impulses and in so doing to supply the dance with energy which it is accustomed to expect from music-energy which in reality the dance will have given itself. And in this method lies the most nearly complete realization of what the dancer has originally set him-self to do.

The composer who would write for the dance has a problem in omission to learn, for if he writes music which is thoroughly independent, he has left no place for the dance. The typical musical composition for dance should (in the opinion of this writer) lack as much as the accompaniment of a song, but in different ways. Whereas the typical song accompaniment may be complete rhythmically but lacking in melody of any distinction, the dance music is frequently complete melodically and incomplete rhythmically. The dance itself supplies rhythm. If the music intended for dancing— especially in the case of highly complex and changing beats—were rhythmically "full," any attempt on the part of the dancer to compose counter-rhythms would be either ineffectual or render the texture unbearably thick.

The composer also must be careful in his use of musical "impulses" such as sudden sforzandi, accents, pointed dynamics. On the other hand, he must not fail to support the dance when these things occur within it. Above all, no element of his music must be so abundantly present that it can possibly absorb too much attention and become foreground instead of background. This latter prohibition is a principal reason why the music of Johann Sebastian Bach will always remain "dance-proof." It destroys anything which is placed beside it.

The present writer has felt a hundred times repaid for the work which he has undertaken in this field. Again, much of the ultimate success of even the music rests with the dancer who has it within his power to be considerate of the composer's efforts. If the two creators wish honestly to set up a true polyphonic structure, they must both learn how occasionally to retire, each in his turn, in favor of the other. For there are times when the dance is building toward and nearing a high point when it is impossible for the composer to do more than follow, but there are other times when the musical fabric which has been set in motion, in order to avoid collapse, must needs pursue a certain idea, perhaps only a measure or two longer before relinquishing it. It may happen coincidentally that at this point the choreography is not entirely inevitable. Certainly then, in the interest of the coalescence, the dancer should try to make an adjustment. If this sort of cooperation exists between composer and dancer, there is little reason to suppose that they cannot create something which would be a reflection of credit to both, and at the same time it is safe to say that their union of efforts should produce in this way the best results possible under a collaborative system of creation.

The inquiring observer of the contemporary dance, having discovered the reasons for the disappearance of certain music from dance programs and having realized that it was due to the rising independence and maturity of the art that it has liberated itself from its former state of dictatorship by music, might also realize that in adapting this comparatively new attitude towards music, the dance has removed itself from the realm of the slight, the entertaining, the purely decorative, and has set itself through this one single gesture on a plane with the best of each of the other serious, independent, creative arts.

SIXTEEN

Relating Music
and Concert Dance

An Idea for Elastic Form

Henry Cowell

W IDELY CONSIDERED A *galvanizing force in modern American music, California composer Henry Cowell (1897–1965) made a transatlantic splash early in life with his inventive use of tone clusters and techniques of strumming, plucking and hitting the strings directly inside the piano. Later on he studied musical traditions from around the globe and used a rich palette of sounds in his symphonic and chamber works. His contribution as a promoter and publisher of his composer colleagues' works was both generous and important in the general artistic scene.[1]*

In the world of dance, scores by Henry Cowell were used early on by Jean Erdman, Erick Hawkins, Martha Graham, and many other choreographers. In our own time, leading artists including Mark Morris continue to draw on this composer's large treasure trove of scores. Cowell invented a concept of "elastic form," a procedure (set forth in this 1937 article) that he felt could be of particular service because it was practical, adaptable, and geared to fluctuations that might occur in dance performances. Younger composers (including Lou Harrison) made substantial use of Cowell's ideas and example.

***

The relation of music and the dance is one of the subjects most discussed by concert dance artists. Yet in spite of the agitation on the subject, all concerned must admit that it has never led to a really satisfactory solution. And even now, the ideas advocated by the leading concert dancers and their associate musicians, and which are practiced by them, lead to a frustrated relationship between the music and the dance.

At first, concert dance was practically all choreographed after the music, and rested on the form and emotional content of the music. Some dancers "interpreted" great music, often with movements that had nothing to do with the rhythm of the music. Usually such dancers fell back, paradoxically, on making motions to the music's rhythm.

Then came various "modern" ideas. Nearly all of these, as far as music is concerned, have arisen from the natural and correct desire of the dance to be independent and not reliant on the music for its form and content. There have been dances without any music or sound. There have been dances to percussion sound only. There have been attempts to write the music in the studio at the same moment that the dance is being invented. There have been dances composed first, after which music was written for them. This reverses the idea that the dance should be made to the music.

All of these methods may lead to some excellent results, and there is no reason why any of them should necessarily be abandoned. There is no need to feel that one solution, and one only, must be found to cover all cases.

Modern composers take for granted that they must compose an absolutely set piece, with each minute detail carefully planned, and that the performer must always play it as near as physically possible the same way. He prides himself on the rigidity to the smallest detail. The freedom of form, as compared to the older classics, consists of more irregular sections and diversity of lengths in the phrases. But once decided upon, these are rigidly set in the composition.

There is no complaint against the composer creating all the details of his own work. There is, however, no reason to believe that all music should be alike, and that there is any stigma attached to music that is free-flowering instead of already set.

One of the elements that have disturbed the modern concert-dancer the most in trying to adjust his dance to already-composed music has been its setness of form, which is incompatible with the greater natural freedom of the dance. That is because the composer knows no other way of working. Either he creates music in a certain form—which may be very new, irregular and made to suit the particular dance, but which once made is set—or his work is formless.

In order to establish a meeting ground for musical and dance composition, in which the dance will be more definite than usual in form, although just as free to make changes, and the music will be less rigid than usual, although no less containing structure, I would propose the establishment of what might be called elastic form. This type of form would be used as a foundation for both dance and music, and either the dancer or the musician could take the first step in making a creation in it. Its relation to older form would be much the same as the relation between ancient and modern concepts of the Universe. The ancients regarded positions as being fixed, and while they recognized the stellar movements, these were thought to be set according to an unvarying plan. Now, we regard the galaxies of Universes according to relativity of motion; and while we may regard the motions as belonging to a greater general plan, the plan makes provision for constant changes in speeds and orbits, and new relations between speeds are found at any given moment.

The practical method of creating elastic form is something which must be studied, and since the subject is in its infancy, anyone who works at it has the opportunity to make new discoveries. Possibilities of infinite elasticity are remote as a practical measure. But a beginning has been made if there are even as many as two possible avenues of expanding a certain form.

Following are some ideas which I feel are practical to incorporate at once into certain musical structures specially written to be adapted to the dance. Since my province is music, I cannot opine what a dancer would wish to invent toward such a form, in case the dance is created first.

1. Each melodic phrase should be so constructed that it may be expanded or contracted in length, by the shortening or lengthening of certain key tones. In writing down, the composer should give the different versions.
2. Each sentence, as well as being capable of varying length, should be so constructed that it may be used as a block-unit in the general structure.[2] This means it may be used and then another sentence may follow, or it may be repeated, either in the same form or in a varied form (which the composer may indicate) if it is desired to expand this portion of the dance.
3. Each section should be so constructed that it may be used in the same way as suggested for sentences; that is, as well as

being capable of being long or short, owing to how many repeats are employed in the sentences, it must be able to repeated or not.

4. Both sentences and sections may be so arranged, in final cadences, so that they may be shuffled about, and not always appear in the same order. For example, let us suppose that three different sections are used. They might appear the first time in the order 1, 2, 3, 1; and follow afterwards in the order 2, 3, 2, 1. In case not all possible orders of sequence are practical, the composer may indicate which ones may be employed.

5. If percussion instruments are used, they should be scored in such a manner that the rhythms may be played on different sets of instruments—that is, one part which may be played on either dragon's mouths or wood-blocks, another which may be played on either Chinese or Indian tom-toms, etc. Also, there should be a full set of parts to use in case of a large performance; but a certain few of these parts should outline the essential rhythms, and be so marked, so that it is possible to cut down the number of instruments used and still preserve the outline. The parts which may be played on alternate instruments enable a dance studio to rehearse the work, irrespective of what type of drums and percussion instruments it happens to possess.

6. The melodic and harmonic part of the work should be arranged so that all of it may be played on a piano, as that is the instrument usually at hand to rehearse with. In many cases it is also desirable to have other melodic instruments used in a performance, since the piano is more colorless from backstage; therefore, optional parts for instruments should be included. These should be so arranged that either one orchestral instrument may be used, in case of a smaller performance, giving the main melody; or several may be used, in case of a larger performance. The scoring should be so arranged that each part may be given to any of several different instruments, owing to what is available. Thus, the high part might be constructed in such a fashion as to be played on either a flute or a violin, the middle part on either a viola or a clarinet, the lower part on either a cello or a bassoon, etc. This means that the work may be performed with the players at hand, instead of having to go to the expense of engaging additional players to

suit exact instrumental requirements for each number, and which may be merely a whim on the part of the composer.

7. The whole work may, then, be short—the minimum length being determined by performing each sentence and section once only—or as long as is desired, by adding the repeats ad libitum. It may be performed with percussion alone, with piano alone, with orchestral instruments, or with one orchestral instrument, or with any combination of these. In this way, the individual rhythm, the phrases, the sentences, the sections, the whole work, the rhythmical and the tonal orchestration are elastic. The whole work will, in any of its ways or presentation, have form; but it may be easily adapted to the changes and freedoms so essential to the dancer's creation.

SEVENTEEN

Sound-Companion for Dance

Henry Cowell's Music

Norman Lloyd

*W*RITING AFTER *Henry Cowell's death, composer-pianist Norman Lloyd comments about his colleague's particular talent for writing dance music and relates his experience with Cowell's use of "elastic form" for one of Martha Graham's dances.*

***

The romance between Henry Cowell and American dancers has lasted a long time—from 1928, in fact, when Doris Humphrey choreographed Cowell's inside-the-piano piece, "The Banshee," right up to the present. During this almost 40-year period, Cowell's music was the sound-companion for the dances of Martha Graham, Charles Weidman, Hanya Holm, Erick Hawkins, Tina Flade, Jean Erdman, Gertrude Lippincott and many others. And of course his music was used for hundreds of dances that were done by college dance groups.

Why have dancers been drawn to Cowell's music? Basically I suspect that the American dancer felt that Cowell was one of them. He, too, was an explorer of new resources. He was always searching for new approaches to his medium, always inventing sounds that challenged and stirred the imagination of the dancer. His music reverberated, suspended itself, cut capers, was thoughtful—and never overcame the dancer with pretentious complexities. There was about it a sophisticated primitivism that was closer to formalism and ritualism than to romantic agonizing.

The music for *Immediate Tragedy* was written by Cowell in California, while Martha Graham composed the dance in Bennington, Vermont. Cowell knew the mood of the dance, its tempo and its meter. Not knowing how long any section of the dance was, Cowell invented a method he called "elastic form" by which his music could be matched to the dance.

I well remember the day the music arrived at Bennington. Louis Horst and I looked at it and agreed that we had never seen anything like it. Cowell had written two basic phrases to be played by oboe and clarinet. Each phrase existed in two-measure, three-measure, eight-measure versions, and so on. All that was necessary was to fit a five-measure musical phrase to a five-measure dance phrase—or make such overlaps as were deemed necessary. The process, as I remember it, took about an hour. The total effect was complete unity—as though dancer and composer had been in the closest communication. Somber and sparse, the music exactly matched the mood of Miss Graham's dance. *Immediate Tragedy* and its companion piece *Deep Song* became two of the finest solos in the Graham repertory.

Martha Graham recalled:

Henry Cowell has been to me, as to so many others, a stimulant and a delight. When I worked with him it was most serious, and yet about it all was an atmosphere of sustained gaiety—torment, too.

The use of percussion in "Deep Song" opened for me a dark, enchanted area of sound experience. Any dancer who worked with him must have felt, as I did, profoundly stirred to a new expressiveness in terms of body movement.

I not only revered his gift, but I treasure his essential, deep sweetness as a person.

There are many of Cowell's works that have not been used by dancers. His enormous output—more than any other American composer—is a vast treasure chest containing enough good scores to keep dancers busy for a long time. The music is always like Henry Cowell himself—to the point, sometimes amused at itself, healthy and imaginative. As good music should, it wears well.

EIGHTEEN

Composing for the Dance

An Overview of Procedures; Personal Experiences; and Advice to Collaborators

Norman Lloyd

A UNIQUE IMPETUS *to the expansion of modern dance as an art form was the Bennington School of the Dance in Vermont, started in 1934 by Martha Hill and Mary Jo Shelly.[1] Among the artists gathered for the summer programs there was Norman Lloyd (1909–80), who collaborated as both composer and conductor for the choreographers Hanya Holm, Doris Humphrey, Martha Graham, and José Limón. Norman Lloyd and his wife, Ruth Lloyd, were also known for their duet accompaniments with both on one keyboard.[2] Esteemed as an educator, he taught at the Juilliard School and Sarah Lawrence College, later becoming dean of Oberlin College Conservatory and subsequently director of arts programs for the Rockefeller Foundation.*

Writing in 1961, the composer presents a framework for understanding what musical collaboration for the dance could involve. He touches upon examples from the history of European ballet and describes his personal experiences in creating a new work with Doris Humphrey over the course of an entire year, contrasted with his composing of a score for José Limón in just thirty-six hours. In conclusion, Norman Lloyd generalizes about what he considers good music for theatrical dance, with examples from works of his contemporaries.

***

FIGURE 18.1 José Limón and Norman Lloyd. Original inscribed "To Norman with gratitude and admiration, José, Dec. 1949." Photographer unknown. From the collection of Ruth Lloyd.

Different Musical Solutions for Different Dances

In the realm of theatrical dance there are the dances that entertain the tired business man in the night club; the spectacle dances in opera and musical shows; the pleasant, the lyrical, the ecstatic, the story-telling, the abstract, the message-bearing dances of contemporary ballet and modern dance companies.

Dance is, above all, a form of theater. And like theater it is unpredictable. Each new dramatic situation demands a new solution. The composer who writes for dance views each dance as a set of new problems presenting several possible solutions. His skill as a composer for dance lies in his ability to choose one of the correct solutions.

Even without knowing too much about the dances of the past, it is possible to categorize the ways in which dance and music come together.

In most cases the dancer has been thinking about his project for a long time. When he has finally arrived at what he believes is the final version of his dance idea, he presents the composer with a scenario. Sometimes the scenario is just a bare statement of a story or mood line. The dancer might have thought of how many minutes he wants in each section. But there is elasticity to his plan. The composer can write a bit more or a bit less than the time allotted to him. The dancer might have specific types of movement in mind for the various sections of the work. These movements often give the composer indications for tempo, dynamics, or even melodic form.

On the other hand, the choreographer often goes to great length to describe what he wants the composer to do. A composer working on a long ballet received a letter from the choreographer, who was on tour (many dances have been composed by correspondence). The letter, four tightly-packed pages of handwriting, told the composer all the thoughts that were to be suggested by the music as a

FIGURE 18.2 Sophie Maslow, Hanya Holm, Charles Weidman, José Limón, Doris Humphrey, Helen Tamiris. From the collection of the Jerome Robbins Dance Division, The New York Public Library for the Performing Arts, Astor, Lenox and Tilden Foundations.

character in the ballet walked slowly across the stage. It told all the inner thoughts of the character, pointed out his psychological problems, flashed back over his past life and brought him up to the present. And all of this had to happen in a comparatively short musical time.

Choreographers are not always so explicit about the motivation of their characters. But they are often most precise in other ways. Petipa, great choreographer at the Maryinsky Theater in St. Petersburg, gave these detailed instructions to Tchaikovsky:

> Soft music: 64 bars. The tree is lit up: 8 bars of sparkling music. The children enter: 24 bars of joyful animated music. A few bars of tremolo depicting surprise and admiration. A march: 64 bars. A short rococo minuet:16 bars. A galop. Drosselmayer, the magician, enters: awe-inspiring but comic music, 16 to 24 bars. The music changes character during 24 bars, becoming lighter and gayer. Grave music for 8 bars. A pause. Repeat the 8 bars. Another pause. Four bars expressing astonishment. A mazurka: 32 bars. A strong rhythmic waltz: 32 bars.[3]

That out of these instructions came the music for the *Nutcracker* ballet is a tribute to Tchaikovsky's genius—a genius which enabled him to write three of the greatest scores for dance [*Swan Lake*, *The Nutcracker*, and *Sleeping Beauty*].

The ballet master Jean Georges Noverre, whose *Letters on Dancing* (1760) served as the basis for most later developments in dance, collaborated with Gluck on the ballet for *Iphigénie en Tauride*. He explained to Gluck how he wanted each phrase of music to be written so as to fit each step, gesture and attitude.[4]

This approach is similar to that of many of the modern dancers who were working from 1930 to 1950. The dancer created the entire dance first. Then the composer was called in. He looked at the dance, notated its general form, its phrase structure, its metric pattern and often the note patterns used by the dancers.

The composer's problem was to write a piece of music that would fit the dance like a tailor-made suit. The dancers and the composer had frequent meetings to "try on" the music. Changes were often made and even whole sections of the music were discarded and the composer told to try again. At times the job of the composer was more like that of a sausage stuffer. An exact amount of music must be stuffed into an exact amount of time. As dancers discovered that their musical scores suffered by such a procedure, they gradually returned to the traditional scenario, allowing a certain amount of freedom for the composer.

With very few exceptions—mostly Stravinsky—no composer has instigated a successful ballet. The moral of this random thought is that a composer should find a dancer who has an idea for dance—unless one is Stravinsky.

A Few Personal Notes

Doris Humphrey had the notion of making a dance to Garcia-Lorca's poem, *Lament for the Death of Ignacio Sanchez Mejías*, for José Limón. She asked me to write the music. We began by discussing the idea for at least half a year until we began to have a sense of the form and style that the work would take. We decided that I should write the music for the opening and closing sections of the poem while Miss Humphrey would work out the big dance section in the middle of the piece.

After several weeks we came together, I to play the music, she to show me her dance. We changed creative places, and I went to work on the middle section, while she began to choreograph the beginning and ending.

We met constantly. As we put the work together we (more correctly, "she") saw that the beginning was too slow in getting started. Miss Humphrey correctly surmised that after the curtain went up, the music had to have the same impact as the opening tableau. We tore the music apart, rearranged its sections, and ran the piece through again. Much as I hated to have my music lose its leisurely buildup, I had to admit that her theatrical sense was right. The total length of time spent in planning and composing the work: about one year.

José Limón's *La Malinche* was written in thirty-six hours.[5] *La Malinche* was scheduled to have its premiere in Boston on a Wednesday. Exactly a week before, the composer who was supposed to be writing the score confessed that the job was too much for him. After all, twenty-five minutes of music is a lot of music to write.

José called me on the phone. The situation was desperate. The dance was completely finished and was needed for the program. Would I try to knock out something? For an old friend I would.

After finishing my teaching on Thursday afternoon, I went downtown to the dance studio where José was rehearsing. I took with me a big batch of manuscript paper. The dancers—José Limón, Pauline Koner and Lucas Hoving—performed the work for me. I took in the general quality of the piece. Next we worked phrase by phrase. I drew bar-lines on manuscript paper, notated accents, cadences and any important dance rhythms. José sang for me the trumpet calls used by the Mexicans in their revolt against the Spaniards. I went home, wondering how to approach the problem. The story was that of the betrayal of the Mexicans by La Malinche, an Indian girl, who helped Cortez. The whole dance had a folk-play quality.

I started writing Thursday night. To simplify matters I decided to use a "village band" sound of trumpet, drums and piano. From there it was easy to identify the trumpet with the Spaniard, the drums with the Mexican and a soprano voice with La Malinche. Contrapuntal or harmonic subtleties were out. There was no time to write much music.

A gay little Mexican folk tune served as the basis of the beginning and ending to the work, as the strolling players paraded on stage and, at the end, took their bows. I sat down and wrote for thirty-six hours, filling up the paper with the stipulated amount of music. After a short nap I took the sketches to the rehearsal studio. We "tried on" the music. With a few minor adjustments it fit, thanks to the great musical understanding and absolute rhythmic precision of the three dancers. I went home, had another nap. Then the music was written in score. Saturday afternoon it was in the hands of the copyist. And on Wednesday night, on schedule, it had its first performance.

Hints and Random Suggestions

The most basic rule for dance music is: if it works, it's good. This has little or nothing to do with the quality of the music as music. A dance score cannot be judged on purely musical terms. It is necessary to know what is happening on the stage in order to judge the true effectiveness of the music. Dance music is not just an accompaniment—but neither is it the whole show. Dance, like all the theatrical art forms, calls for a blending of movement, sound, lights, costumes and stage sets. The value of a dance score lies in its contribution to the total theater form.

This is not to say that dance music cannot be good enough to be listened to as music. Much of it is. But some music, completely right for the dance, does not lend itself to an independent existence, any more than does the piano part of a Schumann song.

The most effective theatrical sound is a snare-drum roll. It creates suspense, heightens the excitement of the moment—and has little or no musical value. The same is true of much dramatic music, such as the frightening sounds created by Carl Maria von Weber in the "Wolf's

Glen" scene of *Der Freischütz*. The score for most Hollywood cartoons is absolutely right when heard with the picture. Away from the picture, the score is likely to be a series of disconnected short phrases interspersed with musical "Pow," "Crash" and "Yeek."

Most satisfactory dance music seems to be built sectionally. Dance seems to call for musical phrases placed in correct juxtaposition, rather than for symphonic emotional sequences. The master of such section writing is, of course, Stravinsky. The score of *Le Sacre* is full of contrasts of tonality, dynamics, orchestration and rhythm. But there is no attempt to modulate, with the feeling of going somewhere that modulation implies. Good dance music *is*. Much good symphonic music is involved with *becoming*.

A dance seen recently was defeated by its accompanying score. The music rose to climaxes, surged passionately and developed its material skillfully. But one looked in vain for anything in the dance that called for such an array of musical forces. As a result, the dance was made to look more pretentious than it really was. The moral here is that too little is better than too much. After all, dances have been performed effectively without any musical accompaniment. (A good example is Doris Humphrey's *Water Study*.)

Dance music does not have to move a great deal to be effective. The brooding opening of William Schuman's *Night Journey* and the bland but warm beginning of Aaron Copland's *Appalachian Spring* give the audience a foretaste of the mood of the dance that is to follow. Such fairly static sounds also allow the watcher to take in the stage set, the lights, and the costumes of the dancers. There is a kind of metaphysical "space" that cannot be filled too completely. Music that is too active crowds out the other sensations. There must be "space" for the dance. A beautiful example of such "space" is that left by John Cage's few assorted noises that are coincident with Merce Cunningham's *Antic Meet*. The hilariously funny dance makes its points in purely dance terms. The "music" does not get in its way. It is possible that music that tried to be as funny as the dance would call too much attention to itself. And nothing is less funny than a performer saying to the audience: "Look folks! I'm being funny!"

Five Dancers, Five Instruments?

Every now and then there is a discussion about the relative number of dancers and musicians. "Does it seem right for a whole symphony orchestra to play for one dancer?" "Can a large dance company be moved by the sounds of two instruments?" These questions reflect a complete lack of awareness of the problem of combining sound and movement. One of Martha Graham's most contrapuntal group dances was *Celebrations*. The stage was active with dancers jumping, falling and weaving intricate patterns. A score which mirrored the complexity of their movements would have reduced the total effect to pure chaos. Instead, Louis Horst wrote a score for trumpet, clarinet and drum. The music for much of the time was a single melodic line with a drum beat to hold the dancers together. There was enough to provide a mood background of celebration—but not so much music that there would be interference.

The opposite approach was used by William Schuman for Martha Graham's solo *Judith*. In this work Schuman utilized all the resources of the symphony orchestra to provide the stormy, terrifying atmosphere for the dance. Many purists—musical or dansical—criticized the work on the dogmatic ground that one dancer does not need sixty to ninety musicians. The truth is that the composer must use the number and type of instruments that he thinks will be most effective for the work at hand.

Theater, Including Dance, Is the Place to Experiment

The history of musical theater and ballet has shown us that many new sounds have come into general usage via the orchestra pit. The experiments in music today are those involving nonmusical resources: the tape recorder and the electronic gadgets. Dancers have been most receptive to the new ideas for sounds. There is no reason (except his own conservatism) for the contemporary composer for dance to ignore such sounds. The orchestra of Haydn-Berlioz-Strauss is usable for many musical ideas. It does not necessarily provide the instrumentation needed for dramatic situations of today. The dancer or playwright who is concerned with the problems of living in a world of outer space, automation, crowded living conditions, canned foods and canned news, eruptive political events, Existentialist thinking—the list could go on—his musical needs will not be taken care of only by the sweet sound of violins.

The music of Varèse was used by Martha Graham and Hanya Holm long before it became popular in the concert hall. Doris Humphrey's *Theatre Piece No. 2* showed the dramatic possibilities of the electronic music by Otto Luening. George Balanchine and Alwin Nikolais have made electronic music the basis of several exciting dance compositions. Merce Cunningham has used John Cage's "prepared" piano as well as the sounds of what might be called his "unprepared" orchestra. There is no sound that cannot properly be used in the theater.

To Be "Ethnic" or Not

A critic once said to me: "Why did you write dissonant, contemporary-sounding music for a dance about something that took place in Mexico in the 1800s?" My answer was that the work was not a costume drama but a conflict between two men and two antagonistic ways of thinking.

In handling historical material in dance, the question always is: how important are the locale and the time? If they color the dance they probably must color the music, at least to some extent. But it is possible to suggest primitivism without writing authentically primitive music (*Le Sacre*) or America of the pioneer days without quoting liberally from *The Bay Psalm Book*.

Is There a Limit of Complexity for Dance Music?

Dancers have made successful dances to every kind of accompaniment. But there is one general rule about complexity that seems to hold true: the more dancers there are on stage, the more apparent must be the pulse of the music. This does not mean that dancers cannot dance to music where the pulse is subdivided fourteen different ways, nor that they cannot cope with constantly changing meters. But there must be a definite pulsation if a large group is moving.

One of the primary functions of dance music is that it is needed to hold a group of dancers together, just as any marching group needs a drummer or a spoken cadence. A solo dancer can be out of step with the music of a complex score and no one (including possibly the dancer) would be the wiser. But with almost forty dancers onstage, as in José Limón's recent *Performance* at Juilliard, it does matter if the dancers are out of step with each other. There is a point of rhythmic subtlety beyond which the composer cannot go. He must constantly have in mind the fact that his music has a kinetic function as well as an emotional, or mood-making, function. Successful dance scores do have a clearly perceptible beat, despite the seeming complexities of the music.

For more than twenty-five years, Louis Horst and I have taught music composition for dance at Bennington College and the Connecticut College School of Dance. Our first advice to young composers is always: "Show the dancer how much time elapses from count one to count two." Once the pulse is established, the composer can indulge in all kinds of syncopations and other rhythmic tricks.

Should Music Imitate Gesture?

Ever since Jean-Philippe Rameau [1683–1764] first wrote sweeping passages during which nymphs ran across the stage, or descending scale patterns while the gods descended from on high, composers have attempted to introduce gesture into music. The effect is sometimes dramatic—and oftentimes ludicrous.

Even a dance which uses dramatic incidents throughout does not have to be handled like a Walt Disney cartoon. (The process of musical imitation of something visual is known in the trade as "Mickey-Mousing.") José Limón's *Moor's Pavane* tells us all the important actions in the story of Othello. But it is set against the highly formal music of Henry Purcell.[6]

Dance music and dance movement co-exist, but they do not have identical functions. If the dance is going to tell the audience exactly what the music is saying, then there is no need for the dance. The same is true of music; sound must add something to the visual event. At the beginning of Martha Graham's solo *Frontier*, she slowly raised her arm to a position above her head.[7] The obvious musical solution was to write music that also rose slowly. But Louis Horst caught the emotion behind the movement and wrote music which opened a vista of the American plains that the dancer was viewing. The dancer's arm moved slowly; the music was active, quivering with excitement. Such is the ideal counterpoint of music and motion.

PART THREE

TOWARD NEW "AMERICAN" STYLES

There is more than one way to speak of America in music.

—*David Ewen*

Overview

*Defining What Makes Music "American,"
and Common Musical Concerns of Ballet
and Modern Dance*

"American" Includes Many Styles

The preceding articles have chronicled collaborations that early modern choreographers embarked on with composers whose background and training were founded mainly on the classical styles of Europe. However, some musicians did branch out inventively for their dance scores, incorporating rhythms and instrumental flavors from more popular veins of contemporary musical styles. As will be seen in Verna Arvey's observations opening this part, at least a few composers were writing ballet and modern dance scores that drew on then-current jazz styles. Latin American social dance music influenced North American composers as well. Additionally, in the early decades of the twentieth century, there were composers in the United States whose experiments were wildly different from anything that went before.

Louis Horst's first piece for Martha Graham was *On Listening to a Flute by Moonlight*, a title that might evoke the very kind of romanticism that he and other American composers wanted so much to avoid. Indeed, after he left Denishawn, Horst himself traveled to Vienna precisely for more training in composition. But he quickly fled back to America, to Martha Graham, and to the continuation of his unique career as composer-collaborator, accompanist, teacher, and champion of both students and leading artists in modern dance.

The kind of ongoing discomfort that composers and some of their audience members have experienced over time in regard to the aesthetics of European musical art has been characterized by the composer-educator Kyle Gann in his book *American Music in the Twentieth Century* (2006). In addressing the question of American traditions, he suggests:

> Let us take as our premise that there is such a thing as "American music" and that it results partly from the clash of European, African, Asian, and Latin American influences. Partly, not completely—for it also results from unfettered Yankee inventiveness and from the freedom Americans have had to create their own music without the restrictions (or benefits) of an assumed, shared culture. Every American composition is a dialogue between inheritance and freedom. Unlike the histories of, say, European classical or East Indian classical musics, which deal with individual contributions to a strong, continuing tradition, American music is a history of originality and innovation. It is the paradox of American music, in fact, that it is a tradition of originality....
>
> Today, as musical society gropes about for a situation of fairer representation in the arts under the banner of multiculturalism, the public perception is that Asian, African, European, and Latin American cultures each have their own musical identity, but that aside from jazz and rock, there is no such thing as an American concert music tradition. America is so distrustful of its own musical creativity that it continues to project musical achievement on the rest of the world, preserving its own cultural inferiority complex. So intense is the focus on the dichotomy between Eurocentric tradition on one hand and ethnic musics—by which the Third World is meant—on the other, that "American classical music" is perceived as just a special case of the European tradition....
>
> For the sake of our national musical self-esteem, it is urgent to show that America is not an empty vessel into which the musics of other societies may be poured, but a culture with its own genius, innovations, and traditions, now long since capable of influencing other cultures as they have influenced us.... The problem is that Americanness in music has been searched for in the qualities of the music itself, music that is far too diverse to generalize about.[1]

As far as modern dance is concerned, it has long been felt that there is no one "right" kind of music and no single method of collaborating. Moreover, even though they were influenced by multifaceted traditions from around the world, early modern concert dancers and their collaborating musicians were also searching to make something different from previous models: something American, something distinctly their very own.

Turn-of-Century Views

The desire to make something with an "American" stamp had been felt earlier, at the end of the nineteenth century, by some composers who felt the weight of European traditions and comparisons—especially in regard to symphonies, chamber music, and opera.

The Metropolitan Opera House opened in New York in 1882 and its presentations soon became regarded as the epitome of accomplishment in art music. A sense of what audiences were hearing there and in concert halls can be gleaned from a huge four-volume set titled *The Music of the Modern World*, edited by Anton Seidl and published in 1895. Seidl had been assistant to the German opera composer Richard Wagner for six years, and so it is not surprising that one focus in the book is opera, with illustrations of well-known Wagnerian singers of the time, in their larger-than-life costumes depicting figures of Teutonic gods and goddesses. And reflecting both the public formality and the sentimentality of the late nineteenth century, the article on American composers is decorated with an engraved drawing of fairies flitting in the moonlight, along with photographic portraits of mustachioed and bearded white male composers in tailored suits and very formal high collars.

What was the view of "the modern world" of 1895 concerning an American style of composing? Seidl called upon Reginald de Koven (composer of the highly popular operetta *Robin Hood*) to write an opinion:

> The American people is now: the American nation is yet to be. Until we shall finally and once for all have done away with hyphenated nationalities and a consequently divided national feeling, we can not expect to have a uniform feeling which shall be distinctly American, and readily recognizable as such in expression. Further than this, until this feeling is generated by the slow process of assimilation and progress, we can hardly hope to have a distinctive national school of music. The Civil War was certainly a national crisis, great enough to have produced some expression of feeling in music which might have been enduring; but as the cause of that strife was a divided national feeling, none of the airs—some of them striking enough—produced at the time have lived.[2]

De Koven went on to refute at great length the suggestion by visiting Czech composer Antonín Dvořák that American composers look more to the folk melodies of Native American peoples and to black spirituals.[3] He notes that the country was just beginning to develop a leisure class that might support art music and concerts, and that traces of the old Puritan feelings lent a lingering mistrust of secular music and dance as enjoyment. Nevertheless, de Koven could be hopeful:

> It is national pride as well as national feeling that begets national art. Confidence in a national ability is undoubtedly an incentive and stimulus to artistic effort in any nation. Perhaps this is what music in this country most needs today. When we are willing to admit…that the work of Americans of itself can be good and considered equal to the works of others when judged by the same standard of excellence, we shall then stand a better chance as a nation of having a musical art in this country which shall be distinctly national, because encouraged and supported by national confidence and pride. Further than this, we must needs first develop a musical atmosphere of our own in which they can work, before we can expect our American musicians, with the foreign training and experience which is at present a necessity, to turn out musical material which shall be characteristically national or even individual.
>
> As a people today we have an eminently original and constructive faculty. This is strongly marked, and when the rapid civilizing and developing processes which we are now undergoing shall have given us more leisure and broadened our perceptions to the extent of enabling us to see in the cultivation of the arts in general, and of music in particular, one of the noblest fields for the exercise of human energy, we can confidently hope to see the American composer take a place in the world of music commensurate with that which has been won by American workers in other branches of Art.
>
> To be recognized and acknowledged as the interpreter in music of the sentiment and feeling of a nation is surely a noble ambition for any composer.[4]

Twentieth-Century Sounds

As the twentieth century progressed, partly because of their collaborations with modern dance choreographers, composers of generations subsequent to de Koven's did produce scores in quite distinguishable "American" styles, even though some of the musicians initially went to Europe for study (including both Virgil Thomson and Aaron Copland, whose writings are included in this part). It can also be observed that choreographers and composers seemingly took a cue from Dvořák and drew upon folk songs of North America, as well as upon African American threads of blues, spirituals, ragtime, and many styles of jazz.

But what sounds can be considered "American"? In this part's first article, Verna Arvey cites a critical opinion that the ballet score *Skyscrapers* (by John Alden Carpenter) sounded "Russian," and she raises the apt questions: "Because of the uneven meters, one wonders? Surely the Russians have no monopoly on that. Too, one might inquire, what exactly is the difference between a Russian and an American dissonance?"

Nevertheless, without going into detailed technical analysis of multitudes of scores, there are several strands of styles that audiences came to feel had generally discernible "American" qualities.

Jazz

Verna Arvey's writing describes how some jazz elements were adapted into symphonic scores written by her husband, William Grant Still, for theatrical ballets choreographed by Ruth Page and others in the early decades of the twentieth century. However, pure jazz was *not* the choice of most of the early modern choreographers for concert dance, though some of their composers did make use of techniques and nuances that originated in jazz of many flavors. By midcentury, Lester Horton would use music such as Duke Ellington's *Liberian Suite* for his concert dance, and over the decades, other choreographers also expanded their musical choices to include jazz-influenced scores as musical partnering for concert art dance.

There were many styles of jazz, and these certainly came to be easily recognizable as "American." By 1968, Norman Lloyd could give this definition in his book *The Golden Encyclopedia of Music*:

> **Jazz:** the American form of dance music which has branched out into so many different styles that it is difficult to define. It can be classified as Dixieland, ragtime, blues, barrel-house, boogie-woogie, swing, bop, or progressive jazz. It has been smoothed out to become "symphonic jazz," mixed with country "hill-billy" music to become "folk-rock," or given a Latin beat to become a rumba, conga, mambo, or cha-cha. Jazz can be "hot" or "cool." It can "swing" and "jump" or be a "businessman's bounce." Almost any kind of popular song in $\frac{2}{4}$ or $\frac{4}{4}$ time, played with a rhythmic accompaniment, can become jazz—whether it is a sweet ballad, a nonsense song, a musical-comedy love duet, or a deepthroated blues.

In the half century since 1910, jazz in its various forms and styles has conquered the world. To many people it is one of America's most important contributions to the world of the arts.[5]

Early in the history of jazz, a singular boost to both popular ball-room dancing and emerging styles of big-band performance was the collaboration of the dance team Irene and Vernon Castle with James Reese Europe and his Exclusive Society Orchestra.[6] Starting with his Clef Club musicians in 1910 in New York, James Reese Europe (1881–1919) won acclaim for his society dance music and for his annual concerts at Carnegie Hall. The Castles broke racial barriers by insisting on having Europe and his musicians play for their performances. When the union objected and cited rules against black musicians playing in pits of New York theaters, the Castles had Europe's musicians follow them onto the stage, thus thwarting the union rules and giving at least one blow to customary segregation in theatrical venues. It was a great loss when the composer-conductor was killed by one of his own drummers, for he was on the verge of taking early jazz orchestras to a new level of accomplishment in relation to dance.

Perhaps that step was left for others such as Louis Armstrong and Duke Ellington to take later on in the 1920s and '30s, with stylish bands and recordings that accompanied several generations of dancers—not only social dancers but also those on theatrical stages and in films.[7] Among Ellington's compositions in collaboration with Billy Strayhorn was *A Drum Is a Woman*, telecast on the United States Steel Hour in 1956 and featuring Talley Beatty as both dancer and choreographer, with Carmen de Lavallade as the character Madame Zajj ("jazz" spelled backward). The dance and the music together presented a miniature allegory of the history of jazz itself.

Regional Folk and Religious Sources

Some choreographers made deeply felt choices in regard to existing music drawn from their own regional and cultural experiences. Such an example would be Alvin Ailey's *Revelations*, the modern dance work that may have been seen more than any other by audiences around the world. The choreographer stated quite simply, in the memoir extract later in this part, that the genesis for his choreography lay in the spirituals that he heard sung in the black churches of his Texas boyhood.

The earlier modern choreographers, seeking to gain recognition for their efforts as a serious artistic form, generally did not incorporate popular tunes of their times. It was felt to be enough of a departure from ballet simply to use folk-style music (as Sophie Maslow did with Woody Guthrie) or religious melodies (as with the Shaker tune "Simple Gifts" that Aaron Copland incorporated into his score for Martha Graham's *Appalachian Spring*).

The score for *Appalachian Spring* (originally titled simply "Ballet for Martha") exemplifies a wide-open sound that came to be labeled "Americana." Another much-applauded "Americana"-style score by Copland was for Agnes de Mille's ballet *Rodeo*. The recognizable effects are achieved in instrumental sounds with wide-spaced, tonally centered harmonic intervals and distinctive orchestral scoring—found not only in scores by Copland but also in those of Virgil Thomson, Roy Harris, and Morton Gould.

Experimental Works

Another strand of American styles can be characterized as experimental. Charles Ives (1874–1954) did not collaborate with modern dancers, but he certainly influenced a great many composers who did. Ives was trained mainly in Danbury, Connecticut, by his bandmaster–music teacher father (who upon occasion played piano for social dances). Ives went on to study at Yale under the tutelage of European-trained composer Horatio Parker (who dismissed Ives's innovations as jokes and cautioned him to write more "correct" work). Leaving academia in 1898, Charles Ives made a brilliant career in life insurance, thus freeing himself to compose whatever he wanted to without commercial restraints, which he did until around 1918. Isadora Duncan and dance artists who followed her immediately did not collaborate directly with this composer, dubbed by many as "the father of American music." But over the years, a number of choreographers used his extant instrumental and vocal works for their dances, including Anna Sokolow, Joyce Trisler, Eliot Feld, José Limón, and more recently, Mark Morris. Jerome Robbins would set a number of the poignant and powerful Ives vocal works in his ballet titled simply *Ives, Songs*. And in 1988, Paul Taylor first presented his *Danbury Mix*. Regarding this last work, Anna Kisselgoff wrote in *The New York Times* that "Ives...is a perfect match for Mr. Taylor. Both are totally American artists, unafraid to stir the darker currents that swirl below the surface of American patriotism and homespun imagery."[8]

Commenting on the impact of Ives, his biographers Henry and Sidney Cowell suggested:

Until after the First World War, American composers of symphonic music were almost without exception trained in Europe by Europeans, and they absorbed the esthetics of the older civilization along with its techniques. At the time that Ives struck out for himself, Central Europe had been the center of the musical culture of the Western world for 250 years, and a composer from raw America who presented himself there as a student would never dream, nor would he have been allowed, to question the canons of musical composition that were given him as absolute law....Americans naively agreed with their teachers that what a composer wrote was right or wrong depending on how exactly it could be made to resemble what was done in Europe, and they could not wait to get home to "improve the musical standards in America." Transplanted to the United States, the rules of harmony and composition took on a doctrinaire authority that was more dogmatic for being second hand.[9]

In contrast, the Cowells continued, Ives's music had its roots in the church, stage, parlor, and dance music of a small American town—the popular music of his time, in short.

There were composers in New England before Charles Ives, but none who questioned the value of European culture for America or who appreciated the music around him at home. If Charles Ives has been called the father of American music by American composers them- selves, this is not so much because he has wired descendants who imi- tate his music, but because he spoke out so strongly his determination to discover what it meant to be a musician as the twentieth century began in America.[10]

Some of the collaborators for modern dance and ballet who could be considered mavericks of inventive music in America early in the twentieth century included George Antheil (whose *Ballet mécanique* is described in Verna Arvey's article); Henry Cowell (especially in his early "inside-the-piano" works); Henry Brant (whose work *The Great American Goof* received positive applause in the *Dance Observer* edito- rial included here); Harry Partch; and John Cage, whose sound scores for Merce Cunningham are given attention in Part Four.

Drawing from the World

Beyond such broad outlines, however, it may be hard to categorize musical styles as "American." Does the fact that a score was written by an American make its sound recognizable as "American"? One com- poser to consider: Lou Harrison, who in his work with percussion for

West Coast dancers could be considered a "maverick," also wrote pieces in the twelve-tone serial procedures invented by the Vienna-born composer Arnold Schoenberg. Later, Harrison explored Korean and Indonesian traditions and incorporated some related sounds and procedures into the personal compositional kits that he devised for each separate composition. Working with choreographer Jean Erdman on mythological narrative dances such as *Solstice*, he achieved effects that can strike one as "universal."

Would the listener necessarily label the music as "American" if one did not know it was by an American composer? Then the question arises, isn't it enough if it is simply theatrically effective for the dance performance? And one is drawn back to wondering why the early moderns made such a point of wanting to be regarded specifically as "American" artists. Did it all, ultimately, have to do with bottom-line considerations of bookings, attention in the serious press, and full respect as artists who were tired of having their dance and music being compared to European works as the only standard of excellence?

Flavors of the Caribbean

Another thread of musical art styles that became important in twenti-eth-century music of the United States emanated from the Caribbean and Latin America. There was a nineteenth-century model to follow, namely Louis Moreau Gottschalk.

In the mid-1800s, America's first internationally touring piano soloist, Gottschalk (1829–69), achieved sensational success with per-formances of his virtuosic arrangements and original pieces in the style of Caribbean (especially Cuban) dances and the Creole dances he heard while growing up in New Orleans.

Gottschalk was of mixed heritage, with a Jewish-English father of German descent and a French Creole mother, who arranged for him to have musical training in Paris. His subsequent travels included "monster" concerts with many pianos and the kind of mass hysterical greetings that are experienced nowadays by rock stars. He described his flamboyant life and musical experiences in his published memoirs. Commenting on why the music of Gottschalk survives, the composer-writer Kyle Gann has observed:

> Gottschalk's piano pieces, modeled after Chopin and with sentimen-tally programmatic titles such as *The Dying Poet*, *The Last Hope*, and *Souvenir de Porto Rico*, can be superficial, but they also represent a bold

and authentic introduction of African and Cuban idioms to the piano repertoire, decades before ragtime would continue the effort. Today, the music of…Gottschalk has retained considerable popularity, for its own beauty as well as for being a symbol of an inimitably American musical sensibility. The contrast illustrates the enormous conflict in American music between those who believe that great art can only come from following the European tradition and those who feel that America's new situation required starting from a clean slate with an attentiveness to the local environment.[11]

Some pertinent observations about the dance-based forms of Gottschalk's works can be found in the book *Music in a New Found Land* by the late British writer Wilfrid Mellers. Gottschalk's music is certainly a nineteenth-century example of cross-cultural blending, and it foreshadowed many aspects of styles that became popular in the twentieth century. As pointed out by Mellers:

> One of the earliest [pieces] is *La Bamboula* which, composed at the age of sixteen, is a pianistic arrangement of an authentic New Orleans dance. In Gottschalk's hands the cake-walk rhythm acquires a self-confident bounce that is reinforced by the bright, resonantly spaced piano texture.…*The Banjo* (1851) begins as a banjo-imitation of the most ingenious character. As a black-note figuration grows increasingly rapid, the piece induces a sense of elevation and spring within its rhythmic momentum. This is even more prophetic of the "swing" of New Orleans jazz.…
>
> Musically, the most interesting of Gottschalk's pieces are those which combine Negroid with Latin American elements: African rhythms meet Spanish tango and habañera, and French folk-tune and operetta. *La Bananier* is a charmingly elegant version of a French Creole tune with an African drone bass; *Pasquinade* has a French gavotte tune, with a striding ragtime-like bass and reiterated pianistic ornaments that anticipate the riffs of jazz; *Suis-moi* most seductively fuses habañera with cake walk—a more refined version of a style later to be explored by Jelly Roll Morton. Perhaps the best piece of all is *Souvenir de Puerto Rico*, which was written in the much-favored convention of the Patrol—a processional music that approaches from a distance, reaches a fortissimo, and then recedes into the distance. Most of Gottschalk's dance pieces are based on the variation principle, as jazz was to be later.…This piece…is physical, connected with bodily (processional) movement, and therefore with the dance.…

The relationship between Gottschalk's positive, incipiently jazz pieces and physical movement, brings us to the overtly functional aspects of music for moving to. In Europe had emerged the first school of composers to dedicate themselves to the production of "light" music as such. In origin the Viennese waltz was revolutionary, as compared with the aristocratic minuet; it was physical, a celebration of the sensual present; and it was addressed to a polyglot public—German, Italian, French, Spanish, Polish, Jewish, even Turkish—since nineteenth-century Vienna, like nineteenth-century America, was a melting-pot of nations. It is not therefore surprising that the Johann Strauss band should have been rapturously received when it toured the United States: nor that the Americans should soon have evolved their own fresher, perkier, less traditionally ripe form of music for moving to.[12]

It can be noted that for one of his early dances, Merce Cunningham used Gottschalk's piece *The Banjo*, with the dance also titled simply *Banjo*.

Later Latin Connections

Other concert-oriented composers after Gottschalk continued to be inspired by dance music emanating from the Caribbean and Latin America, and the interchange between music for dancing and music based on dance types but intended just for listening has been considerable. For openers, there are the Latin ballroom dances that became popular in the earlier decades of the twentieth century and continue to be performed with renewed enthusiasm and variations encouraged by television competition shows today.

Cuban and other Caribbean-based music was also certainly one of the threads of traditions with which early modern dancers were familiar. Among choreographers of a later generation, Trinidad-born dance artist Geoffrey Holder (b. 1930), as well as Jamaica-born Garth Fagan (b. 1940) have infused some of their concert dance works with island-flavored music—though they have been just as likely to draw from the repertoire of European classics or American jazz.

Social gatherings gave rise to a distinct syncopated style of music in Brazil. Among the most beautiful are the tangos of Ernesto Nazareth (1863–1934). When he lived in Brazil early in the century, the French composer Darius Milhaud (1892–1974) heard dances titled variously "Fado Portugues," "maxixe," and "choros," in addition to polkas and waltzes popular with Brazilian social dancers and their musicians.[13]

Milhaud quoted many compositions extensively in his 1919 bitonal rondo *Le Boeuf sur le Toit*, which was used theatrically by Cocteau back in Paris. Among the many European artists who fled to the United States to escape the Nazi threats, Milhaud taught for many years at Mills College in California, and his influence was felt among other composers who worked with dancers.

The Argentine tango, quite different from the Brazilian form, became familiar in North America as well.[14] Mexican flavors also added to the mix heard by American concert dancers and their composer-collaborators. Aaron Copland visited Mexico in 1932, when the Mexican composer-conductor Carlos Chávez led an all-Copland concert.[15] Copland returned in 1941 under the aegis of a State Department tour for cultural exchange, and the music branch of the Pan American Union also encouraged intercultural exchanges.

Carlos Chávez (1899–1978) himself came to leave an imprint on the modern dance and music world of the United States. In 1940, he conducted a series of concerts at the Museum of Modern Art in New York. As a composer, he sometimes injected actual Mexican Indian melodies into his concert works (such as with his *Sinfonía India*). Martha Graham used his starker modernistic music for two of her dances: *Prelude* and *Dark Meadow*.

Norman Lloyd was to compose several scores for Doris Humphrey and the Mexican-born dancer José Límon, with idiomatic musical motifs and techniques used deliberately to evoke a Mexican scene. (These collaborations were discussed in chapter 18.)

Atonality, Angularity, and Tense Harmonies

Among academically trained composers in midcentury America, a sizable number were quite taken with the twelve-tone and serial procedures developed by Austrian-born Arnold Schoenberg, who had moved to California and became a U.S. citizen in 1941. And even if some music was not strictly serial in procedure, the use of angular melodies leaping across wide intervals and dense dissonant harmonies characterized the music of a notable proportion of new concert music works.[16]

In the sphere of theatrical dance, such sounds could complement certain strongly emotional works. José Límon choreographed his 1950 dance *The Exiles* to Schoenberg's music, and Antony Tudor's 1942 tense ballet *Pillar of Fire* was also set to Schoenberg's music. Igor Stravinsky made a notable departure from his previous compositional styles when he composed *Agon* for Balanchine's angular 1957 ballet.

Kinesthetic Concerns in Both Ballet and Modern Styles

In regard to a strict demarcation—ballet or modern dance or musical show—there were from the start what we would now term "crossover" or "fusion" styles. Martha Graham began to refer to her concert dances as "ballets," while ballets such as those presented by Ruth Page's company in Chicago—or Agnes de Mille's *Rodeo* with its score by Aaron Copland, or Lew Christensen's *Filling Station* with its score by Virgil Thomson—all included movement and music that differed from traditions of classical European ballet. As far as collaborations were concerned, there was an important common denominator for composers working in both ballet and modern dance: quite simply, did they have a kinesthetic sense; could they write music that made the dancers want to move and that added to the total theatrical effect without detracting from the movement onstage?

The technical training of ballet dancers and the aesthetics of classical ballet continued to be quite different from those of contemporary dance; but even in the early decades of the twentieth century there were many aspects of subject matter, expressive attitude, and musical styles that they had in common. It is noteworthy that as time went on, in its reviews and editorials the *Dance Observer* covered the music used for both genres. And even if the scores of earlier nineteenth-century ballet music could be characterized by consistent meters, clear rhythms, and regular phrasings, yet in the twentieth century, ballet dancers as well as the moderns had to learn to deal with mixed meters, uneven phrases, extended harmonic frameworks, nonhummable melodies, and, increasingly, extremely complicated rhythmic aspects.[17]

Radical changes in both ballet choreography and music for ballet had been ushered in by Sergei Diaghilev's Ballets Russes in the early years of the twentieth century. The company's stunning collaborative theatrical works used music by Darius Milhaud, Sergei Prokofiev, Erik Satie, Nicolai Rimsky-Korsakov, Igor Stravinsky, and other outstanding composers of the time. As the dance historian Lynn Garafola observed concerning Diaghilev:

> He brought new music to dance and commissioned some of its greatest scores, including works that were equally at home in the concert hall. He reared a whole generation of composers willing and able to write for the dance and totally revamped what was thought of as dance music. His influence was felt throughout Europe as well as in the United States, in modern dance as well as in ballet.[18]

As noted in the following excerpt from Verna Arvey's 1941 book, *Choreographic Music*, scores that the Russian-born composer Igor Stravinsky (1882–1971) wrote for the ballets produced by Diaghilev's Ballets Russes set a new tone and standard in the international artistic world. The richly orchestrated early scores include two choreographed by Michel Fokine: *Firebird* (1910) and *Petrouchka* (1911); and *The Rite of Spring*, choreographed by Vaslav Nijinsky in 1913. Stravinsky's sparser 1927 score for *Apollon musagète* is the one that choreographer George Balanchine always singled out as the inspiration for what he might do analogously in movement: pare down to the essentials. That is an effort that America's modern dancers were also making.

In all genres of theatrical art dance, if one had to pick a single collaborative pairing of creators that stood out in the entire twentieth century, it would likely be Balanchine and Stravinsky.[19] After both men moved to the United States, their long association produced many stunning works for New York City Ballet, including not only newly commissioned scores but also Balanchine's use of Stravinsky's original concert music—altogether totaling thirty-nine works. In her volume on *Choreographic Music*, the author Verna Arvey could not have foreseen the extent of Stravinsky's long collaborative career, but already in the late 1930s she considered his work as a model with which to compare the output of American experimentalists, beginning with George Antheil.

NINETEEN

The Cosmopolitan Scene of the 1920s and '30s

Avant-Garde Experiments; Jazz; and Symphonic Ballet Scores

Verna Arvey

D URING THE 1920S *and 1930s in the United States, there were radical musical changes afoot not only with innovative styles of concert music but also in the flowering of African American compositions and improvisations that passed from ragtime into multiple flavors of jazz and what we now term "crossover" styles. In addition, there were those who skillfully blended non-Western and Western techniques—and then there were the experimenters who fit no known category.*

One excited observer of the creative activity churning around her was Verna Arvey (1910–87). A concert pianist and prolific writer on music and dance, early in her career she accompanied dancers from the Norma Gould studios in Los Angeles, for both classes and area performances. In 1939 Arvey married William Grant Still (1895–1978), widely regarded as the first major African American composer in symphonic styles. She went on to collaborate with him on scenarios and words for some of his songs. Perhaps most pertinent here is the fact that she attended many live performances and through correspondence plus personal interviews was able to elicit observations about collaboration directly from well-known artists of her time.

FIGURE 19.1 William Grant Still and Verna Arvey. From the collection of Judith Anne Still.

Arvey's reflections on the variety of music for contemporary theatrical dance allow us to share her excitement in reviewing various new styles that were percolating during the early decades of the twentieth century. In these excerpts she introduces George Antheil's Ballet mécanique *(which was not a ballet at all but rather a 1924 work scored for airplane propellers, sirens, electric bells, odd percussion, and sixteen player pianos, originally intended for a film). The writer ponders the characteristics of jazz and compares movements of ballet and jazz dance. Arvey then focuses on symphonic ballet scores by William Grant Still and John Alden Carpenter (1876–1951) and expresses optimism for the future of American music for theatrical dance.*

***

The American George Antheil created almost as much discussion with his ballets as did Stravinsky.[1] There was a striking difference: no one was bold enough to insinuate that Stravinsky wrote noise instead of music, whereas such accusations constantly greeted Antheil. Long ago Ezra Pound wrote: "As for the machine shop, Antheil opened the way with his *Ballet mécanique*; for the first time we have a music, or the germ and start of a music that can be applied to sound regardless of its loudness. The aesthete goes to a factory and hears noise and goes away horrified; to the musician, the composer hears noise, but he tries to hear what *kind* of noise it is."[2]

This mechanical trend started when Antheil concluded, upon hearing a player piano, that any unmechanical music had reached its doom. From that moment on, the music he wrote was mechanical: ballets characterized by motion and a steel-like rigidity. *Ballet mécanique*, written in 1923–25, is scored for an orchestra of Antheil's wild dreams: anvils, airplane propellers, electric bells, automobile horns, and sixteen player pianos. Half an hour of this caused ecstatic literary people to dub it "music of the future" and musical people to call it "naive, infantile, passionless, force-less." Once that was out of his system, Antheil began to grope for his true métier, away from violent sounds. His fondness for jazz rhythms and tricks once made him take a trip to collect, in the heart of Africa, native forerunners of jazz. In 1929 he wrote a ballet after W. B. Yeats called *Fighting the Waves*. He also, in 1922 (before the *Ballet mécanique*), wrote two ballets which have never yet been performed. His *Flight*, a chamber opera or ballet for marionettes, was written in 1927–30. His *Les Songes* is noted as the first score to be composed directly for the American Ballet Company. In his opinion, two long dances that he wrote for Martha Graham amount to ballets. One is called *Course*, an ensemble dance; the other is *Dance in Four Parts* arranged from his *One Hundred Preludes to the Woman with One Hundred Heads*, after Max Ernst.

Perhaps Antheil's interest in this form of composition arises from the fact that he is fond of dancing in its theatrical aspects and because he believes that America loves it too and will become a great dance country. Hence his desire to follow the trend of the times.[3]

It has been said that jazz is the folk music of America; that all great national schools of music have been built on the songs and dances of the common people, and that Mozart, Haydn, and Chopin, were they alive today, would write Fox Trots as naturally and as inevitably as they once composed Gavottes, Minuets and Mazurkas.

In spite of the fact that Diaghilev thought jazz in the United States was due to the "Jewish sardonic vein," one thing is indisputable: jazz is based on Negro music-making. Other influences may have come later, but the first impulse came from Africa.

Jazz is not just syncopation, as some people believe. It is a very special "something" that the Negroes added to what we have known as music that enables it to be called jazz. Many definitions of this have been advanced. A curious fact is that the more one reflects upon the excellence of these definitions, and the more one considers the subject itself, the more one wonders whether anyone on earth will ever be able to describe in words exactly what jazz is, why it has taken such a hold upon people all over the world, and why it has influenced so many serious musical works, especially those in the ballet idiom.

It is interesting to note that the dance movements that accompany jazz music have had the same effect on dance movement as a whole that jazz itself has had on music. Whereas in classic dancing, knees and toes were turned scrupulously out, jazz dancers now develop knock-knees to add to what is termed "sex appeal." Whereas classicism developed a beauty of line by extending the foot until one danced only on the point of the toe, jazz dancing uses flat feet and heels to emphasize its intricate taps. Whereas classic arm postures surmounted a rigid body, today the hips, shoulders, and head do the major part of the dancing while the hands dangle loosely. Of course, this is a word portrait of contemporary jazz dancing: but any detailed study of the work of modern concert dancers will reveal that they have assimilated those actions, and made good use of them in quite a detached manner—in such a detached manner, perhaps, that they would even resent the suggestion of such an origin.

Jazz has its pioneers, too. Moreover, just as dancers and composers have accepted the Viennese waltz and other national dance forms as a permanent part of their repertoires or their creative consciousnesses, so they have accepted and will continue to accept jazz. In crude and sophisticated dance music the world over it is a well-defined and undeniably strong influence.

John Alden Carpenter and William Grant Still are among those few composers to stride definitely away from the regular-rhythmed dance music to which the public is accustomed. Their music is at once valuable as music, racially fascinating, not imitative, and choreographic. Both of them first wrote ballets with foreign backgrounds; both of them later came to write ballets expressing the American scene in good-humored, satirical music.

Diaghilev commissioned *Skyscrapers* from Carpenter in 1924.[4] He asked for a ballet dedicated to the modern city. Though Diaghilev's production of the ballet never took place, [it was premiered with great success in 1926 at the Metropolitan Opera House in New York, with choreography by Sammy Lee and] it was once produced in Germany [in 1928 with choreography by Heinrich Kröller] under the title of *Wolkenkratzer*. Later in a 1933 Hollywood production, there were many changes. It appears that one of the reasons for changes was that some imaginary authorities had obligingly opined that life had greatly changed since the ballet was composed. Whereas in 1926 people ate hot dogs for diversion, in 1933 a hot dog constituted a full meal.

Though *Skyscrapers* uses American tunes to depict American scenes, one critic found it Russian in its rhythmic pulse and dissonance. Because of the uneven meters, one wonders? Surely the Russians have no monopoly on that. Too, one might inquire, what exactly is the difference between a Russian and an American dissonance?

Be that as it may, Carpenter is vividly contemporaneous and his works are considered to be the most brilliant that are being produced today in American music, because he is constantly drawing closer to life and constantly growing more mature.

A totally different phase of the American ballet is expressed by the younger William Grant Still, himself representative of all the presumably necessary attributes of an American composer.[5] He is known as an Afro-American, yet the blood of the American Indian also runs in his veins. He studied earnestly with George Chadwick and with Edgard Varèse, opposite poles of musical thought. At one time or another, he has played most of the instruments in the orchestra, whence comes the intimate knowledge that leads to his striking orchestrations. He was once associated with jazz, that typically American expression.

The most American of all Still's ballets to date is his *Lenox Avenue*. For many years, he had been gathering themes and putting them into a little notebook. Suddenly, Columbia Broadcasting System invited him to create a musical work designed especially for radio. Soon, then, *Lenox Avenue* (a series of eleven orchestral episodes with intermittent spoken lines for the announcer) sprang into being [in 1936]. It was seemingly the inspiration of the moment, really the accumulation of years of thought. After the composition was complete in its orchestral form, Still realized that it would also make an effective ballet: a series of choreographic street scenes typical of modern Negro life, and he immediately set to work to give *Lenox Avenue* a new form.

If Still's *Lenox Avenue* is jazz (and many will insist that it is, though it was not intended to be) then the source of jazz is truly established once and for all. For these motives are characteristic, though entirely original with the composer. They were suggested to him by infrequent excursions into night club life and frequent visits to revival meetings in search of little-known spirituals, for which he has a genuine fondness. In this way he succeeded in re-creating the actual atmosphere while not adhering to themes invented by strangers.

Still's approach to the composition of dance music is unique. He had seen Pavlova dance, and though her artistry impressed him deeply, he was even then searching for newer, broader forms of choreographic expression in music. Thus his music is rhythmic in such a distinctive way that it can only be adequately choreographed with modern, free movements: the realization of his mental vision. His music is also conducive to sustained movements, not erraticisms. Instead of mentally picturing actual dance steps, he visualized the general trend and feeling of each dance. While he composed his dance music, he would sometimes rise and dance about the room, not only to ascertain the tempo, but also to determine the characteristics and feeling of the music in relation to the movement.

There is good and bad dance music just as there is good and bad music. But dance music can never be judged from the same standpoint as pure music; it cannot be judged apart from its function. If it is sufficiently strong and vital, it will recall its function even when it is played alone. A changing world of the dance is gradually bringing about an improvement in the attitudes of both dancer and composer. Surely more worthy artistic creations will result!

Other young Americans are following the lead of John Alden Carpenter and William Grant Still. The output of good ballets is increasing yearly in the United States. Both musicians and public are becoming dance-minded. This writer believes it to be a necessary development in the evolution of American music, and an unbounded field for inspired creation.

The Theatrical Thirties

Virgil Thomson

W HEN HE PUBLISHED *his memoirs, Virgil Thomson (1896–1989) counted 1937 as a busy year for collaboration: he had written the score for a documentary film about flooding,* The River *(directed by Pare Lorentz), and was commissioned by Lincoln Kirstein to compose the music for Lew Christensen's* Filling Station, *which was premiered in Hartford, Connecticut, by Ballet Caravan in 1938 and found later stagings with San Francisco Ballet and other companies. The ballet has been widely noted as one of the first—if not the first—with choreography, music, design, and dancing all by American artists, plus a story about everyday American life.*

In the following excerpts Thomson begins by speaking generally about collaboration for both film and theater, sketches his work for Filling Station, *and reflects upon what it was like to be a composer at that particular time. The opera success he refers to,* Four Saints in Three Acts, *was a collaboration with the writer Gertrude Stein, premiered with choreography by the British dancer Frederick Ashton. The composer's 1936 film score with Lorentz was* The Plow That Broke the Plains, *about the Dust Bowl.*

***

Collaborative art, I knew from instinct and experience, can only give a good result when each man offers to the common theme, through his own working methods and at the proper time, his own abundance. An author-director needs to keep all such abundances channelized for

FIGURE 20.1 Lew Christensen in the role of Mac, *Filling Station*. Photograph by George Platt Lynes, from the collection of the Jerome Robbins Dance Division, The New York Public Library for the Performing Arts, Astor, Lenox and Tilden Foundations.

nourishing his theme rather than drowning it; of such are his veto rights. But when he suggests textures he is always wrong. These must come out of each man's own technique. An artist cannot be ordered about or hypnotized, but he can be fecundated by another's faith. Here lies the difference between live art and the commercial, that in live work everybody trusts everybody else.

My other work of 1937, almost wholly for me a year of theater, consisted of a ballet and a Shakespeare play. The dance piece, commissioned by Lincoln Kirstein for his Ballet Caravan, was a slice-of-life called *Filling Station*.[1] That midsummer I had found in

Lew Christensen a dancer and director I knew I could deal with, and in the subject offered us by Kirstein a theme I thought I could at least take hold of.

For *Filling Station* Christensen and I worked out a suite of "numbers" and "recitatives" to tell the story in appropriate timings. And I wrote a score made up of waltzes, tangos, a fugue, a Big Apple, a holdup, a chase, and a funeral, all aimed to evoke roadside America as pop art. The painter Paul Cadmus designed clothes and a setting for it inspired by comic strips. Christensen, as a filling station attendant in white translucent coverall, filled the stage with his in-the-air cartwheels and held us breathless with his twelve-turn pirouettes. At the Hartford opening on January 6, 1938, my music was played on a piano by Trude Rittmann.

The years of 1936 and '37 saw three generations of American composers, from the elders Edward B. Hill and Arthur Shepherd, through my own age group to the still-under-thirty Samuel Barber and William Schuman, all in full command of their powers and at work. Ruggles, though no longer working, and Ives were beginning to be played; and Gershwin, who died in '37, was to become a classic. American music was performed across the nation. And in the League of Composers' magazine, *Modern Music*, Edwin Denby was covering the dance; Copland, records and published music; Antheil, from Hollywood, music in films; Goddard Lieberson, radio; Paul Bowles, exotica from Latin America; Colin McPhee and Elliott Carter, the New York premières; myself, the theater, including opera. Also there were sermons by Roger Sessions, whose learning was to the cause of modern music as Alfred Barr's to that of modern art.

The thirties were also memorable for major jazz developments such as the swing beat and the concert band, for blues more powerful than any heard before, for light music that includes the finest of Cole Porter and of Rodgers and Hart, and for an opera that defies dispute, Ira and George Gershwin's world-famous *Porgy and Bess*. The twenties had been a romance because one was young. The thirties were a time of fulfillment for musicians of my age because we were ready for that, and also because our country was ready for us. That readiness was surely in part a result of the depression. During the first half of the 1930s Alfred Barr and Chick Austin had got together wealth not yet immobilized by the depression and scholars not yet captured by fame, developing out of these elements museums that expressed the time. The second half, through federal intervention, saw modern play writing, modern acting and production, and a public ready for noble subject matter all amalgamated. The *Four Saints* audience, part well-to-do, part scholarly and intellectual, all of it lively, experienced, and not easily fooled, was inherited by the ballet.[2]

TWENTY ONE

Virgil Thomson's Later Reflections

Katherine Teck

*A*DMIRED FOR HIS *eloquent prose writing and wide-ranging promotional activities on behalf of his composer colleagues, as well as for his own music, Virgil Thomson was music critic for the* New York Herald Tribune *from 1940 to 1954 and published several collections of essays. During a personal interview shortly after his ninetieth birthday, he became quite expansive about ballet and theater and made the formative events of American dance seem as if they had just taken place. What the composer-critic had to say about craftsmanship, emotion, and "danceability" in relation to music for choreography is worth ongoing consideration.*

***

The viewpoint of composer Virgil Thomson is of particular interest because the choreographers who used his music include Lew Christensen, Erick Hawkins, Agnes de Mille, George Balanchine, Alvin Ailey, and Mark Morris.

The composer recalled his work on *Filling Station*. Asked if he had any notion, at the time of this ballet's creation, that the collaborators were doing anything path-breaking, the composer indulgently scoffed, "Oh, you don't sit around and criticize your work while you're writing it. You write it and make it work; you don't observe it. However, I *did* enjoy working with Lew Christensen on that."

People who have never composed music often wonder how it is done, and dancers in particular wonder if their collaborators are conscious of movement when they are writing a score for ballet. Mr. Thomson clarified the process: "Look, darling, you don't think about anything else while you are composing but what you are doing—not merely the sounds, but trying to make it work, making it hold together.

"Lew would say: 'Here's a pas de deux, but it cannot possibly last longer than five minutes; I can't think of any more things to do beyond that, so you make it come out.' Five minutes is long anyway in a ballet.

"I've always worked in show business," Mr. Thomson commented. "I've worked in theaters; I've worked in movies, operas, plays, oratorios. I like show biz. I *don't* like the kind of dance that is done after the choreography. Martha [Graham] used to work like that, you know. I think it works better if you work together up to the point where the music has to be written. Then the music should be written, and the choreographer fits the dance to it.

"You *can* talk about it until you get each section in your mind, at least as to the length, or as to the kind of music that you have to write in order to illustrate the kind of dancing that it is. After all, the music's got to move them around."

How did he feel about his concert works set to dance afterwards? "I never know how I feel about anything! If I say that they can do it, then they can do it. I wait until they do it, and then I don't *feel*; I *think*! I think that it works or it doesn't, and sometimes I'm not sure. But if they think they can sell it, I let them sell it. That means their dancers and their audiences take it.

"You see, with a theatrical work, it's not a matter of how you *feel* about anything; it's what you can *think* of to solve the emergency. The feeling is out front—not on the stage."

You can tell whether something works or not, according to Mr. Thomson, by noticing the audience's response. "They'll tell you, oh sure," he remarked. "Applause is always welcome, but tears are the real proof. If they cry, you've got 'em!"

Continuing to speak about emotion and meaning in music for the dance, Virgil Thomson noted the oft-quoted assertion by Igor Stravinsky that music doesn't "express" anything. In Mr. Thomson's opinion, "Music recalls *other* music, a great deal, and how it happens that it stimulates or accompanies emotion, nobody knows how that works. You say, 'I think I'll try that'—and sometimes it works. But *having* emotion on the stage is the worst way to communicate. Follow the story and pattern; the emotion will take place outside. This applies to the musical part, the dancing, everything."

Focusing on the division of labor in the theater, Mr. Thomson noted: "Composers don't think about how dancers work; they think about how *they* work. They are just as amazed as anybody else when somebody takes a high leap and lights like a feather. But they wouldn't be able to tell the dancers just what muscles or leg positions to use in order to achieve that lightness. That happens among the *dancers*.

"Don't talk about ballet as though it were all full of emotions on everybody's part," he cautioned. "Ballet—particularly classical ballet—has a very limited vocabulary. The whole game is to make fifteen or so different things tell the story. It was Balanchine's rule that any movement on the stage which does not advance the story is useless. The movement composition must recount what it says it's recounting. And this works perfectly well too with ballets without a story—though there aren't that many. Though some are *said* to be without a story, they all tell *something*. They are always 'about' something, and we've only got some fifteen different 'words' with which to tell the story."

When asked what it is in music that can help accomplish this, the composer was firm: "Nothing! Music walks down the street beside the dance. Music in a ballet, very much like music in a movie, makes a *structure*, which holds the whole thing together, and it goes on at the same time.

"Music which illustrates the dance is just as boring as dance which illustrates the music," he went on to observe. "They've got to get apart. Got to get the music away from the dancers, and the dancers away from the music. You're not illustrating the music; you're illustrating the *story*. And if the music helps you do that, it's good music."

TWENTY TWO

Editorial

Dance and American Composers

Dance Observer

*T*HE *MODERN DANCE pioneers were sometimes extraordinary in their efforts to elicit new music from contemporary composers. Yet the extent of their work (usually done on a shoestring budget) was not always recognized—as indicated in this 1940 editorial, which singles out several successful collaborations from the late 1930s. Also noteworthy is the inclusion of scores for ballet companies, for the same composers obviously could work for dancers in various styles. It was their kinesthetic sense that was crucial.*

Time and money were also crucial to nurturing new works. Furthermore (as indicated in nearly all the articles of this book), composing for the dance required special considerations that were often outside the realm of the standard academic training of composers early in the twentieth century. For various reasons, therefore, some choreographers opted to keep on using extant music. Here the unattributed editorial takes choreographer Antony Tudor particularly to task for some of his choices and raises the question of whether his ballets might have benefited from newly composed scores specifically made for his choreography. Finally, the gauntlet is thrown down: a challenge for more of America's composers to step up and learn how to collaborate with dancers!

***

A recent editorial in *Musical America* calls attention to the fact that the rapid growth and expansion of the dance in America has opened a rich field to our native composers. Having been soundly belabored in the columns of the daily press in recent weeks for their alleged failure to create a genuinely native idiom and artistic speech, they will scarcely be offended if it is pointed out to them that several of our dancers have done just that.

Some of the best music that has been composed in America in recent years has been written for dancers. Leaders in both the old and new traditions of the dance have turned to our composers for collaboration, and it is encouraging to see how swift and steady has been the rise in the quality of the music used for dance accompaniment. Only a few years ago, and even now in one or two flagrant cases, woeful sounds emitted by piano and percussion were considered satisfactory, not to speak of the saccharine ballet scores that were turned out overnight.

Today it is a different story. Just in recent weeks we have heard admirable music composed for new dances. At the Holiday Dance Festival, Paul Nordoff's score for Martha Graham's *Every Soul Is a Circus* showed how an imaginative composer can carry out and intensify the atmosphere of a new work. And the Ballet Theatre season brought *The Great American Goof*, in which Henry Brant's score shares full honors with Eugene Loring's choreography and William Saroyan's script. Virgil Thomson and Aaron Copland have written brilliant scores for the Ballet Caravan, and no list of music for the dance would be complete without mention of Louis Horst's scores for *Frontier* and *Primitive Mysteries* [for Martha Graham].

The writer of the editorial mentioned above [from *Musical America*] points out cogently: "We need look no further than the inner circle of the great masters to establish the fact that a composer usually produces his best work when he has a definite end in view. From Bach, Haydn and Mozart down the years to Stravinsky, the creative musician has flourished under conditions which imposed certain practical requirements upon him, whether it was a cantata for the Thomaskirche or a score for Diaghilev. The self-discipline and concentration required to write for the dance has had a beneficial influence on many a composer. It is healthful, moreover, for our composers to work in so fresh a medium. The symphonist begins in the shadow of Beethoven and Brahms; the fabricator of tone poems, in that of Strauss. There are fewer barriers in the path of the dance composer, for new techniques, new styles and a whole new philosophy of the dance have opened practically limitless possibilities to him."

Another point to be considered is the fact that no matter how well the atmosphere of a familiar musical work seems to coincide with that of a new dance composition, there is invariably some violation of the spirit of the original. Thus, Antony Tudor's beautiful *Jardin aux Lilas*, though it seems to grow out of the nostalgic longing of Chausson's *Poéme*, cannot avoid a jarring note in the early passages in the work for violin solo, which simply evade any dance setting. Mr. Tudor's remarkable tact and musical understanding have solved the problem elsewhere, but the fact remains that Chausson wrote the work for violin and orchestra and not for ballet. In his setting of Mahler's *Kindertotenlieder*, called *Dark Elegies*, Mr. Tudor is less successful in sustaining the moods of the music. In fact, the dancing would probably be much more effective if a new score were written for it as it stands, in the spirit of the Mahler music, but closer to what Mr. Tudor has evolved.

The dance in America is thriving at the present time in spite of economic obstacles which can be overcome. Our dancers are creating a new language for us and they are saying the things that need to be said in art far more successfully, it may be ventured, than our composers have succeeded in doing up until now. While our composers continue to attempt the combined roles of business men, administrators, teaching executives and creative artists, turning out boiled-over-symphonies in the style of Sibelius and intricate fugal settings of Whitman's magnificently broad and simple poems, our dancers have taken their task more deeply to heart. They know that "American" is simply a much-abused adjective until it is given meaning by something really original and born out of our history and national life. Surely our composers can benefit not only from the stimulation of writing for the dance but also from the splendid example which they will find in the work of our best dancers, as creative artists and personalities.

Overview

Drawing upon Folk Music and Wartime Patriotism

OLLOWING THE TIDE of performance events through the pages of *Dance Observer*, one finds increasing optimism on the artistic front. By January 1938 (just four years after the publication's founding), the editorial titled "Happy Birthday to Us" conveyed this observation:

> When we began, the modern dance found itself groping towards an ideal, which while clear enough in theory, was pretty nebulous in practice. It has grown, we have grown, and dance in America today has undoubtedly attained, in the modern field, preeminence in the world.

But on the political front, throughout the later 1930s *Dance Observer* reflected ominous warnings gleaned not just from journalistic reports of looming dangers in one European country after another, but also through their knowledge of what was happening to artists in Europe such as dancer Mary Wigman. The editorial in the March 1937 issue reported Martha Graham's plea during a public speech, that "dancers be watchful of their world and sincere in their art, carried over the emphasis that the very real and terrible events taking place in the world leave no one unaffected."

By December 1939, the usually cheerful holiday editorials of other years in *Dance Observer* were replaced by gloomier feelings:

> This year, in a larger part of the world, the dance is a dance of death, a clammy horror that takes an unceasing toll of men and minds, relentlessly

beating them into weapons of destruction. A tide of hatred rolls westward, lapping even our distant shores and it becomes increasingly important that we give refuge here to that first outcast of the holocaust, the arts. The world is not a pretty picture this Christmas, but this is our time and our hour. We shall not pass this way again.

Concerning the music world, a wave of desperate European composers and performers flowed into the United States, and we now know that the Nazis even melted down thousands of beautiful church bells to make into guns.[1] Soon the United States was engulfed in World War II, with draft boards, rationing, and a populace strongly behind a war effort. Because of the substantial number of men enlisted or sent into the armed services (including many leading professional dancers), women took their places in factories or entered the armed services themselves (including Mary Jo Shelly, who was so important in founding the Bennington School of Dance). Leading entertainers traveled to dangerous locations to cheer the troops. And the widespread patriotism felt by the general populace is reflected as well in the pages of the *Dance Observer*, for those left on the home front. The magazine reminded readers to buy war bonds; drew attention to the Dancers' War Fund; and ran articles full of heartfelt support for those fighting for freedom. Yet during the war years, somehow dancers and musicians managed to continue some collaborations and performances.

In the following group of readings, Oklahoma-born folksinger Woody Guthrie gives modern concert dancers a pep talk about the importance of what they were doing. Many years later, his daughter wrote the delightful story included here, of how Woody became involved in a dance collaboration with choreographer Sophie Maslow (one of Martha Graham's dancers).

It seems that on all levels people welcomed the cheering effects and the inspiration of music and dance. And so when Martha Graham and Aaron Copland received a commission for a collaborative work to have its premiere in the Library of Congress in Washington, each in their own way drew on some roots of rural America: Graham with her scenario and actual choreography invoking a wide horizon and promise of a farm couple starting out in life; Copland with his suggestive "Americana"-style score that highlighted the Shaker tune "Simple Gifts." The resulting work, *Appalachian Spring*, was heartily welcomed at the time, and it continues to be performed.

In her book on *Martha Hill and the Making of American Dance*, author Janet Mansfield Soares remarked on several wartime works:

Revealing the American spirit through its folk idiom would soon become an overarching theme in the dance field. Dancing as a symbol of national identity suddenly became as jingoistic as it had been for centuries in other countries. Agnes de Mille premiered *Rodeo* with American Ballet Theatre in the fall of 1942, for which *Billy the Kid* and other ballets by Lew Christensen for Ballet Caravan had prepared the way. In 1944, Graham moved with full force into her Americana period with *Appalachian Spring* set to Copland's commissioned score. All of these ballets remain the most significant examples of the period.[2]

In the following grouping of articles, Agnes de Mille provides a general introduction to musical aspects of Martha Graham's work; Aaron Copland's letters provide unusual insight into the practical considerations of composing for dance during wartime; Gail Levin offers insights into the cultural context of *Appalachian Spring*; and Richard Philp (drawing on his perspective as longtime editor of *Dance Magazine*), provides an evaluation of the collaborative work more than a half century later.

TWENTY THREE

People Dancing

Woody Guthrie

*O*KLAHOMA-BORN WOODY GUTHRIE (1912–67) is known for his original *folk songs, social conscience, and legendary travels across America. Less known is the fact that he married Marjorie (Greenblatt) Mazia, a dancer with Martha Graham's company. Together they had four children, including the well-known musician Arlo and the modern dancer Nora.*

Guthrie served in both the merchant marine and the army, and his patriotic and social concerns come across in this commentary about the modern dance scene during World War II. Although he does not explicitly suggest what musical styles would be appropriate, the folksinger has strong opinions about this "new kind of dance" drawing from real-life experiences of both past and present (as his own music did). With references to folk songs, trains, factories, and the earth itself, Guthrie affirms the importance of the arts in bringing understanding and courage to all.

***

In the very first place I ain't no dancer and never thought much about it till just here lately. Besides this is all wrote on first impression—but—

It looks like everything you do has got to fit the cogwheels of the war. This ain't no time to hold back. It would take me a week of solid writing to name all of the kinds of work you've got to do, everything from working on a sharecropper farm to dancing the ballet. (I'd say that one works about as hard as the other), anyway all of us are fighting a war.

FIGURE 23.1 Woody Guthrie playing guitar for Sophie Maslow's New Dance Group, ca. 1942. Tony Kraber on left; unidentified dancers. Photographer unknown. Reproduced by permission of the Woody Guthrie Archives. www.WoodyGuthrie.org.

Ideas have got to be worked out that will help the work of winning this war, quick, fast, and there's no room, no time for an ounce of wasted motion or guesswork.

Production is the job, the main job here at home, and work has got to center on turning out more and more of everything. Show folks have a job to do, and that's to see to it that the show business gets its belt line changed just exactly like the Ford motor plant. Industry needs workers, and workers need show houses to be freshed up and educated, filled with the pep to work and go out of the theatre rearing to battle fascism. There is no room for weak-spined romance, mysticism, complacency, idleness, or laziness. Production is hard steel and solid rock; wind and hot sun and all kinds of blisters and calluses on all colors of hands.

With all of this in my head, I've tried to jot down a few rambling thoughts about dancing, because dancing can be such a healthy gleam in our nation's eye, in these war times when we've got to see the work and the fight quick and do something about it. No matter what kind of work you're doing, it makes it just a shade easier for everybody to find, and know, and feel a little more of the life that comes from knowing.

Do you know, are you making a stab at telling where we've come from, where we are now, where we're all headed for? Has the old road been rocky or smooth, and has it been a picnic, or a pretty tough fight? What are we fighting for today? What all parts make this fight? Where, why, who, which, how and when does your dancing hook on to the train?

There is a new kind of dance budding on our tree. The tree is like people. It digs its hands into the soil, sticks its head up toward the weather, and works up a whole bunch of new limbs to jump out and take the place of the weak ones that died because they couldn't face the fight against things that tried to kill the whole tree.

The job of a dancer (or steel driver, or jackhammer man, or bomber pilot) is all the same. We're working to win a war. We're dancing to help the people and if not, then it would be all stretched out of shape. People want to know people—not for an empty mystic reason, but when folks know folks they can get along better and work and fight better, and it's up to you to dance to teach people what to think in order to know each other better.

Hard times, bad weather, politics, banking, soil erosions, bad housing, slums, superstition, debts, worries, troubles—this is what we're fighting to wipe out. The dance today is more than a war dance; it's a whole fight, and should make every little part of the job plainer and show that we're all working together like a new road gang.

More specific—what has *got* to be done *quick?*

Well, we're a nation grabbing our guns, and grabbing our strength to fight the worst and toughest enemy that ever broke loose out of hell. This means we're finding our real power, in the past, today, tomorrow—and the past has got to be made plain, kept down to earth, told, sung, danced, hollered, and cried. The past has left fresh tracks in the country and on all of the streets—and in little places where people have worked and lived. The fight that's been fought is still alive in the people that fought it, and as long as there's been one loose cog in our machinery, people have fought to fix it. This part of the people is the past still alive. This past that is still living is the biggest part of the present. This is what your dancing has got to be—today sort of riding old yesterday out into the pasture to milk a herd of tomorrows.

Your dancing has just naturally got to tell people about people, their past work, hopes, dreams, aspirations. When people know people, the truth crops out and it is harvested and fed to people, beating down anything that tries to stop them or block their road or blind them and lead them the wrong way.

A dancer is like a railroad worker that knows where the train has come from, where she is now, and where she's booked to go. And the people who built the railroad train love it because you are riding on it. Maybe you're busy at dancing and don't always know just where your coach is wheeling to, but there are thousands of workers throwing switches to get you there. And all a dance is, is a person throwing a switch to keep the whole audience clicking down the shiny irons in the right direction. How do you love your railroad trains? People sing, "She's long, she's tall, she's handsome, and loved by one and all; she's a modern combination called the Wabash Cannon Ball—whow-whow—" And that, for a good word to people that run the railroad, is very seldom equaled. And in this day a good work spoke or danced, or looked out of your eye, is the main line manifest.

There's lots of trouble in the world, and keeping it hid will just slowly make it worse. Trouble and worry grow best when you hide them. If a dance don't tell you what kind of a fight is going on, and what caused it to break out, and what kind of work you got to do to win out, the goods in your costume are wasted.

Dancing is one of the best ways to help something to get said, and this something is all there is to make you dance or me come to look at you—because you couldn't keep me away from your rehearsals and all performances if you told me about a lot of other people. Maybe the whole thing is just being a good average human working along with all the rest of us.

Little lost groups are all over New York, because they lost touch with the rest of us, and in the end, they get to making up all sorts and sizes of dances that tell us about their floating dreams, but not anything about the big country full of plumb sensible folks with both feet on the ground. This is a bad mistake for any talented person to make. This is one of the biggest things you must *not* do.

Some dancing is worse than dead, as it kind of pretends to be alive, and poses also to deal with empty glasses and moon-struck visions, spiritualistic, mystic hokus-pokus, voodoo, hoodoo, and yonder side of death. There is a lot of hard work to be done over on this side, and twisted tales of the empty side only do one thing really good, that's to mess us up and put fog in our eyes. Still, people are awake, and getting tired of all of this blank and fake, worse than useless, junk. A dancer's best stage is old mamma earth. The best subject is the people, or you run the risk of ending up with both feet and your whole body floating off somewhere in the mist, and people leave you, and you gradually get to be your own dancer and your only looker.

> I read the palm of a dancing girl
> And here is what I said,
> "The wind and sun and open air
> Is all right—for your head;
> But in your life of leaping
> And whirling all around,
> You'll find you'll do your very best
> With both feet on the ground."

TWENTY FOUR

Sophie Maslow and Woody

Nora Guthrie

*H*ERE, WRITTEN BY *his daughter, is a delightful and updated tale of Woody Guthrie's introduction to both his future wife and the challenges of collaborating as a musician for a modern dance performance. It seems that it was one thing to create music for his* Dust Bowl Ballads *recording, quite another to improvise on his own songs—and something entirely different to rehearse* Folksay *with Sophie Maslow's dancers. This story also served as a memorial tribute to Sophie Maslow (1911–2006).*

Nora Guthrie, herself a dancer and choreographer, has worn many "hats" on behalf of documenting and preserving the legacy of her father, among them, as director of the Woody Guthrie Archives, producer of recordings, curator of museum exhibits, contributor to the children's book This Land Is Your Land, *and (as underscored by this article), storyteller.*

***

My mother, Marjorie Mazia, and Sophie Maslow were both dancers with the Martha Graham Dance Company in the 1930s–50s.[1] It was an important time in modern dance, as Graham and her troupe were redefining modern dance and how it fit into the culture. Along with her works like *Appalachian Spring* and *American Document*, Graham was looking to American "roots" art for inspiration; incorporating American writers, poetry and music into her collaborations.

Sophie Maslow had formed a small dance company of her own on the side, which Marjorie Mazia was also working in. Sophie's inspirations, like Graham's, were leaning towards American "roots" artists, and delving even deeper, she had choreographed what was to become a historic piece in modern dance history called *Folksay*. *Folksay* brought to life a more authentic American rural life using movements of jigs and hoe downs, along with the rhythms of the southern blues and Appalachia. Included in the soundtrack for *Folksay* were pieces from Woody Guthrie's recently released *Dust Bowl Ballads*.

The dances were all choreographed to records (78s) and the dancers used these recordings to rehearse. What happened then has become part of our family lore—something that we told and retold over the years, a story that, with all its humor and chaos, always seemed to define much of what fueled, and still fuels, our Guthrie family life: chaos and humor! My mother would act it out, with all of us laughing hysterically as she dramatically told the story:

Sophie had heard that Woody Guthrie was in town, living with the Almanac Singers in Greenwich Village, and thought it would be a great idea to invite him to sing the songs live for the opening performances of *Folksay* only a few days away. For support, she asked my mother to go with her to Guthrie's apartment. The two dancers walked up the stairs to the top floor of the Sixth Avenue apartment and knocked on the door. My mother, whose favorite song was "Tom Joad," had imagined her Woody Guthrie to be tall, slim and strong, somewhat Lincolnesque in stature. She figured anyone who could write such moving ballads about the people, such as his Tom Joad, must be larger than life. But when Woody opened the door, there stood instead a slight, 5' 6", 125 lb. man with a twinkle in his eye. (Years later, my mother said that it was at that moment when he looked her in the eye that she said to herself "I'm going to marry that man.") Woody, responding to these two delightful, pretty dancers, immediately responded, "Sure." So the deal was done, and rehearsals with the live musician began.

Woody showed up the next day with his guitar, sat down and began to play as the dancers began their moves which had been carefully choreographed to every beat, note and breath of the record. "I watched their pretty bodies and wished I was a dancer. I swore to quit whiskey and tobacco and start out taking physical exercise." But Woody (who didn't listen much to his own records) played the song totally differently, adding new chords, changing beats and even improvising a few new verses. Unlike highly disciplined and organized dancers, folksingers are known to veer. Woody would simply state: "If you're the same, the weather's different, and if the weather is the same, and even you're the same, you breathe different and if you breathe the same, you rest or pause different." Later he would explain: "If I want to take a breath between verses, I play a few extra chords. And if I forget the lines and want to remember them, I play a few extra chords. And if I want to get up and leave town, I get up and leave town."

The first rehearsal was a complete disaster, as Woody could/would not play the song the same way as he recorded it. Nor could he even play it through the same way twice. Rushing to get to their places, dancers were bumping into each other, falling all over each other, and being thrown up in the air with no one there to catch them on the way down. My dad was having a great time—and something had to be done to stop him!

Sophie pleaded for my mother, who was known for her organizational skills, to go and try to see what she could do. So Marjorie went with a mission: to teach Woody Guthrie how to play a song the same way twice.

Like a patient teacher with a slow, but willing student, my mother worked with him that night. She created flash cards with numbers and beats and words written out which Woody would faithfully follow. He played along, enjoying the company of this pretty dancer, and fascinated by her ability to organize and direct him. No one else had come close. They spent the night together…working, talking. And then the next. And the next. He performed in *Folksay* beautifully, and came in just at the right times, with the right beats, and the right pauses.

The performances were a complete success, and Woody Guthrie learned that sometimes being organized had its points. "I learned a good lesson here in team work, cooperation, and also in union organization. I saw why socialism is the only hope for any of us, because I was singing under the old rules of 'every man for his self' and the dancers was working according to a plan and a hope."

He decided to marry his tutor. Sophie Maslow joined Woody and Marjorie Guthrie at New York City's City Hall, and signed as the witness to their marriage. And so our family life—humor and chaos both—was born with this wonderfully talented and smart lady, Sophie Maslow, who knew who should go rehearse the musician, and who should not.

We are forever indebted to Sophie, not just for our actual existence, but also for all the years of laughter we've had telling and retelling this story. The cast of *Folksay* is now holding rehearsals in heaven. And Woody is still singing the same song—differently.

TWENTY FIVE

Music for Martha

Agnes de Mille

*T*HOUGH THEY HAD *quite different styles, the choreographers Agnes de Mille (1905–93) and Martha Graham (1894–1991) early in their careers shared the stage for a New York season of the Dance Repertory Theater. As time went on, Graham of course was identified with serious "modern dance" (though she began to label her works as "ballets"), and de Mille achieved brilliant success with her choreography for ballet and Broadway theater but was also noted for her wit and the contemporary touch she gave to her solo concert dances.¹ Additionally, she wrote a series of memoirs and other books on dance, including a biography of Graham (published after her colleague's death, though some thirty years in the writing). Despite her account of Graham's difficult behavior, de Mille nevertheless had a deep and abiding admiration for "Martha" as one of the outstanding creative artists of the twentieth century. In the following excerpt, she summarizes Graham's extensive record of collaborations and comments on her choices of already existing music.*

***

Martha was recognized as having made revolutionary changes in dance: in its form and subject matter, in the analysis and examination of her themes, and in the handling of the aesthetics itself. William Hogarth said, "Serious dancing is a contradiction in terms," to which Martha, I believe, would have replied, "Any matter that is not serious is not worthy of dancing." She had a permanently youthful curiosity and approached each project with the innocence and the skepticism of

FIGURE 25.1 Martha Graham, caricature by Aline Fruhauf, originally published in *Dance Observer*, May 1934. Reproduced by permission of Deborah A. Vollmer.

a child, and with a child's bold excitement. And she demanded answers.

The essence of Martha's material, therefore, included fundamental psychology, fundamental emotion, and fundamental physical aesthetics.

She was also a revolutionary in collaborative arts. There has been no other single person equally influential in so many fields—in choice of music, costumes, sets, nomenclature, and subject matter, as well as in dance technique. For instance, she was not a musician and played no instrument, yet she had an instinctive and searching feeling for music. Her choice of music set new styles.

The music Louis [Horst] found for her was fresh, new, and striking, generally not heard before, and certainly not in dance concerts. She had begun first with the moderns, the well-known turn-of-the-century giants, Debussy, Ravel, Satie, Scriabin, Rachmaninoff, Cyril Scott—these were known. But then, under Louis's prodding, she started to work with [music of] the less well known: Bartók, Goosens, Falla, Bloch, Hindemith, Kodály, Honegger, Ornstein, Malipiero, Prokofiev, Mompou, Harsányi, Milhaud, Poulenc, Krenek, Toch. And gradually she began using the Americans: Aaron Copland, Lehman Engel, Wallingford Riegger, Henry Cowell, Edgard Varèse, George Antheil, Paul Nordoff, Robert McBride, Norman Lloyd, Alex North, Ray Green, Hunter Johnson, William Schuman, Norman Dello Joio, Alan

Hovhaness. And always Louis Horst, whose music for her was unfailingly suitable and moving. (At that time, Martha had rarely danced to the greatest modern composers of all, Stravinsky and Richard Strauss, not, I imagine, being able to afford the commissions and royalties.)

Young musicians came to hear the new music, and they came hoping and praying that Martha would use *their* music, because it was an effective way for them to get known.

Martha kept to a lean, acerbic diet of challenging, strange sounds, mainly percussive, which seldom embraced melody. It is no accident that she didn't use melody and that she avoided resolutely all the romantics of the nineteenth century, all the baroque and rococo composers of the eighteenth. There was nothing in her music to suggest past experience to the listener, nothing familiar to cherish, no memories to be stirred, no preconceptions to be affronted. Her music forced attention where Martha wanted it: on the gesture. She made the dancer indicate the atmosphere, the landscape, and the situation, without help.

There are great dangers in this procedure. As with anything very new, the music may not be valid of itself. The restraints and curtailments that great music imposes are dispensed with, it is true, but also all the old crutches and all the old aids and helps. One is therefore forced to take the problems raw, and they had better be solved satisfactorily and truthfully.

In truth, melody is banished at a price, for melody is an extraordinarily persuasive tool. It is a spiritual achievement and it cannot be freely discarded. With it go incalculable kindnesses, easements, endearments, and searchings. Without it the dance can seem dry, even bony, and often unlikable. It is impossible to think of the ballet without melody. The very term *enchaînement* means a linking, an eliding, a slipping from one pattern to another, all sustained and made meaningful by the melodic path. The ballet choreographers mask the primitive joinings and statements with graces—the grease, so to speak, of melody; they're made easy, smooth. In contrast, Martha wished them revealed. In Graham, they stand there like exposed skeletons or diagrams, and we see their authenticity, the verities of line and curve and angle and their shadows in time. I think for this reason Martha could not use anything but the most percussive and stringent of music, a mere intensification of movement.

Martha kept ample notes, not necessarily about dance movement—that came in experimenting—but ideas for the kinds of movements, the atmosphere, the quality, notes on quotations, observations, anything that might give her a point of attack. Because with Martha the gesture and the emotional thought which prompted it were one. But she would not make use of any idea or any impression, any fantasy, until it was a part of her visceral experience. When she had some of this material absorbed, she began making short scenarios, which grew longer and more detailed when she started commissioning scores and had to be specific with composers.

She started physical work always without music or sound, in silence, in order to be free from the hypnotizing audible rhythm and in order not to be seduced by melody. Knowing she was sensitive to both, she wished to train her eye for the visual rhythm, which is less readily perceived. When her pattern was sketched, she would summon Louis Horst for advice on her music, the selection of already composed pieces or the making of new ones. Only after receiving back the finished music did the real choreography begin, for the composer's finished score dictated a new compelling pattern.

As she said, "I am governed by music." There was quite often a struggle between the movement pattern already worked through and the music pattern, but in the end they were reconciled. They had to be. She found this stage of the composition invigorating, the music adding color and accent to the already established design.

Once she advised me to work without the chosen music lest I wear out the inspiration of sound, and she advised that the addition of the finished score to established movement patterns would be extremely zestful to me. Many years later, thirty to be exact, she wrote to a friend that she needed a closer association between music and dance, something that went beyond intellectual association, what she called a breath association.

TWENTY SIX

The Commission for *Appalachian Spring*

Aaron Copland

S OME OF THE *finest scores for theatrical dance would not have come into existence without behind-the-scenes support of individual, organiza-tional, and governmental funding. In these excerpts from letters to Harold Spivacke (then head of the Music Division of the Library of Congress), composer Aaron Copland (1900–1990) offers a chronicle of his wartime project to write a score for Martha Graham, under a commission from the Elizabeth Sprague Coolidge Foundation. It should be noted that Erick Hawkins had initiated efforts that led to this commission and also worked to achieve other funding during his years with Martha Graham.*

The ballet was scheduled for limited performances at the Library of Congress, with thirteen instruments. Martha Graham danced the role of the bride; Erick Hawkins premiered the homesteader; and Merce Cunningham was the Revivalist preacher. Appalachian Spring *has gone on to earn an honored place in the annals of both American dance and concert music. The original score won the 1945 Pulitzer Prize for Music, and the composer arranged the work for full orchestra.*

The following excerpts from letters (written over several years) offer glimpses not only into the artistic effort of collaborating over long distances but also into the business and planning aspects of such a career in the 1940s.[1] Among the logistical considerations was the coordination of instrumentation to fit a relatively small space and service the work by Mexican composer Carlos Chávez, also planned for the program. Copying parts was also a laborious

procedure (done by specialists). At the time, the method of reproducing music was blueprint, with ink written on thin manuscript paper. What emerges here is an reflection of Copland not only as a recognized composer but also as one attentive to practical matters and as a citizen concerned with fulfilling military duty. (However, he was not called to serve in the war.) Copland's title for the score was simply Ballet for Martha, *and he had no idea of the dance title until close to the premiere on October 30, 1944.*

***

Stockbridge, Mass., Aug. 21, 1942

Dear Harold:

As I told you on the phone, I contemplate the giving up of my composing activities with the greatest reluctance, but if I must be used in the war effort, I wish to be as useful as possible. Until this matter takes on clearer shape, perhaps we had better let the question of Mrs. Coolidge's commission ride. Whether or not I can fulfill such a commission depends entirely on how my future pans out.

Sept. 3, 1942

Your letter cheered me up considerably—I mean the part about composers in the Army being given "time for composing." You can't imagine how right I hope you are. But I should warn you that "composing" to me means a private room with a piano and some consecutive time for writing. If the Army can provide that, its set-up is even more intricate than I thought. Well anyway, I'm only too happy to take your word for it that army life and composing are not incompatible.

I'll be seeing Martha Graham in NY., and as soon as I get a clearer picture of what she plans to do for you I'll write you an "official" letter to settle up the matter of the Coolidge Commission.

Sept. 17, 1942

I wanted you to know that I have had my army physical examination and came through with flying colors. Of course my eyes would limit me to what the doctor calls "limited service," but I assume that only improves my case with the Army Specialist Corps.

Thanks a lot for expediting matters in regard to the commission. You would help me enormously if you could tell me what your guess is as to the earliest possible date for my relinquishment of civilian life. In other words, in making plans for the immediate future I badly need to know up to what date I can safely promise to be around. Naturally I know your answer can only be approximate and only a guess, but even that would be a help.

I am seeing Martha Graham tomorrow and will communicate with you again.

[Hollywood, California] April 13, 1943

Your letter, sent to Stockbridge, just reached me out here. Since I hadn't heard from Martha Graham in several months, I was going on the assumption that the idea of a ballet was in abeyance. Your letter now brings the whole thing to life again.

When I last saw her in New York, she promised to send me a scenario which we could discuss. That was around Christmas time and I haven't heard from her since. We also agreed that when the rights to the ballet are released after the first year, she would be willing to pay me a royalty performance fee on a per performance basis. Therefore, as far as Miss Graham goes, everything is set, except that I have nothing to work with, until she prepares a scenario suitable to us both.

Because of the job out here, doing the score for a picture called *The North Star*, my time will be pretty much taken up until the middle of June. However, I can probably sneak in some work on the ballet nevertheless. I assume that the performance date is still planned for late September.

As far as the terms of the commission go, I think the Foundation should take into account the fact that this is a stage work, and therefore ought to be handled somewhat differently from the commissions given for chamber music. I think that the $500 fee should cover three points: 1) the writing of the work especially for the Foundation, 2) the premiere performance, and 3) exclusivity for a year from the premiere performance. I believe, however, that in fairness to the composer, a small royalty fee of $15 per performance should be paid the composer each time the work is given after the premiere. That is the customary procedure with the ballet companies, though of course the rates are about double that for regular commercial outfits. Such an arrangement also provides more incentive for a publisher who might be interested in bringing the work out immediately.

My suggestion is that you write to Miss Graham, finding out the present status of her scenario, and then let me know how the whole matter stands.

May 10, 1943

I'll be waiting with much curiosity to see Miss Graham's scenario. It hasn't arrived as yet, however. I'm also glad to see that the date of the premiere is as late as Oct. 30 now. Don't be concerned about the number of musicians. There is no difficulty on that point since it's being taken into account as early as this. The type of musical instruments needed will depend on the nature of Miss Graham's scenario. I'll try to stick to Chávez' choice of instruments as far as practicable.

Your letter of April 15th was illuminating on the subject of performance fees. Since you state that "the likelihood of the Coolidge Foundation sending the ballet on tour…is practically nil" and that only a few performances are contemplated during the year of exclusivity. I assume you would have no objection if I ask that the number of "free" performances included in the commission fee be limited to five.

June 8, 1943

I received the script from Martha Graham and like it very much, on the whole. I've written to her, suggesting a few changes.

I assume we are now all set, since your letter clears up our "business" arrangements, and is satisfactory to me. If you have occasion to write Miss Graham, please tell her that I have no intention of holding her to a minimum or maximum of ten performances during the first year, but only to the "usual" $15 performance fee whenever she performs the ballet on her own.

I shall assume that the premiere date is October 30th unless I hear to the contrary. Please be sure to let me know if there is any change, as the more time I have the better. Also, if you can find out from Chávez what instruments he intends using, that would be a help.

I think I have my first theme!

July 21, 1943

Two days ago I sent a long letter to Martha Graham, and was just about to write to you when your wire arrived. I can easily understand your anxiety about the score, but the situation was too complex to be taken care of in a wire.

I wrote to Martha because I had just received the final version of the scenario. I had suggested certain changes in the first version she sent me, and she promised to make them. Then there elapsed about a six-week interval. She realized, of course, that the delay was serious because of the pressure of time, but apparently couldn't make the revisions any sooner. The new scenario is an improvement, and I wrote her my acceptance.

In the meantime I was at work on the score, and have perhaps a third done. If I had nothing to do between now and Sept. 1st but write the ballet, I wouldn't hesitate to promise it for that date. But the picture score I am contracted to do is just now getting under way. In another week I shall be in the midst of it—and there are a lot of notes to write!

Because of the nature of the scenario I have decided that the best possible instrumentation for my ballet would be piano and strings. In the case of the premiere that could mean piano and double string quartet. Since you have a flute and clarinet for the Chávez anyway, I may decide to add those two instruments. This means an addition of five players to the Chávez group, and I hope won't cause too much upset in the finances.

Aug. 30, 1943

Your letter announcing the decision to postpone the Graham performance reached me while I was up to my neck in notes for *The North Star*. I'll be out of the woods in another week or so, and can then turn to the ballet score with a free mind. So the postponement is something of a godsend. Also I plan to be back in New York by October first, so can keep in close touch with Martha Graham, which ought to produce better results than long distance correspondence.

I have about a third of the work completed so far. I am going on the assumption that the scoring for double string quartet and piano will be satisfactory.

January 31, 1944:

Thanks for the encouraging words about the part of the ballet you received from me. Martha Graham tells me you are planning for a premiere around October. I really think you don't need to wait to get the score completely orchestrated in order to make definite plans. As far as I am concerned, I think that it is quite safe to go ahead as soon as you get the completed piano sketch. The orchestration is a mere detail.

I have revised my scheme a bit in regard to the instruments for which the ballet will be scored. I told Martha the other day that the ideal combination now seems to me to be the double string quartet with double bass, one piano, and three woodwinds (probably flute, clarinet, and bassoon). That adds up to thirteen men which is one more than your original letter called for. I hope that's OK with you.

June 9, 1944

I have about two more minutes of music to write on the ballet, and am one-third through the instrumentation. Hope to be done by July first.

I'm doing the score on thin sheets so that both Martha and myself can have a copy. Subsequently, I hope I can purchase as many copies as I may happen to need. In the same way, I hope you will be able to copy the parts on thin sheets so that we get independent sets for ourselves if they are needed at some later time.

July 8, 1944

At last I am able to write you that the complete score of the ballet has been mailed to you. Since I put the score on thin master sheets I hope you will send a copy to Martha Graham soon, so that she may have some idea of the sonorities. I am also planning to make some piano records for her, so that she will know my tempi. Unfortunately, she had left for Bennington before I had arrived back here, so I had no opportunity to play the completed score for her.

Martha has the ballet complete already—but since sending it to her there have been some minor changes made, so that she ought to have this final version for comparison. Please return the originals of the piano version to me with the orchestral score copy, as I never know when I may need further copies.

I am about to leave for Mexico for the summer, so hold everything until you get an address from me. That goes for the check also!

I hope the ballet all turns out well, and that you and Mrs. Coolidge will feel properly rewarded for all your pains!

P.S. I wrote Martha that if the orchestration for 13 players is too much for her on the road, the score could be played (with slight rearrangements) with only a single string quartet for the string section, instead of the double string quartet and bass now called for. That would reduce the number of players to 8.

Tepoztlan, Morelos, Mexico, Sept. 7, 1944

I am planning to fly up to Washington for the sole purpose of attending the Festival. Therefore, if anything should happen to change plans for the event at the end of October, please make me the first person to be told about it.

However, on the assumption that all is to go ahead on schedule, would you let me know as soon as possible, what date Martha Graham will be having her first rehearsals in the Library Hall? That's the day I should like to arrive.

Sept. 25, 1944:

I had no idea Martha would be coming for rehearsals as early as five days before the event. Naturally I don't intend to make a nuisance of myself during all that time!

My present plan is to fly up from here on the 25th, reaching Washington the following day. So please reserve a room for me. My budget will stand $4 or $5 a day for a room—but the main thing is to put me where "everybody" will be. Half the fun of going to festivals is bumping into people in your hotel lobby.

Bernardsville, N.J., Sept. 28, 1945

Dear Harold:

I thought you might be interested to know that four orchestras have announced *Appalachian Spring* on their opening programs—NY Philharmonic, Boston, Cleveland, Pittsburgh. Later on performances are scheduled for Los Angeles, San Francisco, Kansas City. Koussevitzky plans to record it for RCA Victor at the end of October. Perhaps you can listen in to the Philharmonic broadcast.

Martha Graham is trying to negotiate a satisfactory contract with Hurok for a tour lasting two seasons, and later Europe. If it comes off, the ballet will be widely seen. I think you have the right to feel just a bit triumphant about your brain child.

Greetings to you!

Aaron

P.S. Perhaps Mrs. Coolidge would like to know about the above.

TWENTY SEVEN

Aaron Copland's America

Gail Levin

N OWADAYS OFTEN HEARD *in full orchestral version,* Appalachian Spring *was one of the works that propelled Aaron Copland to the forefront as a composer of "Americana"-style concert music. Though born in Brooklyn, New York, this modern urban musician was able to evoke both a simpler time and a rural setting in a way that touched Americans deeply during wartime—and which continues to resonate with listeners of today.*

Putting this score and Copland's overall style in a larger cultural context, essays by art historian Gail Levin and music historian Judith Tick accompanied a museum exhibit featuring paintings of rural America, all related to the aesthetic aura of Copland's music. In the following excerpts, art specialist Levin touches upon times past and discusses the traditions of mythic landscape painting and simple lines of furniture that would have been familiar to Martha Graham when she was working on her scenario for Copland.

***

The Composers' Collective, founded in 1932 by the likes of Henry Cowell and Charles Seeger, was a small group of composers who aimed to create proletarian music—in other words, a new music for the masses. An interest in reaching wide audiences also inspired visual artists as diverse as the Social Realists and the Regionalists. Both groups would reject as elitist Paris modernism, and particularly abstraction, as they sought to create a new American art to speak to the masses.

Thomas Hart Benton, Grant Wood, and other Regionalists painted pictures representing ordinary agrarian life, a mythic America detached from the harsh realities of the Great Depression. Wood's *Young Corn* of 1931, even though painted during the Depression, glorified America's fecundity and the simple strength of its farmers. This painting coincides with a growing national interest in American history, folklore, and folk art.

For *Appalachian Spring*, a wartime project, Copland drew upon the folk music of the Shakers, a utopian religious sect that, at its height in 1840, boasted six thousand members spread over eighteen communities in the United States. He adapted a motif from their hymn "Simple Gifts" for the ballet score he composed at the request of Martha Graham.

During the course of their collaboration, Graham sent Copland several scripts. She outlined a scene inside and outside a house with a doorway, a front porch, and a rope swing. On the porch was to be "a Shaker rocking chair with a bone-like simplicity of line." Graham noted that the character of the Mother, whom she then intended to sit in the rocking chair, was "theatric in the way American Primitives are." Having emphasized her interest in folk culture, she then told Copland that he need not use folk material "except as you see fit."

Although Graham played down her wish that Copland incorporate American folk material in his ballet score, her various scripts for what became *Appalachian Spring* are filled with such references. She remarked in one version of her script on "the spare beauty of fine Shaker furniture," noting, too, that "Grant Wood has caught it in some of his things."

Both Wood and Graham sought patriotic images of renewal in a war-torn world. Like the story in Graham's script, Wood depicted a small town, where connections to American tradition and rural life remain unbroken. Graham focused on rural Appalachia by taking her title from a line in Hart Crane's poem *The Bridge*. She chose the words "O Appalachian Spring!" from a section of the poem called "The Dance." The title of the ballet in Copland's mind as he worked was simply "Ballet for Martha." Not until the dress rehearsal did he learn what Graham had chosen to call it, although she admitted that Crane's poem actually had nothing to do with the piece. Still, her choice did not displease him, because of his long admiration for Crane's work.

Graham's taste for folk culture coincided with Copland's own long-standing interest. Thus encouraged, he found in a recently published collection of Shaker tunes the hymn he would make famous. Like

Copland's music and the Shaker hymn he drew upon, Graham's modern dance esthetic was outside the nineteenth-century Romantic ethos of European tradition.

Copland said that "*Appalachian Spring* would never have existed without her special personality. The music was definitely created for her, and it reflects, I hope, the unique quality of a human being, an American landscape, and a way of feeling."

TWENTY EIGHT

Appalachian Spring

An Appreciation Fifty-four Years Later

Richard Philp

*H*INDSIGHT REINFORCES THE *initial approbation that greeted* Appalachian Spring. *Here, Richard Philp (longtime editor of* Dance Magazine*) gives an account of a revival performance set in the same Library of Congress theater and comments on the effect that this work by Martha Graham and Aaron Copland had over the first fifty-four years since its premiere.*

***

As with so many dance journeys, it was a bumpy trip from concept to completion. But the premiere finally happened on October 30, 1944. The producer was the largest library in the world, Washington's Library of Congress, and it took place in a 500-seat theater named for Elizabeth Sprague Coolidge, patron-pianist who commissioned the music. The ballet, *Appalachian Spring*, was created by Martha Graham during the darkest days of the Second World War, when American mythologies desperately needed confirmation. Who are we? Where do we come from? What drives us forward? We needed to know.

Graham selected the American composer Aaron Copland, who a decade earlier had provided her with a dissonant, modernist score for her solo *Dithyrambic*. But since those days, Copland had made a conscious effort to change his composition style to a more accessible, tuneful, "American" sound. He wrote his *Ballet for Martha*, as he called it, to Graham's detailed scenario, but he knew nothing of Appalachia and never gave spring a thought, so Martha attached the now-famous title just days before the premiere. Copland's music, with its open intervals, folk tunes (the Shaker "Simple Gifts" and others), and sonorous suggestions of cool, open space, has become one of the most beloved dance scores of our century. The ballet's Shaker-clean set is a sparse evocation by the American Isamu Noguchi of a fragile frontier shelter erected with great trust against the powerful natural world that threatens to engulf us all. Noguchi's Graham collaborations over thirty years came to define the bare and spare emotions framing many of her mythic dance works. *Appalachian Spring* also marks the first government-commissioned dance work, fueling generations of heated debate over government arts subsidy. It established dance as a major art form, as worthy of mainstream support as the symphony, opera, or theater. For a little one-act modern ballet, *Spring* had an impact way beyond anything imagined.

So. Here we are. Gathered this May in Washington for performances by the Graham Company of *Appalachian Spring* at the Library of Congress, the first revival on Mrs. Coolidge's famous stage—originally designed for chamber music concerts—where it was premiered fifty-four years ago. An event. The ballet is a powerful affirmation of love as the sustaining ingredient in human relations. It is filled with primal force, the exuberance of hope, the dark twistings of Puritanism, and a sweet sense of earth's mystery. A young pioneer couple is able to face the future because the new love they share provides a glowing— and we hope a lasting—shield against the unknown. That Graham created the central role of the Bride for herself and that of the Husbandman for Erick Hawkins, whom she would later marry, adds another poignant dimension. The ballet's final moments of stillness, when he stands behind her and she makes an exquisite, inclusive gesture toward the horizon that embraces not just place but their entire future in it, is one of the great luminous moments of dance—of world theater. It defines us all.

Right down the middle of Washington, for those of you who have not been there, is a vast rectangular mall with such familiar sights on it as the Washington Monument, the Lincoln Memorial, and the National Gallery, a vast collection of art treasures well worth visiting. While wandering among the galleries, we came upon a painting by Johannes Vermeer, a remarkable 17th-century Dutch master whose themes of daily life somehow transcend color, composition, and content and transform simple domestic subjects—moments from everyday life—into profoundly moving meditations on the human condition. The particular painting that drew us back repeatedly on this afternoon was of a young woman holding a balance, a small scale, in which there is—nothing! Or nothing visible. Jewels, nearby, do not concern her. Although there are dark currents present (a painting on the wall behind her is of the mythical Last Judgment), the soft source of light from a high window and her quiet concentration suggest an affirmation to her mysterious measuring; she is absorbed in one of those moments when peacefulness and musings reign to a deep and feeling degree. We feel the moment, its weight; we have been there.

The tingling began at the base of my spine, worked up through my neck, prickled over my scalp, and then my eyes began to burn; there is no explanation for my strong physical reaction to this painting, other than the ability great art has to stir recognition of those moments when we come face to face most intensely with who we are, our being.

That same evening during *Appalachian Spring*, it happened again—the tingling spine, the scalp, the tears. Why? What makes great art? What power do artists such as Graham or Vermeer possess? What witchcraft does genius use? There are imitators, always, but few originals. That artists like these exist at all, however, and can speak with such immediacy and authority, although separated by centuries, techniques, and cultures, is one of the great mysteries of this life. But there is Graham. And there, Vermeer. Observe.

We have speculated for generations on "the great American novel," that unwritten "masterpiece" that should define our national consciousness, that will plumb core feelings and beliefs. What if in this, the century of dance, that great American work turns out not to be a novel at all, but a ballet? Graham's signature work? *Appalachian Spring*? Could it be?

Yes. I am sure it is.

Overview

Building on the Horton Experience

U NDERSCORING THE role of Lester Horton in the development of modern dance, his biographer Larry Warren wrote that Horton "stands with Martha Graham and Doris Humphrey as one of the three American teachers whose methods have established influential schools and whose choreographies are being revived as modern dance classics." He went on to observe:

> The roster of artists he trained should alone assure his place as a prime contributor to the mainstream of the field....
>
> Like so many others at the time, we took Horton and his marvelous little theater for granted. It never occurred to us that the tall, heavy-set man with the worn face and twinkling eyes who sometimes stood at the door of his theater to greet the audience was one of the creative giants of twentieth-century dance.[1]

Dancer-choreographer-teacher Lester Horton (1906–53) was born in Indianapolis and had some ballet training with Adolph Bolm in Chicago. His first forays into modern dance were inspired by American Indian traditions, as well as by Orientalism (both styles he experienced upon seeing the Denishawn productions in 1922). Settling permanently on the West Coast, Horton danced with Michio Ito, then founded his own multiracial troupe, theater, and teaching establishment in Los Angeles in 1934. The flowing technique he developed continues to be taught today, and Horton's style also influenced the outstanding artists he nurtured, including Bella Lewitzky, Alvin Ailey,

Carmen de Lavallade, James Truitte, and Joyce Trisler. With regard to his more than eighty concert dances, to save money as well as to expose his troupe to many facets of culture and art, his "total theater" approach engaged dancers in related aspects, including musical ones. Some of the troupe's programs indicate simply "percussion" as scores, and these were apparently generated by the choreographer with assistance by troupe members. Importantly, first at Mills College and subsequently in Los Angeles, one of his musical collaborators was Lou Harrison, known even then for his inventive percussion scores.

Although his preference was for live music, Horton often had to give in to pressures of time and money and use recordings, drawing from the works of concert composers such as Bartók, Satie, Ravel, Kodály, Tansman, Malipiero, Villa Lobos, Stravinsky, Byrd, Guarnieri, Copland, Gershwin, Bloch, Respighi, and Palmgren. Additionally, he elicited performance scores from the composer-accompanists who worked with his classes.

In a 1936 interview, Horton spoke about his ideal collaboration:

We believe that a situation…fertile in possibilities is the making of new music simultaneously with the making of choreography.…In welding the two elements, movement and sound, it is possible to achieve a homogeneity which is a stronger entity than either separate one. To make a unified composition on this basis it is necessary to find a composer whose views and methods are compatible with those of the choreographer. The composer who can overcome the limitations and problems of dance accompaniment without sacrificing musical form must possess a unique ingenuity and invention.[2]

After Horton's death in 1953, the theater was kept going by Frank Eng for seven years. Subsequently, the choreographer's legacy has been kept alive by the artists he nurtured, by a foundation, and by various festivals. Today, the Horton technique is taught in studio classes across the United States, notably by former dancer Ana Marie Forsythe, who has also written about the technique and made films. For those seeing such exercises for the first time, perhaps the overwhelming impression is of fluidity and supple control of all parts of the body.

In the realm of music, Horton was innovative in using jazz for concert dance, such as Duke Ellington's *Liberian Suite*, at a time when most other modern dancers still had a preference for predominantly classically oriented styles. This precedent had an influence upon choreographers who followed Horton. When one looks at the repertoire of his artistic offspring, the musical choices are notable for ranging widely in genre, from classical to jazz to experimental, with both traditional and inventive instruments, and with both live and recorded performances. Because of Horton's influence, dance theater nowadays has a more varied soundscape.

The following group of articles focuses on some of the artists whose later careers were also touched by their legacy from Horton—including the dance artists Carmen de Lavallade and Alvin Ailey and the musician Kenneth Klauss.

TWENTY NINE

Lester Horton

Of Money, Music, and Motivation

Larry Warren and Others Who Knew Him

*I*N THE FOLLOWING *passages, biographer Larry Warren (1932–2009) chronicles the efforts expended to enlarge the cultural references that found their way into Lester Horton's dances, and he elicits recollections from a few other artists whose careers were touched and influenced by this choreographer.*

Warren himself had worked as dancer, choreographer, and teacher since his youth in California, then went on to teach, first in Wisconsin, and to cofound and direct the Maryland Dance Theater. He and his wife, Anne, received a special lifetime achievement award for nurturing dance in the Washington, D.C., area.

Originally from Portland, Oregon, the composer Lou Harrison (1917–2003) early in life moved to the San Francisco area with his family. He studied with Henry Cowell in San Francisco and later with Arnold Schoenberg in Los Angeles. Harrison also worked as a dance accompanist at UCLA and other studios, sometimes even performing as a dancer himself, and exploring ways of expanding percussion music. From 1936 to 1939 he taught at Mills College, and his California experiences included collaborating with Lester Horton—as he recalls in his 1968 letter to Larry Warren, reprinted here. The composer notes particularly the way Horton had involved artists in creativity outside of their specialties, and the way he had sparked interest in Mexican culture. Harrison's scores for Horton included Conquest *(1938), with a*

FIGURE 29.1 Lester Horton dancers with percussion: Eleanor Brooks, Bella Lewitzky, Mary Meyer, 1937. From the collection of the Jerome Robbins Dance Division, The New York Public Library for the Performing Arts, Astor, Lenox and Tilden Foundations.

theme of Mexican struggle against Spanish colonial rule; Something to Please Everyone *(1940); and* 16 to 24 *(1940), with a political theme about unemployed youth.*

Frank Eng worked as a journalistic theater and film reviewer and in addition to his personal relationship with Lester Horton wore many professional hats for the company, including as press agent and business manager. After

Horton's death in 1953, Eng kept the company alive for seven years, finally closing operations in 1960. In 1995, as Horton's heir, he arranged for the purchase of a large collection of Horton materials by the Library of Congress, including many manuscripts of the music used for Horton's dances.

Joyce Trisler (1934–79) was in her youth a member of the Horton troupe and went on to achieve a wide reputation for her own company.

***

From Larry Warren

In the dismal and depressing 1930s, modern dance was many things to many people, and to most it was a harbinger of a new era. The fiercely independent attitude of the pioneers of the new dance attracted such enthusiastic young devotees as the two quoted in a *New York Post* interview in 1936. Asked why they were studying dance at the New Dance League, a male art student said he felt "We must express everyday problems for the betterment of mankind," and a young model replied, "I want to express life today in all its squalor and despair. I want to express the ideas and beliefs of the workers."

But Horton believed dance could not reflect social conditions and at the same time avoid being becoming propaganda. He felt a strong motivation to create dances based not on abstract form or elusive emotion but on what he referred to as "vital experiences." There were enough individual patrons—added to the deprivation the dancers were willing to live with—to make this happen. This period of idealism and dedication resulted in a brief but meaningful golden age in all the arts in the United States. It provided the spirit in which the Lester Horton Dance Group could thrive.

If a dance about a specific culture was projected, the art, music, history, and movement patterns of the people were studied. This work was not intended to affect Horton's choreography directly, but rather to give the dancers a frame of references upon which to build intelligent characterizations.

These explorations also resulted in a growing collection of percussion instruments—which had an invigorating effect on the dancers. What had started out as a random collection of Chinese and Indian drums was extended by a set of unmatched gamelan pieces he had found in San Francisco. Also in the collection were voodoo, Javanese, and Siamese drums; gongs from Java and Indo-China; gamelan bells from the Philippines; a Kaffir piano (or marimba) from Durban, South Africa; temple bells, wood blocks, and fish heads from China.

***

Lou Harrison

I was much influenced by Lester, his magic stimulus, imagination, humor, and general loveliness. Certainly he was much ahead (present theater developments are closer to him than ever) & working with him was always exciting.

Years before knowing Lester I was already full of admiration for the great artists of Mexico (who, in the thirties, could not have been ??) & too, of the composers Carlos Chavez & (by reputation) Revueltas. Chavez's music was early published in New Music Edition, & Henry Cowell even acquainted me with the music to Chavez's ballet "H.P." by means of old aluminum dubbing discs.

But it was Lester who "full-scale" alerted me to the glories of Mexico as "folk-culture" & "classical ancient culture." Through his own singing I first heard La Sandunga & many other such melodies. (I suddenly realize that this aspect of Lester is right now identically alive in the Ballet Folklorico's work—tho perhaps Lester's were the finer choreographies.) I learned the basic outline of Mexican history from him, & continue to this day to fill it in.

I always felt completely "in tune" working with Lester. There was the wonderful matter of working with another male (an infrequent chance for a young musician-among dancers in those days) &, in addition to the sensation of intimate love & support general in the whole group, there was always that fabulous fantasy playfullness—theatric delight. My own feel for the theater seemed perfectly to mesh with his. I think that this has never happened fully to me since—the concern with all aspects of it. As I had pre-adolescently fallen in love with Yeats "Four Plays for Dancers," the masks & the music of Dulac & of George Antheil, it was only natural to find myself "costuming" & "setting" with Lester when we did a large work together. Maybe due to his own driving intensity I have never lost my pleasure in doing all sorts of things other than the music for which I am known. Anyway, it always has seemed real to me that Lester's type—the type of the full artist—should "create all over the place"—have a ball—PLAY!

When we are children we go about our play very seriously & absorbedly indeed—we do this because, of course, it isn't play unless it *is*

serious & absorbing. When we are "grown up" we do the same thing—
we play—& we then call it Civilization.

Lester never forgot that for a moment!

***

Frank Eng

By and large everyone who was more than passingly touched by this
flame knows in his or her heart that in the contact he or she touched
the wellsprings of creativity. The message was literally galvanizing.
The flame of Horton's genius brought both artists and audiences fluttering in relays if not in droves.

For *Salome* Horton wrote his own music, a percussion and human
voice score. According to Horton, Aaron Copland called it the best
percussion score he had ever heard. But in 1958, a bright young composer called it the worst percussion score he ever heard. Musicologically
good or bad, the score for *Salome* glove-fit the choreography as no musical
score can or decently should. It added an aural, almost hypnotic and pal-
pably physical dimension of sensuality to an already lush work.

For *Brown Country*, about a slave and slaver, with Carmen de
Lavallade, a score was commissioned (a pretentious word considering
the paltry fee we could afford to pay, but Kenneth Klauss was one of
the composers who didn't seem to mind). Horton provided the
phrase-by-phrase, count-by-count requirements on the basis of his
blocked-out scenario. Klauss retired to the desert and returned two
weeks later with a ten-minute score. Then Horton discovered he
should have doubled the musical requirement. Bravely, he chopped the
choreography to fit the score—with predictable results.

***

Joyce Trisler

Although funds for production were limited, to say the least, Lester
managed to commission many original scores. Dances were set to
counts, which were then given to the composers. Scores were always
late. Sometimes they would arrive just a few hours before a performance.
Occasionally the music was written for piano and would be pounded
out live on the dilapidated old instrument that stood in the wings stage
right. The ancient upright blended notes together in such a manner
that it was best to just try to follow the rhythm. When small orchestra
ensembles were required, the scores were recorded. Lester tried to use
live music whenever possible, but this became so expensive that he
finally switched to recordings exclusively.

For *Salome*, Lester brought out his huge collection of percussion instruments. It was a sight to see dancers, in every description of rehearsal attire, standing behind exotic instruments that ranged from pieces of a Balinese gamelan to a pot of screws. The vocal sounds were produced by Lester and myself. Since every member of the company was involved in playing the instruments, the work had to be recorded. It never had the same input as when played live.

Audree Covington, who wrote several scores, was also a member of the company. Other musicians sometimes took class. The composers were often accompanists for the classes. It was difficult not to become involved in more than one activity at the theater.

It might seem that everything concerned with the Horton Company was ideal. This is far from true. Lester was a dominating man of indefatigable energy. He expected us to work day and night, seven days a week, and could barely tolerate anything less than complete devotion. And we were expected not only to rehearse and perform, but also to sew costumes, build sets, paint the theater, or work in the office. I wish I could say that I fully understood what Lester was trying to do for us at the time. I didn't. I resented him as much as I loved him. I resented the way he worked us to death and the way he tried to run my life. Not until years later did I understand what he was trying to say: "The commitment is total, or not at all."

THIRTY

Kenneth Klauss

Musician for California Dancers

Katherine Teck

*L*OOKING BACK IN *his eighty-seventh year, the composer-pianist Kenneth Klauss enjoyed pointing out that he shared a birth date with the one alleged to be that of the Buddha: April 8, though some centuries later. Born in 1923 into a musical family in Parkston, South Dakota, Klauss pursued formal musical training first in Lincoln, Nebraska and subsequently at the University of Southern California with a focus on piano, music theory, and composition—which he mastered mainly under the guidance of composer Ernst Toch. He recalled his young self as a "hotshot classical pianist" with a talent for improvising, and that is precisely the gift that enabled him to earn his living mainly by playing for modern dance classes in Los Angeles starting in the late 1940s. This in turn led to accompanying performances and composing for some outstanding artists working on the West Coast at the time, including Janet Collins, Lester Horton, Benjamin Zemach, and Harriette Ann Gray.*

Among the scores by Klauss was one that Lester Horton used twice: first as a solo dance for Bella Lewitzky, titled La Soldadera, *which portrayed a woman soldier from the Mexican Revolution mourning her soldier-husband's death; and subsequently as the male-female duet* Dedication to José Clemente Orozco, *which many observers consider one of the true classics of modern dance.[1] In addition, as Kenneth Klauss recalled, at midcentury Los*

Angeles was rich in modern dance activity, and he was asked to create much original music for both studio classes and theatrical performances.

***

Reflecting on his long career encompassing composing and improvising for dancers on the West Coast, Kenneth Klauss described generally three ways that music can deal with motion: "First it underlines the motion. In this case, music accentuates and imitates the dance movement almost exactly. Secondly, music can elaborate on that motion. And thirdly, music can be used to *contradict* the motion—a fact that so many people are not aware of. Of course, all three things can be happening at the same time. That's the magic of it."

As with so many musical collaborators for dance, nobody taught him specifically how to evoke such magic. But after he completed his composition studies with Ernst Toch and his degree at the University of Southern California, Klauss explored his options in the Los Angeles scene of the late 1940s and found that because he was a skilled improviser in classical musical styles, playing piano for dance classes was a way that he could earn his living, supplemented by teaching privately.

"I started playing for dancers on campus at USC and got into playing for Melissa Blake. Later on in Hollywood I played for Carmelita Maracci, who was a tough cookie and very temperamental. But I had iron nerves, and for the dancers I mainly played for, I was basically the best because I was inventive. I was good at improvising in modern and classical styles to begin with. And so my career went along mainly by word of mouth. Among the dancers for whom I played classes later in the 1960s was Benjamin Zemach.[2] He became a longtime friend."

Addressing a common misconception, the musician observed, "It isn't as simple as you might think to be a dance accompanist. You may think that if you just play the rhythms that's OK; but you have to go further than that. You also have to pick up on the texture. And mainly you have to be *empathetic*. I did not study dance myself, but I was empathetic. I enjoyed the vicarious thrill of it. But you did have to evolve your own way. Nobody taught me."

The composer reflected about his composition teacher, Ernst Toch, who sometimes bemoaned that one could not really teach composition either. A student could learn technical skills and procedures, but then one should listen to many kinds of compositions, whether you like them or not.

His openness to wide-ranging stylistic explorations served Kenneth Klauss well. Improvising in dance classes, he would start simply, to support the dancers' exercises. Gradually he would elaborate and embellish. With skilled dancers, he particularly enjoyed devising contrapuntal music and playing "games" with those taking class, thus emphasizing the interaction of music and motion. On occasion he would devise challenges to keep himself mentally alert. Once he even accompanied an entire class with improvised variations on a two-note motif.

Mastering the skill of accompanying on his own, Klauss was soon requested to compose original scores for concert dance choreography. For such collaboration, he considers that there are "four and a half" ways of working with choreographers.

"First, your composition already exists, but isolated from motion. The choreographer comes along and uses the music as it is." Klauss himself rarely found this to be the case with his own music (one exception being the request for his harp sonata for use by dance artist Sheila Corregos). Instead, most of the dancers he worked with wanted something tailor-made.

The second way of collaborating was for the dancer to give a general description of what she wanted. This was how Klauss worked with Janet Collins, for whom he accompanied dance concerts in Los Angeles before she went to New York to dance at the Metropolitan Opera and elsewhere. Collins requested a new score for a three-movement piece to be titled *New Land*. She provided general timings for each section and suggested that the first movement should have the feeling of a spacious horizon; the second, of conflict; the third, of triumph and transcendence. These directives gave the composer both a framework and freedom, plus a sense of the textures that might be appropriate. He found that to be almost the ideal way for a composer to work with dancers.

"Thirdly," continued Klauss with his consideration of collaborative methods, "you actually work consecutively with the dancer." In his experience, this was frequently the way he worked with a number of choreographers, including Harriette Ann Gray, for whom he first played dance concerts in 1948.[3]

Twenty years later, at the Perry-Mansfield Camp in Steamboat Springs, Colorado, Gray had just returned from a trip to the Greek Islands and Crete. "She wanted to create a Minoan Suite," recalled Klauss, "and wanted to incorporate irregular $\frac{5}{8}$ and $\frac{7}{8}$ meters that one finds in Greek dances." She also wanted it to be a long suite: forty-five minutes; and it was to be performed by clarinet, violin, cello, and percussion.

The composer set to work, devising a score (just in case) that could also be performed by a single pianist, though it featured three distinct melodic lines for the instrumentation originally specified. At the crucial moment, it turned out that the traveling musicians did not arrive in time, and the composer-pianist had to become the performer as well, moving around behind a screen to incorporate percussion effects specified in his own score.

Turning to his work with Lester Horton, Klauss touched on financial aspects: "I did not play classes for Lester Horton. I was earning my living as a studio pianist as well as by teaching piano privately, and Horton was always operating with financial difficulties. When I was composing for dance, I think I was paid ten dollars per page of manuscript.

"But the fourth way of collaborating—the method that Horton used with me in *La Soldadera*—was to give me counts. Horton choreographed *La Soldadera* on Bella Lewitzky in 1949. We met under rehearsal lights. He gave me specific counts for a dance that would last eight minutes. I went home and composed the piece in two days, and when we tried it out, it worked perfectly. For *Brown County, Indiana*, Horton also more or less gave me quite specific counts, and I went to a high desert cabin in Lucerne Valley to compose the work."

Klauss also performed as pianist for the premiere of *La Soldadera*. But subsequently Lester Horton choreographed a brand-new duet to the same music, with a dedication to the Mexican muralist José Clemente Orozco. The dance has come to be known simply as *Orozco*, and it has been revived a number of times with notable success.[4]

Turning to the "half" in his four and a half ways of collaborating, Kenneth Klauss outlined what he considers the least satisfactory way: "You could take the rhythmic patterns of existing music and write a new piece. For example, the choreographer Karen Burke had a dance set with music of Morton Gould's *Satiric Dance* for solo piano. It was simply too difficult for her then-current accompanists." So the composer mirrored the rhythmic content of the Gould work, but with simpler pianistic realization.

In response to requests from dance students at the Idyllwild School of Music and the Arts, Klauss developed brief pieces that he called "Tokas," related to the Italian musical term "toccata," that literally translates as "touch," but which the composer feels also can imply various textures—a consideration of tremendous importance for musical collaborators.

Very keen on his definitions of words, Klauss does not like to use the term "creations" for his music; instead, he refers to "articulations," a word that can suggest "expressions." Just consider: if one is asked to "articulate" something, that could mean giving voice to a thought or feeling. It could imply saying something with clarity, giving a precise form and character to something that did not exist before. Perhaps the inspiration could be a mood, a subject matter, or in the case of working with dancers, a simple gesture or a larger movement in space.

These two terms that Kenneth Klauss draws attention to, articulation and texture, can be especially important in collaborating with dancers. In music, "articulation" also has the connotation of defining the various ways of beginning and ending sounds. Consider, for example: short (*staccato*); smooth (*legato*); gently pushed (perhaps as with *louré* on strings); accented (sharply, not so sharply); loud then immediately soft (*sfzando*); and so on. Such details can vary enormously, but along with texture they can contribute a distinctive flavor, style, and mood.

Consider also the immediate impact of an initial musical motif: soft or loud in terms of dynamics; fast or slow in gradations of pace; with a melody or essentially rhythmic in intent; a beautifully evocative single melodic line—or one perhaps "doubled" in pitch at one-, two-, or even three-octave range, or at other intervals; chords with ever-changing unusual harmonies. All these aspects of even the most brief musical sounds can inspire a kinesthetic response if skillfully presented. This brings up one of the most noticeable characteristics of the *Tokas* by Kenneth Klauss: sparse textures that allow room for musical breath, as well as room for the dancers to move either in tandem with the music, or in contrast with it, or in denial of the sounds. Each of his *Toka* piano pieces has a distinctive character; each offers its own possibilities for imaginative development. "Here is a germ of an idea," each one seems to say. "Where shall we go with it?"

As a collaborating musician, Kenneth Klauss had to be very aware of visual effects produced by moving dancers. He developed a concomitant appreciation for the spatial relationships in the architecture of buildings. For seven years at the Southern California Institute of Architecture, he taught a series of fifteen seminars for architects, on the history of music and art. Later in life, he brought all his sensibilities together in an unusual way to return something to the Parkston community that nurtured him in South Dakota, by purchasing a historic bank building and turning it into a museum for paintings by the Tennessee-born artist Bernard Albert James, as well as an archival home for the composer's life work, now literally safe in the bank's old vault.[5]

To make any work of art possible at all, Kenneth Klauss reminds aspiring students, "You must first have technique. Don't worship it; but you must have it." The composer also touched upon the endlessly beckoning possibilities of beginnings—which certainly suggest analogies for the processes of improvising and composing music for the dance, and for the germs of ideas that are complete in his *Tokas* while being also open to many ways of development.

"If you know what something is going to be like at the end, it will be dead as a doornail," remarked the composer. "Think of Michelangelo. You take a block of marble and scrape till you feel the spirit in it, but when you start out, you don't know what it will be when you finish."

THIRTY ONE

Carmen de Lavallade

Dancing to Many Musical Styles

Katherine Teck

O NE OF THE DANCERS *nurtured by Lester Horton is Carmen de Lavallade (born 1931). Growing up in Los Angeles, she studied and performed with Horton while still a teenager, and was cast in several Hollywood films of the 1950s* (Carmen Jones, *for one). She made her first New York appearance with Horton's company. Shortly after that, she had a leading role on Broadway in* House of Flowers *along with Alvin Ailey and the Trinidadian dancer-painter Geoffrey Holder, whom she married. When she toured the Far East with Alvin Ailey and his dancers in 1962, the billing was the "de Lavallade–Ailey Dance Theater."*

Presented as a soloist noted for her sense of lyricism and drama, Carmen de Lavallade performed with the Metropolitan Opera and American Ballet Theatre. She was featured in telecasts with a wide variety of musicians (from Duke Ellington to the Boston Pops Orchestra) and had roles created specifically for her by choreographers Lester Horton, Alvin Ailey, John Butler, Geoffrey Holder, Agnes de Mille, Donald McKayle, Gus Solomons Jr., and Glen Tetley. She has also performed and coached revivals of works by Horton and by Ruth St. Denis.

Expanding her career, de Lavallade taught movement for actors in the School of Drama as a professor at Yale University and went on to act professionally in several dozen plays. As a choreographer, she has staged dances

for the Metropolitan Opera's productions of Porgy and Bess and Die
Meistersinger. In 1998 she began to choreograph and perform with Gus
Solomons Jr. and Dudley Williams in their company, Paradigm.

Celebrating the tenth anniversary of Paradigm at the Dance Theater
Workshop in New York in 2008, Carmen de Lavallade performed in Player
& Prayer, a trio with Solomons and former Cunningham dancer Valda
Setterfield, choreographed by Jonah Bokaer—who also devised the sound to
include the three performers' recollections of how they came to be dancers. And
so, accompanying de Lavallade in her expressive movements, the audience
heard interjections of "Hollywood Boulevard" and "Melrose Avenue." That is
indeed where she started. Better to let her tell things in her own words.

***

"Ah, yes, the famous Melrose Avenue," laughed Carmen de Lavallade. "That's where Lester Horton's theater was. And then I had my first little dance classes with Melissa Blake on Highland Avenue near Hollywood Boulevard, around the Chinese neighborhood, where the Kodak Theater is now."

In contrast to the sleeker, faster-paced urban setting of today, the dancer conjures up an image of a Los Angeles with fields of multicolored wildflowers, modest dance studios, and considerable personalized attention. Did she recall any general musical aura from those days, along with the memory of the streets?

"Melissa Blake's was just a little storefront class. But she had live pianists. Carmelita Maracci did too, usually classical.[1] Carmelita had wonderful music. The pianist used to play Schubert, Beethoven, Vivaldi. She had the best music, because she was so picky about it. Unfortunately, Lester couldn't afford very much, so we used more hand drums and percussion, and when we could, a piano. It was different, but there was always live music around.

"Lester had a whole rack of gamelan-like drums and bells, and sometimes he would use that for class. Then for *Salome*, it was all percussion: all those drums and bells and his collection of things. He had an old zither, and he had me take a rattle and hit it against the zither. I remember a very agitated kind of sound which was really quite marvelous. We were set up behind the curtain to play drums and other percussion. We could see the dance past the curtain. It really worked very nicely, and was quite an experience."

Bella Lewitzky originally danced the part of Salome. After she left his company, Horton restaged the dance with Carmen de Lavallade in the role, making changes to accommodate the physical differences and styles of the two dancers. She knew the score well because she had been present at previous rehearsals.

As a child, Carmen had been introduced to percussion. "In the 'old days' everybody had a rhythm band and they had music in school. There is often nothing like that now; it's different, just sad. But I was always around music. My aunt played piano. She wanted to be a classical concert pianist, but you know, in those days that was just unheard of. I played piano too; all 'nice young ladies' played piano! And in both my dad's family and my mom's, we always had recordings, mainly classical. Light opera was a big thing. And then the pop music would have been Ellington and Lionel Hampton, but that was kind of frowned on. I had one cousin who wanted to be a jazz singer, and she would have been a good one. One of the big jazz names wanted her to come—she was in her teens—but that was a big no-no. Nope; not allowed. But I have always been a music nut since I was little. Music and me: we're buddies! I like all kinds."

Another cousin, Janet Collins, was the first in the family to make a successful theatrical career: initially as a noted concert dancer in California, later in Katherine Dunham's troupe, and still later as a soloist on the stages of both Broadway and the Metropolitan Opera in New York.[2] Collins, ten years older, would long be the inspiration for the young Carmen—who in subsequent years literally followed in her cousin's footsteps upon the stage of the Metropolitan Opera.

Carmen de Lavallade laughs with amusement as she recalls what it was like to be the one onstage there. "I could see the conductor at the old Met, and they had those little prompters' boxes. I did *Samson and Delilah* and *Aida*, and both my costumes were rather bare. So you were dancing away and you look in the prompters' box and see this little face smiling at you. Sometimes you see the people in the pit trying to give a little look at the action onstage too."

Artistically, things could get pretty challenging both onstage and in the pits. Who had to adjust to the events of the moment regarding that always-important aspect of tempo: musicians or dancers? The dancer recalled as an example the bacchanal scene from *Samson and Delilah*: "You rehearse and try to get the tempo and come to some agreement, but in performance, the music is the music, and as the dancer, you sometimes have to adjust. And when you're the one choreographing, you can't slow the music down just because you feel like it; the composer *wants* a certain tempo."

But dancing with the full orchestral complement of the Metropolitan Opera was only one among many of the musical highlights in de Lavallade's career. Another was performing with Geoffrey Holder as part of Josephine Baker's show in Paris, using Baker's live orchestra at the Olympia theater to offer the music of Quincy Jones for a witty duet Holder had choreographed, titled *Dear Quincy*.

For various performances of Holder's choreography of *The Creation* for de Lavallade (based on a poem by James Weldon Johnson), there have been various transformations in the musical backdrop: "I've done it with all kinds of musicians, from the eighty-piece orchestra, to once with Willie Ruff on the French horn. I had somebody do it with the flute, with quartet, with other musical combinations, and sometimes with no music at all."

Though dance can have great impact in silence, nevertheless, the injection of live music into a dance program does add to a total evening. For example, in *Three Scenes from Archy & Mehitabel*, a recent duet created jointly by Carmen de Lavallade and Gus Solomons Jr. for their Paradigm programs, the original music by saxophonist Jane Ira Bloom added just the right flavor to this evocation of friendship between cockroach and cat through the years.

Looking back over a long and varied career, Carmen de Lavallade recalls with special fondness the live performance of the folksinger Odetta, for the dance *Come Sunday* choreographed by Holder.[3] "We did that suite at the opening of the Ford's Theater in Washington, D.C. Odetta was onstage, and it drove her crazy. She was worried about *me*, and I said, 'Don't worry; just sing; I will follow you.' It made her nervous. She felt responsible for me and wanted to do it right and wondered if she was going too fast, too slow. But I said, 'Odetta, it doesn't matter to me; I can follow you!' But she worried about me, and that was so sweet." Subsequent performances of that dance were done with Odetta's recordings.

When using recorded music, tempo can be one reason for particular choices. A favorite of this artist is Madeleine Grey's recording of *Songs of the Auvergne* by Canteloube, another work choreographed for his wife by Geoffrey Holder. "That's the one I love. It has a lot of life in it. It might not have been the greatest recording, but the *tempi* are good," observed de Lavallade.

A highlight for Carmen de Lavallade was the live singing of Brother John Sellers during the Pacific tour taken by the de Lavallade–Ailey Dance Theater. The dance was a duet choreographed by Alvin Ailey for the two of them, called *Roots of the Blues*. For that, de Lavallade recalled: "Brother John was extraordinary. Alvin and I at that time were taking acting lessons at Stella Adler's, and so we decided we would have our little drama going on. We put our little story together of two people who would dress up on Friday nights with no place to go, and watch the train go by to Chicago. Brother John was a master with the blues, and Alvin picked wonderful music. To us, we were all people stuck in a town and couldn't get out. So it had a wonderful quality to it."

Long before all these successes, Carmen de Lavallade's musical knowledge and sensitivity were nurtured in her years with Lester Horton, starting when she was fourteen years old. As part of his dancers' training, he included study of the basics of music, having his apprentices write out some examples so as to understand various rhythms and so forth.

The young student also enjoyed Hollywood films, including the Jack Cole movies, operettas, "Our Gang" films, and sparkling musicals such as *Seven Brides for Seven Brothers*. Looking back, de Lavallade also recalls the popular light operettas filmed with Jeanette MacDonald and Nelson Eddie. Additionally, through school there would be trips to children's concerts at the Los Angeles Philharmonic auditorium, orchestral programs with Alfred Wallenstein. And opera: they would see such operas as Wagner's *Tristan and Isolde*.

For someone who later was to perform with an extraordinary range of musical styles, the Los Angeles of her childhood offered an introduction to cultural variety. Many Mexican children attended Carmen's grammar school, and she recalls that the first dance she ever learned was the Mexican hat dance. "As I progressed at Lester's," she related, "that's where jazz came in. Lester choreographed Duke Ellington's *Liberian Suite*, also dances to music by Stan Kenton and Les Baxter. It was very unusual for that time, because most of the modern dancers were using classical music, and Lester started using pop and jazz. During that time, at least, Duke Ellington and Stan Kenton were considered progressive jazz. That was a very interesting period, I felt."

One piece that Lester Horton set to music by Les Baxter was *Sarong Paramaribo*. About this, the dancer recalled: "It was all coordination! Our feet were doing one thing, our torsos and hips something else, our fingers something else, our heads something else. Lester Horton took two cultures, African and Balinese, so you had the hips a certain way, the head and shoulders another. We had a lot of coordination things that we used to do."

Even though a film made during a performance presents dancers as tiny images, a sense of Carmen de Lavallade's vivid dancing and musicality in *Sarong* can be gained by watching the DVD made of the twenty-fifth anniversary celebrations by the Alvin Ailey American Dance Theater, with the shimmering music by Les Baxter, scored for vibraphone, violins, harp, oboe, drums and vocals.

Such physical identification with a wide range of musical styles is an unusual gift. Indeed, one has the feeling that this artist's sensibilities are so finely tuned that she does not normally need to analyze what she is doing, but rather goes deep within herself to identify physically and emotionally with the role she is dancing. This can be observed briefly in a film made of Carmen de Lavallade warming up for her both alluring and gut-wrenching evocation of the singer Billie Holiday as choreographed by John Butler. She stands in black warm-up clothes with back to the camera; her hands flutter in agitated ways; she clicks her fingers as a "come-on." She swings her hips. Turned about, her face becomes a kaleidoscope of battling emotions; she vocalizes some rhythms, and one senses the spirit of Billie Holiday herself entering into the dancer. She goes onstage in a white dress and high heels, to gift the audience with a dance that by turns sparkles defiantly and moans in agony. It includes a barefoot love duet with Ulysses Dove to the words "What makes me treat you the way that I do....Gee Baby, ain't I good to you," and ends with the disoriented Billie figure curled up on the floor in despair even while the sounds of a recorded song are upbeat. Loud applause follows in the sound track: an ironic accompaniment to what the audience sees at the conclusion of the dance.

Portrait of Billie was choreographed to existing recordings by the singer Billie Holiday. But Carmen de Lavallade also had some unusual experiences of dancing to newly made scores, with the music performed live, some created especially for television. A number of these were dramatic narrative dances choreographed by John Butler, including *Jephthah's Daughter* with music by Peggy Glanville-Hicks; and *David and Bathsheba*, with music by Carlos Surinach. Watching these black-and-white films today, one is struck by the seemingly total merging of the music and the movement of all the dancers. The drama was so intense, the unfolding so immediate, it seemed impossible that the choreography had come into being through counts. Were there counts at all?

"Well, you do count, but—" added Carmen de Lavallade with a knowing laugh, "I always discount the counts! The best thing I ever did with John Butler and music was *Carmina Burana*, with music by Carl Orff, first performed at City Center. That caused a great sensation."

FIGURE 31.1 Carmen de Lavallade in *Sarong*, choreographed by Lester Horton. Photograph © 1983 Lois Greenfield. Reproduced by permission.

That is strongly rhythmic music. "Was that particular choreography done with counts,?" the dancer is asked. Her reply:

"You have to count it out. You count things out, but as I said, *I* discount the counts. The music is telling me what to do. It's like good Shakespeare: the words are telling you what to say. Today there exists what I call bang-bang dancing: everything is on the beats; you can see the counts. That's like an actor saying 'to-be-or-not-to-be-that-is-the-ques-tion,'" de Lavallade intones in a monotone of equal syllables.

"You don't want to hear that. You want to hear the words and the thoughts and the feeling. Music has its own personality. You *have* to count sometimes, when you have to check on something, and that's OK. But once you start doing that 'one-two-three-four,' you might as well forget it.

"It's not just about the words; it's about the content of what you are doing. Sometimes if the rhythm is really intricate and I'm not sure, then I count it out. But once I get the rhythm physically and mentally, I throw out the counts. Once I hear it, then I get the flow."

In the premiere of Jonah Bokaer's *Player & Prayer*, the dancers had state-of-the-art technology boxes strapped to their arms. "Our own voices came out of those," explained de Lavallade. "There is no rhythm; there is no music; so your tempo is approximate. There is nothing that you can hang onto. Once you start your tempo, that's it, and then you hope: you have words and feel, oh, that's good, I'm right on it, or whoops, I'm behind. You just have to adjust."

One source of pride for Carmen de Lavallade was her quickly acquired skill of lip-synching for a live telecast. "There is an art to lip-synching," she explains. "You have to do all the words properly, and you have to do the breathing and so on so that it looks as if it's your voice." This skill was called for on her part as the enchantress Madame Zajj ("jazz" spelled backward), in the 1957 telecast of Duke Ellington and Billy Strayhorn's *A Drum Is a Woman*, a series of delightful vignettes that serve as an allegory to the history of jazz music and dance.[4]

Summing up general audience reactions to Carmen de Lavallade's performances, the prominent arts critic John Gruen once stated simply: "She went on the stage, and there was a *presence*, something very unique."[5]

Her sensitivity to an exceptionally wide variety of musical styles—first nurtured by Lester Horton—has been one facet of this dancer's artistry that brought her from Melrose Street in Los Angeles to the stages of New York, the Far East, Paris, and elsewhere.

THIRTY TWO

Instructions

How to Play the Drums

Alvin Ailey

Be born in Africa
(even centuries ago)
Run free on the white sand of
the beach—
Laugh! Throw your black body
against the white sand—
Pick up a tiny stone—
Throw it out toward an island—
(a world you know is there
but cannot see—)

Wait and see if the waves
bring it back—(they do not)
Splash in the water like a
Black Fish—walk slowly
home thru the green leaves
Becoming emerald with nite—
Then—
    Try to run away when they
come for you with whips &
guns & nets

Feel anguish & terror as they
lash you together with others of
your kind in a dark ship's hold—
Sweat, get sick, vomit—
Become thin & weak &
your eyes yellow & empty—
No more sand
no trees—
only perpetual night in a
forest of malignant Black
Bodies—caged like sweaty
panthers in a cave without light—
Then—
Arrive & be sold
Stand on a block

Work

Do not speak your own language
Sing his songs—not yours
Do not dance—it's bad they say—

wonder

think
going home to "<u>his</u>" Jesus—not Obatala

Go to Memphis, New Orleans, Atlanta

sing

blues

spirituals

Be jazz

and that is how to play drums.

THIRTY THREE

Alvin Ailey's *Revelations*

Jennifer Dunning

*A*LVIN AILEY (1931–89) *was among the artists nurtured by Lester Horton, and after Horton's death, Ailey continued with this West Coast theater company for a few years. A native of Texas, Ailey later studied also with Martha Graham, Hanya Holm, and Charles Weidman. He appeared (with Carmen de Lavallade) in the Broadway production of* House of Flowers. *In 1958 he formed the Alvin Ailey American Dance Theater company, which after its founder's death continued to flourish under the direction of Judith Jamison, and which is now set to continue under the artistic leadership of choreographer Robert Battle.*

In regard to music, Ailey drew on the heritage of African Americans for his Blues Suite *in 1958. Shortly thereafter he created what is certainly one of the landmark dances of the entire twentieth century:* Revelations. *It was first performed at the 92nd Street YM-YWHA in 1960.*

The suite of music for Revelations *was drawn from Negro spirituals and includes the following, in three groupings. First,* Pilgrim of Sorrow: *"I Been 'Buked," "Weeping Mary," "Poor Pilgrim," "Round about the Mountain," "Wonder Where," and "Troubles." The second section, titled* That Love My Jesus Gives Me *includes the spirituals "Fix Me, Jesus," "Honor, Honor," "Wade in the Water," "Morning Star," "My Lord What a Morning," and "Sinner Man." The final section,* Move, Members, Move, *features, "Precious Lord," "God A Mighty," "Waters of Babylon," and the finale "Rocka My Soul."*

In this abridged excerpt from her biography of Alvin Ailey, the dance critic Jennifer Dunning presents informative background about Revelations, *places it in the context of a longer look at modern dance in America, and seeks to identify the source of this work's continuing appeal.*

***

The first reviews of *Revelations* were generally positive, but the audience's rapt silence said most about what the new dance was and the classic it would become. *Revelations* would one day be performed in theaters around the world. Night after night after night it would draw tumultuous applause, cheers, foot stamping and general mayhem in even the most circumspect of cultures. By the late 1980s, it was estimated that *Revelations* had been performed more often than the nearly century-old *Swan Lake*.

What is the magic of *Revelations*? It is simple and direct, but so is Doris Humphrey's *Day on Earth*, a modern dance classic in which a man and woman and their child move with gentle inexorability through the life cycle. It is theatrical, but so, certainly, is Alvin's *Blues Suite*. It addresses the life of the spirit, in hope, and in despair—like José Limón's powerful *Missa Brevis*. It is enjoyable fun, but so are any number of dances by Paul Taylor.

The spirituals to which *Revelations* is danced have a powerful, primal appeal. There is in the songs—and in the dance's choreography and scenic and costume designs—a bustling interplay and juxtaposition of complexity and simplicity. Most of all, however, *Revelations* was and remains the work of a community, from the larger worlds of black Americans to the worlds of the individual dancers who helped create *Revelations* and passed it on to later generations.

Dance is, like the other arts, assimilative. Nothing is ever really very new in it. The freshness of a dance lies not only in what the choreographer brings to it, with honesty and expertise, but in how the elements are combined. Alvin borrowed from the world, a habit he cheerfully acknowledged, making a virtue of eclecticism, and in the process creating something that was more a dance style or way of moving than a technique.

An observant outsider in choreography as well as life, Alvin consciously appropriated and fused elements from the techniques of Lester Horton, Martha Graham and the jazz dance of Jack Cole to create a style that could express the visions of a humanist, a poet, or even an anthropologist. *Revelations* is a dance that contains the history of blacks in America.

A shared history is not necessary, however, to understand the piece. Alvin understood that the universal lay in the smallest, most everyday details of particular lives. The religious themes in *Revelations* meant little—or too much—to many of the Ailey dancers. Nat Horne, the southern-born son of an evangelical minister, at first felt a little sacrilegious dancing to the spirituals and worried, unnecessarily as it turned out, about his father's reaction to the piece. Some of the dancers, born up north, had had no experience of the southern black Baptist church. Claude Thompson, who rehearsed but did not perform in the premiere of the piece, recalled that he felt at first like "a Catholic nun at a Baptist convention." He was, after all, someone who passed by the black church in his neighborhood, heard tambourines and thought merely, "Nice rhythm!"

The success of *Revelations* dogged Alvin all his life. He knew the worth of the dance and cherished it in spite of himself, allowing only one other company to dance it, and that for a limited time. But he worried that impressionable young dancers, hearing the wild applause that invariably greets the piece, would assume that their performances were perfect. He worried that they could not understand its soul, coming as they did from worlds so different from those of the dancers for whom it was created.

In the early years, however, *Revelations* brought Alvin as close to a pure and joyful satisfaction in his work as he was ever to come. The future promised much. It was still possible then to envision successors to this outpouring of his heart and soul and craft. And there were later masterworks. But none was ever to have the same impact.

Revelations was a phenomenon, a work of raw emotion rendered with the innocent wholeheartedness and urgency of a first work into which all the experiences, thoughts and emotions of a young life are siphoned in an unquenchable, cathartic flow. At the same time, however, the dance captured the heart of Alvin's greatest gift and made it clear that he alone could have created it.

THIRTY FOUR

How *Revelations* Came to Be

Alvin Ailey, with A. Peter Bailey

*I*N HIS MEMOIR, *the choreographer Alvin Ailey recalls some of the musical inspirations that led to the creation of* Revelations *and explains how it evolved to its final format.*

***

Revelations began with the music. As early as I can remember I was enthralled by the music played and sung in the small black churches in every small Texas town my mother and I lived in. No matter where we were during those nomadic years, Sunday was always a churchgoing day. There we would absorb some of the most glorious singing to be heard anywhere in the world.

With profound feeling, with faith, hope, joy, and sometimes sadness, the choirs, congregations, deacons, preachers, and ushers would sing black spirituals and gospel songs. They sang and played the music with such fervor that even as a small child I could not only hear it but almost see it. I remember hearing "Wade in the Water" being sung during baptism and hearing the pastor's wife sing "I Been 'Buked, I Been Scorned" one Sunday during testifying time. I tried to put all of that feeling into *Revelations*.

My plan was to make *Revelations* the second part of an all-black evening of dance. First would be the blues in *Blues Suite*, then spirituals in *Revelations*, then a section on Kansas City jazz, then a section on contemporary music. The aim was to show the coming and the growth and reach of black culture.

FIGURE 34.1 Alvin Ailey performed his *Revelations* at Jacob's Pillow in 1961. Photograph dbMS Thr 482, by John Lindquist © Harvard Theatre Collection, Houghton Library, Harvard University.

I had also decided that I wanted to develop a black folk dance company that would combine the work of Katherine Dunham and a Filipino dance company I once saw. We would present a concert based on Black American material—songs from the Georgia Sea Islands, New Orleans songs with old blues singers, work songs, folk songs. I planned to do a suite of blues and then a suite of spirituals.

I did extensive research, listened to a lot of music, dug deeper into my early Texas memories, and came up with the piece that I would call *Revelations*. I phoned Hall Johnson, a wonderful man who lived uptown, and said, "We want to do this dance two to three months from now from all these spirituals. I would like you to sing." He had a choir and led me to a lot of music, including "I Been 'Buked, I Been Scorned," which he had arranged. He decided not to do the concert, and I ended up with a group from the YMCA in Harlem. I had to have live music; for me there was no other way.

I divided an hour of these pieces into three sections. First I did it chronologically, leading off with the opening part of *Revelations*, which was the earliest in time. It was about trying to get up out of the ground. The costumes and set would be colored brown, an earth color, for coming out of the earth, for going into the earth. The second part was something that was very close to me—the baptismal, the purification rite. Its colors would be white and pale blue. Then there would be the section surrounding the gospel church, the holy rollers, and all that, the church happiness. Its colors would be earth tones, yellow, and black.

The first version of *Revelations* was quite long, an hour and five minutes, and it had three sections. The first was called *Pilgrim of Sorrow*. I took all the songs dealing with black people's sorrow and put them in this section; at the time there were about five or six songs. The middle section was to be wading in the water. Songs such as "Honor, Honor" had all these extraordinary words. I was moved by what spirituals say as words, as metaphors. So I found these short songs for the middle section.

There were quite a few songs for the last section, *Move, Members, Move*. The whole ballet was a gigantic suite of spirituals. I poured in just about everything, every beautiful spiritual I had ever heard. From the beginning I thought the first version of *Revelations* might be too long, but nobody ever complained about the length. The critics and audiences had nothing but the most delicious praise from the beginning in 1960, when *Revelations* was premiered.

Revelations didn't reach its real popularity until it was edited. When we were invited to Jacob's Pillow in 1961 to do an evening of our entire repertoire, I had no music for *Revelations*; it had always been done to live music. But we couldn't afford to take the singers to Jacob's Pillow, so we had to hurriedly come up with taped music. In those days you couldn't just run to a studio, start taping, and come up with something usable. I approached Howard Roberts, a wonderful black choral conductor and an associate at Clark Center. Together we took bits and pieces of this and that and put them together in order to be able to take *Revelations* to Jacob's Pillow. I had to make do with the music we created, so the first section became three pieces instead of six. There was another song after "Rocka My Soul" called "Elijah Rock," a beautiful song about faith. It was my favorite of the two, but the audience liked "Rocka My Soul" better, and that's what they got.

After I snipped, cut, pushed, and pulled *Revelations* down to a half hour, we went off to Jacob's Pillow. The sequence I settled on was "I Been 'Buked," then "Didn't My Lord Deliver Daniel," "Fix Me, Jesus," and the processional, and finally, "Wading in the Water." When we went offstage after "Wading in the Water" the audience jumped up and screamed, and they've been jumping and screaming over *Revelations* ever since.

PART FOUR

INSTRUMENTS, TECHNOLOGY, AND THE AVANT-GARDE

Making an instrument is one of music's greatest joys. Indeed, to make an instrument is in some strong sense to summon the future.... Nor are all instruments invented & over with. The world is rich with models, but innumerable forms, tones & powers await their summons from the mind & hand.

—Lou Harrison

Overview

Expanding Timbre Possibilities with Percussion,
Vocalization, Electronic Instruments,
and the Sounds around Us

MODERN DANCERS HAVE performed to a greater diversity of instruments, vocalization, and sound scores than had their predecessors in ballet and other theatrical styles. One departure from the traditions of the nineteenth-century ballet was to perform in the absence of all musical accompaniment. Although there is no such thing as absolute "silence" in a theater environment, Doris Humphrey's unaccompanied *Water Study* (1928) was notable for using the breath phrasing of the dancers themselves, with stunning theatrical effect quite different from dance works that used strictly metered musical accompaniment.

Progressing from silence and the visually perceived rhythms of bodies in motion, dancers also incorporated body percussion and vocalization. Such practices had already become highly developed in older traditions such as the *flamenco puro* of Spain, but they were new for concert dancers in America. In this part, Lehman Engel relates his experiences with nonverbal "choric sound" for his collaboration with Martha Graham.

Drums and exotic percussion instruments from around the world were also seen to provide fresh impetus for concert dance. One artist who urged students and colleagues to explore such possibilities was Franziska Boas, daughter of the anthropologist Franz Boas and herself a collector of instruments from various cultures. In her work at the Bennington dance gatherings with Hanya Holm and also independently, Boas introduced many new effects. In her article here, she notes the challenge of new percussion ensembles that (unlike the case with orchestral or jazz band percussion sections) had no standardization. Each group would have a unique set of instruments, precluding a scoring that would allow for repeated performance by other ensembles. She also draws attention to the melodic implications inherent in using multiple percussion instruments and emphasizes that each instrument or set has its distinctive character. Therefore, she suggests, choreographers and collaborating musicians would be well advised to try and match the character of a particular percussion timbre to the character of a specific dance work.

Strictly percussive music was found to be especially invigorating for dancers because of the strong rhythmic impact and subtle nuances that can be achieved with a variety of instruments ranging from the simplest rattles to expensive manufactured cymbals, Latin American marimbas, strange-sounding flexatones, and exotic drums from around the world. But it was not enough for curious dancers and musicians to pick up mallets and beat drums randomly. Effective ways had to be found to put sounds to work for artistic advantage and dance purposes. Consequently, physical drumming techniques drawn from traditions around the world were studied, as well as diverse methods of grouping rhythmic patterns, experiments with diverse metrical structure, and techniques of creating melody and longer phrasing. These are topics addressed here by both Boas and Henry Cowell, who went on to suggest that just because musicians might borrow from Asian traditions, for example, the resulting music need not sound "Asian." So it was not only instruments that Cowell urged musicians to explore but also various mathematical methods used in other cultures for organizing rhythms. In his article here, he draws attention to Indian tala traditions.

When varied instrumental sets or skilled percussionists were not available, choreographers upon occasion turned to recorded percussion, as Hanya Holm did for her *Trend*, presented at Bennington College in 1937. She surprised audiences by concluding her dance to a recording of *Ionization* by Edgard Varèse (1883–1965), which was scored for thirty-seven percussion instruments, including Chinese cymbals, gongs, bongo drums, bass and snare drums, military field drums, slapsticks, guiro scrapers, woodblocks, claves, maracas, sleigh bells, tambourine, anvils, triangle, suspended cymbals, castanets, piano, chimes, celesta, and electric sirens.

Studio accompanists around the country soon found that in their desperation for varied new sound qualities, sometimes a radiator or other things at hand could be used effectively to deliver percussive timbres suitable for the dancers' needs of the moment. For choreographed performances, especially with the collaborations by Lou Harrison and John Cage on the West Coast, effects made by hitting automobile brake drums and other "found" sources of sound were formally included in scores for percussion ensembles. Dancers were intrigued by such timbres as those heard during the Harrison and Cage percussion ensemble concerts when the Bennington dance programs moved to Mills College in California for the summer of 1939.

Harrison had previously used percussion ensembles in concerts when he worked with dancer Bonnie Bird in Seattle. Back in California in later years, Harrison and his life partner, Bill Colvig, went on to build large gamelan sets of tuned gongs in the traditions of Indonesia, and he used these for both concert performances and dance purposes, with tuning plans and scoring very carefully worked out beforehand.

Harry Partch (1901–74) was another composer who built remarkable sets of instruments, which he used for his dramatic theater works, incorporating his unique tunings that involved pitches calibrated at microtonal intervals.[1]

An especially appropriate use of percussion for concert dance was for choreography that drew on traditions of Africa and the Caribbean. Notable examples were the performances of Katherine Dunham in Chicago after she returned from her studies of Haitian culture, and the concert dances of Pearl Primus, for instance in her *African Ceremonial* first performed in New York at the 92nd Street YM-YWHA in 1943.

Along with percussion, pianos quickly became instruments of both convenience and choice for modern dancers. Studios were commonly equipped with pianos, and if two musicians performed at one keyboard, a fullness of sound suitable for theatrical performance could be produced. A few woodwinds or strings could be added at modest cost, and using Henry Cowell's system of elastic form, the instrumentation for a dance score could be varied from performance to performance.

Before his involvement with modern dance, Cowell had concertized in both the United States and Europe, performing his inventive pieces that made use of the *insides* of a piano: strumming, plucking, thumping, combined with keyboard effects using arms and fists, along with quite complex rhythmic organization. Modern dancers found these strange new sounds quite effective in the theater, and among the choreographers who used music by Cowell was Jean Erdman (originally one of Graham's dancers).

Pushing the envelope of generating sound with pianos much further, John Cage (longtime collaborator for Merce Cunningham) invented what he called the "prepared piano," utilizing screws and other objects strategically placed in the strings, with the results being curiously evocative of Indonesian gamelan music. Lucia Dlugoszewski also developed what she dubbed the "timbre piano" and, with artist Ralph Dorazio aiding in the design and building, amassed a sizable collection of unique percussion instruments for use in collaborative performances with the Erick Hawkins Dance Company.

John Cage became known for his avant-garde stretching of the boundaries in making music for dance. Some of the results are described from the point of view of a dancer in Carolyn Brown's memoir in this part, and several excerpts from Cage's writing challenge both performers and listeners to be open to sound in new ways.

In addition to using vocalization, body and instrumental percussion, piano, chamber ensembles, and experimental sound sources, modern dancers also followed the example of Isadora Duncan in performing with full orchestras. Despite the high costs financially, Martha Graham enjoyed the luxury of live orchestral sounds for many of her company's performances. For many years so did Paul Taylor—at least for his New York City seasons.

Improved recording technology offered modern choreographers a less expensive way to provide acceptable music for their performances and allowed them to offer audiences the sounds of full orchestras or other large ensembles, with consistent expected tempos, and also enabling choreographers' increasingly wide-ranging choices in musical genres. However, for some—notably Erick Hawkins—live music was an artistic choice that was not to be dispensed with, regardless of cost or convenience. Nevertheless, as the years progressed during the twentieth century, increasingly dancers (especially touring troupes) would come to substitute recordings and sound systems for live musicians—or else draw upon music that was electronic to begin with.

The invention of tape recording lured inventive minds to explore new technologies for creating music for dance. John Cage and his colleagues tried many ways of doing this and found that synchronization of multiple tapes presented problems, which they solved in various ways, among them, by measuring music in inches of tape as well as with a stopwatch.

The first electronic music used for concert dance performance was Otto Luening's score for Doris Humphrey's *Theatre Piece #2*. The composer describes the premiere of that work, in this part's excerpt from his memoirs. Subsequently, an artist who expanded the role of electronic music in his dances (composing it himself) was Alwin Nikolais, who describes his concept of "total theater" in the article included here. Although such electronic scores as those of Nikolais now are accepted and admired by both dancers and audiences, when they were new, even Louis Horst raised questions. After the premiere of *Kaleidoscope*, he asked: "Where does music end and noise begin?"[2]

Some artistic creation would depend precisely on the invention of new equipment, a fact recognized by composer Edgard Varèse.[3] As documented by Paul Griffiths, as early as 1916 Varèse had been calling for new scientific instruments. By 1939, he suggested a few benefits to be discovered: "liberation from the tempered system, a pitch range extended in both directions, new harmonic splendors, increased differentiation of timbres, an expanded dynamic spectrum, the feasibility of sound projection in space, and unrelated cross rhythms."[4]

Since those days, with many improvements in synthesizers and sound samplers, and with the means of composing and scoring via computer, the job of the collaborating composer for dance has changed substantially. Initial "sketches" can be provided much more quickly now; changes can be made instantly or overnight; and musical components for dance performances can be provided relatively inexpensively (if one compares the cost of a full orchestra, as continues to be the norm for major ballet companies). Indicating the new diversity, composers for dance in the twenty-first century may refer to their collaborations as "sound-art" rather than as "music."

Yet the sound of a single drum played live can still motivate dancers to move, and through some of the following articles we can share the excitement and interest that the early modern artists felt during their sometimes tentative and sometimes bold explorations with varied vocalizing and instrumental music-making.

THIRTY FIVE

Percussion Music and Its Relation to the Modern Dance

Franziska Boas

*S*TEEPED IN KNOWLEDGE *about non-Western cultures, Franziska Boas (1902–88) became known in the dance world as performer, chore-ographer, dance therapist, teacher, and activist against racial bar-riers. The daughter of noted anthropologist Franz Boas, she also studied arts from traditional cultures around the world. Her dance training included studies in Germany with Mary Wigman and in New York with Hanya Holm, for whom she served as both assistant and percussionist. She ran her own school from 1933 until 1949.*[1]

In this 1940 essay, Boas touches upon the challenges created due to non-standardization of newly formed percussion ensembles and calls attention to the importance of long musical phrases as a complementary function for dance performance.

***

Percussion music must cease serving as a time-keeper or as a mathematical problem for division and subdivision of beats arranged in arbitrary meter mosaics. We must think of percussion as a polyphonic euphony instead of a polyrhythmic cacophony.

It is characteristic of our time to stay on the surface and try to accomplish through superficial inventiveness and noise that which can be achieved only by means of inner concentration and an understanding of craftsmanship.

Percussion composers should purposely favor the long phrase, in which the rhythmic detail is incidental to the rise and fall of melody, and to changes in dynamic tension. Melody can be evoked from any objects surrounding us in ordinary life, even from a radiator or a wooden bench. Variation in tension and dynamics may be produced through different intensities of sound or changes in meter. Rise and fall of melody occurs through changes in tone, inherent in instruments made of different substances, made in different sizes and shapes, and with varying degrees of surface tension.

It is not the rhythmic spacing of beats alone but also the quality of tone that indicates tension. It is not enough to use as many or as few different instruments as possible regardless of their pitch. It is necessary to find that particular instrument which most closely reveals the theme, just as the dancer must choose the particular gesture best suited for that which he wishes to express. It is therefore necessary for the percussion composer to study his instruments carefully and know them as a music composer knows the instruments of the orchestra. Like the choreographer who deals with the individual members of his group, so too the percussion composer has many personalities in the instruments of his orchestra. He must find for each its proper place and strive for that which can be accomplished with the material at his disposal.

Of what instruments is this orchestra composed? At present there is no standard. Anything is used. We have access to the already tried instruments of all countries and all tribes in the world. Aside from that we can make new instruments out of anything which has a sound or tone that will carry any distance. How shall we ever find and organize our orchestra? That is the question which must be answered before percussion music can be used in a practical way. At present there are no two percussion orchestras which are alike. Therefore no composition can be truly rendered by any other percussion orchestra unless it has access to the identical instruments used in the original composition. This is due to the fact that each instrument has its individual pitch or quality. We cannot afford to limit ourselves to the tympani, bass drum, snare drum, chimes, vibraphone, xylophone, temple blocks and sizzle cymbal, as the mainstay of military bands, for jazz work and swing bands. There exist too many potentialities for melody and dynamic material in the instruments of other cultures.

British Columbia has box drums made of cedar steamed and bent. In South America, where there is an abundance of hard woods, we have slit log drums hollowed out of one solid piece of a tree. Among the basket-weaving Indians we have basket drums. In New Mexico and Arizona we have drums made of cottonwood logs, hollowed out, with skins of animals stretched over both ends. We could continue enumerating examples for rattles, bells, whistles, and we could consider such substances as clay, bone and claws, reed, shells, etc.

There is no comprehensive scientific material on the problem of preference for certain instruments. Yet there must be a reason why the instruments of each tribe are as they are. Perhaps it is the geographical situation, the type of vegetation, types of animals, or perhaps it is the purpose for which the instrument was made. It might even be all four reasons or any combination of them.

I can conceive that the orchestra of the pure percussion musician may be very different from that of the composer for dance, just as his music may be different. The composer for dance must be guided by the demands of the dance and must find those instruments which will reproduce the tensions and melodies of dance. As an illustration of one orchestra I should like to enumerate some of the instruments in my collection: tympani, tunable tom-toms, hollow log signal drum, Chinese and African tom-toms, tambourines, and experimental drums made of barrels; Burmese, Tibetan, Chinese and Italian gongs; Turkish, Chinese and American cymbals of various sizes; Korean temple blocks, Chinese wood blocks, an African marimba; bells, brass bowls, numerous rattles, a zither, the strings and sounding board of an old piano, and of course, one piano in its natural classic dignity. Some of these instruments are useful in our work with the dance. With others, we are still exploring possibilities.

Theoretically, a successful modern percussion group should be able to accompany a contemporary dance composition by means of a musical improvisation within a pattern. However, a tradition of such a contribution is not yet established due to the varying approaches to the dance of our civilization. Our concert dance has not emanated from folk dance, nor has it as yet crystallized as folk dance, and percussion composers or players who should cooperate in an intuitive rapport do not exist so far.

The musical percussion accompaniment must first create by means of sound the illusory substance within the physical space where the dancer performs. Secondly, the percussion should externalize (project) that part of the emotional content of the dance which is not expressed by movement. Thus the percussion has a complementary function. It may at times go against the dance gesture or seem to go against the emotion carried by the dance movement, thereby creating purposeful conflict, or the percussion may directly conform to the dance emotion, thereby creating a harmonious atmosphere.

Percussion may now drive the dancer on or now subdue him. However, only when the fusion of the movement with its percussion music is completed, is the act of creation between both art forms, dance and music, realized. Such a realization will carry its message to the audience.

THIRTY SIX

East Indian Tala Music

Henry Cowell

*T*HE *COMPOSER HENRY COWELL felt deeply that one should live in "the whole world of music." In this article he suggests that the mathematical principles used by drummers in India could be applied for dance purposes by American musicians as well—resulting in music that need not sound distinctly "Asian" in style.[1] Cowell offers some simple examples as models for rhythmic form and raises questions about awareness of larger sections within a piece of percussion music.*

***

It seems to me unfortunate, yet understandable, that the reaction against too much Oriental influence in the modern concert dance has led to a lack of study and understanding of some excellent values in the science of rhythm. This reaction seems to have arisen simply because these values have been adopted and studied in the Orient, particularly in India. Not to make use of something so valuable is nonsense. There is no question here of doing something in Oriental style; it is a matter of applying the mathematics of rhythm to the dance. The way in which such mathematics are applied may be American, European, Oriental or universal in style.

The whole thing is included in what East Indians call the Tala system of rhythmic study. It is quite possible that not all of the Tala could be applied to modern dance without an Oriental feeling creeping in; but the general principles would, I think, be a great asset in the use and understanding of larger rhythmic sweeps, percussion playing, form of percussion works, and form of the dance rhythmically. Perhaps the greatest asset

FIGURE 36.1 Henry Cowell playing one of five tablas presented to him for his *Symphony No. 13* (*Madras*) by the Music Academy of Madras, India. Photograph by Sidney Cowell, New York City, 1959. Reproduced by permission of the David A. Teitelbaum Foundation, from the collection of the Music Division, The New York Public Library for the Performing Arts, Astor, Lenox and Tilden Foundations.

would be a consciousness of larger aspects of form in which both the percussion player and composer as well as the dancer would participate.

In spite of all that has been said on the subject, it is still noted that music for modern dance, including much percussion accompaniment, and also much in the way of percussion solo, is hazy in outline so far as larger form goes. It is improvised-sounding, and often lacking in sense of climax. It is also distressingly evident that dancers are too much aware of the beats of the music within the measure, and even of the time of each individual note, but are unaware of the rhythm of the larger and longer sections in the form. Some dancers make a movement of the body to go with beats, or note-lengths; some deliberately avoid doing so; in either case, they are influenced by them. What dancer makes the entrances of the different longer sections evident by bodily movements? Either in harmony or in counterpoint? Are they aware of such sections of form? Do the composers of percussion works have any sense of the rhythm of longer sections as they flow one after another? Do they have any sense of some of these sections being rhythmically more important than others, thus making a rhythmic sequence?

Training in Tala increases perception of such things. The simplest illustration is that of $\frac{4}{4}$. The first beat strong, third medium, second and last weak. Everyone knows that, feels it to some extent. But also in a section of four measures, the first measure may be strong, the third medium, the second and fourth measures weak; and in building up in four-measure sections, the whole first section may be strong, the third section medium, the second and fourth sections weak. This is the simplest scheme, and very four-cornered; yet it is astonishing the life there is in the rhythm when a percussion work is based on such a scheme. No two notes, measures or sections of music are ever exactly alike following each other. Yet there is a rhythmic, pulsing relation between them. By placing the strong sections in the proper place, a sense of building toward a climax is achieved. And in carrying this out, there is a body movement indicating each change of measure and section; but the actual subdivisions within each measure are free to be improvised within certain limits. This makes things just the opposite from the custom with us, which is to have the general form improvised and hazy, but to be very particular about the individual beats and subdivisions of the beat. In writing percussion music, it is particularly needed to have definite larger form, rhythmically placed sections, and some clearly audible ways of announcing these sections. In Tala practice the sections are often of irregular lengths; but this is a matter of choice, of course.

Another feature of Tala is to be able to sense irregular (uneven) beats within a measure. All our measures are made up of even beats; in Tala some beats may be longer than others. The nearest approach to it in our music is in the rhumba, which is really a rhythm of three beats to the measure: the first two beats $\frac{3}{8}$ in length, the last beat $\frac{2}{8}$. Writing rhumba in $\frac{2}{2}$ meter as we do, is really misleading.

The addition of irregular and changeable beat-lengths within the measure, and a climactic sense of rhythmically proportioned sections which for a clear larger form would be a blessing to percussion music; and an awareness of these things which would be displayed through the body-action of the dancer wouldn't hurt anything either! And since these things are a natural artistic and mathematical expansion of the materials already used by us, they should not be abandoned because they have also been discovered by the East Indians.

THIRTY SEVEN

Choric Sound for the Dance

Lehman Engel

*L*EHMAN ENGEL HAS *been introduced previously, notably as a composer for Martha Graham. In this article he sets forth a source of sound that in his time had not been explored much for theatrical modern dance purposes, namely, the use of "non-musical" vocalization by untrained voices and, indeed, by the dancers themselves.*[1]

After explaining some problems of form when melodic and harmonic music was used for dance, Engel proposes something new: that a conductor of vocalists could become in effect an on-the-spot composer. This type of sound backdrop could offer an advantage over the use of pure percussion because of the human element of vocal variety and emotional suggestion. The results, says the author, offered possibilities "beyond the wildest hope" of most dance accompanists.

***

What the writer has to say about "sound-patterns" for the dance is the result of actual experimentation which he has been carrying through during the current season with a chorus composed of members of the Repertory Playhouse Associates. He wishes it understood in the beginning that he does not recommend this type of accompaniment for all kinds of dances or dancers, but he feels rather, that used for the most appropriate type of dancing, it presents possibilities which are in some respects far beyond the wildest hope of the dance-accompanist.

If we examine a majority of music written for the dance, we observe that it is conspicuously lacking in the elements of form. The reason, of course, is obvious. The composer learns to be dependent on the dance in so many small details that in its larger outlines the music assumes the form of the dance—an assumption which does not help to complete the music as such. The musical rhythms are contained within the limits of the dance rhythms or phrases, and are derived directly out of the dancers' movements. These rhythms, which generally recur in the dance as one means of establishing coherence and form, usually limit melody within their bounds and, in turn, they often check harmonic flow. Thus, every element of the music becomes limited through the dance and, strictly speaking, what often remains of the sound elements, stuck together without any profound consideration for each other, can scarcely be termed "music." Frequently this does not need to be a serious concern of either composer or dancer since in the end, if the composition is good music-for-the-dance, it will not achieve enough prominence of its own to annoy even the composer when he views his work alongside the dance.

Those things which are limitations to music form the very source-ideas to a creation of choric sound-patterns for the dance. In this system, the conductor of the chorus must be the composer of the sound. The writer terms what is created, "sound," with purposeful intentions, for he proposes that all the materials of sound obtainable from the human voice be employed: words, vowel sounds, consonant sounds, song and *sprechstimme* (a speech-sound with the borrowed property of pitch).

From this point forward, we are concerned with the actual composition of the sound-patterns and the relationship of these to the dance. The dance itself will always insinuate at least the theme which, applied to choric sound, will be first of all a rhythm, secondly an "impulse." The writer employed these two elements chorically in *Ceremonials* for Martha Graham. A low, gutteral sound for men's voices, rising within each of a number of measures to an accent in the dance, on which it climaxed and ended, formed a pattern which was repeated with effect again and again through more than a dozen measures. Since we are concerned with so many kinds of sounds, other than purely musical ones, and since, even in purely musical ones, the dance limits all of the elements including melody and harmony, it follows that there is an additional advantage in employing non-musical sound in that the composer need not concern himself at all with problems of melody and harmony. He is therefore unusually free to follow the dance completely unhampered by restrictions which traditions and our accustomed listening rightly impose on us when we compose or participate in what seems to be music.

The question may well be raised in reply to the foregoing ideas that if we eliminate melody and harmony from sound, we might as well employ percussion instruments exclusively in the accompaniment to the dance. Of course, we do employ percussion instruments to a great extent already. But, in the opinion of this writer, in so doing we are even more limited than in the exclusive use of voices by a complete lack of "human" sounds which even instruments (other than percussives) since the beginnings of music have tried to imitate or complement.

If the dance which is to be accompanied can maintain a background of voices, one may evolve a sound theme out of dance rhythm and impulse. That much has been stated before. The emotional quality of the theme and its "color" (this latter a substitution for harmony) must then be decided upon. There are no limits of sound to which a composer may not go. He may divide the chorus into as many sections as he wishes, giving each section either a different "theme" or part of a theme so that several groups may have to function at once in order to produce a complete effect. The variety this sort of arrangement is capable of producing is limitless. The tone may begin low with one motif in only a few voices; other motifs may be added gradually through the introduction of other groups of voices; the tone, on a single indication from the conductor, may rise higher in pitch—higher and more intense; it may break off suddenly and begin again softly. Now the motifs may be subtracted one by one, the tone lowered, and finally stopped altogether.

This is only a bare indication of a most primitive type of accompaniment. The resources, colors, manner of combining colors, inflections, tones, dynamics, are limitless. Furthermore, considering the matter practically, the dancer does not require musicians in his chorus. Anyone may be directed to participate satisfactorily in this sort of undertaking. A little experimentation will reveal a great deal of useful material in a field which is almost completely unexplored.

More, the dancer may use his group to good effect, both as offstage accompaniment to some of his solo dances and as self-accompaniment in group dances where there is a sufficient number of voices to produce adequate sound.

This field, to be sure, has many limitations. The type of accompaniment could smother certain types of dances. But, used wisely and propitiously, it is capable of making sounds more thrilling in themselves than any other the writer can recall. This method is an important addition to the resources of music-for-the-dance and, besides, it presents a type of sound which may employ some of the musicians' most effective materials without the inevitable limiting or distorting of his melodic and harmonic ideas. Unlike music it is something which has no excuse for being except as a complement to poetry, drama, or the dance, and it therefore must dedicate itself wholly and unrestrainedly to the service of each of these stronger and independent arts.

Goal

New Music, New Dance

John Cage

*B*EST KNOWN FOR *his longtime collaboration with Merce Cunningham (1919–2009) beginning in 1942 in New York, John Cage (1912– 92) got his start in the dance world as a studio accompanist for dancer Bonnie Bird at the Cornish School in Seattle. This was thanks to a recommendation from composer Lou Harrison, with whom he participated in adventuresome percussion concerts as part of the Mills summer programs with dancers in 1939. Subsequently he went on to organize percussion concerts in Seattle and did much to encourage the creation of a new kind of repertoire for such groups.*

The following 1939 article reflects the fact that a concert use of percussion by itself was unusual then—to say nothing of using "found objects" as serious musical instruments, as both he and Harrison often did for dancers. Cage advocates experimentation and offers a premonition of his later collaborations, as well as of future drum machines and other electronic inventions.

***

Percussion music is revolution. Sound and rhythm have too long been submissive to the restrictions of nineteenth-century music. Today we are fighting for their emancipation. Tomorrow, with electronic music in our ears, we will hear freedom.

Instead of giving us new sounds, the nineteenth-century composers have given us endless arrangements of the old sounds. We have turned on radios and always known when we were tuned to a symphony. The sound has always been the same, and there has not been even a hint of curiosity as to the possibilities of rhythm. For interesting rhythms we have listened to jazz.

At the present stage of revolution, a healthy lawlessness is warranted. Experimental music necessarily must be carried on by hitting anything—tin pans, rice bowls, iron pipes—anything we can lay our hands on. Not only hitting, but rubbing, smashing, making sound in every possible way. In short, we must explore the materials of music. What we can't do ourselves will be done by machines and electrical instruments which we will invent.

The conscientious objectors to modern music will, of course, attempt everything in the way of counter-revolution. Musicians will not admit that we are making music; they will say that we are interested in superficial effects, or, at most, are imitating Oriental or primitive music. New and original sounds will be labeled as "noise." But our common answer to every criticism must be to continue working and listening, making music with its materials, sound and rhythm, disregarding the cumbersome, top-heavy structure of musical prohibitions.

These prohibitions removed, the choreographer will be quick to realize a great advantage to the modern dance: the simultaneous composition of both dance and music. The materials of dance, already including rhythm, require only the addition of sound to become a rich, complete vocabulary. The dancer should be better equipped than the musician to use this vocabulary, for more of the materials are already at his command. Some dancers have made steps in this direction by making simple percussion accompaniments. Their use of percussion, unfortunately, has not been constructive. They have followed the rhythm of their own dance movement, accentuated it and punctuated it with percussion, but they have not given the sound its own and special part in the whole composition. They have made the music identical with the dance but not cooperative with it. Whatever method is used in composing the materials of the dance can be extended to the organization of the musical materials. The form of the music-dance composition should be a necessary working-together of all materials used. The music will then be more than an accompaniment; it will be an integral part of the dance.

THIRTY NINE

Electronic Music
for Doris Humphrey's
Theatre Piece No. 2

Otto Luening

*A*MONG THE EARLY *experimenters with manipulated tape and electronic music was Otto Luening (1900–1996). He and his Columbia University colleague Vladimir Ussachevsky explored making music with this new technology independently at first, and later on at the Columbia-Princeton Electronic Music Laboratory in Manhattan.*[1]

Earlier in his career, this Milwaukee-born composer had written prolifically in traditional ways for many combinations of familiar instruments. Additionally active as a conductor and a tireless advocate of American music, he helped to found such organizations as the American Composers Alliance and the American Music Center. From 1934 to 1944 he was chairman of the music department at Bennington College, just as all the modern dancers were gathering there to showcase and hone their talents—including Doris Humphrey.

In the following excerpt from his memoirs, Luening recalls some of the challenges of using electronic technology for theatrical dance, notes some of the criticism that his new music met, and describes his 1956 collaboration for Humphrey's Theatre Piece No. 2.

***

Vladimir Ussachevsky and I were not diverted for long from our main task of advancing electronic music. Most of the members of the Columbia University music department thought that electronic music was a harmless hobby. As we did not let our "hobby" interfere with our teaching duties, and as it cost the department no money, there was no reason for departmental opposition. I urged [composer] Douglas Moore and [musicologist] Dr. Paul Henry Lang to keep in touch with future developments, for I believed that it was something the musical world would have to cope with. Moore was interested in our work, but Lang neither listened, watched, nor visited our laboratory. He seemed to hope that electronic music would just fizzle out.

I learned to communicate with scientists and engineers by observing and working with them and by reading many articles. The best engineers were artistic and were concerned with the human aspects of what we were all doing.

Psychologically, I had to do some balancing, probing, and adjusting. Some admirers of my new work had catapulted me into the avant-garde, while forgetting the early part of my career entirely. New friends knew only of my later work. Circumstances seemed to

FIGURE 39.1 Otto Luening (left) and Vladimir Ussachevsky at the Columbia-Princeton Electronic Music Center. From the collection of the Music Division, The New York Public Library for the Performing Arts, Astor, Lenox and Tilden Foundations.

be carrying my present self away from my past self. This cultural schizophrenia was uncomfortable and was as unacceptable to me then as it is now. I had always considered the old and the new to be interrelated.

The University of California Press asked me to write an essay, "New Sound Techniques in Music," for their book *Art and Artist*. It gave me a chance to straighten out the early history of electronic music and make our work known in new and respectable circles. I tried to relate the experimental developments of the twentieth century with those of the past. I also found it rewarding to search for aesthetic values in the new world of sound. After discovering that although with electronic sound almost anything was possible, it was necessary to meditate about how much of it was possible to perceive, and by what means it could bring human satisfaction along with the novelty of the shock.

Humanists, musicologists, some critics, musicians, and sometimes diehard laypeople liked to ask, even before things were really under way: "But is it music?...But is it really *great* music?...But will it displace music?" Some hated electronic music without ever having heard any. Others proclaimed that it was a great medium, but that we must wait for great composers who knew how to use it before we could develop it.

Some reviewers said the new sounds were not like the music of the past. This remark is still heard nowadays. The obvious answer then and now is, "Why should it be?" The fear that electronic music threatens old music and live music is groundless as long as people keep on playing and singing and are willing to pay for their symphony orchestras, opera companies, and chamber music.

In 1956, Doris Humphrey commissioned me to compose for the Juilliard School's Fiftieth Anniversary, *Theatre Piece No. 2 (Concerto for Light, Movement, Sound and Voice)* for the José Limón Dance Company. The Ussachevsky living room was overloaded with the traveling laboratory, so we moved it to a room in my apartment. My assistant Chou Wen-chung helped me work on my ballet at odd hours of the day and night.[2] Doris Humphrey outlined her story line and made a time schedule for the separate sections. She then made a detailed measure or beat chart for the entire half-hour ballet, indicating to me just what the dancers should be doing rhythmically. She made only one error in the entire score. In two measures she beat quarters instead of eighths. At the rehearsal the dancers were left with their feet in the air waiting for music, but they got them down. She also talked me into writing the spoken text for two 1930 satires: a love scene from a movie and a German poem for a contemporary twelve-tone song.

The rehearsals at Juilliard were difficult. The musical director told me that it was too late to use strings for my performance. I thought it would be effective to use a brass ensemble, percussion, narrator, recorded voice on tape, piano, and myself as conductor, so I did.

The dance company was first-rate and Doris was a fine director. At an open rehearsal, just as the conductor left his stand after the previous piece, the tape recorder emitted an enormous honk. In the intermission the maestro alleged that I had done it on purpose, which I denied, but things went from bad to worse. The pit caught on fire and rehearsals were postponed for a week. Fortunately there was no personal or musical damage, and we actually had more time to synchronize everything further in a rehearsal room.

On opening night Ussachevsky operated the tape recorder. He looked a bit constrained, pale, and worried. I had given the downbeat, so I could only continue and hope that he was well. The performance was smooth and the audience cordial. Later I asked Ussachevsky whether he had been ill during the performance, and he said, "Yes, indeed. There was a loose connection. Had I moved one inch to the left some frightfully loud noises would have brought your premiere to an unhappy end." We shook hands and congratulated ourselves for having pulled the show through.

Walter Terry wrote of the show in the *Herald Tribune*: "The Otto Luening score provides a tonally fascinating and dramatically pertinent basis for the choreography....The initial section suggests pre-human action, growth and metamorphoses through patterns as eerie and as hypnotically remorseless as the accompanying music.... [It] has enormous incantational power."

FORTY

My Total Theater Concept

Alwin Nikolais

QUITE SIMPLY, *Alwin Nikolais (1910–93) created magic in the theater. Coming from an early background that included puppetry, playing organ for silent films in Westport, Connecticut, and accompanying dance classes on the piano, he also learned about percussion from Truda Kaschmann (a former student of the German expressionist dancer Mary Wigman), who suggested that Nikolais study dance. He did so, including at the Bennington summer school.*

After serving in the army, "Nik" worked as an assistant to Hanya Holm and went on to develop a kind of total multimedia theater that was at the time unique in American dance. With a home base at the Henry Street Playhouse in lower Manhattan, he trained his dancers and choreographed the movement. He designed the costumes, lighting, and props. Also functioning as his own composer, he was one of the first to take advantage of tape recording and, subsequently, of the invention by Robert Moog of a relatively easy-to-use synthesizer. With such equipment he was able not only to create his own sound scores to fit his dances precisely in timing and atmosphere but also to supervise the sound systems in actual performances.[1]

In this retrospective article, Nikolais recalls how he came to create his unique dance theater works and offers some amusing observations about the pace of technological change.

***

My total theater concept consciously started about 1950, although the seeds of it began much earlier I'm sure. First was expansion. I used masks and props—the masks, to have the dancer become something else; and the props, to extend his physical size in space. (These latter were not instruments to be used as shovels or swords—but rather as extra bones and flesh.) I began to see the potentials of this new creature and in 1952 produced a program called *Masks, Props, and Mobiles*. I began to establish my philosophy of man being a fellow traveler within the total universal mechanism rather than the god from which all things flowed. The idea was both humiliating and grandizing. He lost his domination but instead became kinsman to the universe.

With the breakdown of story-line, choreographic structure necessarily changed. With the further breakdown of physical centralization—the lid was off. Logic of metronomic and sun time was no longer necessary. Time no longer had to support logical realistic events. It too could be decentralized, but more importantly, breaking the barrier of literal time throws the creator into visions and possible motional itineraries way beyond the literal visions. The time-space canvas was now free. Now we are permitted visions into the world in which we live and perhaps even into the universe. We might even, then, return to the vision of self but placed more humbly into the living landscape, adding grandeur to vision of self—not in proud pigeon arabesque but as consonant members of the environment—enriched by the resonance that surrounds us, a shared energy interplaying with vital discussions rather than domineering argument.

First I had destroyed the fetish of the narrative and realism. Then I began three-dimensional environmental lighting instead of the usual overhead kind.

Along with all of this came the tape recorder, and electronics of a nature that fit into the new stage dimensions of audio-visual impacts. The creative drive of both the artist and the engineer resulted from accumulations of knowledge, new discoveries, new relationships and curiosities.

In my background there is a curious gap—a silent spot—one which now causes rationalizations, embarrassments, and no end of frustrations. I can be buying some splicing tape and racking my brain about the width of the stuff I want when a 10 year old kid will edge me away from the clerk and ask for a super-hederatonated conducer #X21358462 with a hysto-phillico rating of C2X2052 et cetera. Now he doesn't even refer to a notebook—it's coming right out of his little computerized head, and I know he knows exactly what all this is, what it does, how it does it, and why he wants it. For a moment I turn into W. C. Fields and I want to raise my hand and slap the little transistorized demon into the next dimension.[2]

To him the stuff is not a miracle—the voice of god—the utterances of subterranean chemico-dynamic beginnings. To him it's the answer to the dehumanized maiden's prayer—a simple matter of mathematics and matching energies with transistorized plumbing marked his & hers, and it can do anything from programming his libido to changing the Russians' politics.

I had a not-altogether-enviable music background which led to a theater background, which led to a dance background, which led to an early tape machine (to save musician money), which led to *musique concrète* (by virtue of broken tapes, sloppy splicing and punching the wrong speed control), which led to electronic sound, which led to the lousy kid in the electronic shop.[3]

Despite this seemingly incongruous relationship, I and it seem to have spawned some eight miles of offspring. Now one would think that producing some 50 miles of tape and splicing my way thru eight miles might just by electronic osmosis find me somewhat knowledgeable about the #X21358462—but that particular 2 x 2 didn't make 4.

At this point in musical history, and mainly because of electronics together with sociological despair over methods, we are closer to the art of music than since the primitive times of musical art. Primitive musicians selected sounds, not methods. They had no choice of methods; they had only choice of sound. In effect they went directly to their art source: the sound itself. Method came afterwards, and then the tradition and the comfort of pattern. It speaks well of the human spirit that historically we venerate the artist more than the instrument, the result rather than the method—although the methodologists may temporaily confuse the issue.

With the advent of tape music a whole new spirit of listening occurred. Although at first there was a tendency to make electronics imitate violins and pianos, the nature and tremendous score of sound producible electronically quickly overshadowed that Mickey-Mouse stuff and demanded a judgment about sound again on its own terms. As in all such evolvements the traditionalist was outraged and confused. He was not built to hear the art of sound but rather the mathematics of method played comfortably on the familiar flute—his judgment based on loud or soft, fast or slow. The sound was usually easily identified and didn't require any associative Rorschach. A flute was a flute. Now he had beeps & burps, choo-choo trains and clattering garbage pails, and his Rorschach darted to the safest literal experience—an imagination that ran the gamut from A to B.

Already there is a tendency to standardize electronic instruments. From an economic point of view this may be a reasonable compromise, but already the patterns will begin to set. Once this is done, the next step is obvious—standardize the sound—this in turn will lead to standardizing the method et cetera et cetera. It's the old Levittown story—finally the music is prefabricated.

FORTY ONE

Experimental Music

John Cage

*J*OHN CAGE'S INVENTIVENESS *came to the fore early in his career when (in 1946–48) he produced his* Sonatas and Interludes *for prepared piano, creating intriguing new sounds by placing various objects between the strings of a regular piano.[1] Always the experimentalist, Cage made use of traditional instruments played in unusual ways, plus "found" sounds drawn from natural and synthetic materials, and electronically produced or manipulated taped sounds. In his comments here, he touches upon some procedures and limitations in connection with the technology of the mid-twentieth century, with particular attention to the difference between the relative time of notated music and exact time as measured by a stopwatch for both musicians and dancers.*

***

Whether one uses tape or writes for conventional instruments, the present musical situation has changed from what it was before tape came into being. This need not arouse alarm, for the coming into being of something new does not by that fact deprive what was of its proper place. Each thing has its own place, never takes the place of something else; and the more things there are, as is said, the merrier.

But several effects of tape on experimental music may be mentioned. Since so many inches of tape equal so many seconds of time, it has become more and more usual that notation is in space rather than in symbols of quarter, half, and sixteenth notes and so on. Thus where on a page a note appears will correspond to when in a time it is to occur.

A stopwatch is used to facilitate a performance; and a rhythm results which is a far cry from horse's hoofs and other regular beats.

Also it has been impossible with the playing of several separate tapes at once to achieve perfect synchronization. This fact has led some towards the manufacture of multiple-tracked tapes and machines with a corresponding number of heads; while others—those who have accepted the sounds they do not intend—now realize that the score, the requiring that many parts be played in a particular togetherness, is not an accurate representation of how things are. These now compose parts but not scores, and the parts may be combined in any unthought ways. This means that each performance of such a piece of music is unique, as interesting to its composer as to others listening. It is easy to see again the parallel with nature, for even with leaves of the same tree, no two are exactly alike. The parallel in art is the sculpture with moving parts, the mobile.

FORTY TWO

Communication

John Cage

*T*HESE THREE SHORT *samples of Cage's musings are intended as an enticement for people to think about sound in new ways—as this composer-philosopher certainly did.*

***

What if I ask thirty-two questions?
What if I stop asking now and then?
Will that make things clear?
Is communication something made clear?
What is communication?
Music, what does it communicate?
Is what's clear to me clear to you?
Is music just sounds?
Then what does it communicate?
Is a truck passing by music?
If I can see it, do I have to hear it too?
If I don't hear it, does it still communicate?
If while I see it I can't hear it, but hear something else, say an egg-beater, because I'm inside looking out, does the truck communicate or the egg-beater, which communicates?
Which is more musical, a truck passing by a factory or a truck passing by a music school?
Are the people inside the school musical and the ones outside unmusical?
What if the ones inside can't hear very well, would that change my question?

Do you know what I mean when I say inside the school?
Are sounds just sounds or are they Beethoven?
People aren't sounds, are they?

A SOUND IS HIGH OR LOW, SOFT OR LOUD, OF A CERTAIN TIMBRE, LASTS A CERTAIN LENGTH OF TIME, AND HAS AN ENVELOPE.

Is it high?
Is it low?
Is it in the middle?
Is it soft?
Is it loud?
Are there two?
Are there more than two?
Is it a piano?
Why isn't it?
Was it an airplane?
Is it a noise?
Is it music?
Is it softer than before?
Is it supersonic?
When will it stop?
What's coming?
Is it time?
Is it very short?
Very long?
Just medium?
If I had something to see, would it be theatre?
Is sound enough?
What more do I need?
Don't I get it whether I need it or not?
Is it a sound?
Then, again, is it music?
Is music—the word, I mean—is that a sound?
If it is, is music music?
Is the word "music" music?
Does it communicate anything?
Must it?
If it's high, does it?
If it's low, does it?

If it's in the middle, does it?
If it's soft, does it?
If it's loud, does it?
If it's an interval, does it?
What is an interval?
Is an interval a chord?
Is a chord an aggregate?
Is an aggregate a constellation?
What's a constellation?
How many sounds are there altogether?
One million?
Ten thousand?
Eighty-eight?
Do I have to ask ten more?
Do I?
Why?
Why do I?
[Why] did I decide to ask so many?
Wasn't I taking a risk?
Was I?
Why was I?
Will it never stop?
Why won't it?

Are we in agreement that the field of music needs to be enlivened?
Do we disagree?
On what?
Communication?
If I have two sounds, are they related?
If someone is nearer one of them than he is to the second, is he
    more related to the first one?
What about sounds that are too far away for us to hear them?
Sounds are just vibrations, isn't that true?
Part of a vast range of vibrations including radio waves, light, cosmic
    rays, isn't that true?
Why didn't I mention that before?
Doesn't it stir the imagination?
Shall we praise God from Whom all blessings flow?
Is sound a blessing?
I repeat, is sound a blessing?

FORTY THREE

Dancing with the Avant-Garde

Carolyn Brown

*C*AROLYN BROWN (B. 1927) *began her dance studies at a young age with her mother, Marion Rice (who had been trained in the Denishawn school), and finished her training at the Juilliard School. Starting in 1953, she dedicated twenty years to performing as a leading dancer with the Merce Cunningham Dance Company, and additional years to teaching, choreographing, and writing a chronicle of her dance experiences.*[1]

In these excerpts Brown expresses both affection and admiration for John Cage and Merce Cunningham, yet she points out that the composer himself did not dance, and therefore did not experience the effort and movement that dancers were required to put forth even as they were hearing avant-garde scores on occasion for the first time during public performances onstage. Her observations about the musical elements are of particular interest because she was at that time married to the composer Earle Brown and was herself quite knowledgeable about the international avant-garde scene.

An unusual dancer in her day, here Carolyn Brown describes what it was like to perform in Suite by Chance. *She explains how some elements of* Sixteen Dances *were determined by chance procedures; how rhythmic structure was used in other works; and the effect that tape technology had on the measurement of time for dancers. She draws a sharp contrast between avant-garde structures and those produced according to the classroom teachings of Louis Horst. Continuing her extraordinary account, Brown general-*

FIGURE 43.1 Carolyn Brown and John Cage. Photograph © James Klosty. Reproduced by permission.

izes about what it felt like to dance to some of the "far-out" scores (especially when the speaker systems emitted extremely loud sounds).

***

Suite by Chance was the first work whose raison d'être was the desire to explore the use of chance procedures in the making of a dance from its inception, and in Cunningham's own words, "its composition was unprompted by references other than its own life." Just as Cage was interested in letting sounds be themselves, Cunningham was interested in letting movements be themselves, unfettered by content derived from literature, history, psychology, mythology, mood, or music.

With this spare, intractable, yet classical choreography, Merce Cunningham embarked on a journey that has continued to fascinate him for over fifty years—and at this writing still does. The chance procedures opened up possibilities he'd never considered before and led to different ways of seeing. Certain decisions arrived at in the early fifties still inform the works he produces today: 1) the relationship between dance and music is one of coexistence: dance and music are unrelated in the majority of his works; they simply exist at the same time; 2) the choreography is constructed in time, not on or opposed to a metric beat (though often, for practicality's sake, phrases are rehearsed to counts).

Suite by Chance was followed by *Solo Suite in Space and Time*. In 1952, Merce's working methods—that is, his chance procedures, for both these dances—paralleled Cage's chance experiments in, respectively, *Music of Changes* and *Music for Piano*. *Music of Changes* had charts for tempi, duration, sounds, dynamics, and superimpositions (how many events happen at once during a given structural space). Cage's next experiment with chance procedures was to have the notes for the music correspond to the slight imperfections on a piece of ordinary paper (seen when the paper is held up to the light) upon which the piece was to be written. When Cunningham choreographed *Solo Suite in Space and Time*, he, too, used paper imperfections, to determine certain elements in his dance: space and lengths of time for each brief solo and the sequence of movements. During this period, Cage gave a weekly composition workshop for Merce's students, and those of us who attended made dances in similar fashion. We choreographed the movement, but the sequence of steps, the space, and the time (which we discovered by measuring the distances between paper imperfections and equating them with clock time, i.e., inches equals minutes) was "found," as it were. I made *Trio for Five Dancers*. Using my space plan, Earle composed music for it. At Juilliard, we were making "Horstian" allemandes and sarabandes, "cerebrals" and "introspectives." The distance between the two studios was closer to one hundred light years than to the one hundred or so city blocks that separated them.

In the final quartet of *Sixteen Dances*, Cunningham gave each dancer a small gamut of movements whose direction in space, length of time, and sequence he discovered by tossing coins. It must be emphasized, because there has been so much confusion about this, that once the coins had been tossed the order was permanent. Chance was a part of the *choreographic* process only: the dancers were never involved in the chance procedure. Two performances were as alike (or unalike) as any two performances of *Symphony in C* might be. Still, the overriding formal concept in *Sixteen Dances* was the rhythmic structure that linked choreography and music, not chance.

Several years earlier, Cage had written *Sonatas and Interludes* (1946–48), a seventy-minute work for prepared piano, and it, like Merce's *Sixteen Dances*, was described as an attempt to express in music the "permanent emotions" of Indian tradition. This is another instance in which Cunningham's choreography follows a path traveled originally by Cage's music. Musically, Cage's *Sonatas and Interludes* and *The Seasons* (1947) (a fifteen-minute ballet Cunningham choreographed for Ballet Society, later to become New York City Ballet) and *Sixteen Dances* were all the expressions of Cage's then-pervading interest in rhythm—not rhythm defined as individual rhythmic patterns but rhythm as structure—and it is here that Cage's music and Cunningham's choreography were joined. In the 1940s, Cage viewed composition as an activity integrating the opposites, the rational, and the irrational, bringing about, ideally, a freely moving continuity within a strict division of parts. They based their common structure on the use of arithmetical proportions—the whole divided into parts, large and small; it was an "empty" structure agreed upon by composer and choreographer, who then set about filling it, independently of each other, with sound and silence, movement and stillness.

And so Cage began to move away from controlling his music by devising rhythmic structures; he stopped choosing the sounds and no longer submitted his music to his own taste, mind, and will. Nor did he attempt to express in the content of his work Oriental views *about* specific things, choosing instead to have his work be, in and of itself, an expression of the Eastern, specifically the Zen Buddhist, attitude toward art and life as he perceived it. He encouraged Cunningham to do the same.

Suite by Chance was probably the purest chance work Cunningham ever attempted in the years I worked with him. Performing it was both perplexing and frightening. There was only one way for me to approach its abruptness, the going from one isolated movement to another without flow or intended continuity, without a rhythmic pulse dictated by the music, divested of all the dramatic, romantic, sentimental, or sensuous artifices that theatrical dance usually offers as protection from revealing the self, and that was with absolute concentration on each single moment, as though the movements were *objets trouvés*, and in a sense, of course, they were. Did I realize that then? Not in the first performance, certainly. But without knowledge, without thinking about it, and with no direction from Merce, there was no other way I knew how to do it.

Suite by Chance was choreographed and rehearsed in silence. Dance and music met, as if by accident, in the performance space. But by sheer force of habit, I suppose, Cunningham constructed and originally rehearsed it to a metric beat. However, because music for magnetic tape is constructed not in measures but in inches per second, it made sense to unpin the movement from a metric pulse and use instead a stopwatch to relate to the music by means of time units alone. This was, in fact, a giant step forward for dance; or, one might see it as a giant step backward toward the origins of dance. By abandoning meter, rhythmic nuances—complex and capable of enormous variation from dancer to dancer—could be expressed freely if the choreographer so desired and if the choreographer was sufficiently skilled. So it was not, as so many Cunningham detractors thought at the time, an arbitrary, dehumanizing act, this use of the stopwatch, but rather a practical means of functioning with the new music so that dance and music might, if desired, at least start and end together, meanwhile releasing the dance and the dancer from the beat-for-beat or phrase-for-phrase (or the decision to go against the beat or phrase) kind of synchronization most choreographers had accepted as law. One must, of course, admit that this release from the beat could validly be called deprivation.

The most obvious difference between Balanchine and Cunningham is in their attitude toward the relationship of dance to music. Said Mr. B.: "Our movements have to be performed in the composer's time. That's what makes ballet so exciting—this movement of bodies in time. That's why I call Stravinsky 'an architect of time.' His music provides the dancer's floor. It's the reason we move. Without the music we don't want to move." But for Cunningham, the dancer's floor is literally the dancer's floor. He wants to move because he wants to move. It's that simple. In Cunningham's choreography since 1953—though there have been exceptions—it is the choreographer, not the composer, who is "the architect of time." Merce knows that it is hard for many people to accept that dancing has nothing in common with music other than the element of time (and the division of time). But he believes that choreography equated predictably beat-for-beat on the musical pulse may, for the spectator anyway, rob both the dancer and the dance of the subtle rhythms unique to each human body in much the same way as the music imposed on the movements of wild animals (in Disney films, for example) robs them of their instinctual rhythms and leaves them as caricatures.

I won't attempt to defend the music. Certainly some of it I disliked intensely, and among the company dancers I was not alone. If I found it unbearable, I tried to "turn it off," tried to *not hear it*, because it could be disruptive, painful, even violating. For me, those pieces did not coexist with the choreography, they competed with it, even attempted to annihilate it, like an insanely jealous lover. But I think there is no denying the paradox that some of the music, without having much distinction on its own, made a definite contribution to the work *as a whole*. And occasionally the music was truly extraordinary— dynamic and multifaceted.

In order to approach Merce's work sympathetically, one has no choice but to come to terms with the Cage/Cunningham premise regarding the coexistence of the music and the dance. One doesn't have to like it, or agree with it, but one has to, in some way, accept it.

Getting beyond the music/sound in order to appreciate the dance and dancing has remained an ongoing problem for a great many people, and the professional dance critics were no exception. This is unfortunate, for it prevented Merce's work from being seriously analyzed or even properly *seen*. It was so much easier to rant and rail about the music than to write intelligently about the dance, which would have required *serious* consideration of the implications of Merce's chance procedures. Ponder this: *Suite for Five* and *Lavish Escapade* produced strikingly diverse audience and critical reactions, and they are in fact entirely different from each other in form, style, movement vocabulary, continuity, and performance quality. Yet both were composed by chance means. They exemplify the richness, depth, and variety that Merce was able to create through the chance process. And it should be clearly understood: Merce *did* create them. No one else could have or would have made those particular dances, with or without chance methods. They prove—unequivocally—the validity of Merce's use of chance as a choreographic tool...for *him*.

Much has been said and written about the separation or coexistence of music and dance in Merce's work. The idea is sacrosanct, part of the Gospel According to St. John. But what is never said, and should be, is that in many of Merce's dances choreographed in the fifties and sixties—certainly those to Satie but even, for example, with Cage's music for *Suite for Five*—choreography and music were relatively fixed. The dancers did pay attention to the music in its temporal relationship to the movement, and they did rely on it for cues. But more than that, whether the score was determinate or indeterminate, the simultaneous action of the music and dance together had—on us as well as on the audience—a greater effect than the sum of their individual parts. And because we were *not*, after all, robots, neither mindless nor heartless, there was always a deeper, visceral involvement in response to the sound. How could we be human and it be otherwise?

PART FIVE

WELLSPRINGS OF CREATIVE COLLABORATION

Today every composer is faced with the problem I embraced for myself in my youth: How may one learn to live in the whole world of music—to live and to create? No single technique, no single tradition is any longer enough.

—*Henry Cowell, 1961.*

Overview

Diverse Methods and Aesthetic Ideas

B Y THE MIDDLE of the twentieth century, composers could reflect
with satisfaction upon many musical paths that had been followed in order to collaborate with choreographers. There had
been major changes in procedures and aesthetic approaches from the
time of Isadora Duncan: from the custom of considering that dance
was the "handmaiden" of music, to creating the patterns of choreographic movement in silence or before the music was composed; from
using musical classics as both structure and inspiration in interpretive
dancing, to the complete separation of musical and choreographic
creation until the moment of performance.

Stylistically, there had been musicians who continued to seek the
kind of textural sparseness advocated by Louis Horst. There were also
those such as William Schuman and Samuel Barber, who followed in
the paths of symphonists.[1] There were experimentalists such as Henry
Cowell and Harry Partch. There were musicians who drew on traditional styles from other parts of the world and performed without written notation. And then there were the collaborators John Cage and
Merce Cunningham, who (as described in the previous chapter) sepa-
rately wrote detailed plans for their respective arts, based on new
chance procedures for creation.

This part presents some observations of other experienced collaborators concerning differences in relatively concrete matters such as
materials and plans, and about less tangible things such as aesthetics
and taste.

However, before all the method and planning, there had to be the desire to make something new in the first place, and the impetus to work with artists of another discipline. Where did that spark come from? The initial two articles in this part offer some hints, the first written by composer Leonard Bernstein in 1946, the second retrospective reflection by choreographer Paul Taylor in 2008. Following these, the composer Carlos Surinach's essay conveys his concept of what music should ideally provide for theatrical dance—and touches upon some of the aspects that he felt made his own music attractive to choreographers. In the part's concluding articles, composers Lou Harrison and Lucia Dlugoszewski consider various views about collaboration with dancers in both the studio and the theater, ranging from the question of what is primal through the most up-to-date mathematical models.

If a dancer raises an arm, what will happen next? The movement need not be predetermined by traditions of what other people had already done. If a musician sounds a single note, what might happen next? Similarly, the unfolding sounds need not be dictated by what others have done before. Nor need the ways in which music and dance are combined necessarily follow rigid models from the past.

FORTY FOUR

"Fun" in Music and the Dance

Leonard Bernstein

A VIRTUOSIC MASTER *of both classical European traditions and American popular styles, Leonard Bernstein (1918–90) was applauded internationally as pianist, conductor (mainly as director of the New York Philharmonic, 1958–69), and composer (of symphonies, opera, ballets, and musical theater). His scores for choreographer Jerome Robbins included two for Ballet Theatre:* Fancy Free *(premiered in 1944 and subsequently expanded into the musical* On the Town*) and* Facsimile *(1946). For Robbins and New York City Ballet, he composed* Dybbuk, *in 1974. His 1957 work with Robbins for* West Side Story *was a landmark for Broadway theater and subsequent film. Among Bernstein's other collaborations, dances for his theatrical* Mass *were choreographed by Alvin Ailey for the grand opening of the Kennedy Center in Washington, D.C., in 1971. As an educator, he taught several generations of musicians at Tanglewood; his telecast lecture-concerts provided millions of young people with an introduction to orchestral masterpieces; and his legacy includes essays on music in addition to more than 400 recordings.*[1]

In this 1946 essay, the young Bernstein displays his typical exuberance, flair with words, and erudite knowledge. He examines the concept of "fun" in relation to creativity, and indeed the meaning of the word "meaning" in relation to the sounds of music and the movements of dance. Along the way the composer-conductor directs attention to a basic distinction between representational and nonrepresentational art.

***

I remember giving an interview to a New York newspaper in which I replied to the question "Which of your different interests will you eventually choose to follow?" by saying I wanted to do the thing which seemed most like fun at the time. This elicited a furious letter to the paper from one of its more articulate and choleric readers, upbraiding me for my "light" attitude towards music, and for my apparent lack of social responsibility in giving my art insufficiently serious thought. These paragraphs are meant as a rebuttal to that letter of long ago.

The main trouble with these remarks is that the word "fun" is going to appear far too often. The fact of the matter is that the word has no single synonym in our present use of its meaning. If we add up "sense of rightness," "tranquility," "balance," "catharsis," "expressivity," we begin to approach the meaning of "fun." Add to these "participation," "creativity," "order," "sublimation," and "energy-release," and you almost have it. Fun is all the things we find it impossible to say when we hear the opus 131 quartet or witness *Letter to the World*. (Beethoven and Martha Graham must have had this kind of fun *making* these works.) Fun is the final goal of the collected aesthetic searching of David Prall, Dewey, Richards, and Santayana. Fun is the "x" of the equation which tries to solve the riddle of why art exists at all.

To the normal American mind, "fun" carries with it the connotation of a "good time," a party, a relaxation, diversion, a roller-coaster ride, a thriller on the screen, a hot-dog. There is no Dreadful Dichotomy here; we must simply refer these phenomena to the field of art, deepening the experiential values, solidifying the transience to continuousness, even to semi-permanence.

Does it seem strange that a musician, of all things, should be discussing these matters in, of all things, a dance magazine? Not at all. For what other two arts better exemplify this concept of *fun* than do music and the dance?

Basically, the only split that occurs in the various art-media is that which divides the representational from the non-representational. Whatever the technique used, or the medium engaged in, all art is one except for this distinction. It is this which often makes it difficult for the writer to comprehend the basic aesthetic impulses of the musician, and vice-versa. It is this which gives rise to the interminable discussions on technique versus content, form versus functionalism, Marxism versus Ivory-towerism, style versus prettiness.

In the case of music, we find that its inherent meaning, from any of the above points of view, is purely a *musical* meaning. Give it what titles you will, add copious program notes, and you still have only a series of notes, arranged in certain orders and patterns. Call the opening of Beethoven's Fifth Symphony "Fate knocking at the door," or the "Morse Code Call to Victory," and you still have three G's and an E-flat. That's *all* you have. Through some freak in the human animal, these four notes, in their particular rhythmic pattern, have the power to produce a substantial effect on us.

In literature, on the other hand, there is another factor—the concept *behind* the words, the essential transparency of letters and syllables and phrases. In theatre there is the element of story, representation, conceptual meaning. *Simile* in painting and sculpture. (In each of these arts, of course there is an "abstract" movement which comes closer to the musical principle; but this is, after all, a deviation from the basic norm.) In music there is no room for meaning in this extrinsic sense; there is nothing left but the sheer animal enjoyment of organized sound. This I call *fun*.

Dance, because of its proximity to theatre, is not quite so "pure" in this way as is music. Yet it is but one step removed. For, leaving aside for the moment the "dance-dramas" of the last century (which correspond, shall we say, to the programmatic tone-poem of that century's music), we have an art which is basically rhythm, motion, line, tension, release. Whatever representational matter appears belongs to pantomime, superimposed merely, as story-meaning is superimposed upon music. In watching a ballet of Balanchine one feels very close to hearing music itself. A Balanchine ballet is "fun." Likewise, with the inventions of Jerome Robbins.

Certainly there is infinitely more profound searching to be done in any one aspect of this tangled question. These remarks are merely teasers. Only think, for example, of the idea "representational" in terms of the subtle psychic life of the artist: what an unexplored field lies there! Perhaps one day we shall attain to a new meaning of Meaning, in a new frame of reference which is intangible to us now. But for the present we "abstract" artists, we musicians and dancers have this to say to ourselves: Relax. Invent. Perform. Have fun.

FORTY FIVE

Why I Make Dances

Paul Taylor

*T*HOSE FORTUNATE ENOUGH *to have seen* Paul Taylor *onstage earlier in his career recall his dancing as riveting. Over the years, audiences have had the same kind of reaction upon seeing generations of dancers perform in his large repertoire of original works. The 2010 performances celebrating Taylor's eightieth birthday also served to showcase the wide diversity of music he has used—some of it specially commissioned, some extant and spanning medieval religious works all the way to pop tunes.*[1]

Born in 1930, Paul Taylor grew up in Washington, D.C. As an undergraduate at Syracuse University, he focused on swimming and painting before attending the Juilliard School for training in dance. For seven years, starting in 1955, he performed as a soloist with the Martha Graham Company. In 1954 he formed his own first company—and has touched audiences around the world with new works ever since. Taylor wrote an expansive autobiography titled Private Domain, *but in this brief essay, the choreographer focuses on the wellsprings of creativity and touches upon the considerations involved in selecting music for dance purposes.*

***

No one has ever asked me why I make dances. But when flummoxed by the financial difficulties of keeping a dance company afloat, I sometimes ask it of myself. Dance makers are most often quizzed this way: which comes first, the dance or the music? This conundrum was answered most tellingly by the celebrated choreographer George

FIGURE 45.1 Paul Taylor. Photograph © Maxine Hicks. All rights reserved.
Used by permission.

Balanchine, who said: "The money." Nobel Prize winner Orhan Pamuk
has often been asked why he writes. The savvy answer in his *My Father's
Suitcase* was so meaningful and struck such a chord of recognition in
me—his devotion, his steadfastness, his anger—that it caused me to
ponder my own reasons. Motivated by Balanchine's sensible quip and
Pamuk's candid perceptiveness, this is how I might reply:

To put it simply, I make dances because I can't help it. Working on
dances has become a way of life, an addiction that at times resembles a
fatal disease. Even so I've no intention of kicking the habit. I make
dances because I believe in the power of contemporary dance, its
immediacy, its potency, its universality. I make dances because that's

what I've spent many years teaching myself to do and it's become what I'm best at. When the dances are good, nothing else brings me as much satisfaction. When they aren't, I've had the luxury, in the past at least, of being allowed to create others.

From childhood on, I've been a reticent guy who spends a lot of time alone. I make dances in an effort to communicate to people. A visual medium can be more effective than words. I make dances because I don't always trust my own words, or, for that matter, those of quite a few others I've known. I make dances because working with my dancers and other cohorts allows me to spend time with trustworthy people I'm very fond of and who seldom give me trouble. Also because I'm not suited to do the jobs that regular folks do. There is no other way I could make a living, especially not at work that involves dealing face-to-face with the public. I make dances because crowds are kept at a safe distance. That's what proscenium stages are good for.

Dance making appeals to me because, although group projects and democratic systems are okay if they work, when on the job I find that a benevolent dictatorship is best. I don't make dances for the masses; I make them for myself. That is, even though they are meant to be seen in public (otherwise, what's the point?), I make dances I think I'd like to see.

I'm not above filching steps from other dance makers, but only from the best—ones such as Martha Graham and Antony Tudor—and only when I think I can make an improvement.

Although there are only two or three dances in me—ones based on simple images imprinted at childhood—I've gone to great lengths to have each repeat of them seem different. Because of the various disguises my dances wear, viewers sometimes mistake them for those made by other choreographers. My reaction to this depends on how talented I think that person is. Imitating a chameleon has always come easy. Maybe it's genetic, or a protective artifice. The only identity that bugs me is that of the lauded personage. This is because the responsibilities demanded by fame are nuisances that I could easily do without. Ideally, my work would be anonymous.

Stylized lies (novelistic truths) for the stage are what the medium demands. I love tinkering with natural gesture and pedestrian movement to make them read from a distance and be recognizable as a revealing language that we all have in common. Of particular interest is the amorous coupling of men and women, as well as the other variations on this subject. In short, the remarkable range of our human condition.

246   *Making Music for Modern Dance*

Whenever a dance of mine is controversial it brings me much satisfaction. One of my aims is to present questions rather than answers. My passion for dance does not prevent me from being terrified to start each new piece, but I value these fears for the extra energy they bring. Getting to know the music I use is a great pleasure even though toilsome. After making sure that the rights to use it are affordable, each piece needs to be scanned, counted out and memorized. Since I've not learned to read scores, this can take an awful long time.

I make dances because it briefly frees me from coping with the real world, because it's possible to build a whole new universe with steps, because I want people to know about themselves, and even because it's a thrilling relief to see how fast each of my risk-taking dancers can recover from a pratfall.

I make dances, not to arrange decorative pictures for current dancers to perform, but to build a firm structure that can withstand future changes of cast. Quite possibly I make dances to be useful or to get rid of a chronic itch or to feel less alone. I make them for a bunch of reasons—multiple motives rooted in the driving passion that infected me when I first discovered dance. The novelist Albert Camus said it best:

> A man's work is nothing but this slow trek
> to rediscover through the detours of art
> those two or three great and simple images
> in whose presence his heart first opened.

FORTY SIX

My Intention to Serve Spanish Ballet Serves American Modern Dancers Instead

Carlos Surinach

A NATIVE OF BARCELONA, *Carlos Surinach (1915–97) had hoped to follow in the footsteps of the well-known composer Manuel de Falla (1876–1946) and create music for ballet that would be instantly recognizable as Spanish in idiom. Instead, as chronicled in this essay, he gained considerable attention from American modern dance choreographers.[1] Among his original scores were* Embattled Garden, Acrobats of God, *and* The Owl and the Pussycat *for Martha Graham, as well as* David and Bathsheba *for John Butler, and* Agathe's Tale, *commissioned by Paul Taylor. Some of his concert works were also set by choreographers—such as* Ritmo Jondo *choreographed first by Doris Humphrey in 1953 and used in 1963 by Alvin Ailey for his dance titled* Feast of Ashes. *In addition to his composing, Surinach had an active career as a conductor, including introducing the premieres of ballet and opera scores by his composer-colleague Peggy Glanville-Hicks.*

Reflecting upon what inspired him to compose and to collaborate, Surinach touches upon a number of intangibles in addition to considering specific attributes of his music that served to make it attractive for theatrical dance purposes.

***

The music of a ballet should be its most faithful mirror. It should be close to the unconscious and therefore reflect a less controlled and more immediate picture of life and motion than one is apt to receive from any other kind of music. It should be human, with impelling drive, animalizing all intellectual devices, if any.

The music for dance should be, further, a spontaneous creation of the deeper unconscious, or subconscious, inventive powers of the choreographer, which the composer should read in his (or her) mind intuitively, since such deep emotions might not be available verbally. Hence, the music for dance is not subject to the same degree of conscious premeditation as is the straight music, since any deliberate attempt at a certain (musically independent) effect could damage the picture on the stage.

The music for a ballet should be, in fact, at once an expression of a general emotional climate and (necessarily) an expression of the emotions of the choreographer. This does not mean a lack of freedom for the composer, since he has framework enough within the music itself; but he has to do his best to contribute to the general climate, for the dance is above all theatre, and theatre is vision and emotion within a stretch of time.

What I am setting forth are, I think, fair conclusions of my own and in accordance with my experience, but I do not necessarily mean that a composer for dance can be made upon these principles if his personal material does not fascinate the choreographer.

Ballet music, like plants, may grow in very unlikely ways. The material of my music, which seems to have attracted choreographers so much, was born in a very odd manner, for I did not have the dance in mind in the early days of my career. When I was a student in Spain, I was a deep admirer of the earlier works of the musical giant Manuel de Falla. I was determined to follow his lead in my future. Thus (quoting what Gilbert Chase says about my music in his book *The Music of Spain*), I began to "achieve an effect of novelty [in the Spanish idiom] with new technical resources: sharply etched lines, dissonant clashes, emphasis on the sheer primitive power of rhythm and strong reliance on percussion [galvanizing] it into new life by treating it not as romantic atmosphere but as raw material for firmly structured and taughtly textured scores."

I do not know whether Gilbert Chase is right or wrong in what he says about my music, but it is true that these were my principles for a new Spanish music, even before I began to write a single note. I strongly felt, also, that such music could be useful one day for a new conception of Spanish ballet.

The reader may consider my surprise in life when I found out that Spanish dancers are not the least interested in my music; that the main support for it (of course referring only to the dance) comes from the American modern dance movement and some progressive ballet choreographers; that everybody seems interested in the devices I use (e.g., sheer primitive power, raw material [realism], sharply etched lines, etc.), and nobody cares too much about the fact of my music being Spanish!

What did the dancers find in my music to be so fond of it? Trying all my life to do something different with the Spanish music, I had to find for it new devices, new patterns, and new profiles. My intention was to serve the Spanish music. The result was support from modern dancers. They were attracted to my music, not because it was Spanish, but because they were fascinated by the new devices, patterns, and profiles, abstracted from their national flavor. My beliefs about the relation of music and dance have been shaped by this, for it has shown me what it is in music that is useful to dancers.

For the rest, may I say that ballets with unrelated music can be good, as also there can be good ballets with no music at all; but these are separate cases whose genuine value to set a tradition is doubtful. I do believe, further, that the music for dance should have a shape: yes, the very shape of the choreography. If the music can work independently after that as a concert piece, the composer is lucky; if not, it is too bad. For the ballet is a form of theatre, and in theatre all separate elements have to aim to serve the stage and whatever happens there.

Finally, let me apologize for something: It is true that some works of mine have become ballets without having been written for that purpose. To that (and after all my affirmations), I really do not know what to say; but Cervantes said: "In Spain the newborn babe comes dancing forth from its mother's womb." Maybe I was born that way.

FORTY SEVEN

Music for the Modern Dance

Meditations on Melodies, Modes, Emotion, and Creation

Lou Harrison

*E*ARLY IN HIS *career, West Coast composer Lou Harrison (1917–2003) took a course with Henry Cowell in world music. He went on to accompany studio dance classes, using whatever percussion instruments he could make or find, and this interest in different sonorities blossomed into his later building, composing, and organizing of performances for Javanese-style gamelans.[1] Lyrical melodies, evocative timbres, and strong rhythmic impetus marked his earlier music for numerous dance artists such as Lester Horton, Merce Cunningham, Erick Hawkins, Katherine Litz, Jean Erdman, Remy Charlip, Carol Beals, Marian Van Tuyl, and others. Right up until the end of his life, Harrison continued to compose dance scores (including the suite* Rhymes With Silver *for Mark Morris). A meticulous craftsman, he was especially intrigued by the mathematical permutations possible for initial melodic and rhythmic motifs. The composer's calligraphic scores were visual works of art in themselves.*

In this 1952 article, Harrison distances himself from the "chance" approach of John Cage. Yet he offers some insightful comments about both avant-garde and more traditional scores being written for modern dance at midcentury, touching upon rhythmic impetus, the "flavor" of various pitch modes, musical suites, and the way in which a composer might experience features in the dance and imagine music for it.

***

The ancient and beautiful association of dance and music, regarded in some cultures as inevitable and intermingled, is not less today than in the past a birthing ground for musical ideas both fresh and invigorating. Indeed, it has long seemed to me that my fullest stimulation and greatest freedom as an artist has been found in the studios of modern dancers on both the west and east coasts. I find generally among dancers wide, intelligent acquaintance with music of our own time (as well as past times) and generous, creative ideas in the music to which they will dance. I also find the inventive necessities confronting the composer in the way of instrumentation and presentation (for modern dancers are not rich and have not even associations or companies in the sense that ballet has) are invariably stimulating to the imagination. It is probably needless to reiterate these truisms except for the purpose of reminding, perhaps, some of the younger composers; their immediate predecessors, by the listing, are well aware of them.

Led by the inventive and philosophical John Cage, a new kind of music has been evolving more fantastic than those who have not heard it can imagine: rich in fabulous, unprecedented new sounds and organized in ways entirely new to the art—silence as a plastic material (reckoned with in design), sound of the most violent, lush, bespangled, clangorsome and subtle kind, brought together, seemingly, at the least expected moments. It is to be remembered that New York's first introduction to this astonishing music was at Merce Cunningham's dance concert of 1951, at which time, as a prelude to the major work *Sixteen Dances* by Cunningham and Cage, a work by Morton Feldman was played and repeated, as well as a work by Christian Wolff. These latter are both pupils of Mr. Cage, as is Lucia Dlugoszewski, whose remarkable score for Erick Hawkins, *openings of the (eye)*, was heard only recently in its first performance at Hunter Playhouse in New York. This work, while making use of the prepared piano and employing a number of fine authentic native percussion instruments from various cultures, as well as a modern concert flute, follows slightly more conventional and European lines of thought.

In all these works—as in Morton Feldman's fine piano music for Jean Erdman's new *Changing Woman* and my own *Chorales for Spring* for Katherine Litz, a more relaxed attitude has been engendered towards the erstwhile continuous beat-by-beat association of the dance and music. Much time is silently allowed the dancer for the display and feeling of essential motor rhythms undocumented or "associated" by music's special expressive meanings. This presumes two things: a rhythmic impulse in the dancer imperative enough to carry the life beat of the work, and a new, more pointed staticity of musical materials. In this, the Cage school, by its adherence to chance and its disinclination to common melodic or rhythmic formulae or to any reference to "historicity," is at its best. While in concert hearing the same kind of music tends to produce a maximum of "attention-anxiety" by reason of there being simply no expectable time (journey of awareness), the same music—in conjunction with the dance, its anxiety drained off in attention given to kinesis—is often both apt and beautiful. This is in direct conflict with the older idea that, whether for performance alone or with dance or theatre, "music is still music," and probably derives, somewhat remotely, from the earlier German theories and the Louis Horst theory of the docility of good accompanimental music for dance.

I value melody highly and think of it as melos riding on the crest of kinesis. I believe in more traditional formations, on the grounds that form and expression are not accidents of assemblage, and not possible without the first essential, traditional choice. Musically speaking, I would rather "chance a choice" than "choose a chance." Be this as it may, my works are rather more expectable and traditionally expressive than those of the Cage school. And besides, I dearly love music from older times and the ephemeral thought of redolent poetry as "associational" tonal image.

I am quite opposed to Frank Lloyd Wright's remark that just as modern architecture has done away with unnecessary cornice adornment of buildings, so has modern music done away with melody. On the contrary, I feel that essentially and necessarily, music is an adventure in time awareness and that the most singular and simplest route to this beauty is through melody; for herein is form, shape, "recollection," surprise, architecture, and the "take-home-pay" of memorable tune; for few of us are double or multi-minded, and the old "song and dance" idea is presently, as anciently, the most rewarding.

Alan Hovhaness, whose works have been used as accompaniment to choreography and who has indeed written compositions directly for dancers on given subjects, is probably the composer whose apt and singularly direct establishment of "*Rasa*" or flavor (immediate and sustained), brings most suddenly to the dance stage an awareness of tonal "setting." His approach is based on the flavor of the modes.[2] The choice of mode, its tessitura and instrumentation, upon the instant sets a kind of emotional tone which is aurally as direct as costume and decor are to the eye. Now his peculiar rhythmic orientation—one which begins in eternity and stays there, largely abjuring fixed phrasal units and tending, by reason of the intricacy of detailed heterophonic polyphony, to a continuously vibrating pulsation rather than our more accustomed dynamic phraseology (that origin, cumulation, and release of relationships in tone)—tends to be difficult in choreography. Certainly instrumental entrances and departures are discoverable points here and an aid; but his music, as it seems to me, is more apt, and indeed singularly so, for the dramatic than lyric theatre. His tonal imagination, romantic in suggestion of the legend, color, ecstasy, and thundering innocence of the mixed and germinating Middle East (Ah Byzantium!) quite surely sets the stage for one of those grand classic story ballets of royal characters with big doings at stake that we have not had for some time. Nonetheless, his recent score for flute, harp, cello and large gong, written for Jean Erdman and titled *Upon Enchanted Ground*, is among the most beautiful for a dance of lyric nature, and though lacking in the phrasal rhyme of formal lyricism, it evokes, in its few moments, the necessary quality.

I want also to mention here, among what I believe to be the better compositions for dance in recent years, Ben Weber's score *The Pool of Darkness* for Merce Cunningham: possibly the solitary dodeca-phonic ballet score. Its introverted, shuddery, murky, then glassy texture; its withheld then explosive and sometimes hypnotic expres-sivity bring an extraordinary range of tonal variegation to a most complex and inwardly disturbing dance composition (the subject being a hypothetical Oedipus who gave the wrong answers to the goddess-sphinx). The post-expressionist manner here (and it is a latter-day difference) will, I would hazard, require a little space before its follow-through.

The most successful usage of already written music during the past season were Wallingford Riegger's beautiful and imaginative *Duos for Three Woodwinds* (the dance titled *Bridegroom of the Moon*), and the pre-sent author's *Six Cembalo Sonatas* (the dance titled *The Lives of Five or Six Swords*). Both these works are made up of smaller pieces coalesced by the choreographer Erick Hawkins into a larger work—a condition which suggests that the dance suite of earlier times is still, in our own day, an entirely usable and useful invention, and which is not too far in idea from Henry Cowell's specific recipe for flexible modern dance composition, "elastic form," in which a group of connectable and related measures or phrases are presented to the dancer for assemblage as he or she may require, the difference lying only in the greater musical perfection possible when short, but entire, movements are so used (though in the present instance Mr. Hawkins used the individual pieces in the order of the composers' choice).

A few final thoughts and I have done. And these thoughts come from meditation on those moments of astonishment when my unwary self has heard sounds and instruments and tunes while watching in silence the dancer move. We usually look out with one eye and we usu-ally listen in with the ear; we cannot even close them, so important are they for receiving. Now in that amazing vortex of the creative idea, all this is reversed. The eye receives, with what the dancer out of "emo-tion" (emotion is incomplete motion) is expressing. In origin the dancer is one who is capable at later times, and beautifully, to complete our motions for us; for the reservoir of emotion is only one of incom-plete motions (what completed purely functional motion leaves us with an "emotion": none) and so recollects, perfects, and re-realizes us of our perhaps original intents.[3] Then, as the creative act continues to reverse things, the eye receives this, makes possible our own trans-formed and transforming empathy, and finally, for the musician, he "hears out," perhaps, with mind's music. This is, indeed, the simplest form of tonal imagining, for while words, too, may likewise prompt to hearing out, they are in a sense a head start themselves, for they are of themselves sometimes, somewhat of music too, and finally, less essentially imagining than dance movement (for this is primary).

Guarded by the sense of style, the outer wall of the fortress of the creative, then, and open to idea, the musician in the dancer's studio is quite apt to understand what Ezra Pound meant when he said that music is best when closest to dance, and poetry best when closest to music.

FORTY EIGHT

Notes on New Music
for the Dance

Choices Open to Collaborators at Midcentury

Lucia Dlugoszewski

*W*HEN *LUCIA DLUGOSZEWSKI (1931–2000) was only nineteen,
Erick Hawkins sent her a telegram inviting her to be his piáno
accompanist. From then on, though she went on to compose
orchestral and chamber works that won recognition by the most prestigious
awards, it was her longtime collaboration with dancer-choreographer Hawkins
that occupied most of her life: not only as pianist but also as composer, conductor, inventor (with artist Ralph Dorazio) of instruments such as the timbre
piano; as codirector of the Erick Hawkins Dance Company; and as his wife.*[1]

*Although Dlugoszewski began composing music as a child, her college
degree was in physics. She subsequently studied piano with Grete Sultan
and composition with Edgard Varèse, who considered her one of the most
talented composers of her generation. Her first score for Hawkins was*
Here and Now with Watchers, *in 1957; her last one for Hawkins was
a 1994 solo that he choreographed for Mikhail Baryshnikov. Writing
about Dlugoszewski's style in general, the composer-critic Virgil Thomson
observed that she created "far-out music of great delicacy, originality and
beauty of sound." At the end of her life, one obituary stated simply:
"A splendid composer has died."*[2]

*In this essay, Dlugoszewski gives us a vibrant feeling for what it was
like to be immersed in the new dance world at such an exciting time—with*

FIGURE 48.1 Lucia Dlugoszewski and percussion instruments she designed with Ralph Dorazio. Photograph © Daniel Kramer, New York City, 1960.

all the mathematical, philosophical, practical, technological, cultural, and aesthetic choices to consider.

***

The dancer in the year 1957 and the composer involved in music for the dance are confronted with two momentous trends that make more vivid than ever this challenge of what it is to live in the present time of one's life.

First we have as possible material at our disposal the unknown quantity of magnetic tape. And second, at an ever increasing speed, we have a constant barrage of every conceivable culture other than our own. And all this having happened, no matter what we do, we will never be the same.

Now the dialogue of existence for the artist is always between the extent of his material and what he will choose from it, and with our range of material widened to a veritable infinity, we have certainly a problem in reorganizing our attitude toward choice. Some musicians and dancers have chosen to pretend all this does not exist. Others in desperation have proclaimed that "everything is good."

But clearly we always only know "what we are," and now are confronted with a jungle of unknown possibilities which are "what we are not," and to use the word "good" or "bad" implies a moral problem. It presupposes that we first know this something that we are damning or glorifying.

And this "something" we both *do not* and *need* to know. And so it seems the truest direction of music and dance art in 1957 is a sensitive search for *what is*, which is the archaic position—the position of beginning—a most exciting position in the arts of any time. In the archaic position, every element is used for the discovery and illumination of *what it is* and for no other reason.

When modern dance began in America it certainly went back to a discovery of *what is*, and it most certainly proposed that challenge to any composer who was willing to create music for this dance. One of the first of these pioneering composers pointed out that before modern dance, the dancer was always a "handmaiden" to the music. Therefore dance was a subordinate and dependent art. The modern dance did the bold unprecedented thing: composed complete movement structures in silence. And so, the new independent art of dance was born. So too was born the still persisting problem of what music structure would be acceptable to this new dance.

The most imaginative composers working in this field today are still asking: why music for the dance, what music for the dance, and why even consider music and dance as entities that should exist together. This same composer who criticized the old "handmaiden" school noted also that composers often felt that the dancer could encompass only the most elementary musical material of rhythm etc. But the modern history of dance in America certainly indicates that dancers can accept the challenge of any musical material to any degree of difficulty from taped sound to the most intricate polyphonic rhythmic events.

When we ask of music and dance "why together," and "how together," and "what together," we call to mind the brilliant pioneer of the archaic position in the art of words, Gertrude Stein, who asks:

"Does the thing heard replace the thing seen does it help it or does it interfere with it?"

When we are aware of anything (seen, heard, felt, thought, done) we are aware of this "anything," and this "anything" exists on a "ground" which it frames for our contemplation. This act of awareness is sometimes philosophically called bracketing. The first "ground" for a painter is his canvas; for the dancer, the stage; and for the musician, the very fragile ground of the whole sound-laden air that the ear can hear, and so the music's "ground" is a kind of dirty and complicated canvas. Then, some composers consider the empty preconceived time journey that their sounds will inhabit as the "ground."

When dance emancipated itself from music, there became quite an amusing and not so amusing struggle as to who should be "hand-maiden" to whom, and of course, all too humanly the one doing often concluded that the "other" should be subordinate. This made many composers shun the field, and the wail of dancers in the throes of musical problems is still unending.

One kind of music developed (sometimes very beautiful, sometimes incredibly dull) that was really a "ground" for the dance structure—a "musical setting" for the dance theatre. Recently again someone proposed music written that would create a dancer's "rhythm score," and although this does not make dance the music's "ground," it certainly makes it a subordinate structure. The old "handmaiden school" did not think of dance as the music's ground. It was even more subordinate than that: the music truly didn't need the dance *at all*; dance was just a nice frosting that one could eat or leave alone.

The problem today is still the problem of what relationship exists between music and dance, what aspects of musical material and structure fit this relationship, and this very specific way of working by having a complete non-musical time structure as the given point from which to proceed.

It is interesting to review the various solutions that music has proposed in the recent history of new dance concerts. It is a richly varied list including Western classical music, Western romantic music, various ethnic music, jazz, music of the rhythmic structure; twelve-tone, modal, and atonal music; music involving mathematics, tape sound, structures of chance, ostinato structures; music of near silence, pure silence—and the structure of the heard pulse.

One of the interesting problems in music for dance is the use of emotion as "ground." Consider *Swan Lake*. The Tchaikovsky score is melodically motivic. What is called melody, in the dictionary definition, is a succession of single notes or pitches often with a scale or mode as basis (but not necessarily). Actually (ask the boycotters of modern music), what generally creates melody for people is when the pitch intervals are not too far apart and the space of time between intervals is not too taxing to the memory span to permit the ear to link them. When even two pitches are linked we have a high and low journey that is an absolute metaphor for our affective life, and the result is emotion for music. Twelve-tone music in its basic premise emphasized the lack of the linking of pitches, and so the resultant music had heaped upon its head the criticisms of unmelodic, unfeeling, and cerebral. The *Swan Lake* score in its diatonically-pitched and extremely-linked tone progression, creates much emotional content— and emotion can transcend the instant-by-instant listening process to the extent of creating a concept of itself, which is then constant and therefore a "ground." Ballet movement rests upon this emotional ground. Modern dance, when it uses music of an emotional ground, often juxtaposes another emotional ground of its own. Of course *all* melodic music has some possibilities of an emotional ground. Music for the cinema is always in this function. Jazz makes use of the emotional ground as well.

A musical device that always creates a "ground" is the ostinato (or long repetition of something). In the largest sense of the word this ostinato device has been used in many beautiful examples of dance music. Any constant beat (such as one hears in jazz or Hindu and African music) is a kind of ostinato—as is any motivic repetition, whether rhythmic, melodic or timbred (as in *Le Sacre du Printemps*, for example). Even pure silence can be considered as ostinato (since we listen instant silence by instant silence through a long repetition). Erik Satie's experiments in repetition fit this category. The ostinato ground, often, because it destroys its own time sense, makes a very lovely juxtaposition to dance—since then the dancer's time sense is completely alone.

The music of Bach is very far removed from the sense of "ground" for anything else, being complete and self-sufficient in itself. It is somewhat melodic but not in the later motivic sense and so, slightly emotional. But primarily it is using sound to express metaphorically an imaginary architecture, and dancers using this music have often been tempted to create an equivalent architecture metaphorically in motion. This again pulls dance back to a kind of dependent position.

This kind of metaphorical structure includes the later sonata form, much twelve-tone music, the music of the overtone series, music involving mathematical principles, and even chance music when it considers itself a metaphor of life.

Chance music for the dance has, however, interesting other aspects to face and solve. Chance composition in music or dance, to be really successful, must operate in totality. If not in totality, or in a totality it does not understand, then it is mixing categories and creates real eclecticism and superficiality. After all, if you are making ice cream, you can push your range of choice to include everything even to the point of garlic; but ground glass or fire, or thunder, or dance steps mixed in would certainly make you forget the true operating ice cream totality!

So chance must really assume first the archaic position and discover *what is* and therefore what is totality before it can truly operate as chance.

Pitch and rhythm in music and rhythm in movement (that is, the quantitative elements, the most simple totalities) lend themselves more successfully to interesting dance and music structures of chance than other experiments. In such music structures the resulting rhythm is very difficult, or almost too difficult for the dancer to perceive. This also often occurs in a tape score and has led to the accidental method of relationship between sound and movement. Of course the accidental relationship dulls the instant-by-instant time sense of pure theatre, because the audience senses the performer's lack of instant awareness to the happening sound while he performs his instant-by-instant movement.

There are several experiments in music for the dance that attempt to create what seems the most beautiful relationship between the two, and that is the phenomenon of two pure theatres existing independently side-by-side with an instant-by-instant awareness of one another.

Now from Gertrude Stein's searching definition of theatre, "never being able to begin over again because before it has commenced it was over and at no time had you been ready either to commence or to be over," one wonders whether tape, with its fixed and therefore predictable and unperformed sound, is theatre in the purest sense of the word—or is it another more semi-static art material that should have a different relation to movement than performed sound? This is the great problem for the modern dancers who use a tape score, and it badly requires the archaic position.

Among dance scores the "rhythmic structure" does achieve an independent theatre, except that in using an unheard pulse it creates rhythmic hierarchies that do not permit the dancer's own rhythmic composition to exist as independently as it exists in pure silence.

The one structure that seems to permit this independence and still retain its own (two theatres side by side) is the new music structure of the heard pulse, which is especially used for dance that has been first composed in silence. Pulse heard or unheard has been the musical ruler for all performed music all over the world. Only tape does not have this because it is machine-fixed and therefore non-performed. The use of the stopwatch in performance is just another example of unheard pulse. The heard pulse structure makes of itself both a primary poetry and a "ground" on which durational (and therefore non-motivic) rhythms and other musical material rest—and also gives itself as a ground (almost as neutral and fragile as pure silence) on which the dancer can suspend his independent movement structure. Clearly the heard pulse structure permits either music or dance to be experienced alone or in perfect but independent togetherness.

It is interesting to note the increasing use of timbre as musical material, and of structures of timbre for dance music. Western musical development has always suspected timbre of lacking sophisticated possibilities of structure. However, timbre lends itself more to the archaic or *what-is-ness* approach because its very complex, unfixable, almost unnotatable essence precludes its use for any reason but its own existence.

Now timbre permits as intricate and "cerebral" structural solutions as any of the imaginary architectures of Western music, except that they would be different solutions.

It demands the qualitative discipline. That is, an intuitional hearing—instant-by-instant, instantaneously—totals that are beyond the sum of their parts. This particular kind of hearing sensitizes our perception to that delicate range of materials that a Northrop [the philosopher F. S. C. Northrup] or Virginia Woolf would consider the feminine component of art—the component so often lacking in Western culture.

Consider an exercise in hearing with the qualitative discipline. I suggest a New York City garbage truck. How long can you hear instant by instant, undenotationally, and how long can you therefore create this pure theatre of the ear? The longer you can do this, the better you will be equipped to face that new monster, tape—and to experience the dancer's kinesthetic material, and to appreciate the music and dance of any culture. It is then truly the archaic position that one will achieve, what James Joyce so beautifully calls the "epiphany."

PART SIX

DANCE ARTISTS SPEAK TO FUTURE GENERATIONS

The modern dance was to complete the dream that Isadora Duncan's artistic promise had left unfulfilled. The stress in both ballet and the modern dance was on America, on her spirit and folkloric atmosphere, on the vigor and athletic strength of her dancers. The American spirit found its expression in most of the themes and in the approach to subject matter. There was an unvoiced pride in leading America toward the forefront of the dance world.

—*Walter Sorell*

Overview

Postwar Trends, and Music in the Training of Dancers

T HE ISSUE OF *Dance Observer* that included Lucia Dlugoszewski's summation of new music for the dance also serves as an indicator of some trends in performance and education during the post–World War II years and the 1950s.[1]

On the cover of that November 1957 *Dance Observer* was a photograph of the men's "Cool" section from *West Side Story*, which had just opened on Broadway, choreographed by Jerome Robbins to a score by Leonard Bernstein. Also chronicled in the issue was a presentation of composer Harry Partch's dance drama *The Bewitched*, using his unique instruments and with choreography by Alwin Nikolais assisted by Murray Louis, at the Henry Street Playhouse. The Royal Ballet was performing at the Metropolitan Opera House, featuring *The Prince of the Pagodas* to a specially commissioned score by the British composer Benjamin Britten. In lower Manhattan, Cooper Union was offering programs of Afro-Caribbean, Israeli, and Chinese dance styles. Elsewhere, dancers from India, Yemen, and France were also in town.

At Hunter College Playhouse, the Erick Hawkins Dance Company was giving the premiere of *Here and Now with Watchers*, with music by Lucia Dlugoszewski. Critic Robert Sabin gave qualified approval of a new twelve-tone score by Gunther Schuller for dancer, violin, piano, and percussion—performed at Carnegie Hall by dancer Maria Maslova and her violinist husband, Joseph Malfitano. The same issue of *Dance*

Observer also ran a review of a recording of Gian-Carlo Menotti's score *The Unicorn, the Gorgon and the Manticore* (commissioned by the Elizabeth Sprague Coolidge Foundation, premiered in the Library of Congress with choreography by John Butler, with a New York City Ballet cast that included Arthur Mitchell). And in an odd juxtaposition, right next to the review of an appearance by Ruth St. Denis (cited as "one of the rare and most deeply rewarding dance talents of our time") is a now infamous blank space with the headline "Paul Taylor and Dance Company, YM-YWHA, October 20, 1957" signed with Louis Horst's initials. Finally, the back cover showed a full-page ad for Merce Cunningham's company at the Brooklyn Academy of Music.

In summary, it was a time for both honoring what had become mainstream artistic achievement in concert dance and wondering what in the world a new generation of creative artists was up to! Recognizing the achievements of its innovative artists, the dance world began handing out awards, including Capezio citations to Louis Horst in 1955 and to Ted Shawn in 1957. Also with a focus on the past, a wide concern was the visual preservation of dances from earlier years. Several systems of notating dance movement had been devised (including Labanotation), and some documentary films were being made to help pass along the art of the pioneer modern dancers. On the cover of the December 1957 issue of *Dance Observer*, Martha Graham is shown directing a sequence for the filming of *A Dancer's World*, which had been reviewed in the October 1957 issue along with the film that Ruth St. Denis had made of some of her dances, including *Yogi*.

Advertisements in *Dance Observer* signaled improvements in recordings that offered both advantages and disadvantages: as substitutes for live accompanists in the studio and for performances, vinyl LPs could be a cost saver and sometimes a convenience; but there was also a loss in the moment-to-moment interaction of dancers and musicians, of movement and sound.

And then there was television. Agnes de Mille presented several landmark programs about dance on *Omnibus*. But John Cage and others were not so sure about this new blessing, and in the January 1957 issue of *Dance Observer* he began an article: "In this day of TV-darkened homes, a live performance has become something of a rarity, so much so that Aaron Copland recently said, a concert is a thing of the past."

Looking more optimistically to the future, however, organizations were founded to bolster the field of dance in general, for networking over wider geographic areas, and for encouraging both performance and the study of dance as an art form. In 1957, the 92nd Street

YM-YWHA was sponsoring its fourth annual conference "Creative Teaching of Dance to Children," and the Dance Teachers Guild held its first meeting. At the college level, there were concerns about certification of teachers, and academia began asking questions about what counted most as qualification: artistic experience as a professional dancer and choreographer, or a college degree as a dance major? It was considered a turning point worthy of public notice that in 1947 Vassar College had established a credit course in dance history and theory. And after only four years of a program's existence, the May 1957 *Dance Observer* reviewed the report *A Graduate Program in an Undergraduate College: The Sarah Lawrence Experience*, which described an experimental program aimed at future teachers of dance.

Dance in academia continued to expand, as did creative dance and training for children under such teachers as Virginia Tanner in Salt Lake City and Steffi Nossen in New York's Westchester County. Indicative of the level of musical accompaniment was the fact that Tanner enlisted composer-pianist Norma Reynolds Dalby (who subsequently worked with Bessie Schönberg at Sarah Lawrence College and collaborated with more than 200 dance artists including the avant-garde dancer-choreographer Kei Takei). Young dancers in Nossen's classes also enjoyed exceptional live music, provided by Jess Meeker (composer-pianist for Ted Shawn), and by Marjorie Landsmark-DeLewis (pianist for Agnes de Mille and American Ballet Theatre).[2]

Dance Observer's directory of private studios for professional training still counted many well-known names in New York City, but there were also outstanding artists teaching modern dance in other locations around the United States. The best-known of these highlighted the musical component of their studio classes. For example, the Martha Graham School advertised Ralph Gilbert's weekly course in music for the dancer, with an emphasis on "principles of music, of rhythm, timing, and phrase as they relate to the dance movement," and the Graham School continued to have outstanding pianists for technique classes.

But the lack of trained musical accompanists, as well as of funds to pay them, was an ongoing problem in other studios. The need for skilled musicians trained to play for dancers was emphasized by Ann Hutchinson (one of the first faculty members at New York's High School of Performing Arts, founded in 1948). Writing in the January 1950 *Dance Observer*, Hutchinson described the tradition now commonly referred to as the just-throw-them-to-the-lions method for dealing with new musicians. She did not offer a solution and did not begin to address what is perhaps still the overwhelming challenge for accompanists, namely, to improvise in many styles at a moment's notice in order to support dance sequences only just then demonstrated. Even so, Hutchinson had plenty to say about her musical concerns:

> To any dance teacher the idea of teaching large classes for any length of time without the assistance of a pianist is appalling. In order to keep the class going the teacher must either count or beat a drum. The energy of a teacher is divided between keeping an even beat and watching the dancers. The moment he relaxes and stops beating, the class stops dancing. Though modern movement may fit better to a rhythmic drum pattern, a ballet adagio or waltz is completely dead without the melodic line of the music to sustain it. Nor is the victrola the answer. It is often more of a hindrance than a help. Even with a good machine there is the endless running back and forth to start and stop the record at the right place, and the right place is not always easy to find. To use records effectively, the teacher must build the exercises or studies around whatever suitable records can be found, and this means a time-consuming search followed by more time spent adapting the movements to fit the records.
>
> The Music Department at Performing Arts tried to help the situation by sending students to play, with the idea that they would gain something by learning to accompany dance. Since these pianists were only youthful students themselves, they were usually found to be (a) unreliable, (b) unable to play anything but boogie, (c) unable to sight read the music the dance teachers provided, (d) unable to learn anything by heart in a short time, (e) unable to keep tempo, or else a combination of these. By and large the dance teacher found himself spending more time coaching the pianist than teaching the class. To do them justice, one or two music students were comparatively satisfactory, but were whisked away after a few weeks since the music department did not wish to exploit them.[3]

While unfortunately the need for skilled musicians for dance did not immediately spawn formal programs in music departments or certification for specialist accompanists, yet from the time of summers at Bennington with Louis Horst (as well as later on in the West Coast with Lester Horton), music was regarded as important in the modern dancers' own training. And as efforts were made to move dance out of physical education departments and establish independent programs on a par with other performing arts, having live music plus courses in music for dancers was considered a distinguishing asset.[4]

As the twentieth century progressed, modern dance grew—literally, by degrees. The University of Missouri lists the inception of its dance programs as 1907; the University of Oregon began to offer dance in 1911; Butler University dates its dance to 1913; the Cornish School of the Arts in Washington, to 1914. In 1926, the University of Wisconsin in Madison became the first university to offer a degree program in dance, led by Margaret H'Doubler. The University of Michigan's dance department opened in 1929. From 1932 on, Martha Hill spearheaded new departments at both New York University and Bennington College. Arizona State University's dance department opened in 1937; Mills College in California dates its ongoing program to 1938. Other major programs were started in the 1940s, including at the University of Utah. The Juilliard School's conservatory training in its dance division was established in 1951 under the direction of Martha Hill. In announcing this development, Juilliard's president, composer William Schuman, commented on the complementary influences of the two sometimes collaborative arts:

> In establishing a dance department in a school of music, we are well aware that dance, which is dependent upon music for a measure of its effectiveness, has also always exerted a strong influence on music. In contemporary composition, it is perhaps not too much to say that more works are commissioned for the dance than for concert purposes, and in this there is historical precedent in the large number of famous works originally written for the dance or in dance forms. For these reasons, it is important for the art of music that dancers have the highest musical standards. Finally, it is the hope of the School in establishing this department that by giving a thorough training in dance, and at the same time developing musicianship in dancers, it will at once be contributing to both arts.[5]

Other academic institutions kept up the pace. In 1967, New York State authorized the building of its suburban facility now called Purchase College, enhanced by a multitheater Performing Arts Center. While buildings were being planned for Purchase, dancer William Bales (who was appointed as the college's first dean of dance) appeared before government officials in Albany to demonstrate how much space was necessary for diagonal leaps across the floor and to stress the advantages of Steinway concert grand pianos for the studios of the new Conservatory of Dance.[6]

California Institute of the Arts, founded in the 1960s, added a dance degree program in 1971. And so it went. Skipping to the twenty-first century, Princeton University inaugurated its first formal dance program in 2007, offering a certificate for concentration in dance (with an emphasis on modern and contemporary styles), and in the same year Ohio State University replaced its MFA degree program with a PhD in dance.

College guidebooks nowadays count preprofessional BFA and MFA programs in as many as 200 colleges and universities across the United States, and dance courses in more than 600 institutions of higher learning. By 2008 *Dance Magazine* estimated close to 9,000 students majoring in dance across the United States, in addition to another 4,000 or so students with dance as a minor.[7] Added to such numbers, we can note the Bureau of Labor Statistics' surprising figure of 16,340 Americans identifying themselves as "choreographers."

Such numbers would seem to warrant serious consideration by college and university music departments, in regard to including courses focusing on dance and its effects upon music as part of their regular academic curriculum, as well as in offering practical training for composers and improvising accompanists who might find outlet for their talents by collaborating with the ever-widening dance world. In the United States, this did not happen on any broad-scale basis. And despite the fact that so much classical repertoire as well as folk and popular genres are seen to have descended from various forms of music for dance, nevertheless music majors generally were not required to have any formal courses about dance as a closely related art form. Nor were they required to take courses in eurhythmics, which might develop their kinesthetic sense of music. Instead, classically oriented performing musicians continued to focus on instrumental and vocal studies, and many young composers tended toward increasingly cerebral concert genres. Consequently, individual musicians wanting to work as accompanists would seek coaching as apprentices or simply learn their trade via the common previously mentioned throw-them-to-the-lions method offered without academic credit in dance studios throughout the country. All too often, dance teachers were expected to do double duty: not only to teach dance, but also to train their accompanists.

On the more positive side, however, increasingly academic degree programs in dance recognized music as an important facet of the art: one that needed to be addressed in ways quite different from typical "Music 101 Appreciation" college courses. Dancers needed to experience rhythm through their entire bodies, and to imbibe most of their musical awareness through their ears rather than their eyes. But they also needed to understand more about the structure and basic building blocks of what they were hearing. It was also felt that dancers' artistry could benefit from deeper acquaintance with the rich heritage of folk music, the history of various classical traditions from around the world, and theatrical uses of popular genres as well—all styles with which they might be expected to perform in the increasingly competitive world of professional theatrical dance. Additionally, dance students were encouraged to at least try some drumming and, as time went on, to master the technologies of sound systems, recording, and even computer-generated composing of sound scores for their own dances. Furthermore, aspiring choreographers and teachers needed to understand the legalities of "grand rights" in regard to using copyrighted music; how to apply for grants; how to make contractual agreements; and learn practical ways of communicating and working with collaborating accompanists and composers.

All this amounted to a tall order for dance students both then and now, coming on top of the physical demands and time devoted to technique classes and rehearsals. In addition to their formal academic programs in dance, various colleges and universities continued the tradition begun at Bennington, of hosting special festivals and workshops with outstanding visiting choreographers and musicians, and offering emerging artists opportunities to showcase their work in performances. As the years passed, on both regional and national levels, perhaps no other organization has energized student choreography as much as the American College Dance Festival Association (ACDFA).[8] Founded in 1973 with just thirteen charter member institutions, it now has more than 360 college and university dance programs as members and counts annual participation in the neighborhood of 4,000 in recent years.

The dance world was certainly smaller in the 1930s. The 150 or so dancers who traveled from around the country to attend the now-historic gatherings at Bennington College each summer were mainly college-based dance teachers and students, many from physical education departments. Subsequently, what grew into the American Dance Festival (ADF) programs took place at Mills College (in 1939), at Connecticut College (from 1947 to 1977), and at Duke University (from 1978 and continuing into the present). In some years there were special ADF programs to nurture collaboration between composers and choreographers.[9] Additionally the Regional Dance Association (founded in 1988) began to sponsor Craft of Choreography Conferences to encourage new works, also offering the expertise of music advisers.[10]

As witnessed by this collection's last group of readings, for most dance artists and teachers just past midcentury and beyond, music continued to be recognized as a tool that could add energetic support for the performers—as well as atmosphere, virtuosic sparkle, emotional depth, and formal structure. Even if one chose to present some dances in silence, yet music was considered an ingredient worth understanding and using effectively, despite the fact that new scores and live performances might challenge one's budget. Some of the possible rewards are suggested by the articles in this collection's final part.

The first essay offers personal reflections and advice from Erick Hawkins, who made a point of commissioning new scores and always having live music for his performances. Some brief comments follow, from the leading dance educator Bessie Schönberg, who compares music in the training of modern dancers with its use in ballet traditions. Next, the concert tap dancer Paul Draper (known for his use of classical music) offers young dancers advice on musicality, continuing that emphasis begun by Isadora Duncan.

Concluding these readings, dancer-choreographer José Limón contemplates an arc of modern dance experience spanning the innovative art of pioneers in the formative years, through mid-twentieth-century experimenters. Along the way he offers observations about the art of conducting music for dance performances. His general assessment suggests that dance artists and their musical collaborators had indeed achieved some of the aesthetic goals imagined and set forth by Émile Jaques-Dalcroze in this book's first essays. Limón closes his address with a fervent exhortation to the students: the artists of the future, both dancers and musicians.

FORTY NINE

My Love Affair with Music

Erick Hawkins

*I*N THE PREVIOUS PART, *composer Lucia Dlugoszewski provided an overview of musical collaboration for the dance from the vantage point of her
work with Erick Hawkins and her own immersion in the modern dance
and music scene of New York beginning in 1953. Here as a complement are
some aesthetic observations by Hawkins himself, written in 1967 just as the
spheres of mainstream modern dance and concert music alike were being challenged by new generations of experimentalists. Hawkins's emphasis is on the
"now-ness" of dance movement, and in contrast he touches upon how the world
of music had become slightly "unhinged" by recordings, which can lose the
creative impact of moment-to-moment live performance.*

*One of the seminal figures in modern dance, Erick Hawkins (1909–94)
was born in Colorado, majored in Greek civilization at Harvard, and studied
dance first with Harald Kreutzberg in Austria and subsequently at the School
of American Ballet. He performed for a brief time with Lincoln Kirstein's
Ballet Caravan, in choreography by George Balanchine. From 1938 he performed with Martha Graham (whom he married in 1948), but there was a
parting of the ways both personally and professionally in 1951. Hawkins
formed his own company and over the years developed a free-flowing technique that encompassed Eastern tradition, in distinct contrast to the percus-
siveness of Graham's style.*[1]

*As a choreographer, Hawkins was always very proud of the musical aspects
of his dances. Among the composers he commissioned were Henry Cowell,
David Diamond, Ross Lee Finney, Lou Harrison, Alan Hovhaness,
Wallingford Riegger, and Virgil Thomson. As chronicled in this article, the*

FIGURE 49.1 Erick Hawkins dancing with Beverly Hirschfeld (front) and Dena Madole (rear), with composer-musician Lucia Dlugoszewski playing percussion instruments in background. Photograph © Daniel Kramer, New York City, 1967.

collaboration he valued in a special way for its unusual poetic results was his work with composer-pianist-conductor Lucia Dlugoszewski. He outlines their procedures as a suggested model for newer generations to consider and urges that the two arts of dance and music need each other in order to have a vital and expressive relation to the times.

***

I have been called a "loner," a rugged individualist, and a fool because I am one of the very few choreographers and dancers who never has and never will use records or tapes for a live dance performance.

There are at least four reasons why music has been so totally important to my dance and has made me seem more deeply involved with new sound in relation to new movement than perhaps any other choreographer.

1. I cannot see how new dance can be new, when danced to old music.
2. I cannot tolerate the mechanization of records or tapes when used with live dancers in performance.
3. I cannot imagine new dance that is beautiful without being rhythmic, and this presupposes a new music for our contemporary dance.
4. I am involved with a new body discipline and new movement vocabulary that demands a new kind of music.

Expressing Our Own Times

I have never been able to see how new dance can be served by old music. We are living now in December in 1967 and we are everything that makes us what we are now. We are violent. We are bored. We are rebellious about our ingrained puritanisms. We are trying to find our way back to the body. We are resentful of the gigantic, mechanistic gadgetry we have created to imprison us. We are trying to rediscover how to play again, how to feel. We are frightened by our destructive insensitivity. We cannot seem to resolve the conflict between men and women. We cannot find our way clear of ugliness. This is what we are now, and out of all this will come our truly new dance and the dance that truly expresses us. And I fail to see how ideas in movement coming out of our life today can be served well by ideas in music coming out of the life of the sixteenth, seventeenth, eighteenth, or nineteenth century. The composers of those periods were facing different challenges and solving different problems and when we use their works for our dance, we not only defeat it, but we also insult their music.

Records Make Us Deaf

We are practically completely deaf from "Muzak," and we need even louder and stranger sounds to break through our callousness and indifference. For me, the mechanical Muzak-like sound of tapes and records will never promote new dance, and that is why I will never use a record or tape for my dance concerts.

The living musician reinforces the living dancer to make the audience come alive. This is not an easy thing to do. Both challenge the composer to create with originality for our life.

Beautiful Movement and Rhythm

I cannot see how we will escape boredom and the curse of contemporary ugliness without rhythmic movement. For me, unlike other experimental avant-garde dance developments, the essence of beautiful movement, its primal poetry, is rhythmic consciousness, and so, the musical part of dance is especially important to me. I do not want to use music in an unrhythmic way, and I do not want music whose orientation is unrhythmic and thus, unphysical. For me, this unrhythmic development is another inroad on our sensitivity and another path toward boredom.

Not only are we deaf from mechanically produced music; we are deaf from unrhythmic sound. We are bored because we cannot feel and we cannot feel because we are movement-deaf, and we are movement-deaf because we are unrhythmic.

A new dance which would not be boring nor ugly needs a new music that is not a sentimental, swooning unrhythmic mush of romanticism nor an avant-garde arbitrary destruction of rhythmic continuity. We must pass beyond gimmick, tantrum, gadget, or shock to a new theatrical alertness of instant-by-instant rhythmic consciousness in music and movement.

A New Kind of Dance Theatre

Choreographers have been concerned that movement relate to sound emotionally, structurally (one dominating the other or both ignoring the other), even rhythmically. But an entirely new kind of theatre can be achieved by putting movement and music together so that they interrelate entirely and totally with poetry.

While I move and the composer is silent because I have moved, when I jump high and the composer is suddenly very quiet because I have jumped high, when I move my little finger and the composer lets loose with a strong, brave clear sound because it is so important to move a little finger, these are instances of real poetic dialogue between movement and sound, and this is what I find extraordinary in Lucia Dlugoszewski's music for dance. She has created a new standard of music for dance in contemporary history.

How Music and Dance Should Happen Together

Music and movement happen together, but just exactly what happens is what determines the kind of theatre experience. It is like two people being together. One can dominate the other. They can become carbon copies of one another. One can cling to the other for support, strength, and emotional interest. One can use the other for a background to his own importance. They can use each other for distraction, to keep things from being boring. They can be so afraid of losing their individual freedom and individuality that they can ignore each other and end up, often, rather nastily stepping on each other's toes.

But there are rare times when two people are together when each one does an indescribable something for the other and yet no freedom is lost by either. For me, as a living experience, this is what poetry is all about, this resulting situation where everyone is richly, happily alert and clear in their attention and consciousness. I feel this poetry is the only thing that can really "turn anyone on" or make them "high." It has no counterfeit, no chemical crutch, no sentimental illusions. It seems to me to be the very best kind of living experience, the most satisfying excitement, and this is how I feel that movement and sound should happen together.

Contrast with Other Collaborators

Composers for dance have often been only the composers who didn't care very deeply about their art or weren't gifted enough to produce first-rate music for the concert hall, or they were fine composers who had no feeling for movement. Some were fine composers who distrusted the high-handed practices of choreographers who used their music badly and irresponsibly or who felt that dance would always overshadow and obliterate the music, theatrically, and therefore played down their efforts in writing music for the dance.

What do I do differently as far as music for dance is concerned? Generally, choreographers have taken music already written and followed it carefully in terms of the rhythm and in terms of the musical structure. Some have followed and interpreted the score in terms of the musical emotion, or they have ignored the emotion. Some choreographers have ignored the music rhythmically, to the extent of consciously and actively destroying the given musical rhythmic continuity.

Choreographers have taken music already written and used it as a collage either for an emotional bath in which to throw their choreography, or as a structural base to anchor their own shaky dance structures, or have used music as a plateau of distraction to bolster the waning interest of their dance, much the same as radio music serves a dull party.

Choreographers have written a scenario for dance, which is an emotional sequence rather than an independent rhythmic structure, and asked composers to write to this scenario. Then they would fit their choreography to the musical rhythm and structure of this commissioned music. Choreographers have composed dances and then asked composers to fit music to it that would fulfill the dance requirements, but naturally, as a result, limit the creative expression of the music itself.

Choreographers have composed dances and then asked composers to write music that in no way took any notice of the dance. In such collaboration, there was no requirement other than that the music and dance started at the same time and ended at the same time. Such collaborations were deeply suspicious of encroachments on each other's freedom.

Instant-by-Instant Poetic Dialogue

This is what's different in my relation to music. Both the music and dance can stand alone and be performed independently, but both are juxtaposed and related instant by instant, movement by movement, and sound by sound, rhythmically, from beginning to end. And the nature of this relating is instant-by-instant poetic dialogue between the two.

To be true to my dance materials, to find their uniqueness and essence, and to not be misled by musical material, I create the dance in silence. It is structurally and rhythmically quite complete and could be performed in this way. By doing this, I cannot copy and depend upon musical structure. I am not pulled by the cerebral, nonphysical, ethereal, nonrhythmic, and mechanical or emotionally blurring qualities of existing contemporary music, away from my explorations in pure and vivid body poetry.

Then, the composer faces the extraordinary challenge of taking this dance structure and creating a musical structure that relates to it perfectly, but also is an independent piece of music that could equally be performed alone. Contrary to the popular belief, such a piece of music is clearly more difficult and challenging to write than a piece of music for a concert hall.

With such a collaboration of music and dance, each of which could stand alone, you have a double theatrical richness. In my work with composer Lucia Dlugoszewski, she has not only taken my complete dance structures and created music that related to them, but she has also created scores that could stand alone as meaningful musical structures for the concert hall. Her method related these scores to the movements of my dances instant-by-instant, sound-by-sound, from beginning to end. The non-listening callousness of much contemporary and avant-garde dance performance is in this way impossible. Here is a new rhythmic exploration that equally escapes the mechanical tagging along and the mechanistic destroying of all rhythmic consciousness in chance and indeterminate collaborations. Her music challenges the rhythmic vitality of the dancer.

But her most unique contribution was the actual nature of this relating which was constantly in the form of a poetic comment, an instant-by-instant poetic dialogue with the movement. As she has collaborated with me, I feel the musical stature of these works becomes every bit as significant as a new kind of contemporary opera. The Dlugoszewski music for my dance has been praised not only for its poetry, but also for its theatricality.

Theatre is merely the underlining of living physicality. Dlugoszewski has met the challenge of this physicality, of rhythmic invention, of sensitivity and beauty of sound as no other composer, and it is my good fortune to have such a collaborator.

Looking to the Future

Dance needs music, but it has been commonly held that music does not need dance. In an effort for freedom, now a certain kind of dance has decided not to need music, and from my point of view, this makes them both damned. When music has lost so much of its physical vitality that concert halls are empty, we are reaching the era where not only does dance need music, but music needs dance.

It may very well be that challenging a composer with a dance structure that is involved with new attitudes of body experience on the levels of physicality, rhythm, play, and effortlessness or sensitivity can lead music into new, highly original paths away from the exaggerated cerebral, the mechanically callous, the neurotically emotional corners into which contemporary music has trapped itself. Perhaps the greatest new music of the future, the most original and most meaningful, will come from a true, new music for the dance.

FIFTY

Finding Your Own Voice

Bessie Schönberg

*B*ESSIE SCHÖNBERG *(1906–97) discovered modern dance through her study with Martha Hill in Oregon. Going East, she studied and performed with Martha Graham (from 1921 until 1931) until she sustained a knee injury. Undaunted, she went on to teach at Bennington College and then at Sarah Lawrence College (from 1938 to 1975).[1] Through her coaching of choreographers and association at the Dance Theater Workshop in Manhattan and elsewhere, she made such a mark as mentor that an award called the "Bessie" was established in her honor. In this excerpt from an interview, Bessie Schönberg reflects upon the effect that new styles of music had upon modern dancers, in contrast to the place of music in relation to ballet traditions.*

***

One difference, I think, between the training of modern dance students and those in ballet is that even from their early years in the modern dance classroom, the awareness of music has had such an important *creative* place. In many cases, the students had a deep and lasting musical experience with the composer-musicians. There was nothing "comforting" about it! On the contrary, it was something to make you alert, make you learn about music-making; a very active thing.

What I think about music in ballet training, is that it tends to be deliberately rather passive. It goes *with*, it underlies, or it supports. But in my experience of teaching mainly modern dance, the musicians at times would needle the alertness and the abilities of the students. So it was a very lively, altogether creative experience.

It starts at the beginning of learning how to dance. Modern dance has been known for this. With the first class, you are urged to "find something of your own voice," to improvise in solving very simple problem exercises set for the class. This is also why modern dance has enormous diversity—and why it has become a medium that is sometimes hard to understand. Such difficulty arises precisely because there *is* so much individuality.

FIFTY ONE

Music and Dancing

Paul Draper

*A*S STRESSED IN *the preceding remarks of Bessie Schönberg, increasingly, concert art dancers branched out and developed very individualistic styles. Almost unique in his time was Paul Draper (1909–96), who followed the example of Isadora Duncan in using classical music—except that he danced with his tap shoes on and incorporated physical techniques drawn not only from tap traditions but also from ballet and modern dance.*[1]

Tap dancing was a staple of twentieth-century entertainment in both vaudeville and movie musicals, notably in the performances by Fred Astaire, Bill Robinson, the Nicholas brothers, Jimmy Slyde, and others. But Paul Draper presented his tapping as a concert art, and for musical accompaniment he drew upon classical repertoire, jazz, and specially composed scores. In the 1930s and 1940s he was internationally known. In New York he could be seen performing in Radio City Music Hall and Carnegie Hall alike, and his concerts were given consistent praise in the pages of Dance Observer. *He also toured with varied accompaniment, including virtuoso harmonica playing of Larry Adler and the pianistic skills of John Colman (an accompanist for Ballet Jooss and for Balanchine). Further extending his ties to classical dance, Draper was married to New York City Ballet soloist Heidi Vosseler.*

In this speech directed toward dance students, Draper gives advice about things to listen for in both classical music and jazz, offering inspiration for dancers who wear all kinds of shoes, as well as for those who perform barefoot.

***

Thousands of hours are spent acquiring the physical skills necessary to dance, but very few dancers spend even a dozen hours learning about music. An understanding of music is not obtained by osmosis, nor by following the beat of a stick. It is a delicate, difficult and lovely subject, and must be wooed with as much ardor as you would devote to turnout and extensions.

What is it that I would have you understand about music that you don't know already? Don't you have music with your classes? Aren't you exposed to music on radio and TV? Isn't that enough?

What I would have you understand about music is how it is used as one of man's most important ways of describing his life on earth and his place amongst the stars. Whether the music is a primitive cry of exaltation, or the last movement of the Beethoven Ninth Symphony, the aim is similar. It is to define and clarify a reaction to an experience. This aim is shared by all artists, even dancers. But dancers, unlike other creative workers, must make use of the work of other artists in order to complete their own. Therefore they must know not only that they share the aims of another group, but they must also know something of the tools and techniques that this other group of artists uses.

Music is composed in certain exact tonal and rhythmic relationships that are quite formally arranged and learnable. I do not mean that you must become a composer any more than a dance composer has to become a dancer. I mean that you can familiarize yourself with some of the basic rules by which melody and rhythm are combined to produce a sound we call music. The best way to learn this is by listening to music outside the classroom. Just sit and listen to music. If you hate music, either stop dancing or begin with a Mozart piano concerto—say

FIGURE 51.1 Saul Steinberg, drawing of Paul Draper, 1942. Ink on paper. © The Saul Steinberg Foundation/Artists Rights Society (ARS), New York. Reproduced by permission.

the "Coronation" Concerto in D major (K. 537) or the C major (K. 467). I think even the most avid music hater might come to like music from listening to either of these—especially the magical entrance of the piano in the C major. Then perhaps the Beethoven Fourth Piano Concerto. Take note of the second movement particularly. Might not you be the piano? Or the orchestra? This wonder-filled, strong and gentle dialogue between soloist and orchestra is one of the most evocative passages in music. Listen to the rhythms and meter in all the movements of these three works. Are they in, $\frac{3}{4}$, $\frac{4}{4}$, $\frac{6}{8}$, $\frac{2}{4}$, $\frac{3}{8}$? Figure out for yourself, and you will soon hear patterns developing that you didn't hear at first. I haven't selected these three works arbitrarily, or because I happen to like them myself. They are lovely works by any standard, and they are not difficult to listen to. They lead, however, to an inexhaustible fund of music which only you can discover by yourself. The object is to understand the ways and means in which the magic of good music makes itself real. This cannot be done in a classroom, where recordings are used and set to any tempo needed by the particular step or exercise you are doing. Music written to be played fast will have none of its qualities if played slowly, and vice-versa.

An appreciation of music for itself, and relation to dancing, can be acquired only by a considerable amount of conscious effort. When you listen to music with an effort to understand and realize its intent and content, you will also begin to learn a sense of "rhythmic balance," a most important function of dancing. You will learn how phrases in music invariably balance each other. There is always a definite and predictable stopping place for a phrase related to the phrase that preceded it.

You cannot escape finding out about this if you listen with care. The same principle holds true in all jazz and should help you to follow and understand the variations of any good jazz group, both in melody and rhythm.

I think you will find that time spent in examining music by conscious listening will prove most valuable to you as a dancer, and as a person.[2]

FIFTY TWO

Dancers Are Musicians Are Dancers

José Limón

M EXICAN-BORN CHOREOGRAPHER *José Limón (1909–72) began his career as a dancer with the Humphrey-Weidman Company (from 1936 to 1946) and later established his own company, initially with Humphrey as artistic director. His landmark choreography includes* The Moor's Pavane *(1949, to music by Purcell), as well as* The Traitor *(music by Gunther Schuller),* There is a Time *(music by Norman Dello Joio), and* The Exiles *(set to music by Arnold Schoenberg). Works from his repertoire are still performed by the Limón Dance Company, which continues under Carla Maxwell (artistic director since 1978).[1]*

Gifted with strong physical features and an arresting stage presence, Limón was equally eloquent in words, as evidenced here in his advice to young dance and music students at the Juilliard School, where the artist was on the faculty. While generalizing about various historical relationships between dance movement and music, he also touches upon his affinity for Baroque masterworks; looks back to specific dance works that he either performed or witnessed; and considers the challenges of working with conductors for theatrical dance. Finally, Limón's exhortation to his twentieth-century students can inspire young artists of today as well, whether they choose to draw from traditions of the past or explore innovative ways of combining new music with new dance.

***

I have always maintained that musicians are dancers, and that dancers can be good dancers only when they are also good musicians. This does not mean that a composer need perform, literally and physically, all the arduous vocabulary of the dancer, nor that the dancer need be proficient with a violin, kettledrum or harp. No.

The dance has been called the matrix of the arts. Early in our adventure as humans on this planet, we had that supremely instinctual urge and capacity to dance. From this was born percussion and song and music and ritual; painting and sculpture; and from these, architecture and poetry. Let me today only point to that supremely choreographic composer, that incomparable dancer of the spirit, J. S. Bach. He dances not only in his French suites and English suites and partitas and sonatas for the various instruments, with their chaconnes, minuets, courantes, sarabandes, allemandes, gigues and other dance forms, but he could not and did not exclude the dance from the cantatas and oratorios. Dance, as you know, is of all kinds and categories. There is a dance for every single human experience. Bach contains it all in his music, whether secular or religious. He was irrepressively a dancer. Or perhaps we can say that, being a great musician and composer, he could not refrain from the dance.

Dancers, fully aware that the art of music has far outdistanced the dance in dimension, repute and achievement, have attempted to "free" the dance from its subservience to music. It is true that the dance has had its ups and downs, and there is evidence that when the dance was at a low ebb, it made use of inferior music. Whether a degraded dance engendered bad music or whether inconsequential music was the cause of a decadence in the dance, I do not know. The truth is that they have co-existed as accomplices, to the dismay and horror of dancers concerned with the status of their art. The dream of these artists, in their search for a "liberation," was a dance without music. The dance was to be made self-sufficient, creating its own music and its own rhythms.

Doris Humphrey and Martha Graham, in the early days of the American dance, when they were pregnant with an indigenous art, conceived it as gloriously free of the dead hand of an effete and decayed past. Doris Humphrey created dances almost symphonic in dimension, entirely without musical accompaniment. In rejecting the metronomic tempi of the musicians, she searched for the rhythms and phrases inherent in the human entity with its breathing, its muscular dynamics, and emotive range. She accomplished some revolutionary works, the repercussions of which are with us to this day. I was privileged, as a young member of her company, to perform in some of these and observe how her audacity opened new horizons to the human gesture. One day she said to me, "I have learned much in the search for a dance that can stand by itself. I know that the dance can never produce works to equal the symphonies, sonatas and oratorios of the musicians until it can learn to do so. I have succeeded in part; I have failed in part. I have learned that dance and music belong together. But they must meet as equals, not one subservient to the other. They must complement each other."

This she proceeded to prove in a long succession of works of dazzling choreographic mastery and dramatic power. She was another great musician-dancer.

Relations between the musician and the dancer have always been interesting. There has never been a dull moment. The confrontation between these two has not always been face to face. Often a living dancer performs to a score by a defunct composer.

Isadora Duncan, the audacious phenomenon who electrified and scandalized the first decades of this century, would dance, solo, to entire symphonies of Tchaikovsky and Schubert. She was the center of much controversy. There were those who reviled her as a shameless amateur and dilettante. To others, she was a miracle incarnate. In any case, her method of dealing with music was to "interpret" it. There was apparently a good deal of the improvisatory. A musical work was never "interpreted" the same way twice. She had the power to sustain a performance which left her audiences in a state verging on a pandemonium of adoration.

We have seen Martha Graham, one of the towering artists of the dance, use the music of her contemporaries to create fabulous theater. Her fecund creativity has taken movement and gesture, music, decor, lighting and costuming to a magical synthesis. The visual is always so completely arresting that it is only on subsequent seeings that one becomes aware of the music, and the superb use that is made of it.

And here is a curious thing about the relationship between dancer and musician. It has been said often that on first viewing a dance, if you are fully aware of the musical accompaniment, the dance has failed to interest and absorb you as it should. It bored you. It was too long, too tedious, too repetitious, badly composed or badly danced. You took refuge in attending to the music. All dancers and choreographers have had this bitter truth to contend with. Music for dance is successful and effective only when it has been so skillfully utilized that you are not aware of it as a separate component or ingredient. It has blended so perfectly that you are not aware where the dance ceases to be and the music begins.

Not all music can be danced to. Not that dancers haven't tried, at various times, to tread where angels have feared to go. As caustic critics of the predilections and weaknesses of dancers and choreographers have pointed out, nothing is sacred. There was much vituperation when Doris Humphrey had the temerity to compose a dance to the majestic *Passacaglia and Fugue* of Bach. In this case, the dance did not do an injustice to the music, but on its own terms it was equally majestic. Isadora Duncan, in her memoirs, repeatedly made allusion to her dream of making a dance to the Ninth Symphony of Beethoven. This desire seemed to haunt and obsess her. She died with this goal unattained. It would have been a most interesting thing for the world to have seen the result of her attempt.

Leonide Massine made choreographic settings to the Tchaikovsky Fifth Symphony, the Brahms Fourth, the Beethoven Seventh and the *Symphonie Fantastique* of Berlioz for the Ballets Russes de Monte Carlo. Despite the inevitably arresting and exciting results, grave doubts were voiced that he should have done so. Unlike the music of Bach, these works in the romantic idiom seem to leave no room, or at least not much room, for the dancer.

Possibly the most felicitous choices, in recent years of extant music, have been made by our distinguished colleague at Juilliard, Antony Tudor, in using superbly Schoenberg's *Verklärte Nacht* for his masterpiece *Pillar of Fire* and Chausson's *Poème* for his exquisite *Lilac Garden*.

One of the delights of the contemporary ballet repertory is the wit and wistful whimsicality of Agnes de Mille. Her use of the native folk dance and its music is always a refreshing contrast to the cool classicism or impassioned romanticism of her colleagues. Her works have a simplicity and ingenuousness which derive from her sources. In *Rodeo*, with the help of a fine score by Aaron Copland, she brought to brilliant synthesis the elements of the American folk dance. Miss de Mille is a wit of the first order. When asked by an interviewer what was her approach to music, she answered, "My approach to music is with scissors and paste."

Musicians who play or conduct for dancers do so at their own peril. There is that perennial and seemingly irreconcilable controversy over what constitutes the right tempo. As you can imagine, what is right for one person is not for another. What is right in the morning can become just the opposite by late afternoon or evening. A tempo agreed upon at a studio rehearsal can go completely to hell because of nerves on an opening night. Then there is the cleavage in the comprehension of tempo by a human being who understands it from, say a piano bench, or from the conductor's podium, and one who feels it in the more extended, more spatial way of the dancer.

One of the most inspired audacities of the human species is the temerity to take eternity, which is forever, yesterday, and forever, tomorrow, and the ever elusive instant which is the present—and force it into a beat, a rhythm, a phrase. All manner of ingenuities have gone into chronometric devices. We agree about seconds, minutes, hours, days, weeks, months, years, centuries, millennia and eons. But there is still that baffling and subtle human unpredictability which sets us apart from machines.

I have known conferences between dancers and conductors where the arbiter was a metronome and/or a stop watch. Agreements have been made. Notations on scores carefully written: such and such a number equals such and such a note. Come the performance and all this is as if nothing had been arbitrated, agreed, notated, and rehearsed to the point of mutual exhaustion. A very sweaty confrontation behind the scenes is as follows:

"What in God's name happened to the tempo?" demands the frustrated dancer.

"What was wrong? I thought I gave it to you precisely as you wanted it," replies the conductor.

"Well, it was twice too fast," (or too slow, as the case may be).

Musicians sometimes claim that the dancer hasn't the slightest idea of what it is he wants. On a certain performance, if he's feeling fine and can sustain jumps much higher, he naturally wants a slower tempo. If he's low in energy, on the other hand, he wants the tempo just a tiny bit faster.

But how is the poor musician to know all this? Can he read minds? Well, no, but dancers say he can do much better: he can read bodies, and their movements. Which means that he must feel and identify with the sheer mechanics and athleticism of the dancer's craft. He must get to know, just as though he himself were doing it, the pulse, the duration, of a given moment. On the other hand, a good dancer must have the capacity to give with minor and inconsequential deviation from an accustomed or desired beat.

The best thing actually is to have someone play and conduct for you who has worked with you for years, for decades, and who knows you very well, and who is alert to your artistic virtues and defects, and who knows the dance completely. Such a person is my colleague Simon Sadoff, who has gone with me to little out-of-the-way places and played the piano accompaniment, and to Europe, Latin America and the Orient, to conduct the great symphony orchestras for our dances. He can play, brilliantly, the Copland *Piano Sonata* for Doris Humphrey's *Day on Earth*. He can keep the dance, music, and words perfectly timed and balanced in Norman Lloyd's *Lament for Ignacio Sanchez Mejías*. He can conduct the chorus and music in the *Missa Brevis* of Kodály. Because you see, he is not only a brilliant musician and fine conductor, but he has become, over the years, also a dancer.

And so, dancer-musicians and musician-dancers, here you are on the threshold of the next half-century which belongs to you. What music, what dances you will bring into the world! How privileged you are to be artists! Let me salute the puissance of your youth. You are young now, and now is forever. Youth is not wasted on the young: it comes at precisely the right moment. It is the only one you will ever have. It is your magic hour, verdant as spring, golden as sunrise. I adjure you to the courage and probity of the artist, to a terrible daring, to fortitude in the face of the challenge of nihilism and lunatic horror. Some of you here will work with tradition. Others will find new roads. I hope the first will revere and conserve, but not embalm, the treasure of the past. The others, I hope, will not spit in the face of tradition. Be truly a revolutionary, not a mere mutineer or rebel. Remember that art is redemptive, that your life will be half debacle, half apotheosis. You will be wounded. Wear your scars as the most exalted of decorations!

Afterword

Creativity in One's Own Time

Postmodern Dance and Contemporary Music

José Limón was to live only a few more years after delivering his 1967 exhortation to students at the Juilliard School. Yet in many ways, by then the pioneering era of modern dance in which he had played such a great part was already past. Martha Hill, in a fierce battle to keep the Juilliard School's dance division alive, had defended the introduction of classical ballet studies into the curriculum. As time went on, there were increasing stylistic "crossovers" in the performances of ballet and contemporary dance companies. Traditions of mainstream concert dance began to be challenged in other ways by both serious innovators and humorous thrusts, and the parameters of what was considered performance art were expanded. The next fifty years were to be markedly different from the first half century of modern dance in America, yet there were also common denominators between the generations of artists.

With the United States mired in an increasingly unpopular war in Vietnam, some dancers saw their work in the context of political activism (which calls to mind earlier choreographic social comment by members of the New Dance Group, Helen Tamiris, Charles Weidman, Pearl Primus, and Anna Sokolow, for example). In a departure from convention, the newer generations broke out of the confines of proscenium arch stages and presented performances outdoors and in diverse urban locations. Departing further from theatrical traditions, instead of costumes or the familiar tunics and long-skirted dancewear of the earlier moderns, everyday styles of attire were assumed by dancers. Previously barefooted performers put their shoes back on: street shoes, sandals, sneakers, high heels, boots—even pointe shoes. Sometimes there was less of a distinction between "performers" and "audiences," and untrained dancers were enlisted on occasion to participate in public "happenings."[1] With inventions in both visual and aural technology, there were increasing experiments with multimedia productions. Recordings, collages of taped sounds, and electronic music became more widely used.

In addition to making use of technological changes in sound production and sound systems, new generations of dancers were also questioning and redefining the role of music in relation to movement, once again sometimes rejecting it entirely as a collaborative art. For some, music was just another negative thing that could be added to Yvonne Rainer's often-quoted manifesto:

> No to spectacle no to virtuosity no to transformations and magic and make-believe no to the glamour and transcendency of the star image no to the heroic no to the anti-heroic no to trash imagery no to involvement of performer or spectator no to style no to camp no to seduction of spectator by the wiles of the performer no to eccentricity no to moving or being moved.[2]

In a positive view, the focus was on what the body in motion could do by itself, without music or props or theatrical lighting. However, the place of music within concert dance was not lost forever, but rather was expanded in some ways and changed in others, always with the continuing purpose of adding to and enhancing whatever the dancers were trying to achieve.

The informal 1962 showings at the Judson Memorial Church in New York's Greenwich Village have been cited by some writers as the beginning of what was subsequently dubbed "postmodern dance." The Judson experiments originated with workshops led by a musician from the Cunningham studios, Oklahoma-born Robert Ellis Dunn (1928–96).[3] But throughout the 1960s, other explorations were also going on at venues both uptown and downtown in New York and elsewhere around the country. In Manhattan (still mecca for the dance world), Dance Theater Workshop (started in 1965) became exceptional in its nurturing of new choreographers.[4] The New School, with a dance department headed by Laura Foreman from 1969 to 1990, had an ongoing series called Choreoconcerts and Critiques that provided exposure for new works. There were also concerts by Dance Uptown (directed by Janet Soares, working out of Barnard College, from 1967 to 1990) and at the West Side YWCA's Clark Center for the Performing Arts, to give just a few examples. In avant-garde music, there were parallel experimentations, notably involving "crossovers" between jazz and classical styles, the use of electronic equipment, and the injection of theatrical activity.

Previously, ballroom steps, patterns of folk and country styles, or the challenges of the latest popular dance craze would have been viewed as a normal dance outlet for most people; "creative" styles and any staged public performance would have been regarded as something limited to a relatively small number of very agile trained and talented dancers. In the postmodern and contemporary years, however, professional dancers sought ways to introduce their art into more aspects of life. Creative dance was increasingly seen as something that many more people—even those in wheelchairs—could experience.[5] Anna Halprin (working in California) was notable in branching off to combine dance with holistic health concerns.[6]

Another artist who has expanded the community of people in dance is Liz Lerman (b. 1947 in Los Angeles).[7] In Washington, D.C., in 1976 she founded the Liz Lerman Dance Exchange, which now describes itself as "a professional company for dance artists that creates, performs, teaches, and engages people in making art." Its definition of "dance" is as a multidisciplinary art form encompassing not only movement but also words and imagery as well as music.

Other organizations such as the National Dance Institute (founded by ballet dancer Jacques d'Amboise), Lincoln Center Institute, the American Orff-Schulwerk Association, and daCi (Dance and the Child International) became active advocates for arts-in-education programs, not only to encourage appreciation of professional performances and the nurturing of future audiences but also to provide more children and teens with the life-enhancing experience of participating directly in dance, music, and the other arts.[8]

Returning the focus to highly trained dancers, however, a new emphasis on movement *without* music would find a transformation in the genre of contact improvisation, and upon sometimes extreme development of a sportslike athleticism and an impression of ever-increasing speed plus virtuosic physical technique. Some of the styles developed toward the end of the century seemed to require a projection of glazed-looking faces devoid of emotion, accompanied by recordings of electronic sounds that complemented the impassive impression in the dance: quite a contrast to the earlier modern dance that had been so closely related to the expressivity of varied music, performed live. Other dancers, such as the gymnastically inventive troupe Pilobolus, injected humor into their group choreographies, using recorded music in a light vein as a backdrop to enhance the theatricality of their visually unusual concoctions.

Along with waves of change in postmodern dance and avant-garde music, some artists made it possible for contemporary audiences to become acquainted with concert dance styles from the earlier years of modern dance. Annabelle Gamson gave memorable performances evoking the art of Isadora Duncan. Under the direction of Carla Maxwell, the Limón Dance Company continued to present what had come to be considered classics of modern dance. And under the direction of Judith Jamison, the Alvin Ailey American Dance Theater (founded in 1958) continued after Ailey's death in 1989, keeping the heritage of older repertoire such as *Revelations* alive for new audiences to see.

Schools of dance increasingly offered classes that drew on both the dance traditions and unwritten musical styles of the African diaspora, notably in the technique developed by Katherine Dunham.[9] Since 1968 Chuck Davis has encouraged wider activity in African-based styles of ensemble drumming, including with his African American Dance Ensemble based in Durham and the annual "Dance Africa" events over Memorial Day weekends at the Brooklyn Academy of Music.[10]

On concert stages across the country, increasingly descriptions of both dance and its music came to include such words as "fusion," "blending," "crossover." As the 1960s turned into the 1970s and 1980s, there was a proliferation of small dance troupes, injecting a youthful freshness and proud views of diverse heritages, and also enlisting dancers who had developed their techniques to levels and speeds not practiced in the early days of modern dance. Among these were Urban Bush Women founded by Jawole Willa Jo Zollar; choreographer Ronald K. Brown's company Evidence; and the Forces of Nature, headed by Abdel R. Salaam. And growing out of extensive collaborations with dancers, musicians such as singer-percussionist Philip Hamilton could be cited among those who (as Henry Cowell had urged) learned to "draw from the whole world of music," and (as Norman Cazden had urged earlier generations) began to explore innovative combinations of vocal techniques.[11]

The era of the earlier American dance pioneers and their collaborators was indeed passing. Honored in memory, Doris Humphrey had died in 1958; Louis Horst, in 1964; Ruth St. Denis, in 1968; Ted Shawn, in 1972; Charles Weidman, in 1975; Alwin Nikolais and Agnes de Mille, both in 1993; and Pearl Primus, in 1994. A few of the earlier originals continued with their companies for many years, notably Martha Graham and Erick Hawkins well toward the end of the century. Graham died in 1991, Hawkins in 1994. Katherine Dunham passed away in 2006. And just before his death in 2009, Merce Cunningham had been planning a two-year tour for his company, to be followed by its disbanding. Among collaborating musicians, Otto Luening (who had been at Bennington "when it all started") lived from 1900 until 1996; Aaron Copland, who also was born in 1900, died in 1990. And among dance educators, Martha Hill lived until 1995, and Bessie Schönberg until 1997.

New artists claimed the spotlight, continuing some procedures and aesthetic ideas of their predecessors in regard to the use of music but also expanding the musical styles upon which they drew to enhance their works. The sounds heard during contemporary dance performances today still include classical concert works of the past plus scores composed for specific choreography. But the music is just as likely to include popular songs, medieval church chants, chamber music, rock bands, live percussionists drawing from African and Caribbean traditions, or "world" music recorded by musicians performing in other styles from around the globe. It now seems almost quaint that Norman Cazden would have had to defend Doris Humphrey's dancing to Bach.

Considering the role of classical music generally in the development of modern dance, it is also pertinent to point out that in the early days of LP recordings, most of the larger vinyl discs were devoted to classical music, with only a small portion of them representing new works by contemporary American composers. Toward the end of the twentieth century, large chain stores—with a nod toward the commercial convenience of stylistic labels—would typically have a small number of CD bins for classical music (both contemporary and from the past, arranged alphabetically by composer); enormous numbers of bins for rock music (alphabetized by the names of the *performers*); and smaller sections for the genres of rhythm and blues, jazz, folk, rap, country and western; plus large sections devoted to "world music" (arranged by country).

Nowadays, with the increased accessibility of changing recording technology, thousands of contemporary composers and performing musicians are apt to bypass large labels and instead issue their own

CDs and market them online as well as in person at their live concerts, and specialists in music for dance also offer their music for sale via internet computer downloads.[12]

In regard to the multiplicity of current styles and the question of "crossover genres," music critic Anthony Tommasini of *The New York Times* has aptly pointed out:

> Increasingly in recent years classical music, even more than pop, has de-emphasized stylistic categories of composition. This shift has been driven by a new generation of composers who grew up with rock, are disdainful of contemporary music dogma and draw from any system and style that suits their compositional ends.[13]

Yet despite all the wealth of musical styles available, a distressed observation heard not infrequently is that young dancers in our time generally lack familiarity with musical styles outside those of popular rock bands. Whole generations of dance students seem to have missed out on the kinds of broad aesthetic and musical explorations advocated, for example, by Louis Horst and Lester Horton. Furthermore, because of extensive cuts in school budgets around the United States, arts programs have often been the first thing to go, so that students commonly lack basic knowledge about how music is constructed, even though they may have been dancing to its sounds for years in their studio classes.

Limited understanding of basic musical building blocks—plus a lack of broad listening experience—can become a particular concern when students enter into choreographic projects or opt to become teachers themselves. It can also hamper aspiring dancers who are facing the competitive current scene, with its demands for a high level of physical technique, but also involving a global outlook, extensive touring, and the expectation that dancers will be versatile enough to perform in diverse styles of choreography, involving a wide range of musical genres. As observed in 2006 by Harvard University's dance director Elizabeth Weil Berman:

> I am finding a very uneducated group of people musically, and I think that's really hurting our field. We keep turning out these students, and they get jobs and they're teaching the next generation. It's all a pop-culture thing. Nothing wrong with pop culture, but I'd like to see more informed musical choices.[14]

Among contemporary American choreographers who *are* particularly noted for their skill in using diverse styles of music effectively are Twyla Tharp and Mark Morris. Garth Fagan is another choreographer of concert dance who can be singled out for his musicality and wide-ranging choices in musical styles. Meredith Monk (with training in both dance and music) has perhaps been unique in her use of wordless vocalization to effectively convey deep emotion and drama, in such works as *Atlas*, *Quarry*, and *Education of a Girl Child*. And among a younger generation, Robert Battle stands out for his imagination in relating movement to various musical styles, including works commissioned for his own company, Battleworks. It will be interesting to follow what happens as he takes up the leadership of the Alvin Ailey American Dance Theater.[15]

Spanning the generations is Paul Taylor. Seen in his youth as a maverick by some critics (including Louis Horst, who left an infamous blank column in *Dance Observer* to summarize his snubbing reaction to one of Taylor's more experimental concerts), he is now considered one of our leading choreographers, known internationally because of the tours undertaken by his main company as well as by Taylor II. Thinking about the wide musical possibilities open to all contemporary choreographers, Taylor summed up his basic attitude in 1985 (in a personal interview with the author), suggesting:

> I think *anything* can be good for dance. There's no such thing as sound or silence that can't be used for dance! It depends on *how* it's used, how suitable it is, how it's made to sound to the audience (by its relationship to the dance). Whether it's acceptable or not, and whether it's successful, depends on this. There are no rules; there are no laws. The individual choreographer makes his laws; he's selecting what *he* feels would be right. He's wrong lots of times, but nevertheless, he's not to be told that he "can't use that because it's not dance music." Anything is fair game. The sky is the limit. The possibilities that are open to us are infinite, and we choose which ones are suitable—to *us*.[16]

Surely Isadora Duncan's spirit would have been smiling with vindication to hear Taylor's remarks, in such contrast to some of the vitriolic reviews that had greeted her own dancing to Beethoven's Seventh Symphony fully a century ago. She would probably also be surprised by the changes brought about by electronic music.

In the twenty-first century, some people call what is heard during dance performances not "music" but "sound-art," an appropriate term in view of recent technological innovations. One prickly example can be offered, of Alan Terriciano, a collaborating composer who was then also dean of dance at the University of California in Irvine. He made local nightly television news in 2009 with his delicate music elicited by plucking various cactus plants, amplified electronically.

Technology has certainly expanded the kinds of sounds that are available to collaborating composers and choreographers. In studios at colleges and universities around the country, although musicians for dance may still accompany classes on the piano or with drums, they are also apt to use electronic synthesizers, samplers, and even their laptop computers to generate "loops" against which they can vocalize or improvise on various acoustic instruments.

Similarly, when collaborating with choreographers, composers nowadays can generate a menu of electronic samples—literally overnight—and present them on a CD as possible choices for alternate paths that might be followed for the yet-to-be-created soundscore (which may or may not be eventually written on paper).[17] This procedure allows the choreographer to have some immediate input as to the general flavor and style of the composer's music and to make some choices, even about specific aspects such as basic rhythmic patterns that might be stressed. All this is quite a contrast to the kind of long-drawn-out process described by Aaron Copland in his letters concerning the creation of his score for Martha Graham.

Another noteworthy change in our own time is the fact that the enormous expansion in the numbers of trained musicians has made it more difficult for aspiring composers to make their mark. As noted in 1995 by John Warthen Struble in his *History of American Classical Music*:

> Today, with literally thousands of American composers striving in almost complete public oblivion, our situation is not unlike someone trying to make a speech in a room filled with several hundred people, each of whom is also trying to deliver his or her own oration. And the room was originally built to accommodate only a few dozen.[18]

A similar observation could be made in regard to the relative number of choreographers working now in comparison to the early days of modern dance. However, a positive development in the latter half of the twentieth century was the extensive building of large performing arts centers across the United States, often connected with academic institutions. These have provided opportunities for thousands of creative student and faculty choreographers and composers to present their works in fully professional venues. Additionally, such arts centers have enabled larger audiences across the country to enjoy performances by leading regional, national, and international companies—with both recorded and live music.

Life has become more organized, for both audiences and artists. But of considerable assistance on the regional level as well as for nationally touring dance companies was the establishment of the National Endowment for the Arts in 1965.[19] Other funders such as Meet The Composer have made particular efforts to encourage new collaboration between composers and choreographers.[20] In 1990 the International Guild of Musicians in Dance was founded by William Moulton, providing a professional forum for the exchange of information about the specialist art of collaboration with dancers; sponsoring workshops for nurturing skills; presenting public performances of dance works with live music; and in general serving as an advocate for new collaborations between musicians and dancers in our own time.[21]

Thinking about the context of an artist's efforts, Doris Humphrey stated:

> I believe that the dancer belongs to his time and place and that he can only express that which passes through or close to his experience. The one indispensable quality in a work of art is a consistent point of view related to the times.[22]

However, as José Limón suggested to both music and dance students nearly half a century ago, artists *do* make choices about what they want to draw from traditions, even while they are putting their own creativity to work. Or, as the composer Lou Harrison put it succinctly to students:

> *Cherish, Conserve, Consider, Create.*[23]

In this process of learning, reflection, and action, some of the questions about collaboration posed by the authors in this collection continue to resonate with artists and students of today.[24] For though life is more complex and the arts more competitive than they were a century ago, musicians and choreographers still go into bare studios with dancers and ask themselves:

> *What kind of music would be good for our new dance?*
> *And how shall we make it?*

Appendix: Checklist of Composers

Here, for further explorations, is a selected list of composers of music used for earlier modern dance.

George Antheil
Esther Williamson Ballou
Samuel Barber
Robert Russell Bennett
Leonard Bernstein
Paul Bowles
Henry Brant
Earle Brown
Charles Wakefield Cadman
John Cage
John Alden Carpenter
Carlos Chávez
Henry Leland Clarke
John Colman
Aaron Copland
Henry Cowell
Paul Creston
Norma Reynolds Dalby
Norman Dello Joio
Nathaniel Dett
David Diamond
Lucia Dlugoszewski
Halim El-Dabh
Edward Kennedy "Duke" Ellington
Lehman Engel

Charles Farwell
Morton Feldman
Vivian Fine
Ross Lee Finney
George Gershwin
Pia Gilbert
Ralph Gilbert
Peggy Glanville-Hicks
Morton Gould
Ray Green
Charles Tomlinson Griffes
Ferde Grofé
Homer Grunn
Roy Harris
Lou Harrison
Victor Herbert
Paul Hindemith
Louis Horst
Alan Hovhaness
Karel Husa
Charles Ives
Hazel Johnson
Hunter Johnson
Harrison Kerr
Kenneth Klauss

Ernst Krenek

Meyer Kupferman

Ezra Laderman

Eastwood Lane

Eugene Lester

Norman Lloyd

Otto Luening

Robert McBride

John Herbert McDowell

Colin McPhee

Jess Meeker

Gian Carlo Menotti

Darius Milhaud

Freda Miller

Jerome Moross

Nicolas Nabokov

Alwin Nikolais

Paul Nordoff

Alex North

Lionel Nowak

Carl Orff

Harry Partch

Genevieve Pitot

Harvey Pollins

Silvestre Revueltas

Wallingford Riegger

Trude Rittmann

Dane Rudhyar

Erik Satie

Arnold Schoenberg

Gunther Schuller

William Schuman

Cyril Scott

Bernardo Segall

Elie Siegmeister

Robert Starer

William Grant Still

Igor Stravinsky

Carlos Surinach

Alexander Tcherepnin

Virgil Thomson

Gregory Tucker

David Tudor

Edgard Varèse

Clifford Vaughan

Betty Walberg

Christian Wolff

Notes

Abbreviations

LofC   Library of Congress, located in Washington, D.C.

NYPL   New York Public Library for the Performing Arts (including both
            the research collections of the Music Division and the Jerome
            Robbins Dance Division), located at Lincoln Center in New York
            City.

Teck (1989) Katherine Teck, *Music for the Dance: Reflections on a Collaborative
            Art* (Westport, Conn.: Greenwood Press, 1989)

Teck (1990) Katherine Teck, *Movement to Music: Musicians in the Dance Studio*
            (Westport, Conn.: Greenwood Press, 1990).

Teck (1994) Katherine Teck, *Ear Training for the Body: A Dancer's Guide to
            Music* (Pennington, N.J.: Princeton Book Company, 1994).

Preface

1. For a historical study of dance criticism, see Lynne Conner, *Spreading the Gospel
   of the Modern Dance: Newspaper Dance Criticism in the United States, 1850–1934*
   (Pittsburgh: University of Pittsburgh Press, 1997).

Introduction

Epigraph, from Martha Graham, *Blood Memory* (New York: Doubleday, 1991), 120.

1. For detailed historical background, see Kate Van Winkle Keller, *Dance and Its
   Music in America, 1528–1789* (Hillsdale, N.Y.: Pendragon Press, 2007). For this
   author's other books and collected music, go to www.colonial music.org.
   Starting in 1651, John Playford in England published collections of dance tunes,
   which continue to be used also in America for country dances. A modern
   collection is Kate Van Winkle Keller and Genevieve Shimer, *The Playford Ball:
   103 Early Country Dances 1651–1820 as Interpreted by Cecil Sharp and His*

Followers, Studies in Dance History, (Pennington, N.J.: Society of Dance History Scholars, 1990). For information on the Society of Dance History Scholars, go to www.sdhs.org.

The Music of Williamsburg: The Sounds of Eighteenth-Century Virginia (1960) is a DVD that offers a cross section of colonial life, with theatrical opera, slave dancing, chamber music, plus the film *The Musical Instrument Maker of Williamsburg* (1976) offering a demonstration of colonial crafting techniques. Available from Colonial Williamsburg at www.history.org.

For a representative collection of music for "at home" dancing in 1859, see *The Home Circle* (reprint, New York: Da Capo Press, 1980). For an introduction to dance instruction manuals, see the demonstrations directed by Elizabeth Aldrich on the LofC website, http://memory.loc.gov/ammem/dihtml/dihome.html. Also see Elizabeth Aldrich, *From the Ballroom to Hell: Grace and Folly in 19th Century Dance* (Evanston, Ill.: Northwestern University Press, 1991), especially "Music and Musicians" (pp. 125–33).

An overview of what he terms "the cultivated tradition" can be found in H. Wiley Hitchcock with Kyle Gann, *Music in the United States: A Historical Introduction*. (Upper Saddle River, N.J.: Prentice Hall, fourth ed., 2000). Especially see chapter 4 concerning 1820–65 and chapter 6 for 1865–1920.

Among recordings released by the LofC Archive of Folk Culture is *American Fiddle Tunes* (Cambridge, Mass.: Rounder Records, 2000), documenting Appalachian styles of the 1930s and 1940s.

2. In his brief life, Ethelbert Nevin enjoyed success as a composer of songs and short pieces. His song "The Rosary," sold more than 6 million copies, and his portrait was printed on ten-cent U.S. postage stamps of 1940. Recordings of his piano music are available on CDs. The Ethelbert Nevin Collection is located in the Center for American Music at the University of Pittsburgh. For a biography, see Vance Thompson, *The Life of Ethelbert Nevin: From His Letters and His Wife's Memories* (Boston: Boston Music Co., 1913).

3. Henry Cowell and Sidney Cowell, *Charles Ives and His Music* (New York: Oxford University Press, 1969), 16.

4. Michael Broyles, "Art Music from 1860 to 1920," in *The Cambridge History of American Music*, ed. David Nicholls, (Cambridge: Cambridge University Press, 2004), 235–36.

5. Henry Cowell, "How Relate Music and Dance?" *Dance Observer*, June–July 1934, 52.

Part One

Epigraph, from Wallingford Riegger, "I Compose for the Modern Dance," *Dance*, November 1937, 12.

Overview: The Question of Using Old Music for New Dance

1. Regarding "Indianist" composers, see Michael Broyles, "Art Music from 1860 to 1920," in *The Cambridge History of American Music*, ed. David Nicholls

(Cambridge: Cambridge University Press, 1998), 214–254. In the same volume, an overview of actual native traditions is Victoria Lindsay Levine, "American Indian Musics, Past and Present" (pp. 3–29). Also see Michael V. Pisani, *Imagining Native America in Music* (New Haven, Conn.: Yale University Press, 2005), which explores representations of American Indian music from precolonial days to the present, with insights into cultural contexts.

Chapter 1

Émile Jaques-Dalcroze, *Rhythm, Music and Education*, translated from the French by Harold F. Rubinstein (New York: Putnam's, 1921), 231–53; 296–304.

For information about current Dalcroze Society activities, go to www.dalcroze.org.uk and www.dalcrozeusa.org.

1. For a brief introduction to eurythmics, see Monica Dale Johnson, "Dancers, Musicians, and Jaques-Dalcroze Eurhythmics," *Journal of the International Guild of Musicians in Dance*, 2 (1992), 11–18. For information on the journal and organization, go to www.dancemusician.org. An explanation of "Plastique Animée" and an overview by R. J. David Frego, "The Approach of Émile Jaques-Dalcroze," are available through the website of the Alliance for Active Music Making, www.allianceamm.org/resources_elem_Dalcroze.

2. For information about Hanya Holm's Dalcroze training and teaching, see Walter Sorell, *Hanya Holm: The Biography of an Artist* (Middletown, Conn.: Wesleyan University Press, 1969). Holm, who was born in 1893 and died in 1992, came to New York in 1931 to establish a school for the expressive dance approach of German artist-educator Mary Wigman. By 1935 at the summer dance festivals at Bennington College, Holm herself was considered one of the "big four" pioneers of American dance, along with Martha Graham, Doris Humphrey, and Charles Weidman. She went on to have a dual career in concert dance and Broadway shows, with her successes including *Kiss Me Kate* in 1948 and *My Fair Lady* in 1956. For Holm's comments about music (based on an interview late in her life), see Teck (1989), 11–14.

3. *Moving plastic.* The term has been left as in the published translation, but it seems pertinent to consider definitions given in *Webster's 3rd New International Unabridged Dictionary* (1981). The word "plastic" comes from the Greek *plastos* = formed, or molded. Some connotations refer to sculpting of figures, or of images shaped by flow in space. One definition suggests "giving or able to give material or sensible form to conceptions of color, shape, tone, or movement arising from the subconscious."

Chapter 2

Isadora Duncan, *My Life* (New York: Horace Liveright, 1927), 222–25.

Two biographies that offer perspective of time are Walter Terry, *Isadora Duncan: Her Life, Her Art, Her Legacy* (New York: Dodd Mead, 1963), and Fredrika Blair, *Isadora: Portrait of the Artist as a Woman* (New York: McGraw-Hill, 1986). The latter discusses Duncan's use of music (pp. 184–91).

There are a number of groups carrying on the Duncan legacy. For information, go to www.isadoraduncan.org and www.duncandancers.com.

1. There is no film of Isadora Duncan dancing to Beethoven. But a reconstruction of the *allegretto* from the Seventh Symphony in a manner likely danced by her is available in a performance by Pamela DeFina, who learned the dance from Duncan's adopted daughter Maria-Theresa. DeFina performed outdoors at the Trianon Palace in Versailles, in April 2000. The film can be viewed at the Jerome Robbins Dance Division of the NYPL.

Readers can access online the full unsigned review from the November 17, 1909, issue of *The New York Times* concerning Duncan's dancing to Beethoven's symphony. In part it reads:

> It is quite within the province of the recorder of musical affairs to protest against this perverted use of the Seventh Symphony, a purpose which Beethoven certainly never had in mind when he wrote it.... However, if one takes it for granted that Miss Duncan has a right to perform her dances to whatever music she chooses, there is no doubt of the high effect she achieves. Seldom has she been more poetical, more vivid in her expression of joy, more plastic in her poses, more rhythmical in her effects than she was yesterday.

A further sense of the impression made by Duncan onstage can be gained from Nancy de Wilde, "Isadora Duncan's Seventh Symphony in the Netherlands: Reactions to Her Choice and Interpretations of the Music," in Society of Dance History Scholars, *Proceedings*, 10th annual conference (University of California at Irvine, 1987), 166–76. This dance historian searched newspaper reviews from the time of Duncan's three performances of the Seventh Symphony in the Netherlands in 1907, as well as after the initial 1904 performances in Paris, discovering reactions that verged on a degree of anger that today seems surprising. As the author noted:

> The most important question concerned her choice of music: is it allowed to dance to music that is not specifically composed for dance? Most of the critics were definite in their negative answer with as first argument: it is incorrect to use a work of art in a different way than the artist intended. Anton Averkamp wrote: "A symphony by Beethoven is a complete work of art; one is not allowed to add something to it, neither also to take away something from it."...Willem Hutschenruyter called the work of Duncan a sacrilege, and another called it a desecration of the music, and another spoke of an artistic crime.

Contrary to such impassioned views, de Wilde could report that the Dutch critic Louis van Gigch urged audiences to "take her as she is. Because she is sublime when she is able to reach the music."

Another positive contemporaneous view of Isadora Duncan's use of music was offered in a book by Caroline Caffin and Charles Caffin, *Dancing and Dancers of Today: The Modern Revival of Dancing as an Art* (New York: Dodd Mead, 1912). The authors asked:

May the combination of two arts enhance, or must it detract from, the beauty of each? Is the spirit of each a thing so separate and apart that they cannot be combined without confusion? Must we listen to music with our eyes shut and look at dance with our ears stopped? The question seems to be banal, but it was the subject of many of the criticisms which greeted Isadora Duncan's first appearance in New York....

For sheer beauty and gladness of the sort that brings happy tears to the eyes and catches the breath in a sob at the throat, few things in life equal one's first experience of the dancing of Isadora Duncan....The figure becomes a symbol of abstract conception of rhythm and melody. The spirit of rhythm and melody by some miracle seems to have been made visible. (46, 53)

An article that provides historical insight is Kay Bardsley, "The Duncans at Carnegie Hall," *Ballet Review* 19 no. 3 (Fall 1991), 85–96. Bardsley herself was a student of Maria-Theresa Duncan and went on to cofound the Isadora Duncan International Institute. In her article, she traces the importance of New York's Carnegie Hall in Duncan's career.

Closer to our own times, Jack Anderson wrote about Annabelle Gamson's evocation of Duncan dances after this contemporary dancer also performed in Carnegie Hall. In his review for *The New York Times* of August 30, 1981, Anderson observed:

Because modern dancers have always regarded their art as a personal expression, it is easy to fear that once the person who created a dance is gone, the dance's power will also vanish. Intellectual balletomanes have even argued that modern dance's reluctance to separate the artist from the art makes it inferior to ballet, an art in which style and technique are treated as objective considerations that transcend the strengths or limitations of any individual. But Miss Gamson demonstrates that Duncan dancing can exist and be effective without Duncan.

A few films of Gamson dancing are available for viewing at the NYPL.

Other choreographers who have used the Seventh Symphony of Beethoven include Leonid Massine in 1938; Twyla Tharp (for New York City Ballet in 2000); and John Bishop (for Northwest Ballet in 2007). At the NYPL viewers can see a filmed rehearsal and lecture demonstration with the New York City Ballet and Twyla Tharp, who analyzes her own choreography as well as the music and talks about her double training in music and dance, with considerable attention to details of construction. Tharp also offers a capsule memoir of her setting in her book *The Creative Habit* (New York: Simon and Schuster, 2003), 129–32.

Contemporary performances of dances in Duncan style set to Chopin, Schubert, Brahms, Gluck, Scriabin, and songs from the Russian Red Army can be sampled on *Isadora Duncan: Masterworks, 1905–1923*, filmed by the Dance Arts Foundation with the Isadora Duncan Dance Ensemble (Hightstown, N.J.: Dance Horizons, DVD, 2008).

2. These are characters in operas of Richard Wagner.

3. From the 1762 opera *Orfeo ed Euridice* by Christoph Willibald Gluck (1714–87). Witness to the ongoing appeal of dancing with this music, Hanya Holm did the choreography for the 1959 Vancouver Festival production, and the entire opera was staged by choreographer Mark Morris for the Metropolitan Opera in New York in 2007.

Chapter 3

Baird Hastings, "Music for Isadora Duncan's Dance," *American Dancer*, December 1941, 20, 30.

Chapter 4

Helen Caldwell, *Michio Ito: The Dancer and His Dances* (Berkeley and Los Angeles: University of California Press, 1977), excerpted from pp. 4–5; 22, 27, 29; 64–65; and 77.

1. *Michio Ito*. In 1929 Ito moved to California, mounting gigantic productions such as one on September 20, 1929, at the Pasadena Rose Bowl, making use of 200 dancers, full symphony, and chorus, with music by European classical composers Tchaikovsky, Grieg, and Dvořák. He also worked in films. On the eve of World War II, Ito (despite having worked in the United States for more than twenty-five years) was incarcerated in a concentration camp in New Mexico and subsequently deported to Japan by the U.S. government. Although he never returned to the United States, among Ito's work from 1946 to 1948 was the production of revues for the U.S. occupation troops as director of the Ernie Pyle Theater in Tokyo.

   For an account of Ito's activities in California, see Naima Prevots, *Dancing in the Sun: Hollywood Choreographers 1915–1937* (Ann Arbor, Mich.: UMI Research Press, 1957), 179–95.

2. For Ito, Griffes composed *Sho-jo* in 1917, scored for flute, oboe, clarinet, harp, Chinese drum, tam-tam, timpani, and four strings. Subsequently, the composer also made an arrangement of a Japanese melody, "Sakura-Sakura" ("Cherry Blossoms") for one of Ito's dances.

   A particularly lush performance of the music for *The White Peacock* is available on the CD by the Dallas Symphony Orchestra conducted by Andrew Litton on the Dorian label, titled *An American Tapestry*. A pungent performance of the piano solo version, played by Roger Shields, can be found in the collection *Piano Music in America 1900–1945* (VoxBox).

   Representative of reactions to the music of Charles Tomlinson Griffes is this comment from Aaron Copland, in his *Music and Imagination* (Cambridge, Mass.: Harvard University Press, 1950):

   > There are pages in his music where we recognize the presence of the truly inspired moment. His was the work of a sentient human being, forward-looking, for its period, with a definite relationship to the impressionists and to Scriabin. No one can say how far Griffes might have developed if his career had not been cut short by death in his

thirty-sixth year, in 1920. What he gave to those of us who came after him was a sense of the adventurous in composition, of being thoroughly alive to the newest trends in world music and to the stimulus that might be derived from such contact. (102–3)

Chapter 5

Program excerpts, unattributed, from the Denishawn program booklet, 1924–25, for the tour arranged by impresario Daniel Mayer.

1. A book documenting the toured Denishawn dances one by one is Jane Sherman, *The Drama of Denishawn Dance* (Middletown, Conn.: Wesleyan University Press, 1979). A re-creation (by Barton Mumaw and Jane Sherman) of twenty-three Denishawn dances is available on a Kultur 2002 DVD titled *Denishawn Dances On!* performed by Denishawn Repertory Dancers and Vanaver Caravan. Included are *Floor plastique* with "To a Wild Rose" by MacDowell; *Boston Fancy* to music by Eastwood Lake; *Japanese Spear Dance*, with music by Louis Horst; and the "dude" that had been performed originally by Charles Weidman, in *Danse Americaine*, music by Dent Mowrey.

Chapter 6

Norman Cazden, article originally titled "On Dancing to Bach: A Reply to John Martin," *Dance Observer*, March 1943, 31–32.

1. Born in the Bronx, Cazden made his debut as a pianist at the age of twelve at Town Hall in New York City. He studied at the Institute of Musical Art (later the Juilliard School) and City College of New York, continuing composition at Harvard with Walter Piston and Aaron Copland. His doctoral dissertation was titled "Musical Consonance and Dissonance." Cazden's dance compositions included scores for the New Dance Group, the Humphrey-Weidman Company, and José Limón. Though his career was among those of many artists hurt by the House Un-American Activities Committee for a period of years, he was greatly respected for his teaching at Vassar College, the New School, Peabody Conservatory, and the universities of Michigan, Illinois, and Maine.

2. The most powerful critic who covered early modern dance (for *The New York Times* from 1927 to 1962), Martin also was prolific as an author of books about the subject. Among them, *The Modern Dance* (New York: A. S. Barnes, 1936), which discusses how music related to dance, in part IV.

3. For the early modern dancers, older music was simply part of the mix in their total creation; they were not trying to be "historically accurate." Yet if modern dance works set to Baroque music are revived now, perhaps a legitimate concern is *how* the music should be played. A technical guide with samples available via website is Bruce Haynes, *The End of Early Music: A Period Performer's History of Music for the Twenty-First Century* (New York: Oxford University Press, 2007). Commenting on some of the challenges of reconstructing past works, the author suggests:

> Style can jump centuries. It is the only relevant criterion for ascription and for replicating. Of course, there are those who argue that we can't know what music

and even violins were really like in the Baroque; our ideas about these things are always changing. This, we have to agree, is true; art fakes demonstrate that art is captive in its period and place. But if we wait to try to get it completely right, we'll never get it. First, we cannot know if we have succeeded. And whether it's right for all time is not the issue. All we want is to be confident we have realized the style as we perceive it at this particular moment. (120)

4. Extensive materials are available about this pioneer in modern dance. For a time line, go to the website of the Doris Humphrey Society, ww.dorishumphrey.org. The choreographer's autobiography, *An Artist First*, was completed by Selma Jeanne Cohen (Middletown, Conn.: Wesleyan University Press, 1972). *The Dance Works of Doris Humphrey* is a multivideo set with various performers, available from dancehorizons.com. The NYPL has a set of oversized photographs plus a black-and-white film of Humphrey dancing to Bach's "Air for the G String," with Rosario Bourdon conducting, and four other dancers of her company.

A valued text continues to be Doris Humphrey, *The Art of Making Dances*, ed. Barbara Pollack (Hightstown, N.J.: Princeton Book Company, 1987). Chapter 15 is devoted to her thoughts on collaborative music, and in her foreword, Humphrey wrote:

> I think the germ of this book must have existed a very long time ago indeed, probably back to the time when I was a very small child and heard my mother playing MacDowell's "Witches' Dance" and Sinding's "Rustle of Spring" as I was going to sleep. Also about this time I heard Bach's "Air for the G String," which so struck me to the heart that it was almost the first dance I composed as an independent choreographer. So music was my first love and I was led to dance through that.

5. David Ewen, in *Music Comes to America* (New York: Allen, Towne and Heath, 1947), devotes several chapters to documenting American attitudes toward German music (see particularly chapter 6). However, precisely because of both wars, many talented musicians fled Europe, moved to the United States, and enriched the artistic and educational life in various cities. For the second round in a half century, the migration had already started by 1933. As Ewen commented:

> Fascism sucked Europe dry of its genius, and by doing so, has rendered us a service for which we can never be sufficiently grateful. It is not beyond the realm of possibility that the musical historian of tomorrow—in surveying our present turbulent era—will point to this recent influx of musical genius into this country as the final stage in the transformation of America into the musical capital of the world. (253)

Chapter 7

Ted Shawn, *The American Ballet* (New York: Henry Holt, 1926), 54–64, chapter titled "American Music and Composers."

1. Norton Owen has done extensive documentation as the archivist and director of preservation for Ted Shawn's theater at Jacob's Pillow. A brief history plus

photos can be seen online at www.jacobspillow.org. Also suggested is Norton Owen, *A Certain Place: The Jacob's Pillow Story* (Becket, Mass.: Jacob's Pillow Dance Festival, revised edition, 2002). Additionally suggested is the DVD *The Men Who Danced*, which includes an interview with composer-pianist Jess Meeker, as well as two examples of "music visualization" choreographed by Ted Shawn, to piano music by J. S. Bach, available at www.menwhodanced.mpny.tv Also see "Jess Meeker Recalls Years with Ted Shawn," in Teck (1990), 54–59. Among materials preserved at Jacob's Pillow are music manuscripts by Jess Meeker.

2. An intriguing side excursion concerning early human music and dance is Steven Mithen, *The Singing Neanderthals: The Origins of Music, Language, Mind, and Body* (London: Weidenfeld and Nicholson, 2005).

3. A pertinent comment is from Margery Morgan Lowens in her entry on Edward MacDowell in *The New Grove Dictionary of American Music*:

> It is ironic that in his day MacDowell should have been widely regarded as "the great American composer," since it is hard to find anything distinctly American about his music. Indeed he never aspired to write nationalist music; his ambition was to be a fine composer, and he simply happened to be American. He developed an explicit aversion to concerts consisting only of American works and finally refused to allow his music to be performed at these increasingly popular events, insisting that music ought to be presented on its own merits and not on account of its composer's nationality.

4. Among composers touched upon in this chapter, the music of Nathaniel Dett continues to be performed. Denver Oldham has recorded several albums, including a performance of the *Juba Dance* on Dett's *Piano Works* (New World Records, 1992). Typical operettas by Victor Herbert and some of the more popular works by Edward MacDowell are available in various recordings. Some of the other works mentioned by Shawn are seldom performed nowadays. Would-be listeners to music by Stoughton, Grunn, Hadley, Lane, Taylor, and Mowrey might search catalogs of university and performing arts libraries that house early recordings of American concert music.

5. Perhaps Shawn would have acknowledged some sort of fulfillment of his own Whitman dream in the 2008 work *Beloved Renegade* choreographed by Paul Taylor, although it uses the extant *Gloria* of French composer Francis Poulenc. One of the central figures seems to represent the poet Walt Whitman. Writing in *The New York Times* of February 27, 2009, Alaistair Macaulay called the dance one of Taylor's "supreme, and most moving, works" and went on to observe: "The uncanny fit of action to music makes all this poignant, haunting and very Whitman-esque."

Part Two

Epigraph, from Henry Gilfond's interview of Lehman Engel, *Dance Observer*, September 1935, 102.

Overview: Some Challenges of Collaboration, and Composers Debate about What Works

1. For a survey of creative musicians who worked with dancers in the earlier part of the twentieth century, see John Toenjes, "The Composer-Accompanist in the Formative Years of Modern Dance," *Journal of the International Guild of Musicians in Dance* 3 (1994): 24–39. By studying the reviews in *Dance Observer*, Toenjes estimated that in New York City alone during the 1930s and 1940s there were at least 125 composers commissioned for dance scores. These included well-known established composers as well as "emerging composers" and composer-accompanists who became involved with the choreographers initially through their work in classroom or rehearsal dance studios—and sometimes additionally as conductors for professional companies.

2. *Dance Observer* existed from February 1934 until just after Louis Horst's death in 1964. It was a modest periodical, initially only twelve pages monthly for ten months of the year. Horst ran the operation out of his apartment in Greenwich Village. A year's subscription cost one dollar, and the issues listed a handful of street corner newspaper stalls in Manhattan where *Dance Observer* could be purchased, plus a few locations in California. It had limited circulation but marked influence in the initially small sphere of concert dance.

   Lest we forget that *Dance Observer* was launched in the depths of the Great Depression, one opening article is titled "Economics and the Dancer," in which Frances Hawkins warned dancers who aimed to give New York recitals to help launch solo careers. They should, she cautioned, budget at least $100 for rehearsal and performance by a musical accompanist; figure a total cost of $800—and not expect to break even. By the November 1935 issue, composer Dane Rudhyar observed that "the modern dance has still a ridiculously limited public."

3. Louis Horst, "Consider the Question of Communication," *Anthology of Impulse: Annual of Contemporary Dance 1951–1966*, ed. Marian Van Tuyl (Brooklyn, N.Y.: Dance Horizons, 1969), 17.

4. *Judith* was commissioned from William Schuman by the Louisville Orchestra and was premiered in 1950 with Robert Whitney conducting. It was subsequently recorded (on the orchestra's label, reissued as a CD in 2003 on the "First Edition" label). In 1951, Graham again performed the solo, in Carnegie Hall with the New York Philharmonic. For an account of how Schuman considered *Judith* as a concerto for orchestra with the dancer as soloist, see Joseph W. Polisi, *American Muse: The Life and Times of William Schuman* (New York: Amadeus Press, 2008), 159–62.

Chapter 8

Louis Horst, article originally titled simply "Music and Dance," *Dance Observer*, May 1935, 49, 55.

1. See Janet Mansfield Soares, *Louis Horst: Musician in a Dancer's World* (Durham, N.C.: Duke University Press, 1992). The author was an assistant to Horst, then

went on to become a choreographer and to teach both at the Juilliard School and at Barnard College. The volume ties together all the intertwining of public events, private lives, and musical concerns of the early modern dancers who were both colleagues and competitors—and who all benefited from the influence of Louis Horst, whether as pianist, conductor, composer, coach, teacher, or critic. The book includes a listing of Horst's original scores for dances.

The composer's archives are in the NYPL. A booklet still of interest is Ernestine Stodelle, *The First Frontier: The Story of Louis Horst and the American Dance*, with photographs by Barbara Morgan (published by the author in Cheshire, Conn., 1964). Other sources are "Louis Horst: A Centennial Compendium," ed. David Sears, *Ballet Review* 12 no. 2 (summer 1984): 77–98, and Ted Dalbotten, "The Teaching of Louis Horst," *Dance Scope* 8 (1973–74), 26–40.

Louis Horst's much-used text is *Pre-Classic Dance Forms* (1937; Princeton, N.J.: Princeton Book Company, 1987). Also see Louis Horst and Carroll Russell, *Modern Dance Forms in Relation to the Other Modern Arts* (1961; Princeton, N.J.: Princeton Book Company, 1987).

Among Horst's activities were lecture demonstrations at the 92nd Street YM-YWHA in New York City. The importance of this institution in nurturing modern dance is chronicled in Naomi M. Jackson, *Converging Movements: Modern Dance and Jewish Culture at the 92nd Street Y* (Middletown, Conn.: Wesleyan University Press, 2000).

2. For her *Lamentation* of 1930, Martha Graham used Zoltán Kodály's *Piano Piece*, op. 3, no. 2. For her *Two Ecstatic Themes*, Doris Humphrey used music by Nikolai Medtner and Gian Francesco Malipiero. A VHS film of Sarita Smith-Childs performing Humphrey's dance was released in 1997, with the re-creation coached by Ernestine Stodelle and with Vivian Fine as pianist, available from www.dancehorizons.com.

Chapter 9

Henry Gilfond, "Louis Horst," interview from *Dance Observer*, February 1936, 13, 15, 20–21. Extra appreciation is extended to Pamela Gilfond for her attention to the reprinting of this interview.

Special thanks are also extended to Deborah Vollmer for permission to reproduce the caricature of Louis Horst drawn by her mother, Aline Fruhauf (1907–78). Both enjoyable and informative about the era is the artist's memoir, *Making Faces*, ed. Erwin Vollmer (Santa Barbara, Calif.: John Daniel, 1987).

Chapter 10

Gertrude Lippincott, article originally titled "A Quiet Genius Himself: Louis Horst, the Permanent Patron of Modern Dance," *Focus on Dance*, v. 5 (1969): 3–6, published by the American Association for Health, Physical Education, Recreation and Dance. AAHPERD, based in Reston, Virginia, is now known as the American Alliance for Health, Physical Education, Recreation and Dance. Among its affiliates is the National Dance Association. For current information, go to www.aahperd.org.

1. The Gertrude Lippincott Collection is in the Performing Arts Archives at the Elmer L. Andersen Library, University of Minnesota, Minneapolis.

2. Gertrude Lippincott's reference was to Paul Manship (1885–1966), sculptor of more than 700 works, including the Prometheus fountain at Rockefeller Center in New York City. More typical were his *Dancer and Gazelles* (1916), (reproduced in Figure 10.2) or his statue *Indian Hunter with His Dog* (1926) at the Daytona Art Institute (which can be viewed online at http://www.daytonartinstitute.org/collection/am_203_detail1.html)

Chapter 11

Wallingford Riegger, "Synthesizing Music and the Dance," *Dance Observer*, December 1934, 84–85.

1. A detailed account of Riegger's collaborative accomplishments and the New York scene in which he was immersed is Stephen Spackman, "Wallingford Riegger and the Modern Dance," *Music Quarterly* 71 (1985): 437–67. In his opening paragraph the author observes:

> The year 1985 is not only the centenary of Wallingford Riegger's birth, but also the fiftieth anniversary of *New Dance*....Its asymmetrical combination of rumba and conga rhythms hardly suggests its origin in modern dance; its remorseless repetition, Latin ostinato, and brash, streamlined orchestration all suggest that Riegger might easily have made a name for himself on Broadway....There is a strong case for regarding Riegger as the preeminent composer for the modern dance during the years in which it became a major and indigenous American art form. (437)

A DVD of *With My Red Fires* and *New Dance* as performed at the American Dance Festival in 1972 is available from Dance Horizons, ©1978.

An indication of relative monetary values of the time, and of the tightness in dance companies' budgets, is a 1940 letter from Riegger to Doris Humphrey citing standard payments that had been recently agreed upon by the American Composers Alliance and the American Dance Association. The letter can be viewed on microfilm at the NYPL and cites the following fees: $10 minimum for a composition of two minutes or less (with additional rates for longer works); performance fees of 20 cents per minute (but waived for lecture/demonstrations); and three years of exclusive right to performance.

In a subsequent letter to Humphrey (dated June 12, 1941), Riegger apologetically refers to the monetary subject as "sordid" yet notices that there had been a number of performances of *New Dance* and *With My Red Fires* for which he had received no performance fees, which he calculated should have amounted to two dollars per performance at the newly agreed rate of twenty-five cents per minute. Although composers of that era did contribute much time and creative effort to their scores for modern dance, Riegger indicated that the fifty-dollar total would indeed make a difference in his life.

2. That the composition of the music after the choreography had been set was not unprecedented is indicated by this account from Victor Alphonse Duvernoy's 1903 *L'art du theatre* (translated in the earlier edition of Ivor Guest, *The Romantic Ballet in Paris* [Middletown, Conn.: Wesleyan University Press, 1966], 11), quoted here as it appears in Richard Taruskin, *Music in the Early Twentieth Century, The Oxford History of Western Music*, v. 4 (New York: Oxford University Press, 2010):

> In olden days, the scenarist began by finding a choreographer. Between the poet and the dancer, a close collaboration was formed. Once the plan of the piece and the dances were arranged, the musician was called in. The ballet-master indicated the rhythms he had laid down, the steps he had arranged, the number of bars which each variation must contain—in short, the music was arranged to fit the dances. And the musician docilely improvised, so to speak, and often in the ballet-master's room, everything that was asked of him. You can guess how alert his pen had to be, and how quick his imagination. No sooner was a scene written or a *pas* [section of choreography] arranged than they were rehearsed with a violin, a single violin, as the only accompaniment. Even after having servilely done everything the ballet-master had demanded, the composer had to pay attention to the advice of the principal dancers. So he had to have much talent, or at least great facility, to satisfy so many exigencies, and, I would add, a certain amount of philosophy. (4:134)

Chapter 12

Ernestine Stodelle, "Sensing the Dancer's Impulse," *Art Times*, November 1993.

1. An example of Stodelle's stewardship is the series of films produced by Dance Horizons with this artist coaching five of Doris Humphrey's works (including *Two Ecstatic Themes*). The music was performed by pianist Vivian Fine (who also had played for Humphrey's original performances).

Chapter 13

Vivian Fine, untitled essay in *Composer/Choreographer, Dance Perspectives* 16 (1963): 8–11.

1. The composer's family has kept up an informative website at www.vivianfine. org, with sample audio files and Wallingford Riegger's essay "The Music of Vivian Fine" from the *American Composers Alliance Bulletin* 8, no. 1 (1958): 2–3. It should be noted that American Composers Alliance now makes past articles from its bulletins available as pdf downloads. Go to www.composer.com. Also see Elizabeth Vercoe, "Interview with Composer Vivian Fine," *International League of Women Composers Journal*, June 1992, 18–23, and Leslie Jones, "Seventy Years of Composing: An Interview with Vivian Fine," *Contemporary Music Review* 16 (1997): 21–26. Additionally, in 1990 Vivian Fine was

interviewed by Dennis Mullen for the Legacy Oral History Project at the Museum of Performance and Design, San Francisco, California. For information, go to http://www.muse-sf.org/legacyhistory.html. In her interview, Fine mentions that for a 1956 revival of *The Race of Life* she made an orchestration of the piano score, premiered at the Juilliard School with Frederick Prausnitz conducting, and with Doris Humphrey supervising. In 1961 the orchestral version was used with slides of the Thurber drawings for performance by the Hudson Valley Philharmonic, with Claude Monteux conducting.

Chapter 14

Doris Humphrey, essay originally titled "Music for an American Dance," *American Composers Alliance Bulletin* 8 no. 1 (1958): 4–5. The second essay in this chapter, "The Relationship of Music and Dance" is from the collection *New Dance*, edited by Charles Humphrey Woodford (Pennington, N. J.: Princeton Book Company, 2008), 49–56. The essay was originally a speech to dance students at the Juilliard School on November 7, 1956.

1. For videos documenting dances of Doris Humphrey, go to www.dancehorizons .com. These include *With My Red Fires, New Dance, The Shakers, Air for the G String, Day on Earth*, and *Water Study*. Among the films of Humphrey at the NYPL is *The Race of Life* (though, alas, with no sound track), but performed by Humphrey, Weidman, and Limón. Also see *A New Dance for America: The Choreography, Teachings, and Legacy of Doris Humphrey*, DVD written and directed by Ina Hahn, WW Film Company, 2010.

   The VHS film *Charles Weidman: On His Own* is available from Dance Horizons. It traces Weidman's career and includes several full performances by this leading pioneer.

Chapter 15

Lehman Engel, "Under Way: Composing for Martha Graham," in *This Bright Day: An Autobiography* (New York: Macmillan, 1974), 54–58. The second selection, Lehman Engel's essay "Music for the Dance," was published in *Dance Observer*, February 1934, 4, 8.

1. For Martha Graham, Lehman Engel wrote the scores to *Ceremonials, Phobias, Ekstasis, Transitions, Imperial Gesture*, and *Marching Song*. His credits for conducting and arranging some 167 Broadway shows can be seen on the Internet Broadway Database, www.ibdb.com.

2. To balance Engel's verbal sketch, it can be noted that the first issue of *Dance Observer*, February 1934, drew attention to Harry Losee (1901–52) performing at the Metropolitan Opera House in *The Martyrdom of St. Sebastian* (music by Claude Debussy) with the American Ballet Association. In the Ice Capades and Hollywood films, Losee made his mark as a dance director for skating numbers, and his choreography credits include several films with Fred Astaire and Ginger Rogers (such as *Gay Divorcee* [1934] and *Shall We Dance* [1937]).

Chapter 16

Henry Cowell, article originally titled simply "Relating Music and Concert Dance," *Dance Observer*, January 1937, 1, 7–10.

1. Henry Cowell's scores used for the dance include, for Charles Weidman, *Steel and Stone* and *Dance of Sport*; for Martha Graham, *Heretic, Six Casual Developments, Sarabande*, and *Deep Song*; for Hanya Holm, *Salutation*; for Marian Van Tuyl, *Ritual of Wonder*; for Jean Erdman, *Changing Woman*; and for Erick Hawkins, *Trickster Coyote* and *Clown*.

   For those unfamiliar with Cowell's music, an engaging introduction is the 1963 recording of the composer playing his own "inside the piano" pieces, reissued on CD by Smithsonian Folkways, available at www.folkways.si.edu.

   A prolific writer as well as a composer, Cowell rounded up his colleagues to produce *American Composers on American Music* (New York: Frederich Ungar, 1933). The book offers a good cross section of early 1930s art music activities. Some of the composer's other writings have been collected in *Essential Cowell: Selected Writings on Music by Henry Cowell 1921–1964*, ed. Dick Higgins (Kingston, N.Y.: Documentext, McPherson, 2001). Together Henry and Sydney Cowell wrote *Charles Ives and His Music* (New York: Oxford University Press, 1955).

   Joel Sachs has labored for many years on his biography *Henry Cowell* (New York: Oxford University Press, forthcoming). A volume that covers just the early years of the composer's career is Michael Dustin Hicks, *Henry Cowell, Bohemian* (Urbana: University of Illinois Press, 2002). George Boziwick wrote an excellent brief biography plus an introduction to the Henry Cowell Collection at the NYPL, in the Music Library Association *Notes* 57, no. 1 (2000): 46–58.

2. In his directions, it seems to make sense to equate Cowell's use of the word "sentence" to longer phrases or groupings of short phrases—an interesting point for discussion!

Chapter 17

Norman Lloyd, "Sound-Companion for Dance: Henry Cowell's Music," *Dance Scope* 2, no. 2 (Spring 1966): 10–12. *Dance Scope* was a publication of the American Dance Guild.

Chapter 18

Norman Lloyd, article originally titled simply "Composing for the Dance," *Juilliard Review*, Spring 1961, 3–7.

1. A detailed account of the Bennington College School of the Dance summer experiences can be found in Sali Ann Kriegsman, *Modern Dance in America: The Bennington Years* (Boston: G. K. Hall, 1981). As documented by Kriegsman, the music used for new dances presented there in 1936–42 included works by the following composers: John Cage, Henry Leland Clarke, John Colman, Henry Cowell, Lehman Engel, Vivian Fine, Ralph Gilbert, Ray Green, Louis Horst,

Hazel Johnson, Hunter Johnson, Harrison Kerr, Clair Leonard, Norman Lloyd, Robert McBride, Morris Mamorsky, Jerome Moross, Alex North, Lionel Nowak, Harvey Pollins, Maxwell Powers, Wallingford Riegger, Gregory Tucker, and Esther Williamson (later Ballou).

A welcome addition to the literature is Janet Soares, *Martha Hill and the Making of American Dance* (Middletown, Conn.: Wesleyan University Press, 2009), which includes information about both Norman and Ruth Lloyd. Also pertinent is Martha Hill's article based on her thesis, "An Analysis of Accompaniment for the Dance," in Committee of Dance of the American Physical Education Association, *Dancing in the Elementary Schools* (New York: A. S. Barnes, 1933), 87–105.

2. Films of dances with scores by Norman Lloyd can be viewed at the NYPL. A sample of his approach to playing for modern dance classes can be found in his *Accompaniments for the Modern Dance: Technical Rhythmic Studies* (New York: Orchesis Publications, 1960). Growing out of their studio classroom work with dancers, Ruth and Norman Lloyd authored *Creative Keyboard Musicianship: Fundamentals of Music and Keyboard Harmony through Improvisation* (New York: Dodd, Mead, 1975).

   Ruth Lloyd herself had a substantial career working with dancers. For some of her observations, see Teck (1990), 49–54. Ruth Lloyd was interviewed by William Moulton for the International Guild of Musicians in Dance; inquiries concerning his videotaped documentation should be directed to www.dancemusician.org.

3. For complete English translations of Petipa's scenarios for Tchaikovsky, see Roland John Wiley, *Tchaikovsky's Ballets* (Oxford: Oxford University Press, 1985), 321–41.

4. The translation of Noverre's treatise familiar to Norman Lloyd was probably that by Cyril W. Beaumont, *Letters on Dancing and Ballets* (published by Beaumont in London, 1930). It has been reprinted (Brooklyn, N.Y,: Dance Horizons, 1966).

5. For biographical material and an introduction to *La Malinche* and other works, see the film *José Limón: Life beyond Words*, available from www.dancehorizons.com. Also, Patricia Seed, ed., *José Limón and La Malinche: The Dancer and the Dance* (Austin: University of Texas Press, 2008), a collection of essays related to this work, with a DVD of a restaged performance.

6. The English composer Henry Purcell lived a short but productive life (1659–95). *The Moor's Pavane* with music by Purcell can be seen on DVD with the original cast: choreographer José Limón as Othello; and with Lucas Hoving, Pauline Koner, and Betty Jones (from the archives of CBC March 6, 1955). Purcell's music continues to be attractive to modern choreographers: his only opera, *Dido and Aeneas*, was staged and choreographed by Mark Morris, who also directed a pageantlike setting of Purcell's *King Arthur* (originally staged in London and San Francisco; performed with New York City Opera in 2008).

7. Barbara Morgan published her photographs of Graham in *Frontier*, shown in *16 Photographs of Martha Graham* (New York: Duel, Sloan & Peach, 1941). The

NYPL has a video of Graham performing *Frontier* sometime between 1936 and 1939. The film was a silent one, and conductor Jonathan McPhee produced the added sound track in 1987. A VHS tape of Janet Eilber, a member of the Martha Graham Company, performing *Frontier* was recorded in 1976 as a production of Thirteen/WNET, available on Nonesuch.

Agnes de Mille had particular praise for the music for *Frontier*. In her biography *Martha* (New York: Vintage, 1992) she commented: "Louis Horst composed the sparse, marvelous, strange, provocative score, with its magic use of a snare drum calling up all the mettlesome, aggressive, and fighting instincts of a brave people. The melody was like a lost voice, pure and haunting."(220)

Part Three

Epigraph, David Ewen, *Music Comes to America* (New York: Allen, Towne & Heath, 1947), 242.

Overview: Defining What Makes Music "American," and Common Musical Concerns of Ballet and Modern Dance

1. Kyle Gann, *American Music in the Twentieth Century* (Belmont, Calif.: Thomson/ Wadsworth/Schirmer Books, 1997), iii–xiv. For information about Gann's writing, composing, and teaching, go to www.kylegann.com. Mark Morris used Gann's *Studies for Disklavier* for his dance titled *Looky* in 2007.

Two books on the topic of American identity are Barbara L. Tischler, *An American Music: In Search for an American Musical Identity* (New York: Oxford University Press, 1986), and Alan Howard Levy, *Musical Nationalism: American Composers' Search for Identity* (Westport, Conn.: Greenwood Press, 1983). Both volumes deal with concert art music rather than music for dance, but they provide pertinent information about composers' styles in the United States in the twentieth century. The Levy volume has a bibliographic essay on sources and includes this quotation from Virgil Thompson, originally from the *New York Herald Tribune*, January 25, 1948:

> The way to write American music is simple. All you have to do is be an American and then write any kind of music you wish. There is precedent and model here for all the kinds. And any Americanism worth bothering about is everybody's property anyway. Leave it to the unconscious; let nature speak. (130)

On the same subject, in his collection of lectures given at Harvard, published as *Music and Imagination* (Cambridge, Mass.: Harvard University Press, 1952), Aaron Copland suggested that for some composers there is a "universalist ideal" exemplified in the symphonies of Samuel Barber, for example. He commented:

> I realize that there are undoubtedly among my readers those who disapprove heartily of this searching for "Americanisms" in the works of our contemporaries ... [but] not all the composers of any country are to be limited to an obviously indigenous expression. (94)

Nevertheless, Copland recalled that during his years in France:

> Gradually the idea that my personal expression in music ought somehow to be related to my own back-home environment took hold of me. The conviction grew inside me that the two things that seemed always to have been so separate in America—music and the life about me—must be made to touch. This desire to make the music I wanted to write come out of the life I had lived in America became a preoccupation of mine in the twenties. It was not so very different from the experience of other young American artists, in other fields, who had gone abroad to study in that period; in greater or lesser degree, all of us discovered America in Europe. (99)

2. Reginald de Koven, "Nationality in Music, and the American Composer," in *Music of the Modern World*, ed. Anton Seidl (New York: D. Appleton, 1895), 2:191.

   Reginald de Koven achieved considerable success during his lifetime, including the premiere of his opera *The Canterbury Pilgrims* at the Metropolitan Opera in 1917. Born in Middletown, Connecticut, in 1859, he received musical training that was typical of the time: he moved to Europe in 1870 and studied at Oxford and then in Germany, Vienna, and Paris (with Léo Delibes, the composer of the outstanding ballet scores for *Sylvia* and *Coppélia*). Back in the United States by 1882, de Koven found work as a music critic; meanwhile, some of his songs became popular, including "Oh Promise Me," still sung at weddings. His list of operettas is remarkable for the quick pace of output: pretty much one show a year between 1887 and 1913. The composer died in 1920, and his wife, Anna de Koven, published a memoir titled *A Musician and His Wife* (New York: Harper and Brothers, 1926). Recently there was a revival of *Robin Hood* by the Ohio Light Opera Company, whose 2004 CD of the operetta is available on the Albany label. Additionally, on the AEI label are excerpts from a contemporary ensemble, from the 1919 revival cast, as well as one track recorded in 1906 and the famous "Oh Promise Me" recorded in 1898.

3. A book tracing the stay of Czech composer Antonín Dvořák in New York City, 1892–95, merged with a study of African American styles, is Maurice Peress, *Dvořák to Duke Ellington: A Conductor Explores America's Music and Its African American Roots* (New York: Oxford University Press, 2004). Dvořák (1841–1904) had his famous *Symphony No. 9 "From the New World"* premiered in New York's Carnegie Hall, with Anton Seidl conducting, in 1893.

4. de Koven, in Seidl, *Music of the Modern World*, 2:193.

5. Definition is from Norman Lloyd, *The Golden Encyclopedia of Music* (New York: Golden Press, 1968), 261.

   A brief nontechnical history with biographies of major figures and suggested listening is Loren Schoenberg, *The NPR Curious Listener's Guide to Jazz* (New York: Perigree, 2002). A wide spectrum of opinions is offered in Robert Walser, *Keeping Time: Readings in Jazz History* (New York: Oxford University Press, 1999).

6. See Reid Badger, *A Life in Ragtime: A Biography of James Reese Europe* (New York: Oxford University Press, 1995). Two CDs that reissue recordings originally made in 1919 by Europe and his Hell Fighter's Band are *James Reese Europe: Featuring Noble Sissle* (Iajrc Records, 1996) and *Jim Europe's 369th Infantry "Hell Fighters" Band* (Memphis Archives, 1996).

  A good introduction to ragtime is Edward A. Berlin, *King of Ragtime: Scott Joplin and His Era* (New York: Oxford University Press, 1994). Other sources are Rudi Blesh and Harriet Janis, *They All Played Ragtime* (New York: Oak Publications, 1971); and Terry Waldo, with a foreword by Eubie Blake, *This Is Ragtime* (New York: Da Capo Press, 1991). A history with commentary on individual rags is David A. Jasen and Trebor Jay Tichener, *Rags and Ragtime: A Musical History* (New York: Dover, 1989).

  The pianist Bill Edwards has an excellent source of ragtime-related information, on his website www.perfessorbill.com. The Scott Joplin Foundation sponsors a multiday ragtime festival every summer in Sedalia, Missouri, the place where the *Maple Leaf Rag* was born. Go to www.scottjoplin. org. For information on the Blind Boone Ragtime and Early Jazz Festival in nearby Columbia, Missouri, go to www.blindboone.missouri.org. Finally, it can be noted that the very last work choreographed by Martha Graham was her *Maple Leaf Rag*.

7. An enjoyable introduction to jazz continues to be Louis Armstrong's memoir, *Satchmo: My Life in New Orleans* (New York: Prentice Hall, 1954). A recommended recent volume is Thomas Brothers, *Louis Armstrong's New Orleans* (New York: Norton, 2006). And for a popular overview, there is the Ken Burns multidisc DVD set *Jazz* made for PBS (2004) with an accompanying book: Geoffrey C. Ward and Ken Burns, *Jazz: A History of America's Music* (New York: Knopf, 2000). An in-depth study geared to serious music students is Gunther Schuller, *The Swing Era: The Development of Jazz, 1930–1945* (New York: Oxford University Press, 1991).

8. Anna Kisselgoff, "Paul Taylor Borrows Ives to Define Dissonance," *The New York Times*, April 24, 1989.

9. Henry Cowell and Sidney Cowell, *Charles Ives and His Music* (New York: Oxford University Press, 1969), 8.

10. Ibid., 4.

11. Gann, *American Music in the Twentieth Century*, 6.

12. Wilfrid Mellers, *Music in a New Found Land: Themes and Developments in the History of American Music* (New York: Oxford University Press, 1987), 250 ff. Also see Louis Moreau Gottschalk, *Notes of a Pianist*, ed. Jeanne Behrend, foreword Frederick S. Starr (Princeton, N.J.: Princeton University Press, 2006), and S. Frederick Starr, *Bamboula! The Life and Times of Louis Moreau Gottschalk* (New York: Oxford University Press, 1995). Merce Cunningham's 1955 performance of *Banjo* at Jacob's Pillow was captured on film, which is now in the archives there.

13. For a detailed study of the Brazilian tango and Darius Milhaud's use of published sources, see Daniella Thomson, *The Boeuf Chronicles: How the Ox Got*

on the Roof: Darius Milhaud and the Brazilian Sources of Le Boeuf sur le Toit. Go to www.daniellathompson.com.

Milhaud's other ballet scores include *Le Train Bleu, Moyen-Age Fleuri, La Bien-Aimée, Jeux de Printemps,* and *The Bells.* Although it does not focus particularly on his compositions for dance, his autobiography is worth reading, particularly because of his connection with Mills College: Darius Milhaud, *Notes without Music* (New York: Knopf, 1953).

A brief essay on the life of Ernesto Nazareth and musical hints for performing his piano pieces can be found in the introduction to *Nazareth: Brazilian Tangos and Dances for the Piano,* ed. David P. Appleby (Van Nuys, Calif.: Alfred Publishing, 1997).

14. An excellent introduction to the music of the Argentine tango is the 2007 Deutsche Grammophon DVD *Astor Piazzolla: The Next Tango,* which includes the composer talking about the history of the tango and how he changed it during his career, with performances by Piazzolla (1921–92) on the bandoneon, along with his various ensembles. For a detailed biography of this composer (who grew up on New York City's Lower East Side), see María Susana Azzi and Simon Collier, *Le Grand Tango: The Life and Music of Astor Piazzolla* (New York: Oxford University Press, 2000).

15. A biography of this composer is Robert L. Parker, *Carlos Chávez: Mexico's Modern-Day Orpheus* (Boston: Twayne, 1983).

16. A provocative observation about the atonal music written according to Arnold Schoenberg's model (in contrast to the sometimes astringent neoclassicism of Igor Stravinsky) is the following excerpt from James Murdoch, *Peggy Glanville-Hicks: A Transposed Life* (Hillsdale, N.Y.: Pendragon Press, 2002). The reference is to the Parisian teacher of composition Nadia Boulanger, whose students included Virgil Thomson and Aaron Copland.

> Nadia Boulanger firmly believed in the neo-classicism of her musical hero, Stravinsky. That general style dominated American music, mainly through her teaching of the younger composers, until the Nazis squeezed out the Jewish academic composers and musicologists from Europe who then flooded into American universities. They brought with them the dreaded twelve-tone system of Schoenberg. Dreaded, because it seemed to many to be anchored in arithmetic, at times amounting to high mathematics, leading to emotionless and unromantic music. Many despaired of their creative impulse being lost in a mass of technique and rules. . . . For generations thereafter, until the advent of Minimalism, the acceptance or rejection of either twelve-tone music or neo-classicism became the crucial decision for almost all composers. To the rest of the music world—the onlookers—it seemed like the War of the Roses, and the public, not buying into the internecine warfare, remained firmly and happily within the music of the nineteenth century. The sales figures of the recording industry proved it. (24–25)

17. A related study of styles is William Duckworth, *20/20: 20 New Sounds of the 20th Century* (New York: Schirmer, 1999). A CD is included, and the works

considered include Aaron Copland's *Appalachian Spring*; Igor Stravinsky's *Rite of Spring*; and John Cage's *Sonatas and Interludes*. The introductory questions posed along with answers are also a good basis for reflection and discussion. The book includes a selective timeline 1813–1995.

18. Lynn Garafola, "Diaghilev's Musical Legacies," in a collection of her own writings, *Legacies of Twentieth-Century Dance* (Middletown, Conn.: Wesleyan University Press, 2005), 52. A detailed account of the impresario's life and work is Richard Buckle, *Diaghilev* (New York: Atheneum, 1979). Also see Lynn Garafola, *Diaghilev's Ballets Russes* (Cambridge, Mass.: Da Capo Press edition, 1998). A visually rich introduction (in conjunction with a major exhibit at London's Victoria and Albert Museum) is Jane Pritchard and Geoffrey Marsh, ed., *Diaghilev and the Golden Age of the Ballets Russes*, (London: Victoria and Albert Publishing, 2010). Finally, another recent volume, which draws on new research in Russian, is Sjeng Scheijen, *Diaghilev: A Life* (New York: Oxford University Press, 2010).

19. A celebratory book is Nancy Goldner, *New York City Ballet's Stravinsky Festival* (New York: Eakins Press, 1973). It includes statements by both Stravinsky and Balanchine, information on the ballets, and reviews. A book that deals with Stravinsky's earlier collaborations is Minna Lederman, ed., *Stravinsky in the Theater* (New York: Da Capo Press, 1975). A more recent and analytical study is Charles M. Joseph, *Stravinsky and Balanchine: A Journey of Invention* (New Haven, Conn.: Yale University Press, 2002).

Chapter 19

Verna Arvey, *Choreographic Music* (New York: Dutton, 1941). This chapter's reading comprises excerpts in this order, from pages 302–4; 273, 275, 284, 286, 289, 291, 293–94; 411, 300. For copies of the forthcoming new edition of *Choreographic Music* to be released by William Grant Still Music, call 928–526–9355 or go to www.wgsmusic.com.

This book, published when the author was only thirty-one, was unusual in its time for the focus on music written for or inspired by dance. Some of the information about the 1930s scene was drawn from the author's interviews or correspondence with composers. Verna Arvey's biography of her husband, William Grant Still, is *In One Lifetime* (Fayetteville: University of Arkansas Press, 1984). The Still/Arvey archives are in the Special Collections of the Library of the University of Arkansas in Fayetteville.

1. Typical of the relative inattention to music for dance in histories of music is the confession by Richard Taruskin partway through volume 4 of his *Oxford History of Western Music*. Nevertheless, his chapter 3, "Aristocratic Maximalism: Ballet from Sixteenth-Century France to Nineteenth-Century Russia; Stravinsky," provides a nice overview of European ballet and then focuses on three early works by Igor Stravinsky, namely, *Firebird*, *Petrouchka*, and *The Rite of Spring*. Of particular interest to musicians and to dancers who can read scores, there are notated musical excerpts related to the commentary (pp. 131–90).

2. George Antheil (1900–1959) wrote *Dreams* for George Balanchine and *Course, The Cave Within*, and *Dance in Four Parts* for Martha Graham. He would have been pleased today to go online and read about the efforts of Paul D. Lehrman to translate the original *Ballet mécanique* score into MIDI files and finally (in 1999) to present the synchronization that Antheil originally had in mind for the 1925 film by painter Fernand Léger and cinematographer Dudley Murphy. Go to www.antheil.org for information about the performances and the DVD titled *Bad Boy Made Good*, copyright 2006 by The Ballet Mécanique Project LLC.

   A detailed appreciation is Lynn Garafola's article "George Antheil and the Dance," *Ballet Review* 29, no. 3 (Fall 2001): 82–95, reprinted in her own collected writings, *Legacies of Twentieth-Century Dance* (Middletown, Conn.: Wesleyan University Press, 2005), 45–53.

3. Recommended for its in-depth focus on developing concert styles is Carol J. Oja, *Making Modern Music: New York in the 1920s* (New York: Oxford University Press, 2000). Chapter 5 is devoted to detailing Antheil's career and his *Ballet mécanique*.

   Some outstanding composers who collaborated with American modern dancers were trained in Europe. (For instance, Aaron Copland and Virgil Thomson were only two names among the five pages of names listed as students of the famous teacher Nadia Boulanger in Paris, on www.nadiaboulanger.org). Other composers who remained in the United States still drew inspiration from abroad. As noted by Carol J. Oja concerning New York in the 1920s:

   > There, the newest music from all over the Western world was not only heard but discussed and debated, and it provided an environment for wide-ranging experimentation with new ideas. As the decade progressed, the variety of musics classified as "modernist" grew ever more varied, and by its end, a new generation of American composers and critics had come into its own.
   >
   > Perhaps most striking of all was the way that the drive to internationalize dominated. This was not a time of cultural isolationism but rather of reaching out as boldly and ecumenically as possible. With rapid motion, the 1920s turned the Atlantic into a conduit for artistic exchange....Modernism was so deeply transnational that searching for points of origin often misses the point. The nineteenth-century image of young American students dutifully copying from European plaster casts was chucked out the window, replaced by one of them reassembling the models so thoroughly and ingeniously that the original is barely visible—but it is often there. (361–62)

4. The first ballet score composed by John Alden Carpenter (1876–1951) was *Krazy Kat* in 1922, subtitled "A Jazz Pantomime," choreographed by Adolph Bolm (1884–1951). Though born and trained in Russia, Bolm moved to the United States and is often considered a pathbreaker in American ballet with his Ballet Intime troupe. A performance by the Los Angeles Philharmonic is available on CD by New World Records. Carpenter's *Skyscrapers* can be heard in a Naxos

2002 remastering of older 1928–32 recordings, on a CD titled *Skyscraper Symphonic Jazz*. An account about how the ballet came to be is authored by "M. L." [Minna Lederman], "Skyscrapers: An Experiment in Design: An Interview with Robert Edmond Jones," *Modern Music* 3, no. 2 (1926): 21–35. Carol Oja discusses *Skyscrapers* in *Making Music Modern*, 336–40.

Verna Arvey did not mention the U.S. premiere of *Skyscrapers* on February 19, 1926, at the Metropolitan Opera House in New York City, where it received additional performances for two years. The choreographer was Sammy Lee, who in time had great success with Broadway shows such as *Lady Be Good!* and *Show Boat*. For an overview of this choreographer's career, see Frank W. D. Ries, "Sammy Lee: The Broadway Career," *Dance Chronicle* 9, no. 1 (1985): 1–95.

5. Ballet scores by William Grant Still (1895–1978) include *Sahdji*; *Lenox Avenue*; *La Guiablesse*; and *Miss Sally's Party*. A CD of *Lenox Avenue: Music of William Grant Still* reissued the 1938 recording by the CBS Symphony under Howard Barlow, on the Bay Cities label, 1991, and on the Cambria label. Available through www.williamgrantstillmusic.com. *Lenox Avenue* had its premiere as a dance in 1938, performed by the Dance Theatre of Los Angeles. Music for Still's ballet *Sahdji* is available on Mercury CD with Howard Hanson conducting the Eastman-Rochester Orchestra and Chorus.

Ruth Page (1899–1991) danced with Pavlova, Diaghilev's Ballets Russes in Monte Carlo, and Adolph Bolm's Ballet Intime in Chicago. After years of touring, she founded Chicago Ballet. In her own choreography, she incorporated nonballetic movements, and she was responsible for a series of Americana-flavored ballets with commissioned scores from leading composers—including *Hear Ye! Hear Ye!* (1934, with score by Aaron Copland); *American in Paris* (George Gershwin, 1936); and two by Jerome Moross: *American Pattern* (1937) and *Frankie and Johnny* (1938). In her book *Page by Page*, ed. Andrew Mark Wentink (Princeton, N.J.: Dance Horizons, 1978), she had some lively comments about new music for her new dances. Finally, an informative article is Jellen A. Meglin, "Choreographing Identities beyond Boundaries: *La Guiablessse* and Ruth Page's Excursions into World Dance (1926–1934)," *Dance Chronicle*, September 2007, 439–69.

Chapter 20

Virgil Thomson, *Virgil Thomson* (New York: Knopf, 1966), 269–79.

Composer Virgil Thomson was also a prolific writer (as music critic of the *New York Herald Tribune*). His book *American Music since 1910* (New York: Holt, Rinehart and Winston, 1971) provides an overview of musical activities in the early twentieth century, with an appendix of composer profiles that are particularly interesting because these artists were in the midst of their careers. A recent collection is Virgil Thomson, ed. Richard Kostelanetz, *A Reader: Selected Writings 1924–1984*, (New York: Routledge, 2002).

1. A later performance of *Filling Station*, with Jacques d'Amboise in the lead role originally created by Lew Christensen, can be seen on the DVD *Jacques d'Amboise: Portrait of a Great American Dancer* (Video Artists International, 1954).

For a triple biography of Lew Christensen and his brothers Willam and Harold (together responsible for the establishment of ballet companies and schools in both San Francisco and Utah), see Debra Hickenlooper Sowell, *The Christensen Brothers: An American Dance Epic* (Amsterdam: Harwood, 1998). For information about the extensive collaborative career of composer-pianist Trude Rittmann, see Teck (1989), 4–49.

2. Though the creative collaboration took place in the late 1920s, the first production of *Four Saints in Three Acts* was in 1934 at the Wadsworth Athenaeum in Hartford, Connecticut, followed by a six-week run on Broadway, with an all-black cast, direction by John Houseman, and movement and dances set by the British choreographer Frederick Ashton. On February 20, 2009, the seventy-fifth anniversary of the opera's premiere, a series of panels and presentations was held at the Graduate Center of City University of New York, followed by an oratorio concert performance by Encompass New Opera Theatre. A source of information is Steven Wheeler's book *Prepare for the Saints: Gertrude Stein, Virgil Thomson and the Mainstreaming of American Modernism* (New York: Random House, 1999). Mark Morris choreographed an oratorio-length abridgment of the opera, putting the musicians in the pit and the singers on side balconies for the London premiere in 2000.

Chapter 21

This reading is excerpted from Teck (1989), 40–44.

Chapter 22

The unsigned editorial "Dance and American Composers" appeared in the *Dance Observer*, February 1940, 15, 25, 26.

Overview: Drawing upon Folk Music and Wartime Patriotism

1. A stark witness is a photograph of some of the more than 100,000 church bells collected in Hamburg for this purpose. See Mickey Hart and Fredric Lieberman, *Planet Drum: A Celebration of Percussion and Rhythm* (San Francisco: Harper, 1991), 165.

   For an account of music in the context of political events in both the United States and Europe, see Richard Taruskin, *The Oxford History of Western Music*, vols. 4 and 5 on the twentieth century (New York: Oxford University Press, 2010).

2. Janet Mansfield Soares, *Martha Hill and the Making of American Dance* (Middletown, Conn.: Wesleyan University Press, 2009), 143.

Chapter 23

Woody Guthrie, "People Dancing," *Dance Observer*, December 1943, 114–15.

   On the cover of its November 1943 issue, *Dance Observer* featured a portrait of "Sophie Maslow in *Dust Bowl Ballads*"; the magazine also ran Woody

Guthrie's own account of his collaboration for *Folksay*: "Singing, Dancing, and Team-Work" (pp. 104–5).

Chapter 24

Nora Guthrie's memoir, "Sophie Maslow and Woody," is copyrighted © 2006 by Woody Guthrie Publications, Inc.

The Woody Guthrie Foundation can be accessed online at www. woodyguthrie.org, where one can also purchase many materials, including CDs of *Dust Bowl Ballads* (originally released in 1940; remastered for digital release by Buddha Records in 2000); also a remastered recording of Woody Guthrie talking to dance students about music for dance, introduced and questioned by his dancer-wife, Marjorie Mazia (released by the foundation in 2007 as a CD and book set titled *The Live Wire Woody Guthrie in Performance*, 1949).

1. Marjorie Mazia Guthrie (1917–83) was born in New Jersey. In addition to raising a family and dancing professionally, she founded her own school of dance in Brooklyn and made an album for children, *Dance Along*, for Folkways Records.

Sophie Maslow (1911–2006) danced with Martha Graham for twelve years, appeared as soloist in recitals sponsored by the New Dance League (often with political themes), and in 1942 began performing in a trio with Jane Dudley and William Bales. Choreography for her own company included *Woody Sez* in 1980. For an obituary of Sophie Maslow, written by the dance critic Jack Anderson, go to www.nytimes.com for June 26, 2006.

Many New York–based musicians and modern dancers were involved in the New Dance Group, which sponsored not only performances but also classes for both professionals and the general community. For a collection of brief articles plus listings of choreographed works with indications of composers, see Bernice Rosen, ed., *The New Dance Group: Movement for Change*, issue of the journal *Choreography and Dance* 5, pt. 4 (2001). A 2008 DVD of New Dance Group works restaged in 1993 for the American Dance Guild includes *Folksay*, performed by members of the Alvin Ailey American Dance Theater, with musicians Walt Michael and Lana Gordon (available from www.dancehorizons. com). The end of an era was noted in *The New York Times*, February 14, 2009: "After 77 years, New Dance Group will close its doors after classes on Saturday, ending a history of providing a space for modern dance lessons. The organization simply ran out of money."

Chapter 25

Agnes de Mille, *Martha: The Life and Work of Martha Graham* (New York: Vintage, 1991), 206–8, 140–41. The book includes a handy chronological list of Graham's dances, with names of the composers (pp. 434–55).

1. A major figure in twentieth-century dance, Agnes de Mille) is known as author of many books on dance, but primarily as a choreographer and dancer in ballet

and Broadway styles—notably for her success with *Oklahoma!* in 1943 and *Carousel* in 1945 (music by Richard Rodgers), as well as for her ballets performed by American Ballet Theatre. Early in her career, however, she frequently performed as a solo concert dancer. For a brief biography and information about her ballets, see the American Ballet Theatre website at http://www.abt.org/archive/choreographers/de_mille.html.

De Mille's collaborations with contemporary composers included *Rodeo* with Aaron Copland (created originally for Ballets Russes de Monte Carlo in 1942) and *Fall River Legend* with Morton Gould. A detailed account of her work with Gould is her book *Lizzie Borden: A Dance of Death* (Boston: Atlantic, Little Brown, 1968). A performance of *Fall River Legend* by Dance Theatre of Harlem, with Virginia Johnson in the lead role of Lizzie Borden, is available on DVD (RMArts, 1989). An essay by Morton Gould, "Music and the Dance," was included in the second printing of Walter Sorell, *The Dance Has Many Faces* (Cleveland: World Publishing Company, 1951). An account of that composer's career is Peter W. Goodman, *Morton Gould: American Salute* (Portland, Ore.: Amadeus Press, 2000). For further comments about the collaboration of Agnes de Mille and Morton Gould, see Teck (1989), 3–7, 78–82.

Martha Graham's own memoirs were published under the title *Blood Memory* (New York: Doubleday, 1991). Edited by Jacqueline Kennedy Onassis, the book weaves together family and professional pictures and recollections.

John Toenjes wrote an overview, "The Evolution of Martha Graham's Collaborations of Music for the Modern Dance," for *Journal of the International Guild of Musicians in Dance*, v. 2 (1992): 1–10; available through www.dancemusician.org. Also see www.jtoenjes.com for information on other writings by this former president of the guild.

Several views of what it was like to work in the studio with Martha Graham were offered by Greg Presley, who from 1979 to 1984 was accompanist for the Martha Graham School. His duties with the Graham dancers included conducting and recording two revivals of *Primitive Mysteries*. Reflecting upon his experiences as a pianist for Graham, he wrote a double interview for the *Journal of the International Guild of Musicians in Dance* 5 (1996): 30–37, in which he questioned his musical colleague Reed Hanson and then answered the same questions for himself. Looking back in 2008, Greg Presley shared these further thoughts via e-mail with members of the guild (reprinted here with his permission):

> I learned more from and through Martha Graham than through any of my music teachers. Somehow, everything that she taught about dance performance I found completely relevant to music performance. To me, she is/was the dance equivalent of Bach—someone who could take an idea generated by passion, improvisation, and inspiration, and break it down logically into component parts that could be reassembled in the same order or into something completely different for another purpose. Her ability to distill complicated ideas about art into simple, coherent, powerful language was amazing.

The first time I saw a *real* dance class was the company/advanced dance class at the Martha Graham school. I was stunned. The movement seemed so primal, the music was so exciting with changing meters and phrase lengths, that my entire body was spasmodically contracting and releasing right along with the dancers. I was just ten feet away from some of the top modern dancers in the world at that period of time, and to say I had a kinesthetic response would be to make a gross understatement.

Martha used to say that the act of listening was one of the most powerful images on the stage, and that was often the subject of the discussion when she was coaching dancers. Sometimes all she wanted was for them to stand perfectly still and find a way to show in their bodies that they were *really* listening.

Chapter 26

Aaron Copland's collected correspondence is held in the Music Division of the LofC. The copyright is held by the Aaron Copland Fund for Music.

1. Aaron Copland's scores composed specifically for theatrical dance include *Billy the Kid*; *Hear Ye Hear Ye*; *Rodeo*; *Appalachian Spring*; and *Dance Panels*. His earliest work intended for a ballet, *Grogh* (1922), was never mounted, and Copland reworked much of that score into his very kinetic *Dance Symphony* of 1930.

For a general introduction to Shaker music, see Edward Deming Andrews, *The Gift to Be Simple: Songs, Dances and Rituals of the American Shakers* (New York: Dover, 1967).

An earlier modern dance inspired by the rituals of the religious sect also known as the "United Society of Believers" was Doris Humphrey's 1931 work *The Shakers*, with music based on Shaker hymns, adapted by Pauline Lawrence.

Martha Graham was filmed in 1958 re-creating her role in Appalachian Spring, available on a black-and-white Kultur DVD titled *Martha Graham* in *Performance*, with Eugene Lester conducting. A color Nonesuch VHS film documented the Martha Graham Dance Company's 1976 performance of *Appalachian Spring* for WNET's series *Dance in America*.

For further reading, see Richard Kostelanetz, ed., *Aaron Copland: A Reader, Selected Writings: 1923–1972* (New York: Routledge, 2004). For oral histories of twentieth-century American composers including Copland, see Vivian Perlis and Libby Van Cleve, *Composers' Voices: From Ives to Ellington* (New Haven, Conn.: Yale University Press, 2005), with CDs. For an account of how Graham developed the scenario for *Appalachian Spring* in consultation with Copland, see Howard Pollack, *The Life and Work of an Uncommon Man* (Urbana and Chicago: University of Illinois Press, 2000), 388–406. Aaron Copland's own writing on music continues to be enlightening, including his much-used text *What to Listen for in Music* (New York: McGraw-Hill, 1957).

Although he did not seek out large theatrical work, nevertheless composer Roy Harris should be mentioned in connection with "Americana" styles. His *Symphony No. 3* is perhaps his best known, but in the 1940s he also worked with

Hanya Holm when she was in Colorado Springs. His dance scores for her include *From This Earth, Namesake,* and *What So Proudly We Hail.* For a brief description of some of his collaboration with Holm, see Walter Sorell, *Hanya Holm: The Biography of an Artist* (Middletown, Conn.: Wesleyan University Press 1969), 93–95. Also see Claudia Gitelman, "Finding a Place for Hanya Holm," *Dance Chronicle* 23, no. 1 (2000): 49–71.

Chapter 27

This reading by Gail Levin is taken from Gail Levin and Judith Tick, *Aaron Copland's America: A Cultural Perspective* (New York: Watson-Guptil, 2000, in conjunction with the exhibition at the Heckscher Museum of Art in Huntington, New York), 66, 99–100, 102–4. The book itself includes reproductions of artworks plus an essay by Tick titled "The Music of Aaron Copland." Levin is Distinguished Professor of Art History, American Studies, and Performing Arts at Baruch College and the Graduate Center of the City University of New York. She both conceived of the book and organized the exhibition that it accompanied.

Chapter 28

Richard Philp, editorial concerning a revival of *Appalachian Spring,* from *Dance Magazine,* August 1998. From 1999 to 2002 Philp was executive editor of the magazine; from 1989 to 1999, editor in chief; and from 1969 to 1999, managing editor. In addition, he is the author of seven books. His collection of materials related to *Dance Magazine* and his writing is in the NYPL.

Overview: Building on the Horton Experience

1. Larry Warren, *Lester Horton: Modern Dance Pioneer* (Pennington, N.J.: Princeton Book Company, 1991), ix–xii.
2. From the publicity for the Lester Horton Summit held in Los Angeles in 2006, as quoted on http://lhdt.org/lesterhorton.html.

Chapter 29

The memoir of Larry Warren (1932–2009) included in this chapter is reprinted by permission of both Anne Warren and Dance Perspectives Foundation. It is drawn from *Dance Perspectives* 31 (1967): 13–14; and from Larry Warren, *Lester Horton: Modern Dance Pioneer* (New York: Marcel Dekker, 1977), 57, 60, 69. Also from the same issue of *Dance Perspectives,* are the two excerpts included in this chapter, by Frank Eng (pp. 20, 22, 34); and by Joyce Trisler (pp. 60, 61, 62, 64). The letter from Lou Harrison is reprinted by permission of the Lou Harrison Archive, the University of California at Santa Cruz.

In addition to his biography of Lester Horton, Larry Warren wrote *Anna Sokolow: The Rebellious Spirit* (Princeton, N.J.: Princeton Book Company, 1991). Born in Brooklyn, Warren was raised in North Hollywood and both trained in the Ruth St. Denis studio and performed with the studio's Concert Dance Group. He completed undergraduate and master's work at UCLA, writing a thesis on Horton. Warren performed some years in the California area, including with the San Francisco Opera, and was on the faculty of the University of Maryland from 1971 to 1995. His wife, Anne Warren, had early training with leading dance artists, including Limón, Graham, Carolyn Brown, and Alfred Corvino, and went on to cofound the Maryland Dance Theater with her husband, to choreograph and to tour with the group for more than 400 performances. At this writing she continues as professor and chair of the dance department at the University of Maryland in College Park.

For further information on Lester Horton, consult the LofC online guide to the Lester Horton Collection. The collection includes a number of the musical scores used by Horton for his dances. Also see the Horton Summit website at www.lhdt.org. Naima Prevots has a chapter about Horton's staging of Stravinsky's *Le Sacre du Printemps* at the Hollywood Bowl in *Dancing in the Sun: Hollywood Choreographers 1915–1937* (Ann Arbor, Mich.: UMI Research Press, 1987), 221–44. A sense of how Horton's theatrical dances struck his contemporaries can be gathered from Margaret Lloyd, *The Borzoi Book of Modern Dance* (New York: Knopf, 1949), 277–92.

For a visual introduction to his training techniques, see *Lester Horton Technique: Warm Up; Intermediate Level; Advanced Level* (Kultur DVD). A video titled *Genius on the Wrong Coast* was produced by Lelia Goldoni in 1993 and includes brief dance excerpts and still pictures of Horton's work plus some reminiscences of those associated with him. It is available for viewing at the NYPL.

As with so many studio musicians for the dance, information about their careers is not easy to compile. In addition to Lou Harrison, a few names of composers indicated on program listings of Lester Horton's productions include Simon Abel, Constance Boynton, Audree Covington, Sidney Cutner, Gerhardt Dorn, Bertha English, Judith Hamilton, Mary Hoover, Sol Kaplan, Roland Klump, Toni Masarachia, Anita Short Metz, Gertrude Rivers Robinson—and Kenneth Klauss, whose work with dancers in California is described in chapter 30.

For a later collaboration that exemplifies the "total theater" approach that Bella Lewitzky honed in her work with Lester Horton, see the article by her music director Larry A. Attaway, "A Collaborative Process," *Journal of the International Guild of Musicians in Dance* 1 (1991): 17–23.

Chapter 30

Kenneth Klauss was interviewed by phone by Katherine Teck on January 29, 2009. The author retains the taped conversation and transcript, which were supplemented by subsequent e-mails. Mr. Klauss provided the author with a video of his presentation for the Lester Horton Festival cosponsored by the Library of Congress and American University on December 4–10, 1996. Because some topics were covered similarly in both the presentation and the private conversation, this article draws upon both without attribution for specific sentences. Additionally, the composer provided CDs of himself performing his own music, including *Retrospect: Tokas for Piano Solo*, copyright by the Kenneth Klauss Trust in 1996, and two personally recorded CDs with his *Contemplations* (1968 and 1973, 1975, and 1976). The observations about the music are the author's.

1. Naima Prevots was instrumental, along with American University, in organizing the Lester Horton Festival in conjunction with the Library of Congress, December 4–10, 1996. Included was a performance of *Dedication to José Clemente Orozco* with the composer at the piano. Lucy Brown was pianist for a performance of *Orozco* filmed in black and white and featuring Alvin Ailey and Carmen de Lavallade, available for viewing at the NYPL.

    When this dance by Lester Horton had its New York premiere at the YM-YWHA, Louis Horst himself gave it high praise in the *Dance Observer* of June–July 1953:

    > Another dance of a more sustained pattern was the beautiful *Dedication to Jose Clemente Orozco*, superbly danced by Carmen de Lavallade and Jack Dodds. With a minimum of props, a sombrero for the man and a shawl for the woman,
    > Mr. Horton has created a most touching and moving dance, one of the finest this viewer has ever witnessed. (89)

2. Kenneth Klauss was music director and pianist for the 1969 videotape *The Art of Benjamin Zemach*, produced by Miriam Rochlin and presented by the University of Judaism, School of Fine Arts in Los Angeles; available for viewing at the NYPL. For further information about Benjamin Zemach (1901–97), see Naima Prevots, *Dancing in the Sun: Hollywood Choreographers 1915–1937* (Ann Arbor, Mich.: UMI Press, 1987), 197–218. For an overview of Zemach's unusual career, see the obituary written by Anna Kisselgoff for *The New York Times* of June 30, 1997.

3. Originally from Missouri, Harriette Ann Gray (1914–87) was a leading dancer with Humphrey-Weidman, worked in Hollywood in the 1940s (both teaching and dancing in films), and formed her own touring company in the 1950s. She was on the faculty of Stephens College and from 1946 to 1979 was director of dance at the Stephens/Perry Mansfield School in Steamboat Springs, Colorado.

4. Filmed performances of this work (notably the one with Carmen de Lavallade and Alvin Ailey) can be seen at the NYPL.

5. Kenneth Klauss provided the author with a video of the opening ceremonies for the Klauss-James Archive and Art Museum in Parkston, South Dakota, from which some of his comments here are drawn. Parkston is located west of Sioux Falls. A picture of the museum plus reproductions of some paintings by Bernard Albert James (1929–94) can be accessed online at www.musicartsd.org. The website also contains a complete list of compositions by Kenneth Klauss.

Chapter 31

This section was based on a taped phone interview between Katherine Teck and Carmen de Lavallade on February 2, 2009; on the author's observations of live and filmed performances; and on other materials as indicated below.

A documentary film about Carmen de Lavallade and her husband, Geoffrey Holder, is *Carmen and Geoffrey*, produced by Linda Atkinson and Nick Doob (DVD from First Run Features, 2009). See also Jennifer Dunning's book *Geoffrey Holder: A Life in Theater, Dance, and Art* (New York: Abrams, 2001). A brief glimpse of the young Carmen de Lavallade dancing can be seen on the DVD version of *Carmen Jones* (20th Century Fox). That film had dance sequences choreographed by Herbert Ross, who later cast Carmen de Lavallade on Broadway in *House of Flowers*.

A digitalized compilation film at the NYPL includes six works choreographed for Carmen de Lavallade by Geoffrey Holder: *Come Sunday* (spirituals sung by Odetta); *Bachianas No. 5* (Heitor Villa Lobos piece arranged by Lalo Schifrin); *Songs of the Auvergne* (music by Marie-Joseph Canteloube, sung by Madeleine Grey); *Dear Quincy* (jazz by Quincy Jones); *Allegro* (harp concerto by Alberto Ginastera); and *The Creation* (poem by James Weldon Johnson, music, "Venus" movement from Gustav Holst's *Planets*). The first four were originally telecast by CBS-TV on *Camera Three* in 1968; the last two were from the PBS "Evening at the Pops" with Arthur Fiedler and the Boston Pops Orchestra in 1973.

Also at NYPL is a filmed tribute to Lester Horton, that includes 1987 Jacob's Pillow performances of James Truitte, Carmen de Lavallade, and Alvin Ailey in 1987 in the following Horton dances: *Sarong Paramaribo* (music, Les Baxter); *To José Clemente Orozco* (music, Kenneth Klauss); *The Beloved* (music, Judith Hamilton); and *Liberian Suite* (music, Duke Ellington).

Sarong Paramaribo, performed by de Lavallade, was videotaped during the twenty-fifth anniversary celebrations of the Alvin Ailey American Dance Theater. Her 1990 restaging of it for dancers of that company can be seen at the NYPL in a videotape made during rehearsals at UCLA in 1990.

A videotape of John Butler's *Portrait of Billie*, performed by Carmen de Lavallade and Ulysses Dove in 1992 at Jacob's Pillow, has recorded songs with Billie Holiday singing. Additionally, there is a 1973 film made in a studio at Jacob's Pillow in preparation for de Lavallade's performance of two dances by Ruth St. Denis: *Incense* (with music by Harvey Loomis, performed by Jess Meeker on the piano) and *The Yogi* (music by Alexander Alexay).

In keeping alive the knowledge of former collaborations, Carmen de Lavallade was a panelist for "Carlos Surinach and the Creation of Modern Dance in New York," a concert and discussion sponsored in 2008 by the Foundation of Iberian Music. To see her performing in tandem with Surinach's music, see the film of *David and Bathsheba*, a narrative dance choreographed by John Butler with Glen Tetley as David, telecast by the series *Lamp unto My Feet* in 1960. Another biblical drama was set by Butler, also available for viewing at the NYPL: *Jephthah's Daughter*, with a score by Peggy Glanville-Hicks. See comments about this and the composer's view of modern dance in James Murdoch, *Peggy Glanville-Hicks: A Transposed Life* (Hillsdale, N.Y.: Pendragon Press, 2002), 228–30.

The video *Celebrating John Butler* (1918–93) documents panels and film clips shown on December 6, 1993, at the NYPL. During the discussions, Carmen de Lavallade recounts how natural it seemed for her to enter into the dramatic dances choreographed by Butler, because of the training she had had with Lester Horton. Included are clips from de Lavallade's performances in the 1950s, among them *Glory Folk* and *Five Senses*. The video ends with footage from a rehearsal made late in John Butler's life, at Jacob's Pillow, rehearsing *Portrait of Billie* with Carmen de Lavallade and Ulysses Dove.

Among Carmen de Lavallade's own choreographed works for Paradigm are SRO (*Single Room Occupancy*), with music by Astor Piazzolla, and *Sam's Party* (music by Marsalis, Bloom, Strayhorn, Prince). For information about the artists in the company, go to www.paradigm-nyc.org. Other choreography by de Lavallade includes *Sweet Bitter Love* (assisted by Dudley Williams) for Alvin Ailey American Dance Theater in 2000 to several love songs; and *Sensemaya*, to music by Silvestre Revueltas, performed by Dance Theatre of Harlem, which also can be seen in a film funded by the Save Our Treasures project of the National Endowment for the Arts and the National Park Service.

A video interview in which de Lavallade touches upon multiculturalism and her experiences growing up in Los Angeles can been seen online as part of the National Visionary Leadership Project at www.visionaryproject.org/delavalladecarmen/. A condensed transcript of the interview appears in Camille O. Cosby and Renee Poussaint, *Wealth of Wisdom: Legendary African American Elders Speak* (New York: Washington Square Press, 2004), 96–103.

In 2009 the Alvin Ailey American Dance Theater released a CD of *Blues Suite*, premiered in 1958 at the 92nd Street Y in New York City. The CD, conducted by Howard Roberts, features the singing of Brother John Sellers and is available from www.alvinailey.org.

1. For a profile of Carmelita Maracci, see Agnes de Mille, *Portrait Gallery* (New York: Houghton Mifflin, 1990), 51–69.
2. Janet Collins (1917–2003), an older cousin of de Lavallade, was born in New Orleans and raised in Los Angeles. She was a much-admired ballerina and also danced in the companies of Lester Horton and Katherine Dunham, as well as touring with her own solo concert dance programs. In New York she became the first black ballet soloist with the Metropolitan Opera and also performed on Broadway and in Hollywood films. See obituary written by Jennifer Dunning for *The New York Times*, May 31, 2003. Also see Yael Lewin, "Janet Collins: a spirit that knows no bounds—African American ballerina," *Dance Magazine*, February 1997, 66–71. A documentary film titled *To Dance Is To Live* was being completed by M. J. Washington in 2009.

3. For biography and video clips of an interview with the folksinger Odetta Holmes (1930–2008), go to www.visionaryproject.org/gordonodetta. For an obituary by Tim Weiner from *The New York Times*, go to http://www.nytimes.com/2008/12/03/arts/music/03odetta.html.

4. *A Drum Is a Woman* was telcast May 8, 1957 on the *United States Steel Hour*. The music alone is available on an imported CD issued in 2008 by Jazz Track Records.

   Duke Ellington's archives are located in the National Museum of American History, Smithsonian Institution, Washington, D.C.; see http://americanhistory.si.edu/archives/d5301.htm. Also see Vivian Perlis and Libby Van Cleve, *Composers' Voices from Ives to Ellington* (New Haven, Conn.: Yale University Press, 2005), 350–415; and see pp. 400–404 for Alvin Ailey's memoir of collaborating with Ellington. Also suggested is Mark Tucker, ed., *The Duke Ellington Reader* (New York: Oxford University Press, 1993).

5. John Gruen made this comment while introducing Carmen de Lavallade on one of his 1978 programs on New York City's radio station WNCN, broadcast with the title "The Sound of Dance." A tape can be heard at the NYPL. And concluding with praise garnered more recently, in June 2010, the professional organization Dance/USA honored Carmen de Lavallade and the sixtieth anniversary of her onstage debut as a concert dancer. See Deborah Jowitt, "Divine de Lavallade," *Dance Magazine*, June 2010, 18.

Chapter 32

Alvin Ailey's poem "Instructions: How to Play the Drums," drawn from the artist's notebooks, is included here courtesy of the Alvin Ailey Dance Foundation, Inc.

Chapter 33

Jennifer Dunning, "Alvin Ailey's *Revelations*," from *Alvin Ailey: A Life in Dance* (Reading, Mass.: Addison-Wesley, 1996), 122–26.

   Jennifer Dunning's reviews for *The New York Times* can be accessed via online archives at www.nytimes.com. These include, over the years, a number of articles about both the Alvin Ailey American Dance Theater and the Ailey II dancers.

Chapter 34

Alvin Ailey with A. Peter Bailey, *Revelations: The Autobiography of Alvin Ailey* (New York: Birch Lane, 1995), 97–101.

   A video of the Alvin Ailey American Dance Company performing *Revelations* is available from Kultur. *An Evening with Alvin Ailey American Dance Theater* was released in DVD format by Image Entertainment in 2001. The soundtrack for *Revelations* is available on CD from www.alvinailey.org.

   The NYPL held several panel discussions in 1992 in connection with its exhibit *Continuing Revelations*, and the program was videotaped. Speakers who shared their experiences with the first performances of *Revelations* and beyond included Judith Jamison, Ves Harper, Carmen de Lavallade, Dorene Richardson, Ella Thompson Moore, and Liz Williamson. Zita Allen acted as moderator. A book with further details is Thomas DeFrantz, *Dancing Revelations: Alvin Ailey's Embodiment of African American Culture* (New York: Oxford University Press, 2004).

To follow the thread of African American music, see Eileen Southern, *The Music of Black Americans* 3rd ed. (New York: Norton, 1997). And for a dance focus: Lynne Fauley Emery, *Black Dance from 1619 to Today*, 2nd rev. ed. (Hightstown, N.J.: Princeton Book Company, 1988). A more recent volume is John O. Perpener III, *African-American Concert Dance: The Harlem Renaissance and Beyond* (Urbana: University of Illinois Press, 2001).

Part Four

Epigraph, from *Lou Harrison's Music Primer* (New York: C. F. Peters, 1971), 42.

Overview: Expanding Timbre Possibilities

1. Some accounts of Partch's various theatrical projects can be found in Harry Partch, *Bitter Music: Collected Journals, Essays, Introductions, and Librettos* (Urbana: University of Illinois Press, 1991). Also see Bob Gilmore, *Harry Partch: A Biography* (New Haven, Conn.: Yale University Press, 1998).

   For a first acquaintance with Partch, it seems best to suggest that people hear his music and see pictures of his instruments. These have been preserved and can still be heard in some concerts, but such opportunities are uncommon. The website of the Harry Partch Foundation is www.corporeal.com. For a clip of Partch introducing the instruments played in *Bewitched*, go to http://musicmavericks. publicradio.org/features/feature_partch.html. In addition to hearing the music, you can click onto pictures of the instruments and "play" them via computer.

   The reader is also directed to a book produced in connection with San Francisco Symphony's June 2000 festival under Michael Tilson Thomas, *American Mavericks* (Berkeley and Los Angeles: University of California Press, 2001).

2. Louis Horst review in *Dance Observer*, August–September 1956, 101.

3. Apparently the early compositions by Varèse were either lost or destroyed. In terms of total performance time, his surviving works are brief (witness the fact that the Lincoln Center Festival for July 2010 was able to schedule the entire Varèse repertoire for two evenings). Yet because of his experimental explorations, he influenced younger composers. In 1915 he had come to the United States, where he helped to found the International Composers Guild and to organize performances of new music.

4. See Paul Griffiths, entry on Varèse in H. Wiley Hitchcock and Stanley Sadie,ed.,. *The New Grove Dictionary of American Music*, (London: Macmillan Press Limited, 1986), v.4, 447–452. The first edition of this reference set is being updated by Oxford University Press, edited by Charles Hiroshi Garrett.

For now, until publication, many of the new entry articles are available online on a subscription basis. Go to www.oxfordmusiconline.com.

A recommended source about new inventions is *Experimental Musical Instruments*. This magazine ceased publication in 1999, but back issues, books, CDs, and links to other sites on inventive instruments are all available at http://www.windworld.com/newsnw.htm.

Chapter 35

Franziska Boas, "Percussion Music and Its Relation to the Modern Dance: Fundamental Concepts," is from a series in *Dance Observer*, January 1940, 6–7.

1. The Franziska Boas Collection is in the LofC. It includes Labanotation scores plus choreographic notes and other materials documenting the artist's life and work.

The influence of Mary Wigman concerning instruments is beyond the scope of this book, but for information about her protégée Hanya Holm, see Walter Sorell, *Hanya Holm* (Middletown, Conn.: Wesleyan University Press, 1969). Also available is a video, *Hanya: Portrait of a Dancer*, Dance Horizons. For recollections based on an interview with Holm late in her life, touching upon the use of percussion instruments, see Teck (1989), 11–14.

Chapter 36

Henry Cowell, "East Indian Tala Music," from *Dance Observer*, December 1939, 296.

1. For an example of how one contemporary percussionist has put into practice the kinds of suggestions made by Cowell, go to www.tiggerbenfordpercussion .com. Robert ("Tigger") Benford, one of the percussionists heard on the CD *Talamalika*, has had extensive experience using percussion creatively with choreographers and dance teachers. For those who wish to delve into tabla and tala systems, Benford recommends Samir Chatterjee, *A Study of Tabla*, published by the organization Chhandayan, 2006. For information, go to www.tabla.org.

Henry Cowell would probably have been delighted by recent concerts of Indian tabla player Zakir Hussain in combination with composer–double bass player Edgar Meyer and banjo virtuoso Béla Fleck. For information, go to www.momentrecords.com. What is unusual with this trio's music is the seamless amalgamation of Indian techniques and rhythms with other styles, including jazz, bluegrass, spirituals, and their own original composition.

Chapter 37

Lehman Engel, "Choric Sound for the Dance," *Dance Observer*, April 1934, 29.

1. An intriguing book organizing various possible vocalizations is Cornelius L. Reid, *A Dictionary of Vocal Terminology* (New York: Joseph Patelson Music House, 1983).

Chapter 38

John Cage, "Goal: New Music, New Dance," *Dance Observer*, December 1939, 296–97.

Chapter 39

Otto Luening's description of his electronic music for Doris Humphrey's *Theatre Piece No. 2* is excerpted from *The Odyssey of an American Composer: The Autobiography of Otto Luening* (New York: Scribner's, 1980), 546–49.

1. The memoirs of composer Otto Luening (1900–1996) provide a representative slice of concert musical life during the entire twentieth century in the United States. The archival collection of Otto Luening is in the NYPL and includes extensive documentation of the development of electronic music.

    To hear some early electronic works, including some by Luening, a good CD is *Pioneers of Electronic Music* (New World Records, 2006). A three-disc compiled set with an illustrated ninety-six-page booklet is *OHM: The Early Gurus of Electronic Music 1948–1980* (Roslyn, N.Y.: ellipsisarts, 2000). The set includes Clara Rockmore playing the theremin (considered the earliest electronic instrument); the 1955 *musique concrète* piece *Dripsody* that Hugh Le Caine created by manipulating the sounds of a single drop of water; Edgard Varèse's *Poème électronique* dating from 1958; as well as sample works by other composers up to a 1982 piece by Brian Eno.

2. The assistant mentioned, Chou Wen-chung, was born in China in 1923, immigrated to the United States in 1946, and went on to become a well-respected composer as well as later chairman of the Columbia University music department. See Peter M. Chang, *Chou Wen-chung: The Life and Work of a Contemporary Chinese-Born American Composer* (Lanham, Md.: Scarecrow Press, 2006).

Chapter 40

Alwin Nikolais, "My Total Theater Concept," originally untitled essay from *Nik: A Documentary*, ed. Marcia B. Siegel, *Dance Perspectives* 48 (1971): 11–17.

1. The Alwin Nikolais archives, including many documentary films of performances, are in the library of Ohio University. Audiences of today can enjoy some of his works on a multivideo set, *The World of Alwin Nikolais*, released by the Nikolais-Louis Foundation for Dance. For the music alone, a CD sampling is available on CRI 651. The Ririe-Woodbury Dance Company (based in Salt Lake City) has continued to keep some of this repertoire alive in touring performances, especially commemorating the 2010 centenary of the composer-choreographer's birth. For information go to www.nikolaislouis.org and to http://www.ririewoodbury.com/nikolais.php. The NYPL mounted a major centennial multimedia exhibition in 2010 called *Alwin Nikolais' Total Theater of Motion*, curated by Claudia Gitelman.

    A recent collection of readings is Claudia Gitelman and Randy Martin, eds., *The Returns of Alwin Nikolais: Bodies, Boundaries and the Dance Canon*

(Middletown, Conn.: Wesleyan University Press, 2007), especially chap. 8, "The Music of Alwin Nikolais" by Bob Gilmore (pp. 132–53).

2. The reference by Alwin Nikolais was to the silent movie star W. C. Fields, who was reputed to remark that "anybody who hates children can't be all bad."

3. *Musique concrète* was a term for tape techniques involving the tape-recording of natural or man-made sounds and then manipulating and splicing the tape to make a musical composition. A boxed set of CDs with some of the earliest of these is a Philips import (released in 2002), *Mix 03* with music by the French composer Pierre Henry. Included in the CD set is the 1963 work *Variations pour une Porte et un Soupir* (Variations for a Door and a Sigh,) which was used by George Balanchine for his 1974 pas de deux by the same title.

Chapter 41

John Cage, "Experimental Music," was originally given as a speech before the Music Teachers National Association in 1957 and is copyrighted by the John Cage Trust.

1. In 1995 Composers Recordings reissued its landmark 1951 recording of Maro Ajemian performing Cage's *Sonatas and Interludes for Prepared Piano*, now available as a CD from New World Records. A recent two-CD set of John Cage's *Music for Prepared for Piano* was made by Boris Berman, available on the Naxos label. Among available DVDs that offer insights into this unusual collaborative team is *Cage/Cunningham*, a documentary by Elliot Caplan (Kultur).

Chapter 42

John Cage, "Communication," is an abridged excerpt from a lecture given at Rutgers University in 1958. The copyright is held by the John Cage Trust, which gave approval for the publication of the excerpts included here. The complete lecture can be found in *Silence: Lectures and Writings by John Cage* (Middletown, Conn.: Wesleyan University Press, 1973), 41–56.

Chapter 43

Carolyn Brown, excerpts from *Chance and Circumstance: Twenty Years with Cage and Cunningham* (New York: Knopf, 2007), 40–41, 47, 49–51, 172, 233–34. (New title added for this chapter.)

1. For extensive information on the life and work of Merce Cunningham and his company, plus the unusual Legacy Plan, go to www.merce.org. A wonderful gift to viewers is the company's free webcast series of "Mondays with Merce," which can still be seen online and includes clips of Cunningham teaching, performing, and rehearsing, as well as his associates discussing various aspects of their art and experiences. A listing of Merce Cunningham's complete dance works can be found at www.merce.org/archives. The John Cage Collection is at the NYPL.

For Alastair Macaulay's tribute to Merce Cunningham, in *The New York Times* of July 27, 2009, go to http://www.nytimes.com/2009/07/28/arts/dance/28cunningham.html. The Legacy Tour of the Merce Cunningham Dance Company, including performances in more than forty cities around the world, was scheduled to end December 31, 2011 in New York City.

A particularly beautiful book is David Vaughan, ed. Melissa Harris, *Merce Cunningham: Fifty Years*. (New York: Aperture, 1997). Vaughan, archivist for Cunningham, provides chronological commentary, and the large volume features magnificent color photographs, including a number showing Carolyn Brown in performance. Also pertinent about musical aspects of these works are sections of *The Dancer and the Dance: Merce Cunningham in Conversation with Jacqueline Lesschaeve* (New York, Marion Boyars, 1985).

Part Five

Epigraph, from a speech that Henry Cowell made in Tehran in 1961. The entire essay is in "A Composer's World," in *Essential Cowell: Selected Writings on Music by Henry Cowell 1921–1964*, ed. Dick Higgins (Kingston, N.Y.: McPherson, 2001), 311–20.

Overview: Diverse Methods and Aesthetic Ideas

1. The orchestral scores that Barber wrote included *Cave of the Heart* in 1947, for Martha Graham, and *Souvenirs*, a ballet for Todd Bolender in 1955. For his part, Schuman composed large orchestral scores: *Undertow* for Antony Tudor in 1945; and for Martha Graham, *Night Journey* (1947), *Judith* (1949), *Voyage* (1953), and *The Witch of Endor* (1965).

Chapter 44

Leonard Bernstein's essay, originally titled simply "Music and the Dance," appeared in *Dance Magazine*, June 1946, 28, 42.

1. For further information about Leonard Bernstein, go to www.leonardbernstein.com. In addition to his legacy of hundreds of recorded and filmed performances plus his own compositions, Bernstein left his mark on educating audiences through his telecast and written explorations of the aesthetics and craft of music. His book *The Joy of Music*, originally published in 1959, has been reprinted (Pompton Plains, N.J.: Amadeus Press, 2004). For information on the sometimes long-distance collaborations of Leonard Bernstein with Jerome Robbins, see Deborah Jowitt, *Jerome Robbins: His Life, His Theater, His Dance* (New York: Simon and Schuster, 2004), 78–87.

Chapter 45

Paul Taylor, "Why I Make Dances," appeared in the *Wall Street Journal* on February 23, 2008.

1. Indicative of the almost universally held opinion about Paul Taylor's innate musicality is a review by Alastair Macaulay in *The New York Times* of February 29, 2009. Headlined "Dance Weds Music, and the Body Electric Sings," the column begins:

> No mystery in the art of dance runs deeper than that of how movement and music can fit satisfyingly together. And today no choreographer addresses that mystery with more imaginative power than Paul Taylor. He responds to music with a searching innocence that reveals many of its layers, and yet he gives the impression of being the least musically analytical of great choreographers.

For a comprehensive list of Paul Taylor's works, with indications of the music he has used, go to the company website at www.ptdc.org. Paul Taylor's autobiography is *Private Domain* (New York: Knopf, 1987). He was also interviewed about musical aspects of his work for Teck (1989), 8–11. (See also pp. 69–72 for information about Taylor's composer-conductor Donald York.) Additionally suggested is the DVD *Dancemaker* produced by Matthew Diamond. For an interview with one of Paul Taylor's earlier collaborators, see Beth Tyler, "John Herbert McDowell: Composing for the Dance," *Ballet Review* 13, no. 2 (Summer 1985): 23–28.

Chapter 46

Carlos Surinach, untitled essay was originally in *Composer/Choreographer, Dance Perspectives* 16 (1963): 26–28. The brackets and words within them were in the original.

1. For a visit with Carlos Surinach later in his life and discussion of his dance collaborations, see Teck (1989), 36–40.

   On March 31, 2008, the City University of New York Graduate Center's Foundation for Iberian Music presented a series of programs titled "Carlos Surinach and the Creation of Modern Dance in New York," with panels and performances in celebration of the fiftieth anniversary of the score for Martha Graham's *Embattled Garden*.

Chapter 47

Lou Harrison's article was originally titled simply "Music for the Modern Dance," in the *American Composers Alliance Bulletin*, October 1952, 11–12.

1. For information on Lou Harrison's life and works, with CDs sampling his music, see two books by Leta E. Miller and Fredric Lieberman: *Composing a World: Lou Harrison, Musical Wayfarer* (Urbana: University of Illinois Press, 2004); and *Lou Harrison* (Urbana: University of Illinois Press, 2006). Chapter 4 of *Composing a World* is devoted to "Music and Dance" of Harrison (pp. 79–101); chapter 11, "Assembling the Pieces: The Compositional Process," explains Harrison's concept of a "kit" for each work (pp. 205–36). For various tribute memories about Harrison see www.otherminds.org/shtml/Irememberlou.shtml.

The range of Harrison's musical influences and styles has been summed up by Miller and Lieberman in their book *Composing a World*:

> He has absorbed one musical influence after another: Handel, Rameau, Cowell, Ives, Ruggles, Schoenberg, Thomson, Partch; percussion, tuning systems, Gregorian chant, Amerindian song, Korean court music, gagaku, gamelan, Chinese opera; Medieval, Baroque, modern, Indian, Turkish, and Javanese dance styles. As we have seen, he dives headfirst into an in-depth study of each new discovery; learns to imitate it; and then shapes the technique to fit his personal language. (205)

To sample Lou Harrison's music, the listener might explore the following: *Drums along the Pacific* (New Albion, 2003); *Rhymes With Silver* (the suite for Mark Morris Dance Company, on New Albion, 2000); *Perilous Chapel* (which was choreographed by Jean Erdman, also New Albion, 1994); *Lou Harrison: For Strings* (Mode label, 2004); *In Retrospect* (includes *Solstice*, which was originally choreographed by Jean Erdman; on the CD conducted by Dennis Russell Davies on New World, 2007); and an earlier release of *Solstice* (on Music Masters Jazz). A sampling of Harrison's *Gamelan Music* is on Music Masters Classics.

Dance and Myth: The Dance Works of Jean Erdman is a multivideo documentation supervised by the choreographer, featuring some of her collaborative works with Henry Cowell, Lou Harrison, John Cage, and other composers. Erdman's archives are in the special collections of the NYPL. The VHS set includes a performance of *Solstice*.

For further remarks by Harrison on collaboration, see Teck (1989), 56–62, 171–72.

2. Alan Hovhaness, born in Massachusetts of Armenian heritage, lived from 1911 to 2000. Known for his mystical scores with melodies based on various non-Western pitch modes, and with static harmonies and cycles of rhythms, he had success with modern dancers, writing *Circe* and *Myth of a Voyage* for Martha Graham; *Plains Daybreak* for Erick Hawkins; as well as works for modern choreographers Jean Erdman and Pearl Lang, plus the ballet *A Rose for Miss Emily* for Agnes de Mille and American Ballet Theatre. For further information, go to www.hovhaness.com.

3. Lou Harrison has a very particular train of thought here, which some readers have told me they find difficult to follow. The paragraph might well spark some conversations with different views, and I hesitate to comment. That said, here are a few observations. One definition given for "emotion" by *Webster's Seventh New Collegiate Dictionary* is: "a psychic and physical reaction subjectively experienced as strong feeling and physiologically involving changes that prepare the body for immediate vigorous action." We frequently think of "emotion" as being an invisible human sensation. The "e-" even suggests "away from" motion. Yet we move, and in everyday life our movements do express invisible feelings, or emotion. With dance, however, physical motion is extended,

intensified, and focused for theatrical purposes. Both the visible physical motions and the invisible emotions suggested by the dancers' movements can reach audiences, can touch us as we watch. And so we may "re-realize" or feel again and understand in heightened ways, things that we may have known or experienced before somehow, but in more subdued manner. We recognize in the dancers' physical motion "meanings" or feelings, "emotions" that are *behind* the visible. And so the dancers "perfect" or make whole our understanding of particular unseen emotions, precisely through their physical movement which we see. It is interesting that when we feel emotion upon seeing a film or dance or other theatrical presentation, we often say: "It was moving," or "I was moved by it." The reference is to our invisible feelings. But with the dancers, of course, the movement is actual; they are literally moving. Previously in this collection, Virgil Thomson touched upon this phenomenon of eliciting an emotional reaction from audience members. I don't know if all this helps, but offer it as one train of thought prompted by Harrison's.—Ed.

Chapter 48

Lucia Dlugoszewski, article originally titled simply "Notes on New Music for the Dance," *Dance Observer*, November 1957, 133–35.

1. For information on the Erick Hawkins Dance Foundation, go to www. erickhawkinsdance.org. *Black Lake*, one of the many Hawkins-Dlugoszewski collaborations, can be seen on the video *Erick Hawkins: America Dancing*, available at www.dancehorizons.com. For a sample of Dlugoszewski's purely concert works, listen to *Disparate Stairway Radical Other* (with the composer performing, conducted by Gerard Schwartz, Composers Recordings, 2000).

2. It was Mike Silverton who paid a personal salute to Lucia Dlugoszewski as "a splendid composer" in "A Friend's Tribute to Lucia Dlugoszewski," *La Folia*, 2:5, accessible via www.lafolia.com/archive/silverton200007dlugo.html.

Another tribute to Dlugoszewski was written by dance critic Deborah Jowitt. This remembrance, from the *Village Voice*, April 19, 2000, is quoted by permission of the author and the *Village Voice*:

> Lucia Dlugoszewski was more than Erick Hawkins's wife, musical director, and principal composer. The two were artistic soulmates. He was her hero, and often she put her own career—as a distinctive voice in American music—on hold to provide spare yet sensuous scores for his dances. She was found dead the day the Hawkins company, which she directed, began its season at Playhouse 91. She had been struggling to finish the music for *Motherwell Amor*, a two-part dance she'd also choreographed.
>
> Into that work, heroically performed in her honor, she poured all her passion for Erick, and her unassuaged grief over his death six years ago. Building duet after startlingly beautiful duet, she created an anthology of love. Women bore men in complex ways; men cradled women. Partners became mountains for each other to climb. Enlaced like a yin-yang symbol, gentle and strange, they grazed on one

another, exploring the tender claw, the kiss on the back of the knee, the tracing finger. As with all her work, this score for piano, percussion, and small ensemble didn't support the dancing but conversed with it—uttering the turbulence beneath calm, the wondering hush that surrounds fierce endeavor. (Those who loved Lucia could envision her—fervent, disheveled—attacking her "timbre piano.") In what we lament as her final statement, she summed up a rare artistic partnership in a hymn to love fulfilled.

Part Six

Epigraph, from Walter Sorell, *Hanya Holm: The Biography of an Artist* (Middletown, Conn.: Wesleyan University Press, 1969), 54.

Overview: Postwar Trends, and Music in the Training of Dancers

1. The focus in this part is on artistic developments within a general cultural and educational context, but of course all these took place against a larger national backdrop that included dire conditions as well as hopeful and wonderful events: the Cold War; the Korean War; the Vietnam War; the Civil Rights Act; and Apollo 11 landing on the moon, July 10, 1969—two years after José Limón's convocation address that concludes this collection.

2. For profiles of Norma Reynolds Dalby, Marjorie Landsmark-DeLewis, and Jess Meeker, see Teck (1990), 192–98; 54–59; 31–35.

3. Ann Hutchinson, "Idea into Reality: The High School of Performing Arts," *Dance Observer*, January 1950, 7. Since that time, LaGuardia High School of Performing Arts has cultivated excellent musicians for dance, with professionals accompanying all studio classes. In recent years, some of these musicians have hosted mini–conference programs showcasing their special art of collaboration. For current information about the school, go to http://www.laguardiahs.org/home.html.

4. Pertinent to dance and its music being regarded as an art, see William Moulton, "Musicians in Dance: The Struggle for Legitimacy in Academia," *Journal of the International Guild of Musicians in Dance* 1 (1991): 24–32. William Moulton, to whom this book is dedicated, is at this writing associate arts professor in the dance department at the Tisch School of the Arts, New York University. He was on the faculty at the State University of New York, Brockport, when he founded the International Guild of Musicians in Dance in 1990. Subsequently, in New York City, he cofounded the contemporary music and dance ensemble Footnote, which has performed on campuses across the United States, and in addition to being a highly creative improvising pianist, he is the composer of more than fifty works for contemporary dance.

5. Quotation from "Juilliard School of Music Announces Addition of Dance Department," unsigned report in *Dance Observer*, April 1951, 53. The same issue also includes a more detailed report: Arthur Todd, "A New Union of Music and Dance" (pp. 84–85).

William Schuman had a great deal of influence upon art dance in America through his presidential administrative positions at the Juilliard School and at Lincoln Center for the Performing Arts. For a detailed biography, see Joseph W. Polisi, *American Music: The Life and Times of William Schuman* (New York: Amadeus Press, 2008), especially 146–65, for an account of Schuman's collaborations for dance. Also see Teck (1989), 34–36. The composer's talk at the Martha Graham School on November 5, 1986, provided a memorable overview of his collaborations with Graham.

6. William Bales (1910–90) danced with Humphrey-Weidman, subsequently performing with the Dudley-Maslow-Bales trio. He taught at Bennington, NYU, the Juilliard School, and elsewhere before becoming the founding dean of dance at Purchase. The award-winning facilities, the pianos, and dance as an art were certainly championed by him. Suggesting the current tone of study, the website for Purchase's Conservatory of Dance states flatly: "This is not a program for dabblers." Courses in music theory and music literature are required for all dance students.

7. Internet websites offer information about specific college dance programs. Additionally, a handy volume for aspiring dancers, composers, and accompanists is the annual *Dance Magazine College Guide*.

8. For the history of this organization, as well as current information, go to www.ACDFA.org.

9. The website of the American Dance Festival at www.americandancefestival.org includes a history of the gatherings plus a chronological list (in progress) of all its premieres and commissions, since 1935, with indications of both choreographers and the music used.

10. For information about the Regional Dance Association, go to http://www .regional-dance-america.org. Some 3,000 dancers are involved in the association's festivals and programs each year.

Chapter 49

"My Love Affair with Music," written in 1967, was published in Erick Hawkins, in *The Body Is a Clear Place* (Princeton, N.J.: Princeton Book Company, 1992), 78–87.

1. The Erick Hawkins Dance Company has continued to perform under the direction of Katherine Duke. For current information, go to www. erickhawkinsdance.org.

For additional comments by Hawkins concerning the music he used, see Teck (1989), 17–22. For a sample of the choreographer's works, a VHS film is available from www.dancehorizons.com and includes dances with scores by Lucia Dlugoszewski, Virgil Thomson, Alan Hovhaness, and David Diamond.

Among exceptional films at the NYPL is one from the "Speaking of Dance," series released at the American Dance Festival in 1995, titled *Erick Hawkins: Poet of the Modern Dance*, produced by Douglas Rosenberg. It offers dance excerpts as well as interviews with both Hawkins and Dlugoszewski speaking eloquently about how important it is for musicians and dancers to work together in live performances. It is now also available in DVD format; go to http://adfvideo .com/adf.php

Chapter 50

Bessie Schönberg was interviewed by the author on October 6, 1989. The excerpt here was taken from "Bessie Schönberg Contrasts Music for Ballet and Modern Dance," in Teck (1990), 78–82.

1. For a brief biography, photographs, and excerpts from this artist's oral history at Sarah Lawrence College, go to http://pages.slc.edu/archives/schonberg/index .htm.

Chapter 51

Paul Draper, "Music and Dancing," is from his speech accepting an award from the Dance Educators of America, published in *Dance Magazine*, August 1961, 52–53.

Saul Steinberg (1914–99) created the drawing reproduced in Figure 51, of Paul Draper shortly after he immigrated to America in 1942. Although widely known for his drawings in *The New Yorker*, Steinberg enjoyed parallel careers as an exhibiting artist, designer, and muralist. For further biography, bibliography, and news about current exhibitions, go to www.saulsteinbergfoundation.org.

1. For a recollection by Paul Draper concerning his own career, see "Tapping Into the Classics," in *TAP! The Greatest Tap Dance Stars and Their Stories, 1900–1955*, rev. ed. Rusty E. Frank , rev. ed. (New York: Da Capo Press, 1994), 231–40.

In a phone conversation of February 1, 2010, the dancer's daughter, Pamela Draper, underscored the tap artist's eclectic tastes in music. She recalled that although he was known for performing to classical music, in later years Draper came to also like and respect rock music—especially the singing of the Beatles and Sting, as well as the style of singer-dancer Michael Jackson.

Dancers of a later generation continued to hone tap as a concert art, combining it with music in many styles. Among the outstanding artists in this genre have been Brenda Bufalino, with her American Tap Dance Orchestra, and Savion Glover, performing in his Broadway production of *Bring in 'da Noise, Bring in 'da Funk*, and with his own ensembles in touring programs such as *Classical Savion* and *Bare Soundz*.

For an article on current examples of merging various musical styles with tap and other genres of "percussive dance," see Darrah Carr, "Rhythm Mash-ups: Percussive Dance Hybrids Send New Sounds across the Globe," *Dance Magazine*, May 2010, 28–32.

2. An indication that dancers of the twenty-first century continue to have questions in regard to their relation to music is an article by Kristin Lewis, "Musicality Matters: How to Become a More Musical Dancer," *Dance Spirit*, January, 2010, available at http://dancespirit.com/articles/2427.

A compendium of earlier viewpoints about musicality can be found in an article by John Mueller and Don McDonagh, "Making Musical Dance: Robert Irving, Richard Colton, Kate Johnson, Karole Armitage," *Ballet Review* 14 no. 4 (Winter 1986): 23–44.

Chapter 52

José Limón, "Dancers Are Musicians Are Dancers" was a convocation address given to students at The Juilliard School on October 5, 1966. It was published in the *Juilliard Review* of 1966/67.

1. Carla Maxwell joined The Limón Company in 1965, became artistic director in 1978, and has been responsible for many reconstructions of dances choreographed by José Limón. In 1998 she was awarded a "Bessie" and cited for "finding a creative present in the context of a revered past, and thereby offering choreographic opportunity to multiple generations of artists." For some of Carla Maxwell's own musical and pedagogical viewpoints, see Teck (1994), 260–62.

    For updates on the Limón Dance Company, go to the website www.limon. org, which includes a chronology, repertory list indicating music used, photographs, and video clips. Archival materials are held both at the Limón Institute in New York and at the NYPL.

    In her essay "Thoughts on Staging José Limón's *La Malinche*," *in José Limón and La Malinche*, ed. Patricia Seed (Austin: University of Texas Press, 2008), the former Limón dancer Sarah Stackhouse commented:

    > Limón was an accomplished musician and one of the most musical choreographers of the twentieth century. In all of his works, the movement is so integrated with the music that it seems to be another layer of the music—and the music, another layer of the dance. Limón worked "out of his ear" and heard the choreography as much as he saw it. (163)

    Among Limón dances using music of contemporaries were *La Malinche* (Norman Lloyd); *War Lyrics* (Esther Williamson); *Danzas Mexicanas* (Lionel Nowak); *This Story Is Legend* (Ray Green); *Alley Tunes* (Ray Green); *Western Folk Suite* (Norman Cazden); and *Serenata* (Paul Bowles).

    José Limón's manuscript for *An Unfinished Memoir* was edited after his death by Lynn Garafola (Middletown, Conn.: Wesleyan University Press, 1998). To gain a sense of Limón in performance, see *José Limón: Three Modern Dance Classics*, on the Video Arts International label, and the DVD *Limón: A Life beyond Words*, on Dance Conduit (2003). The latter gives a particularly good sense of how political events in Mexico shaped Limón's artistic outlook. Another pertinent essay is José Limón, "Music Is the Strongest Ally to a Dancer's Way of Life," in Myron Howard Nadel and Constance Nadel Miller, ed., *The Dance Experience: Readings in Dance Appreciation* (New York: Universe Books, 1978), 189-94.

1. That this aspect of "happenings" is not totally a thing of the past (nor always welcome) was reported in the June 13, 2010, issue of *The New York Times*. Dance critic Roslyn Sulcas wrote "Drafting the Audience into Very Active Service," which begins: "Audience participation. Is there a more unpleasant conjoining of nouns in the English language?"

2. Yvonne Rainer's "No" manifesto first appeared in her article "Some retrospective notes on a dance for 10 people and 12 mattresses called "Parts of some sextets," performed at the Wadsworth Atheneum, Hartford, Connecticut, and Judson Memorial Church, New York, in March 1965, *Tulane Drama Review* 10 no. 2 (Winter 1965): 178. Also see Sally Banes, *Terpsichore in Sneakers: Post-Modern Dance* (Middletown, Conn.: Wesleyan University Press, 1987), 43.

   Yvonne Rainer went on to develop a successful career not only in dance but also in film, receiving many awards, including a MacArthur Grant. Her later thoughts can be found in two of her own books: *Feelings Are Facts: A Life* (Cambridge, Mass.: MIT Press, 2006) and *A Woman Who...Essays, Interviews, Scripts* (Baltimore: Johns Hopkins University Press, 1999).

3. A book that provides a dance-by-dance introduction to the Judson Memorial Hall performances and workshops led by musician Robert Ellis Dunn is Sally Banes, *Democracy's Body: Judson Dance Theater, 1962–1964* (Durham, N.C.: Duke University Press, 1993).) The author tells a detailed story, even though she herself had not seen the performances described.

   After his series of workshops, Robert Dunn himself worked as assistant curator in the Dance Division of the New York Public Library for the Performing Arts and later returned to teaching choreography, finally as professor of dance at the University of Maryland. Some of Dunn's personal recollections appeared in "Judson Days," *Contact Quarterly*, 14 no.1. (Winter 1989), 9–13. There is also an interview with Dunn in Don McDonagh, *The Rise & Fall & Rise of Modern Dance: The Story of Modern Dance in the 1960s: Merce Cunningham, Paul Taylor, Twyla Tharp, Yvonne Rainer, Alwin Nikolais, and Nine Others* (Pennington, N.J.: a capella books, 1990), 46–59.

   Indicative of varied viewpoints about 1960s dance is Constance Kreemer's comment: "Postmodern dance was never entirely 'one thing,' one presentation of an idea, but perhaps the press emphasized and promoted it that way." (Constance Kreemer, *Further Steps 2: Fourteen Choreographers on What's the RAGE in Modern Dance* [London: Routledge, 2008], 13). Her introduction (pp. 1–40) offers an overview of both "modern" and "postmodern" dance.

4. For a history of Dance Theater Workshop, go to www.dancetheaterworkshop .org. For an obituary of Laura Foreman, see *The New York Times* article by Jennifer Dunning, July 5, 2001. Foreman's archival papers are in the NYPL. Dunning also wrote a review April 2, 1989, of a retrospective concert by Dance Uptown, with special mention of a dance by Janet Soares titled *Things Are Looking Up*. As suggested by Dunning, the choreographers in Dance Uptown

programs tended to have "highly developed senses of craft." Dance Uptown archives are housed in the Barnard College Library.

5. Mary Verdi-Fletcher was indeed a pathbreaker, founding the Dancing Wheels Company in Cleveland in 1980. A decade later, a professional studio was opened, and a partnership with Cleveland Ballet initiated performances and workshops that have reached millions of people. For information, go to www.dancingwheels.org.

6. For a listing of West Coast artist Anna Halprin's dances with the music she used, go to www.annahalprin.org. When Ruedi Gerber's documentary film *Breath Made Visible* was about to have its first showings in New York in 2010, critic Jeannette Catsoulis commented: "It portrays a woman with angels in her feet and innovation in her blood" (*The New York Times*, April 23, 2010).

7. For information about current site-specific performances and residencies of the Liz Lerman Dance Exchange, go to www.danceexchange.org.

8. For current information about the National Dance Institute, go to www. nationaldance.org; about Lincoln Center Institute, www.lcinstitute.org; about the American Orff-Schulwerk Association, www.aosa.org; and about Dance and the Child International, www.daciusa.com.

9. Writings by and about Katherine Dunham are extensive, but articles focused solely on musical aspects of her performances have not been located by this editor. Dunham's own comments about music are tucked here and there into her published writing. Unpublished writing includes a 1963 draft with the intriguing title "This Historic Necessity of Music," in the collection of the University of Illinois at Urbana-Champaign, and there may well be other pertinent materials in Dunham's archival collections. A useful introductory timeline of Dunham's life and career can be found on the LofC website.

   The music to which Dunham performed spanned solo and group percussionists, especially using Caribbean, Brazilian, and African instruments and techniques; sung spirituals; piano and percussion; jazz ensembles with various instrumentation; Broadway and Hollywood orchestras; and performances by San Francisco and Los Angeles symphonies. According to biographer Joyce Aschenbrenner in *Katherine Dunham: Dancing a Life* (Urbana and Chicago: University of Illinois Press, 2002), 128, the Dunham company took written arrangements on tour for locations where orchestras would be available. Further explorations might also include studying programs and information about individual musicians who worked with Dunham.

10. For current information on events and in-school touring of Chuck Davis's company, go to www.africanamericandanceensemble.org. For information about Dance Africa programs in Brooklyn, now in their 34th year and counting, go to www.bam.org. The online Wikepedia website actually has a good list of past Dance Africa festival programs from their inception, a list that suggests names of many companies to explore further. A DVD that offers a good introduction to African American concert dance is *Dancing in the Light* (Kultur, 2007), with dances by Talley Beatty, Asadata Dafora, Katherine Dunham, Pearl Primus, Bill T. Jones, and Donald McKayle.

11. Philip Hamilton was recognized for his work as a contemporary composer of music for dance, with a 2004 "Bessie" (New York Dance and Performance Award). Blending jazz singing with his own virtuoso drumming, he has evolved a cutting edge style that now encompasses a group composed entirely of vocalists, named Voices. When Voices performed at Hamilton's alma mater, Middlebury College, observers noted on the college's website that the singers' style "fuses global rhythms and influences. Voices combines international vocal tones and techniques—such as Tuvan throat singing, Balinese monkey-chanting, and hip-hop's beat-boxing—with the rich sounds of diverse a cappella (unaccompanied) singing styles, including doo-wop, Bulgarian choirs, barbershop quartets, South African miners' songs, and Gregorian chants." This is cited as just one example of the way contemporary composers and musicians draw extensively from styles well outside the concert traditions that were practiced in the United States at the time of the early modern dancers. For a few clips of Hamilton's Voices performances, go to you tube online. His 2004 CD *Blues, Rhythm, Rhythm and Blues* on Montenegro Records offers a sampling of his solo singing with backup.

12. Of particular interest is the website www.asimplesound.com founded by Michael Wall of Ohio State University. Geared to the special needs of dance educators, it offers music categorized by duration and meter, as well as ambient and non-metered songs, all in lengths and styles suitable for use in the classroom. The music was created by outstanding specialists in the field of dance accompaniment, and before purchasing and downloading, dance teachers can first listen to samples online to determine exactly which styles and pieces are appropriate for them.

13. Anthony Tommasini, "Even Sopranos Get the Blues," *The New York Times*, May 30, 2010.

14. From Janet Mansfield Soares, "The Landscape of Dance: Five Professionals Assess the Field," *Juilliard Journal*, 21, no. 6 (March 2006), 5.

15. For a report on the designation of the thirty-six-year old Robert Battle to replace Judith Jamison as artistic director, see Daniel J. Wakin, "Ailey Company Names New Director," *The New York Times*, April 28, 2010.

16. Paul Taylor made his remarks to the author in a taped interview in New York City, June 25, 1985; the quotation is taken from Teck (1989), 8.

17. Stephen Rush, professor at the University of Michigan, explained his process of collaborating, at several workshop presentations for the International Guild of Musicians in Dance. Rush, who has composed more than 100 scores for dancers, also has to his credit international performances of multimedia work, four operas, plus chamber and orchestral music. He is also director of the Digital Music Ensemble at the university. Among the equipment he has students work with are touch sensors (with dancers triggering sound and light); light sensors (using glosticks to play music), dancer-played mercury switches (which trigger music); and infrared garage door openers rigged to make sound. For further

information about the ongoing experiments of the Digital Music Ensemble, go to http://www.music.umich.edu/current_students/perf_opps/dme/index.html.

18. John Warthen Struble, *History of American Classical Music* (New York: Facts on File, 1995), 344.

As documented by the readings in this book, some composers discovered that a satisfying outlet for their talents lay in collaborating with dancers—for both modern styles and classical ballet. In our own time, the acceptance of new music by ballet audiences was addressed by music critic Anthony Tommasini in his article for the June 13, 2010, issue of *The New York Times*. Titled "Bending a Knee to a Modern Sound," it begins:

> Spare us that dreadful modern music!
>
> For decades such pleas were voiced by a sizable segment of the classical music audience in America....
>
> Things have changed. A new generation of musicians committed to the music of their time has come to the fore, along with younger listeners naturally curious about anything new....
>
> From what I can tell, no comparable resistance to contemporary music has afflicted ballet.

Tommasini went on to report about the commissioning of scores by New York City Ballet over the years and to convey the opinion of director Peter Martins that at least with his company, the music really does come first—to the extent of giving composers' names immediately after ballet titles in printed programs, even before names of choreographers.

19. For current information about the National Endowment for the Arts, go to www.arts.gov.

20. Founded in 1974 as a project of the New York State Council on the Arts, Meet The Composer provides funding nationally, as well as publications helpful to choreographers and composers. For a report on a national project, see Katherine Teck, "Meet The Composer's Composer/Choreographer Project: A Bold Vision with Far-Reaching Results," *Journal of the International Guild of Musicians in Dance* 1 (1991): 2–16.

21. Participation in the International Guild of Musicians in Dance is open to both musicians and dancers. See www.dancemusician.org. For information (in English) on the European branch, see http://home.swipnet.se/svenskaigmid/eng/Startsida.htm.

Among presentations at the 2010 Guild conference in Tucson was one by David Karagianis (Los Angeles–based composer and music director for dance at Loyola Marymount University) in which he showed films of graduate students' choreographic projects—in each case first with the dancer's own choice of recorded music, then repeated with different sound possibilities chosen by Karagianis. Those viewing commented that there could be no better example of the powerful effect (either positive or negative) that music can have upon dance performance. For information about Karagianis, go to www.sounddance.net.

Many Guild members have years of experience in creating scores for student and professional choreography. Their output leads to a staggering total number of original scores for dance. For example, Robert Kaplan, music director for dance at Arizona State University, has composed more than seventy-five scores for dance. Natalie Gilbert has been music director of the American Dance Festival for more than twenty-five years. Larry Attaway was composer-in-residence for the Bella Lewitzky Dance Company from 1972 to 1997. Richard Schenk at Connecticut College numbers his dance scores in the "dozens" and still counting. Claudia Howard Queen (now at the University of North Texas), formerly accompanied more than 200 dance instructors in New York and Chicago and has composed thirty-eight scores for dance. And so it goes: a great contrast to the more limited collaborative involvement of most musicians in the formative years of modern dance.

Unlike the situation in former days, collaborating composers are no longer concentrated in New York and California but are found in other cities around the United States, often at academic institutions that offer both undergraduate and graduate degrees in dance. Among such musicians is Christian Cherry at the University of Oregon, where his teaching duties are typical for musicians-in-dance: courses in fundamentals of rhythm; music for dance; accompaniment; dance improvisation; production technology; aesthetics and choreographer/composer workshops; and artist marketing.

Another indication of the expanded expectations in regard to musicians for dance is a 2010 posting from the dance department at Florida State University. For the entry-level position of "music specialist," requirements include "knowledge of the concepts, principles, and practices of musical composition and accompaniment; knowledge of and ability to perform audio engineering and recording." Duties include not only daily accompanying of classes but also upkeep of audio equipment, management of licensing, training students to use electronic lab equipment, and other technologically oriented responsibilities. It is no longer sufficient to just play the piano or percussion.

Academically based musicians specializing in dance also involve themselves in further collaborative efforts. For instance, a project spearheaded by Manjunan Gnanaratnam—Open Source Dance in Minneapolis, Minnesota—is intended to provide an environment in which both composers and choreographers might engage in multidisciplinary explorations (see www.opensourcedance.org).

On some campuses, music students can now pursue for-credit academic studies in dance accompaniment and composing. For example, under Karen Follet, a program in accompaniment was initiated at Shenandoah University in Virginia, and under Suzanne Knosp at the University of Arizona, a full-fledged MA program in dance accompaniment was established, with components for both percussionists and pianists.

22. From Doris Humphrey, *New Dance: Writings on Modern Dance*, ed. Charles Humphrey Woodford (Hightstown, N.J.: Princeton Book Company, 2008), section titled "Declaration" (pp. 5–6).

23. The composer's advice can be found in *Lou Harrison's Music Primer* (New York: C. F. Peters, 1971), 33–34.

    A recent example of such a process is the reconsideration that the Martha Graham Company is giving to its double role as "living museum" and as an impetus for the creation of choreography with newly commissioned scores—including not only professional dance performance but also activities with high school students. See Julie Bloom, "On Dance: A New Direction for the Martha Graham Company," *The New York Times*, June 9, 2010. The reporter interviewed artistic director Janet Eilber, who commented: "It's important to encourage new talent. We were not slavishly tied to Martha's vocabulary in these creative new works. We are of course dedicated to it in our core collection of works, but our dancers need to be quite versatile."

24. For experienced collaborators and for uninitiated musicians who want a preview of what might be involved in working with dancers in our own time, a most informative and inspiring book is Stuart Hodes, *A Map of Making Dances* (New York: Ardsley House, 1998).

    For an insightful research paper that reflects contemporary concerns of musicians who collaborate with dancers, see Van Stiefel, *A Study of the Choreographer/Composer Collaboration*, Princeton University, Center for the Arts and Cultural Policy Studies, Working Paper Series, 22 (Princeton, NJ: Princeton University, Fall 2002). Also available as a PDF file online at the musician's website: www.vanstiefel.com. The paper (which provides an excellent brief history of music in modern dance plus an overview of working methods for collaboration) was based on Stiefel's informal interviews and group discussions with musicians, choreographers, producers, presenters, and critics gathered at the 2000 Bates College Dance Festival (in Maine), as well as upon his own experience in working with dancers.

    Stiefel notes that most composers still are not conversant with dance, nor do they understand what is required for making effective music for theatrical art dance. He makes a convincing case that among the best collaborator-composers for choreographers are musicians who already know and understand the needs of dancers, based on years of working with them closely in studio classes, rehearsals, and performances. This brings to mind observations made in the early years of modern dance by Louis Horst, who liked to use the label "composer-accompanist" for what he did.

Bibliographic Essay

The following are basic resources for research and historical information. Suggestions for materials pertaining to specific topics are included in the chapter notes.

General Reference Works

Selma Jeanne Cohen, founding editor, *The International Encyclopedia of Dance* (New York: Oxford University Press, 2004). Attention is directed to entries under "United States (History of Dance)" and "Music for Dance."

Taryn Benbow-Pfalzgraf and Glynis Benbow-Niemier, eds., *The International Dictionary of Modern Dance* (Farmington Hills, Mich.: St. James Press, 1998).

H. Wiley Hitchcock and Stanley Sadie, eds., *New Grove Dictionary of American Music* (London: Macmillan, 1986). See especially the entry by Pauline Norton for "Dance." For information about online access to some articles from the forthcoming second edition edited by Charles Hiroshi Garrett, and about the other Grove Dictionaries of music, go to www.oxfordmusiconline.com. Also suggested is *The New Grove Dictionary of Jazz*, 2nd ed., ed. Barry Kernfeld (New York: Oxford University Press, 2003), and the extended reference set edited by Stanley Sadie and John Tyrrell, *The New Grove Dictionary of Music and Musicians* (New York: Oxford University Press, 2003), which includes succinct historical subject articles under entries for both "dance" and "ballet," as well as composer biographies under individual names.

Four handy paperbacks are Debra Craine and Judith Mackrell, *Oxford Dictionary of Dance* (New York: Oxford University Press, 2004); Michael Kennedy, *Concise Oxford Dictionary of Music*, 5th ed. (New York: Oxford University Press, 2007); Horst Koegler, *The Concise Oxford Dictionary of Ballet*, 2nd ed. (London: Oxford University Press, 1982); Ted Libbey, *The NPR Listener's Encyclopedia of Classical Music* (New York: Workman, 2006), in tandem with Naxos offers online listening excerpts related to various composer articles.

Collaboration, History of Ballet and Dance

For those new to the history of Western theatrical dance, a compact introduction is Susan Au, *Ballet and Modern Dance*, 2nd ed. (London: Thames and Hudson, 2002). An accessible history of ballet, its precursors, and its music is Lincoln Kirstein, *Four Centuries of Dance*, (New York, Dover Publications, 1984). A recent history of just ballet is Jennifer Homans, *Apollo's Angels* (New York: Random House, 2010). A volume focused on modern styles is Nancy Reynolds and Malcolm McCormick, *No Fixed Points: Dance in the Twentieth Century* (New Haven, Conn.: Yale University Press, 2003). The decade of the 1960s is the focus of Don McDonagh, *The Rise & Fall & Rise of Modern Dance* (Pennington, N.J.: a capella books, 1990). Also see Robert Coe, *Dance in America* (New York: Dutton, 1985), published to accompany the PBS series by the same title.

History of American Music

For a general history of American music, see H. Wiley Hitchcock with Kyle Gann, *Music in the United States: A Historical Introduction*, 4th ed. (Upper Saddle River, N.J.: Prentice-Hall, 2000). Another volume, which includes a useful timeline from 1562 to 1993 plus a listing of composers by their state of birth, is John Warthen Struble, *The History of American Classical Music: MacDowell through Minimalism* (New York: Facts on File, 1995). A slimmer volume with two CDs of samples plus website links is Barrymore Laurence Scherer, *A History of American Classical Music* (Naperville, Ill.: Sourcebooks/Naxos Books, 2007). For a topical approach, highly recommended is David Nicholls, ed., *The Cambridge History of American Music* (Cambridge: Cambridge University Press, 1998). Also of interest is the anthology of readings collected by Judith Tick and Paul Beaudoin, *Music in the USA: A Documentary Companion* (New York: Oxford University Press, 2008). An earlier study is Wilfrid Mellers, *Music in a New Found Land: Themes and Developments in the History of American Music* (New York: Oxford University Press, 1987). Another nontechnical book that covers not only classical music but also folk and some popular styles is Richard Crawford, *America's Musical Life: A History* (New York: Norton, 2001).

For modern concert styles, a thoughtful volume is by composer Kyle Gann, *American Music in the Twentieth Century* (Belmont, Calif.:Wadsworth, 2006). Another engaging introduction is Alan Rich, *American Pioneers: Ives to Cage and Beyond* (London: Phaidon, 1995).

Other Resources

For those pursuing research on a particular collaboration, two good places to investigate are the online catalogs of the New York Public Library for the Performing Arts (both dance and music research divisions; www.nypl.org) and the Library of Congress, where many composers' manuscripts and papers are kept (www.loc.gov/performing arts/index.html). For West Coast artists, there is the Museum of Performance and Design in San Francisco (www.sfpalm.org).

The Smithsonian Institution recordings include many types of American music. For information by genre, instrument, and style, go to www. smithsonianglobalsounds.org and to www.folkways.si.edu.

For a catalog of folk music in the Library of Congress archive, go to www.loc.gov/ folklife/folkcat.html. Categories suggest a spectrum of music-making in America and include fiddle tunes, American Indian music (by tribe), African-American spirituals, humorous songs, animal songs, sea songs and shanties, cowboy cattle calls, lumberjack tunes, Negro blues and hollers, Negro work songs, railroad songs, Sacred Harp hymns, miners' ballads, dance music for reels and waltzes, ragtime, jazz—and more.

Index